Morgan O´Connell

The last colonel of the Irish Brigade

1745-1833. Vol. 1

Morgan O´Connell

The last colonel of the Irish Brigade
1745-1833. Vol. 1

ISBN/EAN: 9783337124878

Printed in Europe, USA, Canada, Australia, Japan

Cover: Foto ©ninafisch / pixelio.de

More available books at **www.hansebooks.com**

THE LAST COLONEL

OF

THE IRISH BRIGADE

OF

THE IRISH BRIGADE

COUNT O'CONNELL

AND

OLD IRISH LIFE AT HOME AND ABROAD
1745–1833

BY

MRS. MORGAN JOHN O'CONNELL

IN TWO VOLUMES
VOL. I.

LONDON
KEGAN PAUL, TRENCH, TRÜBNER & CO., Ltd.
PATERNOSTER HOUSE, CHARING CROSS ROAD
1892

TO THE

BELOVED MEMORY OF MY HUSBAND,

MORGAN JOHN O'CONNELL.

PREFACE.

A BOOK consisting largely of the letters of one Daniel O'Connell suggests to the possible reader a similar work wherein the famous bearer of the name paints his own portrait in scores of familiar letters. His editor has modestly confined himself to such a thin thread of narrative and comment as is required to make the letters intelligible to a later generation.

Now, I have pursued a precisely opposite course. Helped by two kinsmen, who were able to supplement my lack of special lore, I have endeavoured to depict old Irish life at home and abroad. The hoards of faded papers at Darrynane and many another old Munster home have been ransacked; a whole collection of Count O'Connell's letters were lent me by Mr. Fitz-Simon, of Glancullen; old tags of verse in English and Irish have been written down from the dictation of old ladies and old followers; old smuggling bills and legal opinions, wills, and marriage treaties have been laid under contribution. From this somewhat chaotic mass we have endeavoured to evolve a sort of counterfeit presentment of the old native Irish gentry, the O's and the Macs, fighting abroad and struggling at home, and likewise to depict the high-spirited mothers who bore them. A matron and two of her sons will be described in these pages.

Daniel Charles, Count O'Connell, was a distinguished cavalier of fortune abroad, and one of the prime movers in the transfer of the Catholic Irish French officers to the English Service without loss of faith or honour. He may fairly claim to represent the best type of the refined, scholarly, and scientific officer of the old time.

His brother Maurice, witty, wealthy, and wise, was a remarkable man in his own way. He lived in seeming seclusion and voluntary obscurity, yet amassed a great fortune in spite of the anti-Popery laws, and carried on a most interesting political correspondence with the leading Protestants of his county. We find him about to be tried for his life in 1782, and appointed a Deputy-Governor for Kerry a few years later.

Their many-childed mother, with her weird gift of Irish improvisation, her practical shrewdness and good house-wifery, and the extraordinary influence she wielded in her family until her death at near ninety years of age, seems to me a figure of no common interest.

In the letters of ninety years, dry and formal indeed for the most part, we see the real life of the old Irish people at home and abroad. I confess these old letters upset most of our preconceived notions. Here we find Irish-folk abhorring drink and debt, and living on the best terms with their heretical neighbours. Some of them are fighting against England abroad, others defying English laws at home; yet they share one sentiment, and in these pages they show a most curious desire to be suffered to be loyal.

These neatly traced letters are written by all sorts and conditions of men—generals and schoolboys, bishops and priests, lawyers, merchants, and politicians. My dear husband remembered his grand-uncle, Count O'Connell; and I have met many other old people who had a lively recollection of a tall, straight, handsome old man, who was kindness personified.

The vicissitudes of Count O'Connell's long life seem to me worthy of a careful record. I purpose to chronicle his escapes in battles and sieges and during the Revolution; his honourable poverty and interesting negotiations with Pitt during the Emigration; his late, though happy marriage; and his delightful family life among his French kindred. He had step-daughters who were devoted children to him, "wealth, honours, troops of friends," Irish and French, and among his personal friends he could count his king, Charles X. I fancy few of the veterans of the old heroic Irish Brigade have left a fairer record.

As chronicler of the last set of Munster officers of the Brigade, I have collected such verses, old stories, and old pedigrees as are floating about among the southern shores and lovely hills of Kerry and South-West Cork. The critic may laugh at some of them; yet I venture to say there are scores of Irish homes in the greater Erin beyond the seas and in remote colonial tracts, where these identical stories and pedigrees will give a keen sense of pleasure to offshoots of old historic stems.

Our task is threefold—the life-story of an honourable and honoured career; an attempt to reproduce old Irish life without either sentimentality or caricature; and an attempt to preserve old pedigrees, stories, verses, and traditions that otherwise would soon be hopelessly lost. In these pages we have stored such flotsam and jetsam as we could rescue from the waters of oblivion.

The articles signed "R. O'C." are contributed by Mr. Ross O'Connell, of Lake View; and Mr. O'Connell, of Darrynane, has given a general revision and supplied those marked "D. O'C.;" and a girl-cousin has given precious help.

I grieve to record the death of two kind helpers. While this work was going through the press, the Liberator's daughter Kate, Mrs. O'Connell, of Ballinabloun, and the venerable Miss Julianna, oldest of all the O'Connells, have passed away to their reward.

MARY A. O'CONNELL.

Longfield, Cashel.

THANKS.

I TENDER my thanks to the following kind helpers who aided me in various ways:—

To my three fellow-workers: Ross O'Connell, of Lake View; Daniel O'Connell, of Darrynane; and a young kinswoman who wishes to be nameless.

For letters, State papers, and traditional information, to Christopher Fitz-Simon, of Glancullen; Sir Maurice O'Connell, of Lake View; Mr. Fitz-Patrick, Fitz-William Square, Dublin; Mr. Leyne, Registry of Deeds, Dublin; La Marquise de Sers, of Madon, near Blois; Judge Kelly, of Newtown; Mr. Lecky, the historian; Mrs. Ffrench and Mrs. O'Connell, daughters of the Liberator; Miss Julianna O'Connell, Darrynane; Miss Evelina McCarthy, Vögelhaus; Mrs. Anne O'Mahony, late of Cullina; Miss O'Geran, Rushmount; Miss Lizzie O'Sullivan, Kenmare; Mr. Mahony, of Dromore; Mr. Marshall, of Callinafercy; Mr. Morrogh-Bernard, of Faha; Dr. George Sigerson, Dublin, who has given some notes over his initials; Mr. Hickie, of Killelton; Rev. L. Gilligan, C.C., Labasheeda; General Sir Martin Dillon, and others.

For information on Irish topics, Irish verses, translations, and Celtic lore generally, to the Rev. Peter O'Leary, C.C., Doneraile; Rev. John Martin, C.C., Cahirdaniel; Professor O'Loony; Mr. McSweeney, R.I.A., Dublin; Sergeant O'Connor, R.I.C., Cork; Mr. O'Sullivan, Maylor Street, Cork; Michael Houlahan, Cork; to Daniel Sullivan, John James Gallavan, and Mary Sullivan Lia, all from Darrynane.

CONTENTS OF VOL. I.

BOOK I.

OLD IRISH LIFE AT HOME.

                                                                                     PAGE

Birth and parentage of Daniel Charles O'Connell—Short sketch of his family—Darrynane a century ago—Donal Mor O'Connell and Maur-ni-Dhuiv O'Donoghue, his wife—How Maur-ni-Dhuiv ruled her household—One verse of her spinning-song—Rhymed dialogue with a tenant—Her elder children—Maurice goes to a finishing school—Descriptive letter to John—John marries Mary Falvey, of Faha—Letters to and from Maurice (1748-49): educational, admonitory, descriptive, amatory—Death of John—Maurice's statement about the young widow, with five of her letters (1751-53)—Anecdote of Daniel's boyhood—Fisheries—Connell goes to France—Then goes to sea—Curious absence of bigotry in Kerry—Letter from Arthur Blennerhassett to John O'Connell—From Connell to Maurice—From Connell to F. O'Sullivan—Marriage of Maurice O'Connell to Mary Cantillon, of Ballyphillip—Smuggling—Natural facilities of Darrynane for the purpose—Smuggling letter from Maurice O'Connell (1751) 1

NOTES TO BOOK I.

Note A.	Pedigree of **Donal Mor O'Connell**	...	48
" B.	**Fish in Kerry** ...	...	49
" C.	**O'Mahony** ...	...	50
	Mahony of Dunloe	...	51
	Sugrue ...	...	52
" D.	**O'Falvey** of Faha	...	53
" E.	"The Poor Scholar's Blessing"	...	57
" F.	**Weather-slated Houses in Munster**	...	60
" G.	**Cantillon** of Ballyheigue	...	61

BOOK II.

IRISH BOYS ABROAD.

1761-1769.

How the young cousins, Daniel O'Connell of Darrynane, and Morty of Tarmons, went to serve abroad—Maur-ni-Dhuiv's parting lament—

English rhymed translation—How Chevalier Fagan got Daniel into the French Service and the Royal Swedish Regiment—Brief account of last campaign of the Seven Years' War, wherein the boys smelt powder on opposite sides—Chevalier Fagan's letter to Maurice O'Connell, describing Dan's admirable conduct during it, and prophesying his future eminence—Morty gets taken prisoner—Father Guardian O'Brien helps him, and writes to Maurice O'Connell, enclosing a letter from Morty, and consulting Maurice about the feasibility of making a match between Marshal Browne's son and Lord Kenmare's daughter—Dan's letter (Fort Louis-on-the-Rhine, February 12, 1764)—Answers to Maurice about his going into the Spanish Service—His reasons for not doing so—Money matters—Letter from brother Connell (1764) to Maurice—Satisfaction at Dan's conduct—Shelbourne leases—Irish pilots—Letter from Dan to Maurice (Schlestatt, in Alsace, April, 1765)—Friendship of Captain Fagan—Brother Connell's death—Notice of him—Some of his letters—Letter (Schlestatt, August 6, 1765) from Dan to Maurice—Wants help to accept colonel's offer of a place in Academy—Expectations of wars—Hopes of promotion—Kindness of his colonel—He expects to join the staff—Offer of place in Carabineers—His studies—Looking forward to serve his own king and country—Letter (Strasbourg, December 27, 1765) from Dan to his father, deprecating his displeasure—Death of the Dauphin—Loyalty of the French—School letter (Strasbourg, February 12, 1766)—Military School—Probable advancement—Some hopes of war—Letter (Schlestatt, June 16, 1766) from Dan to Maurice—Joins his regiment—Gets commission as first lieutenant—Sets out for Switzerland with his colonel—Anecdotes of Morty of Tarmons—Letter (Cambray, 1766) from Dan to Maurice—Marching with his regiment—Sister Abigail abroad—Cousin John FitzMaurice—Talks of wintering in Paris—Letter (Aire, August, 1767) from Dan to Maurice—Movements of the regiment—He acts as "Officier Major"—Meets relations—FitzMaurice—Mahony—His cousin the Abbé—Daniel Swiney—Robin Conway—Talks of a trip to Ireland—Orders to appear before the King—Cousin Maurice Jeffrey—Notice of Burkes of Cornabulliagh—Letter of Father Guardian O'Brien to Hunting Cap (Buttevant, December, 1767)—Sir Walter Esmonde—Influenza—Chapter in Athlone—Blakes—Intends setting out for Spain—Mrs. Blake's visit to Darrynane—Rev. James Bland to Hunting Cap, on roads—Outlaws in Iveragh—Dangers to respectable Catholics—Smuggling—Letter from Dan to Hunting Cap (dated London, January, 1768)—Accompanies his colonel to London—Impressions of London roughs—A letter from Gravelines (March, 1768) to Hunting Cap—The post of "Sub-Aide Major"—Colonel's kindness—Letter (Gravelines, May, 1768) to Hunting Cap—Movements of the regiment—Indisposition of the Queen—Sister Nelly's marriage to Arthur O'Leary—Robin Conway—Penal law enforced against Tim McCarthy—First letter of 1769, dated from Mauburge—The affairs of Corsica—Paoli—Regimental affairs—Armorial bearings—Matrimonial letter from Captain Robin Conway to Maurice O'Connell from Bergues (January, 1769)—The Sheriff goes smuggling—Letter from Dan to Maurice (dated Paris, August, 1769)—The camp—Captain Fagan—Paris and the gay world—Claims of preferment—Hopes of going home—Movements of the regiment—Stephen Fagan 66

Notes to Book II.

			PAGE
Note A.	Irish Pilots and Seamen	...	131
,, B.	**O'Sullivan**	...	132
,, C.	**Conway** of Bodrhyddan	...	135
,, D.	Shevaun-ni-Dhuiv's Vengeance	...	136
,, E.	The Two Red Roquelaures	...	138
,, F.	Penal Papers in 1775	...	139
,, G.	Hunting Cap's Visit to London	...	141
,, H.	Louis de France	...	145

BOOK III.

IN THE IRISH BRIGADE.

1769–1779.

Daniel Charles O'Connell joins as aide-major to "Clare's" (October, 1769)—*Kerry Chronicle* on Dan—Colonel Meade—Royal Swedes—First letter from Dan on entering Brigade—No promotion in Royal Suédois Regiment—Succeeds Conway as aide-major in "Clare's"—Regimental affairs—Debts—Chevalier Fagan helps—Lord Kenmare's advice—Chevalier Fagan to Hunting Cap—Dan's sense of honour—Series of letters to Maurice O'Connell: from Dan, Rochefort (December, 1770)—Sailing for East Indies—Captain aide-major—His father's death—Letter from Chevalier Fagan—From Dan (the Road of Rochefort, January, 1771)—Farewell letter—Dan's first letter from Mauritius (July, 1771)—Six months' voyage—Hopes for war—Provisions scarce—Hard times—Chevalier Fagan again—Hunting Cap at home—Morgan O'Connell of Carhen's marriage—Catherine O'Mullane—Morgan of Carhen—Maur-ni-Dhuiv again—Romantic anecdotes—Arthur O'Leary, "the Outlaw"—Fair Mary Baldwin's love-story—Niece Abby—1772: James Gould writes to congratulate Maurice on the major's return—Smuggling—Hugh Falvey, of Faha, the friendly "discoverer"—From Daniel (Clonakilty, April, 1773)—Tralee—Cork—Finds a ship for Dunkirk—Hopes to march in June for Poland or Italy—Jerry McCrohan—Ample sea stores—Dunkirk (April, 1773)—After a passage of four days—Military acquaintances—Alliance with England—Military movements—Setting out for Bethune—Jerry Falvey—Family affairs—Bethune (April, 1773)—McCarthy Mor, the real chief of the family—Charles McCarthy—Margaret McMahon—Lawsuit with Herberts—Lord Clare—No war at present—South Sea discovery—Late for Indian promotion—Arthur O'Leary, "the Outlaw," shot—Eileen's grief—Vengeance—Bethune (June, 1773)—Poor Arthur—His widow and orphans—Preparations for war laid aside—Military gossip—Tom Conway—Bethune (September, 1773)—McCarthy Mor—Irish Parliament—Certificate in favour of a rebel—Nancy's marriage—Hunting Cap's wife—Leaving for Rocroi—Eugene McCarthy—Affairs of the nation—Chevalier O'Mahony—Count O'Mahony—Lord Clare—Rocroi (February, 1774)—The Duke d'Aiguillon and military affairs—Mighty changes expected—Miss Browne's marriage—Talk of visiting Ireland again—Rocroi (July, 1774)—Death of the king—Duke d'Aiguillon—A well-wisher to Ireland—Military gossip—Fears a dissolution of the Brigade—Hopes of going to court—Eugene McCarthy—Colonel Meade—Lord Thomond—Rocroi (August, 1774)—Visit to Ireland in October—Colonel Meade—Clohina—Death of Colonel Meade—Rocroi (October, 1774)—Going home—Regimental movements—Death of Mrs. Fitz-Maurice—Major Sullivan—Paris (October, 1774)—Trip to Ireland postponed—Military affairs—Friendship of Doctor Mahony—Administration in France—Mr. Crosbie, of Ardfert—Lord Shelbourne—Colonel James Conway—Abbé Connell—Episcopacy of Kerry—Doctor Mahony and the chevalier—Paris (December, 1774)—Money matters—Mr. Hickson—Military constitution—Changes in the Brigade—"Bulkeley's"—"Clare's"—"Dillon's"—Major Conway—The Marquis of FitzJames—Gloomy forebodings—Lord Kenmare—Marquis de Syvrac—Paris (January, 1775)—The critical situation of the Brigade—Courtly acquaintances—Evil forecasts—Bishopric of Kerry—Abbé Connell—The prince at Rome—Obligations to Doctor Mahony—The last of "Clare's"—Dan pays a visit to his family—He hopes to serve his country—The Count de Maillebois—Sir John O'Sullivan—Cork (March, 1776)—Clohina—Abby Gould—Passage in the Havre packet—Troops marching—Cork the rendezvous for troops bound for America—Dr. Connell—Jemmy Baldwin—Letter from Robin Conway—Morgan in Cork—Mr. Wise—Havre (March, 1776)—Passage takes six days—Denis McCrohan—Going to Paris—Cambray (June, 1776)—Expectation of military changes—Formation of regiments, etc.—McCarthy Mor—Walsh's regiment—Dan on other people's small boys—Introduced to the Ministers—Studies—Calais (July, 1776)—Family affection—Bad health—Eugene McCarthy in Count Walsh de Serrant's regiment—Jeffrey Maurice O'Connell's boy—Death of Daniel O'Connell, of Ballinablown—Intercedes for Arthur O'Leary's widow—Calais (September, 1776)—Quite well—Regimental movements—Talks of a trip to Paris—Le Comte de Maillebois in command—His kindness—Young Falvey—Mick Falvey—Birth of Morgan's second son—Gravelines (December, 1776)—Military preparations—Flattering offers of the American Congress—Major Conway—A tour to Paris next month—Jeffrey Maurice's boy—Abbé Moriarty—James Baldwin—Notice of "Berwick's"—Paris (January, 1777)—Forms a design of going to America—He is refused permission to go—M. de Maillebois presents him to the Ministers—Faction and intrigue—Chevalier O'Mahony—Rickard O'Connell—Gambling—Tom FitzMaurice—Cousin Morty in Germany—Paris (March, 1777)—Roguery of Dan's servant—Presented at court by M. de Maillebois—Difficulties of promotion—American plan—American War—Chevalier O'Mahony—Mr. Trench—Mrs. Mahony—Mr. Mahony, lieut.-colonel in the Spanish Service—Count Mahony, ambassador at Vienna—Burses founded by Dr. Connell—Certificate of baptism—Arms—Pedigree—Gravelines (May, 1777)—Where to send a boy (in reply to Hugh Falvey)—Dijon—Jerry Falvey—Major Conway—Florence—James Mahony—Captain Rick O'Connell—Paris (October, 1778)—Pleasing news of laws in favour of Roman Catholics—Sighing for the liberty of spilling his

blood in defence of the English king—Friends and distinguished
acquaintances—Some advantages offered in the East—Refused—His
sister's illness—The pedigree—Paris (October, 1778)—Rick Connell
arrives—Linen and genealogy required—Rumoured death of Tom
Conway of desperate wounds—His recovery—Campaign in Bohemia—
Military talents of Lacy—General Dalton—Army gossip—Sister Nancy
—Captain Rickard O'Connell takes up the pen—His personality—His
flirtations—Captain Rickard on Dan—Rickard's relations, etc.—Plot to
murder him—His letter to Maurice Leyne—Waits on the Earl of
Inchiquin—His friendship—Religion a bar—Daniel Charles O'Connell
a major in "Berwick's"—Major O'Connell's advice—Hunting Cap lends
money for Rickard's advancement—"Alps of difficulties"—Gratitude—
His adored patron (our hero)—Camp near St. Malo (September, 1778)—
Captain Rickard to Maurice Leyne—Joins the Brigade—Regimental
duties—Colonel O'Connell—Chevalier O'Mahony—Colonel Conway—
The drum beats!—March, 1779: Captain Rickard writes to Colonel
O'Connell in Paris—Rickard to Maurice Leyne—Illness—Rickard sen-
timental—Approbation of the colonel—A letter from Colonel O'Connell
to Rickard, telling him of Count Walsh de Serrant's favour—Captain
FitzMaurice—Offer of a commission in "Dillon's"—Going to Martinico
—Wants Colonel O'Connell's approval—Colonel O'Connell says No—
Rickard's commission in "Walsh's"—Captain O'Connor—August, 1779:
Captain Rickard writes again to Maurice Leyne—Rickard a rebel
—French war news—Cousin Conway—Dr. Sheehy—Père Felix
O'Dempsey 146

NOTES TO BOOK III.

Note A.	McCarthy Mor and O'Donoghue of the Glens	...	...	...	225
„ B.	O'Donoghue of the Glens and O'Donoghue Dhuv; and Female Descents of the O'Donoghue Dhuvs	...	...	...	232
„ C.	The Strong Chieftain and the Smith	...	...	...	237
„ D.	Dirge of Arthur O'Leary	...	...	...	...	237
„ E.	Baldwin of Clohina	...	...	246
„ F.	A Century and a Half of Dr. Leynes in Tralee	...	...	246

BOOK IV.

COLONEL O'CONNELL.

1780–1783.

No letters from Daniel Charles O'Connell from October, 1778, to March, 1780
—Captain Rickard and others fill the void—Rickard's first letter of 1780
dates from Cambray—Recruiting—Marching—Colonel O'Connell's kindness—A true friend—Flanders—Robin Conway—Eugene McCarthy—
Little Maurice Jeffrey O'Connell—Sir Maurice (Charles Phillip) O'Connell and other small boys—Captain Robin Conway to Hunting Cap
(Bergues, February, 1780)—A little cousin—The colonel gone to Strasbourg—Robin loses his mother-in-law—Little Robin to play the pipes for

promotion—Colonel O'Connell, "my best and worthyest of friends"—
Mrs. Seggerson—The Cross of St. Louis—Our hero's portraits—Paris,
March, 1780 : Colonel O'Connell to Hunting Cap—Thanks for money—
Knowledge of the affairs of the country—Going to Strasbourg—Little
Maurice to be presented to Duke de FitzJames—Eugene McCarthy
gone to Martinico as captain in his regiment—Chevalier O'Mahony—
Doctor Connell—Account of Colonel Eugene McCarthy—Strasbourg,
May, 1780: Dan to Hunting Cap—Old friends—Royal Swedes—
Genealogy—Earl of Glandore—Counsellor Fitzgerald—Little Maurice
gone to college—The O'Connells at home and abroad—Irish gossip—
Knight of Kerry to Maurice O'Connell, on roads—Iveragh, the asylum
of rogues and vagabonds—Maurice's reply to Knight of Kerry—
On the affairs of the barony—Volunteer corps—Account of a shipwreck
—Captain Rickard writes from Cambray (January, 1781)—Sentiment—
An exile from Erin—Rickard's cold and cure—Colonel O'Connell, as
usual, the best of friends—Poor Conway—No letters from Colonel
O'Connell from May, 1780, to April, 1783—He is mentioned as with the
battalion at Minorca—Quite well in Captain Rickard's letter—A letter
(1782) mentions his brilliant prospects—Chevalier Bartholomew O'Mahony
—Port Phillip and Gibraltar—Daniel is invited to serve in Russia—
Later in Portugal—O'Callaghan on our hero—Port Mahon—The siege
of Gibraltar—Allied forces of Spain and France—Drinkwater describes
the times—News from Portugal—The Spanish Fleet—Fort St. Phillip
besieged—Surrender of Fort St. Phillip—Lieut.-Colonel O'Connell to
Rickard O'Connell (December, 1781)—Grant's account of the landing
of the Duc de Crillon—O'Connell specially and honourably noticed—
Account of Minorca from the "Annual Register"—General Murray's
description of the fall of Port Phillip—Captain Rickard to Hunting Cap
(December, 1781)—Is in Ireland, ill—Dan with the battalion in Minorca
—Dan's letter to Rickard from Gibraltar—Dan's pedigree—Captain
Rickard pedigree-hunting—"Flirting the mother of mischief"—Colonel
O'Connell's "College"—Chevalier O'Mahony—Captain O'Connor writes
to him—Rickard speaks of Dan's brilliant success at Gibraltar—The
Liberator on his uncle—Anecdotes of the Colonel—Old Kerry newspaper
—Count de Vaudreuil—Fine friends—Vaudreuil on O'Connell—Our
hero at Cadiz—Siege of Gibraltar, and list of officers there—Duc de
Crillon-Mahon—O'Connell a member of the council of war—Names of
the battering-ships—Count Fersen—"Le Beau Fersen"—Fersen's ge-
nerosity—Account of the floating batteries from the "Annual Register,"
—Contemporary account of our hero on board the floating batteries—
Prince of Nassau—"That day of wrath"—O'Connell's coolness in danger
—Plot on his life—Saves his friends and others—Wounded—A shell
bursts—"Annual Register" continues—Captain Curtis—Letter of a
French officer—Family tradition—Mr. James Roche—Chevalier Bartho-
lomew O'Mahony writes (Paris, October, 1782) to Hunting Cap—Con-
gratulates him on Dan's promotion—Pedigree a necessity—Cambray,
October, 1782: Chevalier O'Mahony again—Dan wounded, but recovered
—Brothers in arms—Perils at home—The penalties of smuggling—
The mysterious crooked knife—Captain Whitwell Butler—The smugglers
caught—Gallantry of Captain Butler—Young O'Sullivan of Couligh—
Owen McCrohan writes to Morgan O'Connell—Plots—Informers—Mr.

Contents. xix

PAGE

Dominic Trant, M.P.—Trants of Dovea—Maurice O'Connell to Counsellor Dominic Trant—Foul plot against Hunting Cap—Honourable conduct of Judge Henn, Dominic Trant, Lord Annaly, and other Protestants—Several letters about this matter—Triumphant refutation of all calumnies, and perfect vindication of Maurice, Morgan, and Daniel O'Connell ... 249

NOTES TO BOOK IV.

Note A.	Alexander Ross's Siege Diary	314
„ B.	Count **Bartholomew O'Mahony**, with **Trant** and **FitzMaurice** Pedigrees	316
„ C.	"**Le Brave O'Mahony**"	320
„ D.	Dominic Trant and his Jacobite Kindred	325
„ E.	Sir Nicholas Trant, K.T.S.	329

THE LAST COLONEL OF THE IRISH BRIGADE.

BOOK I.

OLD IRISH LIFE AT HOME.

Birth and parentage of Daniel Charles O'Connell—Short sketch of his family—Darrynane a century ago—Donal Mor O'Connell and Maur-ni-Dhuiv O'Donoghue, his wife—How Maur-ni-Dhuiv ruled her household—One verse of her spinning-song—Rhymed dialogue with a tenant—Her elder children—Maurice goes to a finishing school—Descriptive letter to John—John marries Mary Falvey, of Faha—Letters to and from Maurice (1748-49): educational, admonitory, descriptive, amatory—Death of John—Maurice's statement about the young widow, with five of her letters (1751-53)—Anecdote of Daniel's boyhood—Fisheries—Connell goes to France—Then goes to sea—Curious absence of bigotry in Kerry—Letter from Arthur Blennerhassett to John O'Connell—From Connell to Maurice—From Connell to F. O'Sullivan—Marriage of Maurice O'Connell to Mary Cantillon, of Ballyphillip—Smuggling—Natural facilities of Darrynane for the purpose—Smuggling letter from Maurice O'Connell (1754).

DANIEL CHARLES, COUNT O'CONNELL, was born in an eventful year—on the 21st of May, 1745. Born the very year of the last Jacobite rising, just two months before Charles Edward's splendid banner had lured so many high-spirited Catholics to destruction in Scotland and England, his life was prolonged until Queen Victoria's girlhood. He had served three King Louises, had first borne arms against Britain and the great Frederick, yet died in the prosaic modern days of Louis Philippe, in the curious position of a French general and an English colonel. He was the uncle as well as the namesake of the famous Daniel O'Connell, whose remarkable gifts he had soon perceived, and over whose early career he watched in France and England.

The convolutions of a Munster pedigree are not of much interest except to the parties concerned therein; so suffice it to say that the O'Connells were among the lesser clans who followed the great chieftain McCarthy Mor, the Celtic rival of the great Norman Geraldine, the Earl of Desmond. Elizabeth's iron hand crushed both these hereditary foemen and Desmond, and South Munster knew their sway no more. The O'Connells were hereditary constables of McCarthy Mor's great ocean stronghold of Ballycarberry, near Cahirsiveen, in Kerry.

From these long-established custodians my hero descended. Cromwell "transplanted" Maurice O'Connell, the head of the family, a very aged man. He died on the way; but his family proceeded into exile with their servants, flocks, and herds, and settled beyond the Shannon, in a district called Briantree, near Lisdoonvarna, in the County Clare. The second branch of the family remained unmolested, and contrived to preserve some unforfeited lands in Glancar, in the barony of Iveragh, held by the family by the unwritten tenure of immemorial possession.

The second brother of this Maurice, who died on the way to exile, was John, an eminent barrister. He was seneschal to the great Duke of Ormond, who, though a Protestant, had a fancy for employing Catholic lawyers to transact his private business. He obtained from his patron not only a confirmation of the Cromwellian grant to his eldest brother's descendant and namesake, but a licence for this younger Maurice to set up a few Franciscan friars at Briantree.

Daniel O'Connell, great-grandson to Maurice, rented what is now called Darrynane from the Earl of Cork, and thereon his grandson and namesake, some time, it is supposed, early in the second quarter of the last century, built the old portions of the present house. It was the home of their famous descendant and namesake, the Liberator, grandson to the Daniel who built it. My fellow-worker, Ross O'Connell, appends a genealogical note.[1] The father of this Daniel,

---

[1] Note A, *infra.* p. 48.

John O'Connell, a captain in the King's Guard, served at the sieges of Limerick and Derry, and at the battles of the Boyne and Aughrim. His first cousin, Brigadier Maurice, nephew to Councillor John, fell on that last fatal field. Captain John, having the good luck to be included in the articles of the Capitulation of Limerick, lived unmolested at home for nearly fifty years after.

Darrynane is really in O'Sullivan's country, in the barony of Dunkerron; but it is only seven miles from the borders of Iveragh, where the old lands of the O'Connells are situated, and the family have been always called the O'Connells of Iveragh. The late Sir James O'Connell, of Lake View, bought Ballycarberry and the ruin and much adjacent land, now belonging to his son, Sir Maurice. Thus, by a curious coincidence, the old home of the castellans of Ballycarberry, whence Maurice O'Connell was driven forth by Cromwell, belongs now to his namesake and direct descendant.

There are so few anecdotes of my hero's childhood that they would not fill a page, and I request any reader who only wants to know about the cavalier of fortune and the inner life of the Irish Brigade to pass on to Book II. I shall devote the rest of this chapter to an account of the settlement of the O'Connells and to old-world family life. My object is less to transcribe and translate from biographical dictionaries, histories, and army lists, the adventures in which my hero was concerned, than to describe how people really lived in Ireland, and out of it too, over a hundred years ago. Of course, I shall give the historical extracts as they occur; but these are easily seen elsewhere. What it seems to me Irish people ought to study is the real inner life of the old native Irish Catholics. Old Maurice O'Connell, of Darrynane, had as great an objection to burning written matter as a Mahometan, and to this peculiarity I am indebted for the means of letting the old folk depict themselves.

Kerry was in many respects a very curious place.

Quaint old Dr. Smith, the learned historian of Kerry, visited Darrynane in 1751. His chapter on the southern baronies gives a singularly pleasing picture of both gentry and peasantry. He tells how the gentlemen, by subscribing among themselves, had opened, shortened, and repaired the roads.

"They have at great charge," he continues, "shortened many of the old roads, and carried them on in straight lines over rocks and morasses and heretofore impassable mountains and deep glens, as the new road from the lakes of Killarney to the river of Kenmare, and others, carrying on along the side of that great arm of the sea into the barony of Dunkerron and Iveragh, whereby they have rendered tedious and toilsome journeys for travellers not only cheap and easy, but also extremely pleasant and entertaining. Several of the gentlemen of Kerry, since the spirit of improvement hath appeared in Ireland, have laid themselves out in building, planting, enclosing, improving, and reclaiming waste and unprofitable ground, and enriching themselves and advancing their country. The gentlemen and inhabitants of this country are all of them remarkable for their hospitality to strangers, generosity and courteous carriage, which characters, should I refuse them, must be attributed to the highest ingratitude; and lastly, there are few among them but whose breeding and parts, and I might say learning also, are eminently more conspicuous than in many other places in this kingdom; notwithstanding, Ireland may vie in this respect with most of the civilized countries of Europe. It is well known that classical reading extends itself even to a fault among the lower and poorer kind in this country, many of whom, to the taking them off from more useful works, have greater knowledge in this way than some of the better sort.

"The common people are extremely hospitable and courteous to strangers. Many of them speak Latin fluently, and I accidentally arrived at a little hut in a very obscure part of this country where I saw some poor lads reading Homer, their master having been a mendicant scholar at an English grammar school at Tralee."

The learned doctor thus describes Darrynane and its surroundings—

"At Cahirdonel [now Cahirdaniel] is a circular fortification built of large stones seven feet high, and said to be the work of the Danes. At Aghamore, towards the western extremity of the parish, are the remains of a small abbey of Canons Regular of St. Austin, founded by the monks of St. Finbar, near Cork, in the seventh century. It stands on a small island near the mouth of the river of Kenmare, having its walls so beaten by the sea that they will be soon entirely demolished. About a league to the south-west of this island, which is at low water joined to the shore, there are two islands called Scariff and Dinish. The former is a high mountain in the sea, and hath one family on it, who take care of some cows and make a considerable quantity of butter. These islands, with the adjoining continent, are farmed from the Earl of Cork and Orrery by Mr. Daniel Connell, who has, on part of the said land called Darrynane, built a good house and made other improvements—the only plantation thereabouts."

Sir James O'Connell used to tell a story about Dr. Smith, namely, that he, when at Darrynane, fancied a certain admirable pony, the property of his host, and offered, if it were presented to him, to give a full account of the family of his entertainer, whose wise son Maurice instantly besought him to accept the animal, but for the love of Heaven not to say a word about them, but to leave them to the obscurity which was their safeguard.

Concerning the name Conell, or O'Connell, the suppression of the O was a matter of policy. People at home did not use it openly until the relaxation of the penal laws in 1782. People abroad used it always. The rough rendering I have made of Maur-ni-Dhuiv's Irish verse explains this—

> "Connell is Connell the gentlest born,
> Connell is Connell sprung from the dust."[1]

Darrynane means "St. Finan's Oak-wood." A small ruined church on the Abbey Island, so accurately described by Dr. Smith, was a dependency of a great abbey in the County Waterford, whose possessions were granted to Sir Walter Raleigh. At the fall of that splendid adventurer, Darrynane passed into the hands of Boyle, first Earl of Cork, whose

---

[1] Connaill ap Connaill 'na Luaire
Agur Connaill ap Connaill v'a uairle.

descendants let it, on very favourable terms, to the O'Connells. In those days the only chance a Catholic had of saving any remnant of his own fee-simple property was by renting a large tract from a powerful Protestant. "My lord" would always protect his tenant, and the property of the middleman was a good security for the landlord. The middleman could sublet what he did not want; and the great man, if he had small profits, had neither risk nor trouble.

Farming, sporting, and smuggling attracted several old Catholic families to these wild and remote shores, where they could worship unmolested, and earn something to boot. Their faith, their education, their wine, and their clothing were equally contraband.

We must not suppose, however, that smuggling was peculiar to the down-trodden Papists.[1] There are old papers at Darrynane showing nearly every name on the grand jury list as engaged in these ventures, and one in which the countenance and actual bodily presence of the sheriff are promised on some especial occasion. The rock on which Mass used to be said in a hollow of the sand-hills which form the beautiful beach at Darrynane, and the wonderfully dry smugglers' cave among the rocks above the garden, are pointed out to this day, and likewise the Smuggler's Sound, through which the fleet little craft bore my hero and a band of young kinsmen to seek service abroad. Most contraband of all goods were the boys who were going to be trained for the service of foreign powers—the "wild geese" of tradition, song, and story.

[1] Smuggling was not even peculiar to Ireland, for it was carried on with great activity and daring along the British coasts, in continental products. What is less known is the fact that a vast contraband commerce existed between England and Scotland on the one hand, and Ireland on the other. Both Scotch and English smuggled over Irish products, and many of these were of a nature the modern reader may wonder to find on the contraband list. "In salt, for instance, an essential element in fish-curing as well as in diet, there was a stirring trade all along the west coast of Great Britain. Half a million persons in Scotland never used any other than smuggled (Irish) salt, and, as the duty was still heavier in England than in Scotland, the movement thither was brisk. Again, in the article of soap and candles, none were exported into Ireland, and none were officially admitted into Britain from Ireland, but great quantities were certainly smuggled into all the western counties of England and Wales, and from thence, by inland navigation, into other counties" (Sigerson, "Two Centuries of Irish History," p. 103. London: 1888).

My hero's parents were Daniel O'Connell and Mary O'Donoghue. Donal Mor and Maur-ni-Dhuiv, the people call them. Donal Mor, or "Big Daniel," refers to the commanding stature of the elder Daniel. Maur-ni-Dhuiv[1] does not mean "Dark Mary," but "Mary of the Dark Folk"—Dhuv, "Dark," being the suffix of a younger offshoot of the O'Donoghues of the Glens. The great clan pedigree of the O'Donoghue chieftains is in the Royal Irish Academy, $\frac{23}{G1}$. The senior branch, whose head was The O'Donoghue Mor, Chieftain of the Lakes, and whose seat was Ross Castle, is extinct. The O'Donoghue of the Glens (in Irish, O'Donoghue Glynn) exists in the person of my grand-nephew. Mr. McSwiney, the learned Assistant-Librarian of the Royal Irish Academy, informs me that the O'Donoghues of the Glens branched off at the thirteenth generation of O'Donoghue Mor at a man named Amhlaoibh (Auliffe), fifth in descent from Donnchad, from whom the O'Donoghues took their clan-name. Some cadet of the family of the Glens was called as a nickname "Dhuv," or "Dark," and his family retained the name. They were settled in Glanflesk at a place called Anees,[2] near Brewsterfield. Maur-ni-Dhuiv died aged about ninety, nearly a hundred years ago, so there is absolutely no tradition as to who her mother was; however, my fellow-worker, Ross O'Connell, in looking up a Mahony pedigree, discovered that lady's name. "She was the daughter of Donell Mahony, of Dunloe," he tells me, "the great and terrible Papist" of Mr. Froude, "who ruled South Kerry with his four thousand followers" (Froude's "English in Ireland," vol. i. p. 452). He left, with other issue, a daughter, to whom, "as the only person in the barony worthy to wear them," he bequeathed his velvet breeches. This daughter was the wife of Donal O'Donoghue Dhuv, and the mother of Maur-ni-Dhuiv, Count O'Connell's mother [R. O'C.].[3] The symbolic gift might have fitly descended to Donal Mahony's granddaughter, who, having in-

[1] Boeté Ⅵ.ιιρα or Ⅵ ιρι' αι Ϥυιɓ.

[2] Called Awnys in a biographical sketch in Grant's "Cavaliers of Fortune."

[3] See also vol. ii. p. 203.

cited her easy-going spouse to build her a good house, the first slated house built in the barony since Cromwell's time, ruled it and him and their children for some seventy years or more.

The O'Donoghue Dhuvs seem to be extinct, for I never met any one who had ever known of any of them. Mr. McCartie, of Headfort, near Glanflesk, who is descended from two sets of O'Donoghues, tells me that his father, who was born in 1786, knew in his boyhood a very aged Mr. Geoffrey O'Donoghue, an old bachelor, who was remarkable for his knowledge of Irish poetry, and who was supposed to be the last O'Donoghue Dhuv. Maur-ni-Dhuiv had a brother Geoffrey, but no one knows if he were this old gentleman or a namesake. Maur-ni-Dhuiv's own descendants, however, are as plentiful as leaves in Vallombrosa.

The present owner of Darrynane is an architect, and he pointed out to me the original plan of the quaint old grange, modernized and added to almost beyond recognition. It must have resembled the House of the Seven Gables. It resolutely turned its back on sea and sunshine, and looked into a walled courtyard planted with trees. It had dark parlours with deep wainscoted window-seats at either side of the hall-door. It was three stories high, and had gables and dormer windows in the roof. Out-offices formed one wing abutting on the courtyard, and there were kitchens and servants' quarters at the back. A bridle-road ran along outside the courtyard wall, and a beautiful garden lay beyond, where a mulberry tree, erroneously said to have been planted by the old monks, still exists. Old people say the flower borders produced such lovely polyanthuses, like gold lace on dark velvet, that the servants used to call a neighbouring lady, who was very handsome and dressy, "Polyanthus," after the flowers. Bees, seldom seen in the mountain region, thrive there too.

The O'Connells of Darrynane were prosperous people, though their affluence consisted rather of flocks and herds and merchandise than of hard cash. The small mountain tenants mostly paid their rent in labour or in kind. Little money changed hands, unless on special occasions. Strapping "boys," sturdy girls, and hardy "garrons" (the strong little mountain horses) could give work instead of the rent.

This patriarchal system of living, with its rude plenty, rendered large families less burdensome than elsewhere. Of the enormous progeny of twenty-two children born to Donal Mor and Maur-ni-Dhuiv, four sons and eight daughters grew up. Mr. O'Connell gives me the following details:—

"Miss Julianna, eldest surviving member of all the O'Connell 'gens,' says only eight of Hunting Cap's sisters married. Their names in order of seniority are as follows. She is not sure if Honora or Joan was the elder; they were the third and fourth at all events:—

"1. Elizabeth m. Tim McCarthy, of Ochtermony, before 1744.

"2. Alice m. John Segerson,[1] Ballinskelligs Manor, about 1750.

"3 & 4. { Honora m. Morty O'Sullivan, of Couliagh, 1751.
{ Joan m. Chas. Sughrue, of Fermoyle, in 1744.

"5. Mary m. James Baldwin, of Clohina, 1762.

"6. Eileen m. (1) Mr. O'Connor, of Firies; (2) Arthur O'Leary the Outlaw, 1768.

"7. Abigail m. Major O'Sullivan, 1766.

"8. Nancy m. Maurice Geoffrey O'Connell, August, 1773.

"Elizabeth and Alice were both older than any of their brothers. Their settlements are here."—[D. O'C.]

John, the eldest son, died young, and for many years the working, organizing, practical head of the family was the next brother, Maurice, who lived to be ninety-seven, and only died in February, 1825.

Daniel O'Connell was a big, handsome, jovial, kindly man, amiable, as big, handsome men generally are, and no exception to the rule by which they seem to like being more or less dominated by small, fair wives. He was liked by his neighbours and idolized by his children. His son Maurice, who was a man of great natural capacity and well educated, worked up the family to a high social position, and, childless himself, was as a father to his young kindred. He was

---

[1] This name is written *Segerson* and *Sigerson*; even in Domesday Book we find Filius Sigari and Filius Segari, dating from Edward the Confessor.

always most devoted to the clever, keen-witted mother from whom he derived so much of his practical shrewdness.

Maur-ni-Dhuiv was small, slight, fair, and active, though the mother of sons remarkable for height as well as good looks. Though she was a blonde, her eyes were not blue, but bright hazel. The Liberator told a great-granddaughter of hers, when a little child, that she had Maur-ni-Dhuiv's very eyes. I happen to know this lady as a mature but still handsome matron, and she has very sweet and expressive light-brown eyes verging on hazel, like Longfellow's description of the lady in "Hyperion"—"of the colour of the brown depths of mountain streams." That shrewd and close observer, Oliver Wendell Holmes, calls fair-haired, fair-skinned, hazel-eyed women "blondes of the leonine type," and says they are usually among the most energetic beings in creation. This old-world Kerry gentlewoman certainly bore out his theory.

Her enormous family and her large household did not overtax her energies. True, each child which survived of the twenty-two was sent out to a tenant's wife to be nursed; but then it came back in due time, and there were its feeding, training, and clothing to be seen to. In these remote places every article of common use had to be prepared. The corn was threshed with flails, winnowed by hand on the winnowing-crag, ground in the quern, and made into various sorts of bread—fine white cakes for the family; "brack bread" (*i.e.* "breac," speckled or spotted cakes) of whole meal, baked on the griddle, for servants' use. The flax and the wool were carded and spun. Pumps being unknown, the servant-girls had to carry all the water from wells; turf had to be cut, saved, and carried in. Besides our modern picklings and preservings, there were wholesale slaughterings and saltings of beeves in autumn, salting of hides, candle-makings of the fat. Every labourer used to get a salted hide to make two pairs of brogues. Add to this the ordinary toils of the laundry, the dairy, the kitchen, and the stable, and you get some idea of the gangs of people an old-fashioned Irish lady had to rule over. What Count O'Connell, in later letters, jestingly terms "the multitude of our followers and our fosterers," had to be added to these.

This most notable dame was a famous Irish improvisatrice, and frequently commanded her forces in rhyme. One verse of her spinning-song is yet remembered in her home. The lady is setting the spinners to work after their dinner, and the verse may be roughly rendered—

> "Now hasten, ye women,
>   You want not for bread ;
>   The good wheels are steady :
>   Go, spin the fine thread."

In Irish the verse runs as follows :—

> Brostaig, a mná!
> Caolaig a ṡnáṫ,
> Mná gan ocnur
> Ar tunainn rocaine.

Sergeant Michael O'Connor, late R.I.C., an "Irishian,"[1] to whom I am much indebted, procured for me the following rhymed dialogue[2] between the strong-minded mistress of Darrynane and a tenant. He remembered it since his boyhood :—

> Máiṙ' ní Ḋuiḃ 'r a Tenáncoiṫe
>
> M. Cread ar tura?
> T. Ua Ḋromṫanaḃan, a ḃean uarall
> M. Ir maiṫ an feilm irinn
>   Ta coir aiṁa riorainn,
>   Ir ta coir aiṁa 'nall ain,
>   Ta a h-aġaiṫ leir a n-gneim
>   'S a cúl leir an rioc.
>
> T. Ta tura go maiṫ cum i molaḋ
>   Aċḋ tainre coiṁ-maiṫ cum i caineaḋ
>   Ua ir againre na cuir a cainte
>   Ta buirge 'n alan, 'r ta baḋ 'na boin
>   Ta a cúl leir a n-gneim
>   'S a h-aġaiṫ leir an rioc
>   Ta an cior no anḋ
>   'S an topaḋ no loin
>   'S ní feidin liom tiol leat ain.

[1] A name given in Munster to one knowing the Irish-Gaelic language.
[2] The Irish has been revised by Mr. Fleming, the distinguished Irish scholar.

Mr. O'Sullivan, Maylor Street, Cork, kindly wrote down the dialogue, and rendered it thus—

Lady. "Where are you from?"
Tenant. "From Dromcaravan,[1] madam."
Lady. "That is a good farm.
You have a riverside below,
And you have a riverside along it;
It faces the sun, and has its back to the snow."
Tenant. "You are well able to praise it, but I can dispraise it just as well.
There is a quagmire at its foot,
And a brake in the centre;
It is exposed to the snow, and it turns its back to the sun.
The rent is very high, and the produce rather stinted,
Which causes me to be far short of the rent."

The point of the dialogue is the rhymed inverted meanings of words very similar in sound and termination.

"Go to your spinners" was a favourite reproach of eighteenth-century husbands in Munster, if they thought wives took too much on themselves. But the mistress of Darrynane had an eye to the tenants too. I quote these quaint rhymes and trivial details because a mother is generally supposed to have much influence over her sons, and here is a very interesting case of strongly marked heredity, a woman of the most remarkable energy and capacity in her own sphere, the perfectly legitimate woman's kingdom of home, bearing a son who, by the same qualities of indomitable energy and perseverance, added to the natural and common manly quality of pluck, achieves distinction abroad.

Even at the risk of prolixity, I must keep my hero waiting somewhat longer, while I briefly describe the marryings and buryings which went on before he was out of petticoats.

This is essentially a study of Irish life, and chance has

---

[1] It has always been a tradition that the O'Donoghue Dhuvs lived at Droumcarbin, but no ruins of the house now remain. A comfortable farmhouse stands close to the field shown as the site of the O'Donoghue dwelling. This farmhouse faces about north-east, has mountains very near at the back, and a river flows beneath. This must be the Dromcaravan of the dialogue—Drumcarvan spelt in Irish with *bh* for *v*. When a fortune was not paid off at once, it was customary to assign rents of certain farms, so that would bring Maur-ni-Dhuiv into direct contact with her brother's tenant. Her niece, Mrs. McCartie, of Churchill, is called Joan O'Donoghue, of Droumcarbin, that being the English form of *Dromcarabhan*.

opened a rich find of materials. In old Maurice O'Connell's secrétaire, brass-handled and many-drawered, the present owner of Darrynane has found a great bundle of letters, several of them in the delicate Italian hand of the young widow of Maur-ni-Dhuiv's eldest son. Now, in the hundreds of papers that have passed through my hands, I have never seen so many letters by a woman. She and her child, who was only four or five years younger than her uncle Daniel, figure constantly in my hero's letters. Oddly enough, one was found the other day in which he mentions the death of "our poor niece Abigail," who in her babyhood was so spoilt and petted by her uncles that her mamma had to complain to them. Let the military student skip this chapter, but let him who believes that "the proper study of mankind is man" peruse these old-world epistles, where the inner life of Catholics in penal days is depicted by themselves.

I visited Darrynane in the lovely spring-time of 1890, when the woods were blue with wild hyacinths and the hillsides golden with gorse. My coming had stimulated my host and fellow-worker, Daniel O'Connell, of Darrynane, to fresh rummagings for documents; and he made the aforesaid precious find of early eighteenth-century letters.

Two young nephews of his great-great-grandfather and namesake write from France, where Maurice seems to have been soldiering and Morgan studying for the Church. They were first cousins to each other and to the young men at Darrynane. Writing to John, the eldest, they talk of the kindness of his parents to theirs. Maurice O'Connell writes from Paris, May 9, 1744—

"This help from your father argues full well how truly sincere a relation he is, and confirms me in the favourable ideas I always conceived of him, viz. of being the only [man] of my name, as aught I know, who in his good intentions is more really sincere and constant. It is true he alone is blessed with a happy companion, who, far from barring his good dispositions, spurs him on, if ever he fails, and generously herself his place supplies."

The previous month the young student, Morgan O'Connell, writes to his cousin Jack—

"I cannot set a sufficient value upon your Father's Good

Nature and Kindness, of which that bill [for £3] is not the first mark He gave me. I shall not be wanting in thanks and good Inclinations to Him till it pleases God to put me in a capacity of showing my gratitude otherwise, which, if it should never happen, I hope he'll take the will for the deed. You are good enough to think £3 a Trifle; but for my part (tho' it be small in comparison with Many Calls I have for it) I look upon it as a great Matter, when I consider how rare it is to find a man in that country who would be as mindful of an absent friend as your family is of me, without any obligations thereto but the Motions of Him who is the Inspirer of good thoughts and the great Remunerator of good Dispositions. You say he has already ten children, and all but two a Dead Charge. By speaking thus you seem to misapprehend the Blessings of Heaven for Misfortunes, for a Numerous Issue has been ever looked upon as one of the greatest Blessings of the married state, especially when Providence has furnished the parents with a competent share of wealth for the subsistence of their children."

The future divine proceeds to wish Donal Mor and Maur-ni-Dhuiv "had fifteen times the number, upon condition they were as well able to do for them as for their present charge; and so please God, if it be His will, to add every year one to the number of your father's children, with a child's portion of his worldly inheritance."

I found an amusing letter descriptive of the mighty fuss my Lord Kenmare's advent created at Killarney, and treating of things in general in that more civilized district. As it amused me, I will give my reader the benefit of it.

Of the twenty-two children of Maur-ni-Dhuiv and Donal Mor, nine must have died in infancy or early childhood. My hero and two sisters were born in 1745 and ensuing years. Two of the elder daughters of the house were already married, for the student says, "I am glad your sister is married to Mr. Sughrue, for I believe her well off." And in sending his formal budget of greetings desires his love "to your sister MacCarthy." John and Maurice O'Connell were near in age, and among the elders of the surviving thirteen children. Morgan, the Liberator's father, was the third son. Connell was much younger than they, but somewhat older than Daniel Charles, my hero. The two younger lads strikingly resembled each other, and were very handsome. All were fine, tall men, considerably above the average stature.

I have never heard but two anecdotes of my hero's childhood, and have no precise information as to his early education. All the brothers seem to have been conversant with French and Latin. These acquirements they probably imbibed from Father Grady, a foreign-bred priest, whose head-quarters were at Darrynane, and whose piety, simplicity, and queer sayings, in very defective English, are still remembered. The eldest brother, John, was most kind and warm-hearted, and, according to a formal letter of counsel to his younger brother Maurice, had imparted to him the first elements of knowledge. The old letters mention "pushing masters"—no doubt a species of "grinder"—besides the hedge schoolmaster.

My hero, according to his own sworn declaration, was born on May 21, 1745; but, oddly enough, his mother seems to have forgotten the date, and for years he was supposed to have been born two years later.

He was only three years and a half old when Maurice, his lifelong correspondent, went to school at Cork. The first letter addressed by John, the eldest brother, to Maurice, and Maurice's reply, are so quaint that I shall append them. John wrote a small legible Italian hand, almost like a foreign lady's. Maurice's is as large as a modern British hand, rather round in boyhood, and becoming taller and much more angular than most eighteenth-century writing as he advanced in life.

I cannot find any letters about John's marriage; so I infer that Maurice may have been present at it. It took place in January, 1748, according to Maurice's own statement.

I shall now give an amusing letter to John from his kinsman Mahony, of Dunloe.

John Mahony, of Dunloe, to John O'Connell.

Dunloe, March 9, 1750.

DR. JACK,—I am much obliged to your Father for ye kind present of fish. There was but one Salmon taken here that I know of since Xmas.

Our minds are all taken up here with ye coming of Lord Kenmare and his Gang. They were expected last Thursday. A great Deal of Whiteboys and Girls, and all ye inhabitants in and about Killarney, in their Best Array, ready to meet him, when an account came that he would not come this Fortnight. I believe he intends surprizing us to avoid any Frolic or extraordinary Cavalcade. I can't tell you with any Certainty any thing about Dr. Crosbie, and heard Lord Shelbourne starts some new obstacles against renewing, some think by the instigation of Geoffrey Maurice. However, Crosbie is pushing on his suit with vigor. It will soon come to a Hearing. Doubtless he knows no more of it as yet. Sister Lawlor got a young son last Wednesday. He is not much bigger than a Rabbit. I hear she has been very weak since, but I hope will soon get ye better of it. I have been in Corke for 3 weeks in last month, where the People were highly entertained with a Turk, who danced and sang, and did the most surprizing equilibres on a wire hung across the stage in the playhouse. 'Twould take up too much time to tell you ye particulars. Our Assizes here is the 8th of April, in Limerick and on here. The Judges Hassett and Dawson. Friends at Faha and ye Point are well. There are a great many Candidates putting up for Grenagh. Nobody knows here yet who'l have it. My Bror. Jerry intends for Corke abt. the later end of this month to take Ship. I shall get as far as Corke and . . . Good Family at Darinane.

I am yrs. affectly.,

JOHN MAHONY.

John O'Connell, of Darrynane, to his brother Maurice.

Darrinane, January 4, 1748.

DEAR MAURICE,—I lay hold of this oppertunity to open a correspondance with you, which, as this is its commencement, we may date from Christmas, 1747. To obviate y^r first curiosity, I am to inform you that all friends are, God be praised, well, and that nothing new has happened here since y^r departure. We have had a Merry New Year; doubt not but you had the same, and hope We shall all see many happy ones. I am now to ask how you spend your time, and give me a just account. I shall then be able to Judge of y^r taste in ye disposal of ye fleeting days. I believe you sometimes sit to rescribe the book I gave you; and, whenever you doe, be certain to refer to the sphere in ye geography, to reckon thereby the definitions of ye book to yourself. Questionless you sometimes goe to the Change to observe ye Custums there, and you probably Now and then visit ye Coffee Houses to read ye News and see ye various modes of address and behaviour. In the Course of y^r Remarks, I fancy you'll own y^t a cheerful Mien, an easy, free deportment, and a courteous, affable behaviour is ye most graceful and most recommending [manner] Man can conduckt himself in; the three means [of] improvement a Man has are writing, reflection on what is heard, and read[ing]. And in these Methods the great art is to select and glean out what's good, and leave ye bad behind. Y^e Choice of Company is one of ye most essential things for youth, and which they ought to be very nice in, for external appearances often, too often, deceive us; and which may at first seem to have no impression on us, will in Course of time get deep into us, if Wee don't speedily see into, and when ye evil communication [is] y^t [that] sets us the evil example. Young Company is the most dangerous, and consequently the most to be taken care off; y^t is, a man must be cautious in imbibing none of ye criminal qualifications wch young men are frequently infected with, and which they mistake for gallantry and high breeding, it being, indeed, ye lowest and most servile; and ye best caution a man can keep is to use this kind of loose, idle Company very sparingly, and never at unseasonable hours. It must at ye same time be confessed y^t [that] if a man looks out he'll meet several young men whose minds are sound, and conversation improving and gay; and these are such as I should like.

Please my compliments to Mr. and Mrs. Conway, and kind service to Doctor Connell, who, I presume, is friendly to you. Join to it my Father and Mother's Blessing, and ye kind remembrance of ye other Friends.

Dr Maurice,
Y^r most affect. Bro.,
JOHN CONNELL.

P.S.—Pray is Cornelius Connell gone yet?

The boy Maurice [Hunting Cap] to his brother John.

Corke, February ye 3d, 1748.

DR. BROTHER,—I received Yours Dated the 18th Ult., wherein you charge me with being doubly in y^r Debt. I've, In Answer to y^r former, wrote to Owen MacCarthy, to wch I refer you, and shall use my utmost Efforts to adhere to ye rules of Beheaviour laid down in both. I send ye Hat, w^{eh} I wish may be agreable, and have traversed ye whole City (to no purpose) for a 'Directorium ad Canonicas horas.' You'll please to tell my Mother I chuse a riding Coat, wch pray may be sent off by ye first oppertunity. I am infinitely obliged for y^r repeated presents and Admonitions, and Do pray you'll Continue the Latter. With regard to ye Cash for Coats, my father ordered I should pay 5s. 5d. for shoes, and remainder I kept, being all he was pleased to leave me. I have this day agreed with a pushing Master, wch I hope won't be Disagreable to him. Dr. Connell is in no shape friendly to me.

I am, with duty to my Mother, and compliments to all friends,

Y^r Very Affectionate Brother,
MAURICE CONNELL.

P.S.—I have y^r Breeches by my Uncle Maurice's people.

In January, 1748, John married Mary Falvey, of Faha, a young lady of very ancient family. I spent a day at Faha, and beheld, in the modern house, hoards of the loveliest old Indian china, which probably belonged to Mary's mother. I append to this chapter some account of the family,[1] as it is specially typical of some phases of old Irish life; and I heard a good deal of it from a follower of theirs, whose father rented the old house of Faha when the family ceased to reside there. Sergeant Michael O'Connor procured for me the "Poor Scholar's Blessing"[2] to Mary Falvey's sister-in-law. I heard him recite a considerable portion of it.

I am sorry not to have found the wedding letters.

In a letter of March, 1748, John O'Connell begins, in the style of the period, by expressing his edification at the manner in which the younger brother proportions his time between the school, recreation, and reading. He congratulates him on the opportunity of forming his manners and improving his mind. He discourses in the same strain on the advantages of different branches of education, casually remarking, "I gave you the little taste I could of ye elements of knowledge." Then follows the news of the country-side. The good-natured elder brother then says, "My Mother sends you the riding coat, and the enclosed note to Mr. Conway will prevail with him to buy you the trimmings, and pay ye Taylor. [I fancy it was cloth to make the coat.] I have ventured in it to order Velvet, tho' I shall be one time or another rattled for it." The postscript says, "We have got a pushing Master, Mr. McCarthy; of whom do ye learn, and what does it cost you?"

"Pushing master" was the old phrase for "grinder," or "coach." Besides grinders in towns, peripatetic sages lived

---

[1] See Note D, p. 53.
[2] See Note E. p. 57.

about in the gentlemen's houses, tarrying a few months here and there, working up pupils who had had the hedge schoolmaster and the old foreign-bred priest to teach the "elements."

A third sister was then married, as John mentions, in March, 1748 (same letter), that brother Segerson was likely to get a good *quantum meritus* in the shape of salvage, he and his father having saved a Dutchman, laden with butter, which stranded in Ballinskelligs Bay.

In June Maurice returns. John writes—

Darrynane, May 29, 1748.

DEAR MAURICE,—I send you my horse and furniture to bring you home. The pannels of the Saddle want stuffing, which you will get done, else the horse's back will suffer. I also send you my Stock Buckle, with one of its Buttons, which got loose, and which you'll get fastened by a Silver Smith. I assure you I am quite void of Cash at present, or w^d send you some. Father Grady greets you, and sends you by Bearer 4s. and 4d., for which he prays you'll buy him a good bridle, stirrup leather, and a leather girt, wch don't neglect. [How relatively cheap leather goods must have been in those days!] I am told your Foster-father sends you some money, and suppose my Father likewise orders you some. If so you ought to buy the little Conveniences necessary for the Country, as Boots and spurs and a whip, etc. There is Cloath here, to make my Father and you Coats. My Mother sends money to buy the under particulars [list missing] for me, which you'll doe. Bring all the Current News, put the two Letters for Carlow into the Post Office. You'll strive to make as genteel an Exit as you can, and take leave of y^r good acquaintances and friends, and in ye journey home take Care of ye horse and things.

I am, y^r truly Affect. Brother,

JOHN CONNELL.

My compliments to Mr. and Mrs. Conway and Mr. Fuller.

Every spring and summer, big Daniel O'Connell and one of his sons went to the Tralee Assizes, and on to the County Limerick fairs, buying and selling great droves of cattle, and staying at friends' houses. On these occasions John's wife used to stay with her family during her husband's absence. She also often visited them at other times.

There are two pretty letters of hers in March, 1748—one to "My Deare," the other to "My Deare Life." She is longing for St. Patrick's Day, when he will come to her, reproaches him for not having been more impatient to come and see her, who esteems him above all the world, and sends her mamma's thanks for a present of oysters and scallops. Poor John, in the absence of Maurice, had doubtless been busy about the spring tillage. These young people were probably told by their elders to marry, but they seem to have been truly in love with each other.

Maurice, who appears so unsympathetic to the tender passion, did not escape scot-free after all. The venerable Miss Julianna O'Connell, his cousin, who kept house for him in her youth and his extreme old age, tells me he was in love with a member of the Falvey family, but sacrificed inclination to duty, and was fond of telling his young relatives he had done so, as a hint to them to do likewise. We actually find him, a year after his visit to Cork, employing his cousin, Mr. Mahony, of Dunloe, to write verses for him.

James Mahony, of Dunloe, to Maurice O'Connell.

Dunloe, March 19, 1749.

Dr. Cousin,—I had the pleasure of y^{rs} of the 17th, wth ye very agreable present of fish, for which we return y^u a great many thanks. I am very glad to hear of y^r safe return from the East. I believe the road, for more reasons than one, seem'd more fatiguing on ye Coming back than when I had the Satisfaction of travelling wth y^u. However, I hope ye heart as well as all other parts of ye Body, is yet entire. I am not unacquainted with Conflicts of this Nature, and therefore I am the better qualified to prescribe rules upon these occasions, and should readily do it for y^r advantage, if I was not fully satisfied of y^r own Judgement and penetration to give up too much to that Wily and Fascinating Deity.

I'll Draw out the poem you require, as well as one made on this place, and wish they may help to amuse you in a thoughtful and melancholy hour, absent from your Dulcinea. If any mistakes in transcribing them occur to you, I begg y^u may amend 'em, for I've done the two in a hurry. As the latter is in some Measure a Poetical Panegyrick on us, I should hardly trouble you with it, but that I Imagine the Flights of a luxiriant brain which so apparently present themselves in this Poem, might not be to you, a Votary of Parnassus, disagreable. My Brother gives ye all his kind service, to whom I likewise wish all imaginable happiness;

and whenever y^u see our agreable acquaintance at the Fishery and Tarmons, I beg y^u may make my best Compliments to 'em, for which I shall acknowledge myself,
Dr. Sr.,
Y^r Obliged and affect. Kinsman and hble. Sert.,
JAMES MAHONY.

Maurice O'Connell, in after-years the most practical hard-headed of men, who devoted his life to amassing wealth for himself and managing the affairs of a huge connection in so far as their easy-going, unthrifty ways permitted, appears here as a love-lorn swain, and in the next letter as an indolent bookworm. I fancy his powers had no scope during this period of his life, when he was a mere subordinate to father and brother, and that it was when he got real practical control of affairs that his great business capacity developed and asserted itself.

"Babby," doubtless Barbara, who comes on a visit, must have been the Dulcinea of the previous letter. There were three families of Falveys; so if she were not Mary Falvey's sister, she may have been her cousin.

The formal installation of the young couple at Darrynane seems to have been deferred till the fine weather, as it would have been most difficult and disagreeable for a lady to ride across the mountains in winter.

Faha, May 7, 1749.

DEAR BROTHER,—We arrived last night from traversing ye County of Limerick, where at different ffairs we gott 93 yearlings. My ffather says Molly and I are soon to goe home, and promises to send you, Tim Carthy, and my Uncle Geoffrey for us. Y^e horse y^t I bought will be able to carry Molly and you, and I'll ride whatever you bring; but, as Babby goes, my ffather promices to send his black padd for her, wch you'll not forget. Bring no luggage at all, as you'll have but one night's delay, and y^t all ye Cloak bags will be necessary for her things and mine. I prayed him to send a man and horse to us as soon as he gets home wth Tim Carthy's Cloak bag, y^t we may send off some of our Things directly, wch put him in mind of, when you are coming you must bring either my Mare or ye Bay Horse for Molly's maid to ride. See, as much as you can, y^t matters be well prepared; and I hope my Mother has a Cannister of green Tea. Babby and ye lads may possibly stay a Month; and it will be necessary to have a stock of flour, flesh, and drink, *sat. sapienti.*

I am now to tell you that my ffather has in our travels complained of you to me, in both his sober and drunken capacity. He says y^t you never look to any thing if you are not specially commanded, y^t you doe nothing but read from morning till night, nor exercise yourself any way. He says y^t, being destined for neither ye army nor sea, you know you have nothing to depend on but industry in ye ffarming way, and therefore is dissatisfy'd y^t you don't apply to learning some Experience on those things while you have youth and leisure; not y^t he w^d at all disapprove of y^r reading at convenient times, but now y^t ye have a good foundation in books, and y^t you are grown up, he is provoked at y^r being a mere recluse and caring for nothing but your Room and Reading. I argued a good deal with him on ye thing, and told him it was happy you were so studious in acquiring of knowledge and improving y^r understanding while yet disengaged from ye Cares of Life; but, to speak my thought to you freely, I am of opinion you should alter y^r Methods somewhat, y^t you shd. appear more assidious in ye affairs of my ffather, and learn ye Methods of ye Country wth regard to dry and dairy Cattle—how got and disposed off, etc., etc.; how ye ground is till'd and manag'd, etc., etc. I begin to perceive my own mistake in not seeing into those things more than I did while I might, and probably I shall perceive it more and more by degrees. You can read at Night and sometimes by day. Goe visit ye workmen; goe fish of a fair day in ye Boat; sometimes ride and see ye herdsman and Cattle; see Waste grass, and corn, and sometimes Rush, leap, run, play ball, etc., etc. By this you'll inform yourself, you'll doe ye ffamily a service, you'll exercise yourself, and, wch is more than all, you'll please your ffather thoroughly, upon whom you know your future welfare depends, and whom (believe me) you can not otherwise please.

My Duty to my Mother, and love to ye rest,

I am, Dr. Maurice,

Y^r most Affect. Bror.,

JOHN CONNELL.

The next letter contains a comical list of old-fashioned garments which Maurice is to receive by messengers from Faha, and stow away. Unhappily, the chest is locked, so we only get a small inventory—

Faha, June 4, 1749.

DR. BROR.,—I have the pleasure of y^{rs} of the 1st in answer. Y^e fish was most acceptable. You have taken ye hint setting things to right. Mr. McCarthy is gone, sorrowful News! I am glad my precepts with regard to attending to Business have weight with you. Molly, who desires her love to you, has made ye Ladyes promise to pay off y^r kisses with interest when they see you. Whenever you come, you'll see y^t she does. . . .

We are to go home from ye ffair. You can come here some days beforehand, if you have a mind to have a proper acquaintance with the Ladyes.

Here follows ye Inventory of wh^t are in the Portmanteaus, for ye trunk is lock'd and consequently secure. In ye large bag are my white Coat, Waiscoat, and britches, my old brown coat and blew britches, 6 ruffled shirts and 6 stocks, 5 pair of wove silk, thread, cotton, and worsted stockings, and a silk gown of Molly's, all wch you'll stow handsomely in my Chest. In ye small bag are 3 gowns, a dozen shifts, and a dozen Aprons, all wh^{ch} let my Mother put together into one of her Chests. I send a pair of Shoes of mine in the fflap, and 2 brandes, all wch I beg and pray you will take proper care of, and put out of ye way of being mislaid.

      I am, y^r most affect. Bror.,
         JNO. CONNELL.

Just going to Mass in haste.
My Respects to ffather Grady, and Service to the Rest.

The young couple lived principally at Darrynane, keeping a maid and a servant-boy, probably a precursor of our "buttons" of to-day, and having their own horses, cattle, etc. This youth was not only clothed, but taught; and John O'Connell's account-book shows the quaint item—

"Paid Jasper Lisk, the School Master, for teaching my boy to read, write, and siffre, for a twelvemonth, 1s. 1d."

According to the custom of the time, their little girl Abigail was nursed out, but we soon see her mentioned in the letters. She seems to have been a special pet of her uncle Maurice. Some disagreements arose about land between a relative of his and Mary's brothers, in which Maurice took his kinsman's side, and he drew up a statement of the life and conversation of the family with Mary Falvey. This is a most graphic picture of old-world life. Ross O'Connell found fragments of the narrative at Darrynane, and the old letters supply the rest.

John and Mary seem to have truly loved each other; and,

though left a widow very young, she never married again. She was expecting the birth of a child when he died of one week's illness. Maur-ni-Dhuiv's grief was intense when her son was stricken. She besought him to forsake the family burying-place in Cahirsiveen, and suffer his remains to be laid in the Abbey ruins on the island, where she could often go and say her rosary above his grave. Yet so strong was the feeling among Irish-people about burial in family sepulchres, that he refused this most reasonable request, saying, "Kindred ashes love to mingle."[1]

When the poor young fellow died, the mother's grief found a vent in elaborate funeral rites; but she shed no tears. She sent messengers far and near, bidding friends and tenants to the wake and funeral, and recited laments over him, in which it was customary for all who entered the death-chamber to join.

A relative's wife, Mrs. Charles Philip O'Connell, of Riverstown, in the Glen, near Ballinabloun, newly settled in the wilds, and ignorant of this primitive usage, fell on her knees in silent prayer. The bereaved mother violently reproached her for uttering no words of praise and sorrow above her dead. She clapped her hands, and called out in Irish, "Where are the dark women of the glens, who would keen and clap their hands, and would not say a prayer until he was laid in the grave?"

The new-comer excused herself by stating that she had spent most of her life in Cork, where no keens[2] were recited, and where it was etiquette to pray in silence around the dead.

Maur-ni-Dhuiv called out in Irish, "Do foscail an Peadair me!" *i.e.* "Your prayer has opened the flood-gates of my heart!" And the pent-up tears gushed forth, as if the lady's prayer had melted the stoical pride of her heart.

The young widow spent a good deal of her time with her husband's parents, and her little Abby was as a daughter of the house. By local tradition, and by her subsequent behaviour, we see that Mary Falvey, of Faha, was a high-spirited, impetuous woman, yet, living with her people-in-law,

[1] Miss Julianna says the dying man repeated a Latin line, and translated it thus to his mother.
[2] In Irish, caoine, "a dirge."

she curbed her spirit, and charmed them by her "prudent discretion and recommending modesty." This young creature coming among them is stated to have inspired *what?* "Y⁰ tenderness and respect due to y⁰ rank she held in y⁰ family." There is not a bit of warm natural feeling in Maurice's statement. He does not say a word of any real human liking. The eldest son's wife, the mother of his possible son, was to be tended and respected. In her sorrow and loneliness she wants to rush off home to her own mother; and here is the youthful sage—he cannot have been twenty-five years old —lecturing her on *les convenances*. Ladies should not be seen beyond their gates so soon after bereavement, etc. When nature proves too strong for the iron bonds of eighteenth-century etiquette, he puts the best face on the matter, solemnly escorts her a suitable distance, visits her at her mother's, sends to inquire after her, induces her to come back for a while, and, failing to prevail on her to remain for the birth of the expected heir, rides near a day's journey with her, and arranges to come to the christening. Hunting Cap shall tell it all in his own words, worthy, indeed, of Dr. Johnson. "Sister Mary's" letters, scrupulously preserved and docketed by him, fill up the picture. It is rare to find a woman's letters among the hoards in old houses. Mary O'Connell, born Falvey, writes and spells well. The little girl, Abigail, after her grandmother Falvey, was called Abby when she grew up. As a little toddler, she rejoiced in the hideous appellation of Gobby, short for Gobbinette, the Irish for Abigail. Maurice writes—

"Account of the Death of my poor Brother, with the subsequent behaviour of his Widow.

"My brother, John O'Connell, was seized with stitches of a violent pleurisy on the 2nd day of May, 1751. He languished therewith till y⁰ 9th under y⁰ most intense and grievous pains, and y⁰ 8th day died in y⁰ 26th year of his age. He had since January, 1748, been married to Mary Falvey, of Faha, the eldest daughter of John Falvey. This lady brought him a fortune of £300 stg. They had hitherto resided with his father at Darrinane, where Mrs. O'Connell met with y⁰ tenderness and respect due to y⁰ rank she held in y⁰ family from every individual thereof. Her conduct was hitherto conformable to a prudent discretion and recommending modesty, which, added to ye sense of respect which was universally conceived for ye place she enjoyed, rendered ye family quite studious to oblige her. After the interment of my brother, she immediately discovered a disposition to accompany her brother Hugh, who had arrived in ye family 14 or 15 days after ye sad occurrence, to Faha, his and her mother's habitation. She communicated her resolution to me; to which I replied that it was too early after soe severe a shock as ye death of her husband to undertake so long and irksome a journey, that it was not practised by persons in her condition to go abroad soe early, and further added that ye world would conclude that a separation soe very sudden must have proceeded from some dissentions between her and her husband's friends, as it tended to their mutual . . .

"All my efforts proved vain. She set out with her Brother in 2 or 3 days after, and carried with her every thing belonging to her, a circumstance not a little aggravating, as it must have confirmed the world, as I before observed, in the opinion of her being unfriendly treated by the family, and she quitted 'em in a perfect belief of her intention utterly to seperate from 'em, and forget the ties which had formerly subsisted between 'em.

"Notwithstanding this unkind, and, I must say, unnatural proceeding, and the manifest disregard of my sentiments, I attended her to Bannilians, which is about two parts of the way. At parting I promised soon to visit her, and in a few days sent expresly to see her, and wrote a consolatory letter penned in ye tenderest and best-natured terms that a slender capacity, led on by a profusion of the most sincere respect and esteem, could devise."

The "consolatory epistle," I regret to say, has eluded my search; but here is the poor young widow's reply—

Faha, June 7, 1751.

My Dr. Bror.,—I had the pleasure of your letter yesterday, and do assure you no person can be better pleased to hear from you than I am, and that as often as you can. I am proud, Dr. Bror., to find y^t y^u have not forgot y^r promise in coming to see me very soon. I am just as when we parted, most part of my time unwell, tho' I do all I can to follow your good and friendly advice in bearing my crosses and misfortunes with ye greatest patience and resignation I can. I need not tell you how great they are in ye loss of ye best of husbands. I am very sensible, Dr. Bror., of yᵣ great loss, and how dear you were to that sweet companion the Great God has parted me from. Welcome be His holy Will. Gobby is very well, thank God, but she seldom parts me, as she knows nobody else here yet. I shall say no more at present, but conclude with sincerest affections and respects to my ffather and Mother, and kind service to all yᵉ rest of that good family.

My Dear Maurice,
Your most afftd. and much afflicted Sister,
MARY CONNELL.

All this family desire their best respects to you.

I broke in on Maurice's narrative to give the simple and pathetic reply to his letter to his brother's widow. I now resume it *verbatim*—

"In a few days after I made her a visit, and remained with her for 15 or 16 days. From thence I went to Tralee, where I remained till after the ensuing Assizes, which was about yᵉ 15th inst. After the Assizes I returned to Faha; and, after using my best entreaties, prevailed with her to come hither.

"We set out yᵉ 10th, and arrived here yᵉ 20th. She was met in yᵉ most warm and affectionate manner by my Father and Mother. They discovered entire comfort and satisfaction at her appearance, and studied constantly to console and please her. I took every oppertunity yᵗ offered to please and render her kind offices, and divert her from her trouble, tho' quite overwhelmed therewith myself. All yᵗ was not sufficient to engage her to make any stay.

"She parted for Faha the 1st of December, in company with her brother Hugh, who came (as was, I presume, before concerted) for her a day or two before. I attended her as far as Glenbeigh, assured her of a lasting continuance of my respect and esteem, and engaged for her to let me know when she should be delivered, in order I should wait on her to represent her deceased husband on this occasion. To this she agreed; and after mutual endearments, we parted.

"In yᵉ latter end of January following, she sent an express to let me know yᵗ she had been delivered of a daughter. I set out yᵉ following day, notwithstanding that the weather was very rigorous, and remained till she . . ."

Here several pages are missing.

By her letter of the previous month, we see Maurice arranging and advising, and Maur-ni-Dhuiv ruling, for the mother and expected child. The young widow writes—

Faha, 22 Xber, 1751.

My Dr. Bror.,—I had the pleasure of your kind letter with £7 0s. 3d., which is by 8 shillings and 3 pence more thⁿ ye half-year's interest. I would be glad to know what it is for, as ye made no mention of it in your letter to me. Inclosed I send you a receipt for what y^u desired. As for my ffather-in-law, I don't in ye least doubt his willingness to serve me. I would be the most ungrateful person on earth if I had harboured any [doubt] either of him or of any of ye ffamily.

My Dr. Bror., I am greatly obliged to you for considering me in a double light, and it is more than I deserve, otherwise than by being the relict of y^r most worthy Bror.; and since it has been God's will to make me that unfortunate woman to loose soe good and fond a Husband, it gives me great comfort that he has left behind a most kind and affectionate Brother, as I have always found you to be since our first acquaintance. You shall hear from me next month. I am very glad to hear Sister Nonny [1] is married, and I hope and wish it may turn out for her happiness.

I am satisfied to have a Nurse of my Mother's chusing, as I find it is most agreable to her and my ffather, tho' I would not willingly have my child nursed at so great a distance from me. I am glad to hear ye boat has got off soe safe as ye say.

My best respects to my ffather and Mother, and am, with most tender love and duty,

   My Dear Maurice,

      Your most affect. Sister,

         Mary Connell.

P.S.—The half guinea you sent is light, and I believe won't pass. Gobby is very well, thank God.

As I could not help feeling a certain sympathy for this unconventional dame, I set to work to find out *what* she could have carried off. Perhaps she may have had some of her cattle driven before her. Her husband's will mentions some for her and the child, and he gives her all her own possessions, his and her own furniture, and his riding horse and its furniture (this would include her pillion), and his linen, which might be useful for the babies. He leaves his whips and buckles to Maurice; and his gilt snuff-box to her, to be kept for the baby. Some silver spoons, a wedding gift from Maur-ni-Dhuiv, appear in his account-book.

[1] Mrs. O'Sullivan, of Couliagh, whose wild son, Captain Mark, of the Irish Brigade, is so often mentioned in the old letters. Her son John married his cousin Mary, daughter of John Segerson and Alice O'Connell.

In a list of things belonging to their daughter appear, years later, five rings, a gold watch-cover, and "my great-great-grandmother's rosary." Most of the old rosaries were of handsome agate, with heavy silver mountings; some, indeed, were all silver or gold. Poor John O'Connell also leaves his wife the indentures of his serving-boy, whose education was duly provided for at thirteen pence per annum. The silver spoons and snuff-box and rosary, the "buttons," the horse and furniture, and her little daughter Abigail, would not have been such a large collection of belongings, even with nurse and maid and ponies to carry them thrown in. So I fear the inconsiderate woman must have had some black cattle driven off before her.

I don't quite see how Maurice could have *represented* her husband at the christening, as he said, unless he meant to pay all expenses. This may have been his meaning; for, although exceedingly close in money matters in general, he was always ready to behave generously and handsomely on great occasions.

In poor John's account-book "tips" figure largely. To servants at different houses, to the priest at a wedding, to pipers and servants at "my sister's hauling home,"[1] and at two different christenings the nurses get 3s. 6d. and 4s. 6d.

The cambric linen, lawn, and thread for the first baby's clothes cost £3 19s. 8d.; the christening suit, £1 11s. 8d.

"Gown my wife bestowed on her mother, and christening clothes, £2 18s. 11d."

The young people, living with the young man's parents, bought no food in general, but the happy father supplied—evidently for the christening party—29 lbs. of beef at 2¼d., 5s. 11d.; one side of lamb, 11d.

I fancy the first baby was born at Faha.

A mysterious set of entries were for *caudle*, which I feel sure would kill any modern lady under the circumstances. A charming and most intelligent old lady, the late Mrs. Deborah Grubb, explained them, and told me that she had tasted it as a child. "A pint of cinnamon-water for my wife"

---

[1] "Hauling home." The bride was escorted home by a great crowd of friends and followers. In a country with roads, horses were taken from her coach, and the peasants drew her part of the way home. She was usually carried over the threshold of her new dwelling.

is a different item. Brown sugar, almonds, barley, nutmegs, white wine, and oranges, for caudle, amount to 9s. 4d.

The patient got none. It was served to the ladies who visited her out of wide, fine china cups. For the gentlemen, rum, wine of three prices, fruit, and sugar were supplied on this occasion.

Doctor Cronin only gets half a guinea. Mrs. Carr, "ye midwife," receives a whole guinea.

Maurice duly presided at the christening, but the poor babe soon joined its father. Lively, wilful Abby, whom her grave uncle found it hard to manage afterwards, alone survived, and she had a hard struggle for existence—flying from small-pox in one page, stricken with ague in another.

To my mind there is one bit worthy of Baring Gould in what comes next—the lady mounting up on the pillion of the borrowed horse, behind the toil-stained foot-messenger set up for her "fore-man," and Hunting Cap's implied rebuke in the lament over his inability to personally attend her, and the statement that he sent servants and horses to convey her. How she must have winced under his tender and protecting care, and the perpetual vigilance with which he watched over her, expecting such marvels of deportment, graceful, modest dependency, and mild, continued affliction, which no eager, impulsive woman could feel with any great intensity for two years, though Mary Falvey never forgot the lover-husband of her youth, and never cast away his name! They say in Irish that she never changed his name or the colour of her gown; and black, except during the actual period of compulsory mourning, was little worn a century and a half ago.

There was some litigation, as I said before, between Hugh Falvey, of Faha, and one of the O'Connells, in which the widow and her people-in-law took opposite sides. Maurice's elaborate statement was evidently drawn up to show she had had no personal cause of complaint, which her letters to him prove to be true. Owing to loss of the missing portions, I can only give a brief summary of their dealings; but it is exceptionally valuable as a life-study of our ancestors.

"I solemnly declare," writes Maurice, "it is very far from my thoughts to misrepresent her [Mrs. John O'Connell], or to derogate from her merits. No; what I hereby intend is only an indication of mine and Family's beheaviour to this lady, which could not be affected without giving the general knowledge of the whole affair. The chiefest motives for it were to prevent the severe and hard notions of this affair; which narrative of the facts may beget in the mind of the most inconsiderate individual to whom we should not be known."

To resume our former account—

"About the middle of August following, I called to see her in my way hither, but, from reasons before mentioned, I made no way there, and should have previously told this."

It would seem that she had been with them before, as a June letter describes a return journey. She writes—

Faha, June 12, 1752.

I had the pleasure, my Dear Maurice, of your kind letter yesterday, which, you may depend, was very agreable to me. I had just finished a letter I was sending to John Crohon when yours arrived, but I would not let slip ye opportunity of letting you hear from me.

I am too well acquainted, Dr. Maurice, with your disposition and regards for me; and, tho' we have those frequent seperations, to my great loss and affliction, yet my regard and affection for your Family shall never lessen; otherwise I would be most ungrateful. My Dear Maurice, y^t pleasure I have in y^r letter is next to seeing you. I shall now give you an account of our journey. The night you parted us, wee were to stay in a house neare ye River, where I was feasted with salmon. You may judge how wee lay. Wee got to Faha next day. Gobby was very easy with my Bror. Jack. She is every day going to see you. Cornilius has observed y^r directions in calling to see ye child. He tells me shee is well. I am pleased my Father has arrived safe from Dingle. Killarney is now a merry place. I wish you would come and take share of their diversions; but would not have you think of going to Tralee, as they have got ye Small Pox there. I have nothing worth relating. I conclude with Dutiful Respects to my ffather and Mother, and kind affections to all ye good family.

My Dear Maurice,
Y^r most sincerely affec. Sister,
MARY CONNELL.

All ye family desire their best compliments to you and family.

Mary O'Connell writes again in a few days. The baby, whom she had suffered to be nursed so far away from her by a nurse of Maur-ni-Dhuiv's choosing, sickens, and she writes to bespeak her brother-in-law's good offices about it. Fancy having one's baby sick, and having to trust to a countryman's report of it!

Faha, July 9, 1752.

My Dr. Bror.,—This morning I was eased of great uneasiness I have been in since my last to you. It was too great to be expressed. I thought you were resolved to forget me quite, tho' I could not imagine what your reason was, as I never intended to give you any, nor never shall. I am now convinced the cause of y^r not writing to me was entirely owing to the man who carried my letter; for I thought, Dear Maurice, I know your good dispositions and esteem for me too well to think you would neglect doing me ye satisfaction of letting me hear from you as often as you could, and hope you believe nothing could give me greater pleasure.

I had an account about nine days agoe of ye child being very ill. The man I sent to see her told me she was then mending. He told me my Mother had got there a little before him, and that you ware to see her y^t day before, for which you have my sincere thanks. This man tells me she is still in a bad way. I fear she will never do well. I wish she could be carried to Darrinane. I would have gone to see her before now, but that I can't leave Gobby. I shall soon begin to discipline her, as you desire. My ffather has been here with me a copple of nights. You will please to give him and my Mother my Dutiful respects, and best affections to all the Family,

And am, Dr. Maurice,
Y^r most sincere and affect. Sister,
Mary Connell.

P.S.—The Ladies and my Brother John desire their respects to you. I pray you'll tell my Mother I got ye sheep and wool she sent me, for which and many other things I am greatly obliged to her. I am soe taken up with Gobby, I hardly know w^{ht} I write.

A fortnight earlier the young widow had written the following letter:—

Faha, June 23, 1752.

My Dear Brother,—I take this oppertunity of writing to you, tho' any other would be much more agreable to me than this, as he goes to serve my ffather with some papers about this land in dispute between Charles Connell and my Bror. Hugh. Dr. Maurice, it gives me vast concern to think that my ffather or Uncle Jeffery would be brought to any trouble about this affair. I hope and sincerely wish they may not. I know my Bror. Hugh, who is the person concerned in this, would be as unwilling to hurt or disoblige my ffather as he would be his own Bror.; and is shure he has noe hand in this affair; but he says he hopes my ffather can't take it ill of him to take all ye fair methods he can to come by his own.

I would be glad my ffather would send me a little money now, if it be convenient, as my Mother here desires. I would lay it out for yearlings, which she will give me grass for. I should not call for this till he had thought proper to give it, but y^t I am to buy them at ye next ffair. Y^e bearer's receipt is sufficient. I thought I should have ye pleasure to hear about this time. Tho' short a time it is since I parted from you, it seems long to me. Let me know if you had any late account from ye Child. Give my dutiful respects to my ffather and Mother, and affections to all y^r Family, that

I am, my Dr. Bror.,
Y^r most sincere and affect. Sister,
MARY CONNELL.

P.S.—All my Family desire their best compliments to you and ffamily. Gobby is well, and desires her respects to you.

Notwithstanding the litigation between Hugh Falvey, referred to in the preceding letter, and the O'Connells, the families continued on fairly friendly terms, and certainly stood by the young widow when she wanted them. All sorts of worries beset her. Maurice catalogues them in a very unsympathetic manner, but he helped her in every way, and was certainly devoted to her child. The second baby did not live long. The letter above quoted is thus referred to by Maurice—

"In ten days after parting she wrote pressingly for money that became due to her the 11th of May, and that by a person who was sent by her brother to give my Father with some papers relative to the above-mentioned suit. About the middle of August her Brother John was seized with ye small-pox. She, for ye preservation of her child, my little niece, from malignant disease, retired to my Uncle Geoffrey O'Donoghue, to Killarney. I, on hearing this, wrote in a strain very warm, to pray she would agree to come hither. Herewith necessity rather than choice caused her to comply, which was very visible from her manner of acting at this juncture . . .

for, before she answered my letter, she went to Faha, though under the difficulty of borrowing a horse, and making the fellow I had sent her her foreman."

This last sentence, perhaps, requires some explanation. The man behind whose saddle the lady's pillion was placed was called her "foreman." He was usually a relative, or, failing such, the most respectable of the menservants, in his best broadcloth. This unconventional dame did a fearful thing in riding through the country town behind the rough peasant stained with travel, who had carried the missive. The ensuing paragraph about servants and horses to attend her shows what the family respectability felt on this breach of *les convenances*.

Having described the very undignified manner in which the fair widow visited Faha, Hunting Cap goes on to say—

"She went there to consult whether or no she would go at my request. Nothing could remove the defference and regard which I thought due from me to her; and when I despatched horses and servants for her, and wrote an apologetic letter for my not personnally waiting on her, she arrived here about the 10th of December, to the infinite satisfaction of this family. The winter coming on obliged her to tarry till the 1st of April, 1753. She prepared to travel early in March with one Daniel Falvey, a kinsman of hers, who happened here at that time. But the weather, proving too severe, forced her to desist from ye project. I attended her with ye utmost care and dilligence during her abode here, in which I was seconded by all my friends, who joined in signalizing their uncommon attatchment and esteem for her. I saw her safe to Faha, not without considerable trouble to her and to me, occasioned by constant rain, where, after a night's delay, I left her, making ye most persuasive and sacred protestations of ye permanency of my kindest respect for her. To this she replied that my Family, and I in particular, had, since the death of her husband, carried themselves to her in such a sort as rendered our tender kindness to her, and ye defference we preserved for ye memory of my brother, unquestionable facts, and all of which she had and would retain ye most lively and gratefull sence. That she was perfectly satisfied of our resolution to persevere in this laudable and beneficient conduct, which greatly allayed the trouble she was wrapped in; and, finally, that a suitable return of ye unlimited benevolence would ever be the most predominant object of her care and attention, and particularly towards me, whom she considered as the delegate of her very worthy consort, consequently as her ruler and admonisher. Early in ye month of May her little daughter was taken with an ague that held her for two months. She herewith acquainted me. I visited her, and duly sent over once in six days to see her during the time."

Here ends the fragment. Does it not seem as if Baring Gould had written it? The messengers duly brought back bulletins of the little maid's progress, and what Dr. Cronin, who had brought her into the world, said of her in one letter. It appears her uncle Maurice had so spoilt her that no one could make her take her physic. Then the doctor ordered port wine. Maurice at once sent over a considerable quantity "of both kinds of wine," which, of course, had paid no duty, and which seems to have finished the cure.

By a letter of the young widow's we see that Maurice took the sickly baby to Darrynane. I fancy it died there, as there is no further mention of it; and Miss Julianna never even heard of its existence.

Big Daniel O'Connell had always been an indolent, easy-going man, not averse to riding about and inspecting, but disinclined to taking other forms of trouble. Maurice soon assumed the reins of actual government in the family: he reflected, weighed, compared, inquired. We hear little in the letters about his next brother, Morgan, the Liberator's father, because, as he was wanted at home to help to oversee the farming, smuggling, and fishing, there was no need to write letters about him. He was tolerably near in age to Maurice; Connell was much younger; and Daniel, my hero, younger still. These two lads, however, were devoted to each other, while they regarded Maurice as a second father. Perhaps Connell's early death led to the treasuring of every scrap about him, for, in proportion as information about my hero's early years is scanty, it abounds concerning the sailor-brother, drowned in the flower of his young manhood.

Only two anecdotes of Count O'Connell's childhood have reached me. He told one of his grandnieces that he had never slept in a four-post bed all to himself until he went to France; and to another he mentioned that from the time he was a very little fellow he had set his heart on being an officer in France, and making his fortune with his sword, and knowing King Louis. As his brother Connell had gone to sea when he was very young, the only boy at hand to whom he could confide these aspirations was his foster-brother. As the two boys rambled and sported over the mountains and cliffs, Daniel would pour forth his dreams, which were realized after all. The peasant lad, who was of a less venturous spirit, would try and dissuade him, especially observing, What did he want with King Louis? What finer place could King Louis have to live in than a "slate house"? and had he not a slate house to live in at home? From the long rambles of his boyhood the soldier of foreign lands derived the most passionate love and recollection of every rock and cliff and lovely view about his home. In his old age he would describe them to young relatives at school in France, and repeat long passages of Irish poems.

Darrynane is a perfect Paradise for boys. The noble mountains are alive with hares; woodcocks come to the woods which clothe the feet of the hills; grouse to the open moors; while the sea teems with fish. I saw *eight kinds* of fish [1] once together on the table at Darrynane on a Friday. At that time there were herds of ponies and plenty of good-sized horses, too; boats of all kinds abounded, as the population were practically amphibious.

The sea-board was pretty populous, and the smuggling-ships constantly brought over visitors, whose finer clothes and finer manners and travellers' tales of courts and cities would naturally inflame the imagination of a boy. I find by the letters that eighteen young and old kinsmen were serving France, Spain, and Austria at one time.

Farming and smuggling naturally occupied the elders of families, and the younger boys had to choose between trade, or physic, or the Church at home; and soldiering, sailoring, or doctoring, or a religious life abroad. I find mention of my hero's friends, Dr. O'Mahony, one of Louis XVI.'s physicians, and Dr. O'Connell, who endowed a "bourse" (or "free place") in the Irish College of Paris. Count Dease

---

[1] See Note B, p. 49.

was surgeon, over a century ago, to the Empress Catherine of Russia, and John Sobiesky's body-physician was a Kerry man, whose adventurous career is set forth in Smith's " Kerry."

For medicine, however, my hero seems to have had no fancy. The family had relatives serving in France and in Austria, and O'Sullivan kinsmen who were pilots—"masters," as they would have been styled in England—on board the King of Spain's galleons. One, whose letters I have also perused, and who guided the frigate which carried a new governor to the Netherlands, could earn more than a contemporary captain in the Spanish Navy. Then they had correspondents who disposed of outgoing cargoes of hides, wool, salt pork, salt beef, and butter, and freighted the fleet little smuggling craft with wine, brandy, tea, tobacco, and such like costly goods, and settled with the underwriters, and managed that the craft should sail under French or Spanish colours.

Before planting out his young brothers, wise Maurice had much correspondence with friends abroad. Connell had a passionate love of the sea; Daniel, an equal desire to go soldiering on land; but both were evidently obliged to do what they were told, though, happily, their brother was able to dispose of them according to their wishes. Curiously enough, he seems to have had a great hankering after Spain for their future abode. His representative found last year a letter of Gyles O'Sullivan in 1758, dissuading him from sending Connell there; and he would have made young Daniel quit the French for the Spanish Service but for the prudence and resolution the lad himself displayed in the matter. Failing any account of Dan's early training, I give some particulars of Connell's; doubtless the two boys learned the same things.

Mr. Daniel McCrohan, of Nantes, to whose care young Connell was committed, writes to his home in 1754—

" I received a letter from Cousin Connell from Caen, with an enclosure to be sent to his Father; and as he gave no account of anything in his Letter but of his voyage from Ireland, I was desirous to know further. I opened his Father's Letter, the substance of which is that he is very well where he is.

Mr. David Cary is very kind to him. He found him fit for philosophy, and made him enter y⁶ Colledge without loss of time. He also goes to the French School."

This, of course, shows that the boy knew French as well as being considerably advanced in weightier studies. He was a most warm-hearted lad. Before he got his heart's desire of embarking on a "letter of marque," in 1756, he stayed with Mr. McCrohan to study navigation. During his visit his host lost a little son; and the bereaved father writes to Darrynane, "My poor little Johnny died with Connell's name on his lips."

The two handsome, high-spirited young brothers were passionately devoted to each other, as many passages in yellow faded letters testify to this day. The feeling of "family" was very strong long ago. In households of the virtuous and decorous type, to which the Darrynane household belonged, an immense sense of filial reverence and duty, a formal courtesy and most strict discipline, prevailed. This respect extended not only to the parents, but to the acting head of the family in the person of the elder brother, who was always ready to help with money and influence, not only younger brothers, but nephews and cousins.

The extraordinary lengths to which parental authority was carried in the matter of disposing of the hands of daughters, and shaping the careers of sons, shocks our modern notions. Thank Heaven, nowadays we may choose our own husbands, and must rejoice at the emancipation of the younger generation. Still, we cannot refuse to admire the spirit of family affection and reverence for parental authority which prevailed in those olden times. When my hero was an elderly man, his eldest brother wrote him a sharp rebuke for leaving their mother without tidings of him during the early days of the French Revolution. He writes thus in reply—

"I am heartily sorry to find this circumstance has been the cause of terrors and apprehensions to our dear and much-Respected Mother. Nothing in nature could make me so unhappy as to think that I might have been the wilful occasion of giving her the smallest uneasiness. Pray assure her that her happiness is far more to me than my own life, and that I never passed a day since I quitted her and you without the most tender and the most lively remembrances of her virtues and her goodness. I am sure this sentiment is indelible, and can never be impaired within my breast."

Next to their strong sense of filial piety, the most remarkable thing about these old Catholics is their absence of bigotry. This absence of bigotry, which distinguished the relations of the old Kerry Catholics and Protestants, is strikingly exemplified in many letters from the Rev. James Bland, of Derryquin, to Maurice O'Connell, of Darrynane. "The Rocks" he styles the lovely place to which his descendants have given back its old Irish name. No one is so indignant as this honest Protestant parson when the "lowders"— a gang of imprisoned highwaymen—trump up charges against the O'Connells, who had been instrumental in their capture after they had nearly murdered one of the Mahony kinsmen of the Darrynane family. The Rev. Mr. Bland sent Hunting Cap copies of several different letters about this affair, which the timid editors of that day had refused to print. Another proof of his total absence of bigotry is in the care he takes to provide Lenten fare for his guest. The Derryquin oysters are renowned through the district. Before the great outbreak of cholera, all the healthy practical Catholics abstained from meat all the week-days of Lent.

The Rev. James Bland, in a letter from "The Rocks," Lent, 1769, to Hunting Cap, says—

"If you can spare Time to come and help us in Farming, you shall have salt Herrings and Oysters in Plenty."

Twenty-six years earlier, a future divine, then a student, had written the following graphic boyish letter to Maurice O'Connell's brother John.

With truly diabolical laws, calculated to set man against man, the southern gentry, differing in religion and in origin as they did, continued on the best terms. Bundles of letters from old Knights of Kerry show how they stood to their Catholic neighbours of Darrynane; and there are boyish letters from a young Herbert, studying in Trinity College, to John O'Connell, at Darrynane, showing the closest intimacy.

Trinity College, 9ber 22, 1743.

My Dear Jack,—You could never have contracted a greater uneasiness at our suden departure yn I did, occasioned by the time being so long since I had the satisfaction of seeing you so as to talk upon the inocence of our former days, when murder, such as is here committed by mere children, was quite unknown. Your uncle, with whom I had the pleasure of being once in Company since his arivall here, gives an acct of you equal to the wish of your sincere friend. I lead a most pleasant life this winter. Every Monday and Saturday I goe to the assembly, and once a week to the play. The girls are all of a green complexion. What takes up the attention of the town now is this Tryall between my Lord Anglesey and young Onslow, the son of the late Ld Altham, transported (as was proved in court) by the present Earl, in order to come in to his property, which he is like to loose. The Kerry [case] will, 'tis thought, be put of till next term. Last night one of the scholars run away with a girl in Peter's Street. I would write much more, but am just going to visit Sr Maurice and other friends who are come to town. I make bold, begging it a request, your representing my service & complyments agreable to yr father and the rest of your friends. Arthur Hassett has moved for a petition, as has also his brother, yesterday. Adeu, Drest friend, and believe me to be as ever,

Your affect. and obdient.,

Arthur Herbert.

N.B.—Don't neglect writing to me whenever you are at leasure; and, what's more, when you do me that pleasure, direct to Robt FitzGerald[1] in Nicolas St, at the sign of the Seven Stars, Dublin.

[This Arthur Herbert, who finds the complexion of the Dublin beauties somewhat tarnished after the lilies and roses of the Kerry ladies, was the eldest son of George Herbert, of Currans, and Jane FitzGerald, daughter of Maurice, Knight of Kerry. He was Rector of Tralee; and dying September 30, 1760, aged thirty-six, left by his first wife, Helena, daughter of Richard Townsend, of Castletownsend, a son Richard Herbert, of Currens, who succeeded his great-uncle, Arthur Herbert, at Cahirnane, in 1781, and was M.P. for Kerry in 1783. He married Amelia, daughter

---

[1] Robert FitzGerald, uncle to the writer; as M.P. for Dingle, he franks the letter. He succeeded his nephew Maurice as Knight of Kerry in 1780.

of Thomas Herbert, of Muckross, and was grandfather of the present Henry Herbert, of Cahirnane.—R. O'C. |

John O'Connell indited a Christmas carol to Mrs. Butler, of Waterville, full of praises of the charms of her sister-in-law, a fair but heretical Cinolda Butler, who died a maid, and I rather think an old one, over a hundred years ago. The late Mr. Butler showed me her signature to an old deed.

Maurice O'Connell was enabled to buy lands through the connivance of a Protestant connection, Councillor Hugh Falvey, of the Faha family; but when he got old, the Protestant trustee declined to perjure himself any longer. Every letter I have read written to, from, or about the old respectable Protestants of Munster showed the same friendly spirit. At the same time, while nothing could be kinder or more considerate than the demeanour of the really respectable Protestants, the "Shoneens," the petty Protestants, were odious and unendurable. Their impudence and spite, however, rather affected the people in towns than the denizens of the wilds. In after-years, Count O'Connell had many opportunities of being useful as well as agreeable to Kerry Protestant gentlemen visiting Paris on the grand tour.

The following letter of Connell's shows one horrid risk the young Catholic lads ran. If caught on a craft sailing under hostile foreign colours, and naturally to be supposed engaged in smuggling, they could be "pressed" as common seamen in the British Navy. There was no chance of promotion or money-making then. On the other hand, if they volunteered for eighteen months as sailors before the mast in the Spanish Navy, they could qualify as pilots—as before shown, a very lucrative career.

Connell O'Connell to Francis O'Sullivan.

St. Sebastian, 7ber 19, 1757.

Mr. Fau. O'Sullivan,—Dr. Cosn., I have ye pleasure to pray you'll acquaint all friends of our safe arrival, ye 5th inst, after a passage of f. . . . days. We were only met by ye *Tiger* and *St. George*, privatares of . . . who brought us too. Ye first in ye Latt. of 46·3°. We were only registered by ye former, as wee were brought too by her. They behaved mighty well to us, for they never looked far within our holt or papers. They took two barrels of beef, two casks . . . and these victuals from us, for wch they paide. We found y^e *Mary* here before us, Silvy Mahony pilote of her. She was brought here by a pilote on board of her in Guernsey, when poor Daniel was taken out and put on board a King's shipe. His Dirty Captain refused him at parting for either an anker of his own brandy, or any part of ye money he raised on ye vessell. J . . . is here now, . . . by ye intendant for . . . cor . . . to y^e . . . as ye p.p. works only from here to Ireland and back. We are to unload for a day or two, in all ye delay we are to . . . merchant tells me to hear from Nantes. You may depend on my doing all in my power to hasten . . . As to our cargoe, ye beef and fish I believe may sell well, but ye butter I fancy will lye for some time.

I write in haste for ye post, but remain, as always,
Y^r Affect. Kinsman,
CONNELL O'CONNELL.

While the brothers at home write *Connell* without an *O'*, the moment the young boys get abroad they start the Celtic prefix.

Early in 1759 Maurice O'Connell, of Darrynane, brought home his bride—not the Dulcinea of his boyish fancy, but a lady whoses charm were of a more substantial kind. The marriage treaty, now in the possession of Sir Maurice O'Connell, at Lake View, bears date December 5, 1758. It informs us of the intended marriage of Maurice O'Connell with Mary, eldest daughter of Robert Cantillon, of Ballyphillip, County Limerick, to be solemnized two days later. The bride has for that time a considerable portion—£1000 bearing interest at £100. They are to live at Darrynane, where the bridegroom's parents covenant to find "for said Maurice, Mary, and one servant, good and sufficient meat, drink, washing, lodgings, and firing in said Daniel O'Connell's dwelling-house, freely and without the said Daniel being entitled to any demand as any kind of payment for the same." She is the kind "Sister Molly" of so many of the young soldier's letters. She spent the winter at Ballyphillip, and did not go to Darrynane for six months after the marriage. All her married life she was overshadowed by her husband and her mother-in-law, born rulers both. She got on very well with every one except her brother-in-law's wife. She showed considerable jealousy of her sister-in-law, "the fruitful mother of children," one of whom was the famous Daniel. The childless wife of the eldest son was not a personage of much weight, though treated with great civility. Except where the natural feminine jealousy of the blessing denied her appeared, she was very gentle and amiable, and kind to the young creatures among whom her lot was cast. Of this kindness Daniel ever entertained the most grateful recollection. She was by no means clever—seemingly a lady-like and simple-minded nonentity.

I append some notice of the Cantillon family,[1] whereof Ross O'Connell, of Lake View, supplies the genealogical portion. Mr. Cantillon had no son, and his daughters were co-heiresses of his property at Ballyphillip. The three Miss Cantillons were said to have married three of the finest men in Munster. Maurice O'Connell, commonly known as Hunting Cap, was about six feet three, and very handsome, with long, straight features, blue eyes, fair complexion, and an oval face. The two other handsome brothers-in-law were Mr. Phill Blake, of ——, near Ennis, and Mr. Burke, of Cornabulliagh, County Tipperary, who bore the mediæval designation of "McWalter," being descended from an Earl Walter de Burgh, of the Clanricarde family, as the extinct McWilliams descended from an Earl William. In a letter from Hamburg, March 21,[2] 1760 O.S. (March 21, 1759, of our reckoning), Connell congratulates his brother—

"You can better conceive than I can express ye satisfaction it gave me to hear of y^r being married in a creditable ffamily, and to ye satisfaction of my Parents and you. As to ye Unlimited Letter of Creditt you were good enough to Send me, as it Comes from y^r Hands, whom I always looked upon as my Better half, I shall only say that I expect, with ye Assistance of ye Almighty, never to be guilty of anything y^t may incur y^r Displeasure or in ye Least alienate y^r affection you always had and at present shew for me."

[In the eighteenth century, as most of my readers know, to be concerned in smuggling was not regarded as in any way a disgrace. Indeed, few gentlemen living near the coast but were more or less mixed up with "the traders." If this were

---

[1] See Note G, p. 61.   [2] 1760 O.S. began on March 25.

so in England, it was but natural that in Ireland, where a legitimate foreign trade was discouraged in every way by law, the gentry should carry on an illegitimate one. The south and south-west coasts of Ireland, too, remote as they were, and indented everywhere with harbours large and small, besides creeks innumerable, offered great facilities for smuggling—facilities of which the inhabitants were not slow to avail themselves.

Among the most active of these smuggling gentry in Kerry were the O'Connells and their relatives, the numerous O'Sullivans and Goolds. I have still in my possession letters, invoices, bills of lading, etc., of various dates from 1745 to 1780, referring to their transactions, from which I have thrown together a few facts which may possess some interest.

And, first, as to the goods usually brought over. They were chiefly tea—usually "bohea, or black tea"—sugar, and tobacco, with, in earlier years, rum, and later, brandy. Small quantities of claret were imported, and always for the O'Connells; I only see one single consignment of that wine, indeed, to any of their partners. The ladies got silks and velvets, and once, at all events, Maur-ni-Dhuiv imported a mirror from France, which is still at Darrynane Abbey. The vessels employed were, of course, small; large craft could not enter the out-of-the-way nooks which suited the trade. So far as I can make out from the cargoes and crews they carried, the vessels do not seem to have been of more than forty to fifty tons. At first they were hired, and were of various nationalities—Irish, English, and one, at all events, the *San Juan Baptista*, was Spanish, as I suppose was the *San Antonio*; eventually "the company," as the old papers call them, procured a craft of their own, the sloop *Prince Ferdinand*, which ran a couple of cargoes annually for many years.

The cost of a cargo in France—at Nantes usually—was from £200 to £300; unfortunately, the papers I have do not show what the profit was, but it must have been large. English smugglers, I believe, considered they cleared expenses if they successfully "ran" two cargoes out of three, which would mean a profit of something like fifty per cent., and this on imported goods only; for no return cargoes were sent from England, while they were by the O'Connells and their "company."

Butter, salt hides, and salt fish were the principal items exported; wool was sent at times, but it and linen seem to have been usually private speculations of the ladies; horse-hair occurs a few times. One item never is mentioned, though I make no doubt it might have been—"wild geese," which I may explain to English readers was the name given to recruits for the Irish Brigade.

At first trade seems to have been carried on quite as much with Spain[1] as with France; subsequently with the latter only, the O'Connells' principal correspondent there being a Kerry man named McCrohan, settled at Nantes. Still later, in the seventies, I find cargoes sent from Guernsey.

It may seem strange that return cargoes could be shipped, but the smuggling craft seem to have lain sometimes for weeks in the little harbour of Darrynane. The place even now is very out-of-the-way, and a hundred and twenty years ago was as much so as any corner in the United Kingdom. The harbour is, to use a sea phrase, a "blind one"—no stranger passing it would detect its existence from the sea. Then, if by any chance an underling of the Revenue did turn up, he was not always proof against a bribe; so I find in one account of expenses in landing a cargo: "To ——, the boat-man" (meaning Revenue boatman, or coastguard), "who came here seeking a prey, 5s. 5d."—5s. 5d. Irish being 5s. English money.

On the land side, the only approach was by a road im-passable for wheeled vehicles, and not traversed by any stranger save at long and rare intervals. The neighbouring gentry, too, even though not partners in "the company," were ready and willing purchasers of its goods, and not likely

---

[1] That there was in old times a very large trade between Spain and the west and south-west of Ireland is well known. Smith, in his "History of Kerry," makes frequent references to it.

A venerable relative of mine, now verging on ninety, narrated to me that her grandmother told her she remembered when women from the neighbourhood of Ballinskelligs, in Kerry, used to borrow one another's cloaks to go to Spain with "slaucan" (i.e. "sloke," or "laver," an edible sea-weed) for sale, the Spaniards being extremely fond of it. Smith alludes to the cloak-borrowing, but does not seem to have known what the motive for a trip to Spain was.

to interfere with its operations, and, until comparatively a late date, there was no officer of the Revenue or Preventive Service anywhere near.—D. O'C.]

The following copy of a letter from Maurice O'Connell to the smuggling correspondent of the firm gives us an idea of the exports as well as of the imports:—

Maurice O'Connell to Mr. McCrohan.

Darrinane, 7ber 22nd, 1754.

Dr. Sir,—I have Wrote to you ye afternoon the *Alexander*, Captain John FitzGerald on brd, which have shipped — for account of Messrs. Seggerson and Company[1]—2 Large sacks C. W.,[2] one of wch is for the Captain and Crew; 58 firkins butter, and 65 Salt hydes, on all which, as Well as the Vessel, you are to insure as follows: viz. on one pack C. W., £18; on the butter, £48; and on ye Hydes, £24; and on the Vessel, £68; in all, £153. . . . She set out with a Very favourable Wind, and the strongest appearance of a continuance of it.

I refer you to ye forementioned letter for y^r Government relative to ye returns, hoeever shall repeat to you that the whole proceeds are to be invested for Teas, half Green and half Bohea. As to last commodity, it promices pretty well. Brandy is in noe demand, nor is there a likelihood of a Call for it for a considerable time.

I mentioned to you in said letter to send 13 Ankers Brandy, 3 of which Cherry. A Cask powder Sugar, and 2 Tierces good Claret for ye private consumption, and seperate account of Messrs. Seggerson and my ffather, which please to observe, and am ord'red to direct you to send 2 Quarter-casks small White St. Martin or Rhenish wine for ye same purpose and account. The costs and charges of all wch place to a seperate account.

You have in charge £10 or £17 for Butter, ye property of my ffather. He thinks proper, in consequence of ye stuff, to order home the proceeds of the Butter in Teas, as before.

---

[1] Mrs. M. J. O'Connell mentions that the names of Hunting Cap's partners were James and Francis Segerson, of Cork. In 1724 James Segerson, merchant, Cork, held by lease for 980 years a portion of "Dunscombe's Marsh," bounded south by Benj. Winthrop's holding, west by a street leading to King George's Street, with river frontage on the north, and privilege of shipping and landing goods gratis. Subsequently his widow married Mr. P. Prosser. In the same year John Segerson, jun., held a house and garden in Bridge Street, in the South Liberties. In 1761 Francis Segerson, merchant, Cork, married Mary Aghern; the marriage settlement is in the Registry of Deeds Office, Dublin. [G. S.]

[2] Wool.

This you are to note, and, as it's made over on me, The Goods are to be mark'd wth the Intitial letters of my Name. There are ffourteen Hydes of my own and 160 bandles flannell of my Mother's, in 2 bundles. Out of which pay Cornilius 60 livres, and send the 4 Aunes Velvet mention'd. The price of the Looking . . . deduct from proceeds of ye last-mention'd Butter. Advise us speedily of ye Vessel's arrival and course of the Markett, and dispatch her with all possible Expedition. We'll endeavour to send her Back immediately after her arrival. Mr. Tim McCarthy prays you'll ensure £30 stg. on 35 hydes, 3 firkins butter, and a pack C. W. he has on board. Your brother Jemmy has shipped himself according to your Directions. I fancy my Brother Connell has ere now advised you of his arrival in Caen.

I am Dear Cousin,
Your sincere Kinsman and Obedient Servant,
MAURICE CONNELL.

[C. W. stands for wool.—D. O'C.]

A bandle is twenty-seven inches, the length of a man's arm—the old English ell, or Italian *bracchio*. Home-spun flannel and linen are still measured by it in West Clare. The very odd conglomerate of measures—the anker and its compounds, are Dutch measures, though applied to other liquids than hollands.

"1 *anker* = ¼ *awn*, and contains 2 *stekans*; each *stekan* consists of 16 *mengles*; the mengle being equal to two Paris pints" (Rees' "Cyclopædia," vol. ii.). The anker, therefore, contained sixty-four Paris pints.

A tierce is forty-two gallons, or one-third of a pipe.

"Looking . . ." evidently refers to a looking-glass, of which there are two yet at Darrynane, said to have been smuggled by Maur-ni-Dhuiv. The plates are oblong, very thick, and bevelled, and set in rococo gilt scrollwork, forming a sort of long flattened oval. The gilding is so good that it has retained much of its lustre for nearly a century and a half.

NOTES TO BOOK I.

Note A.

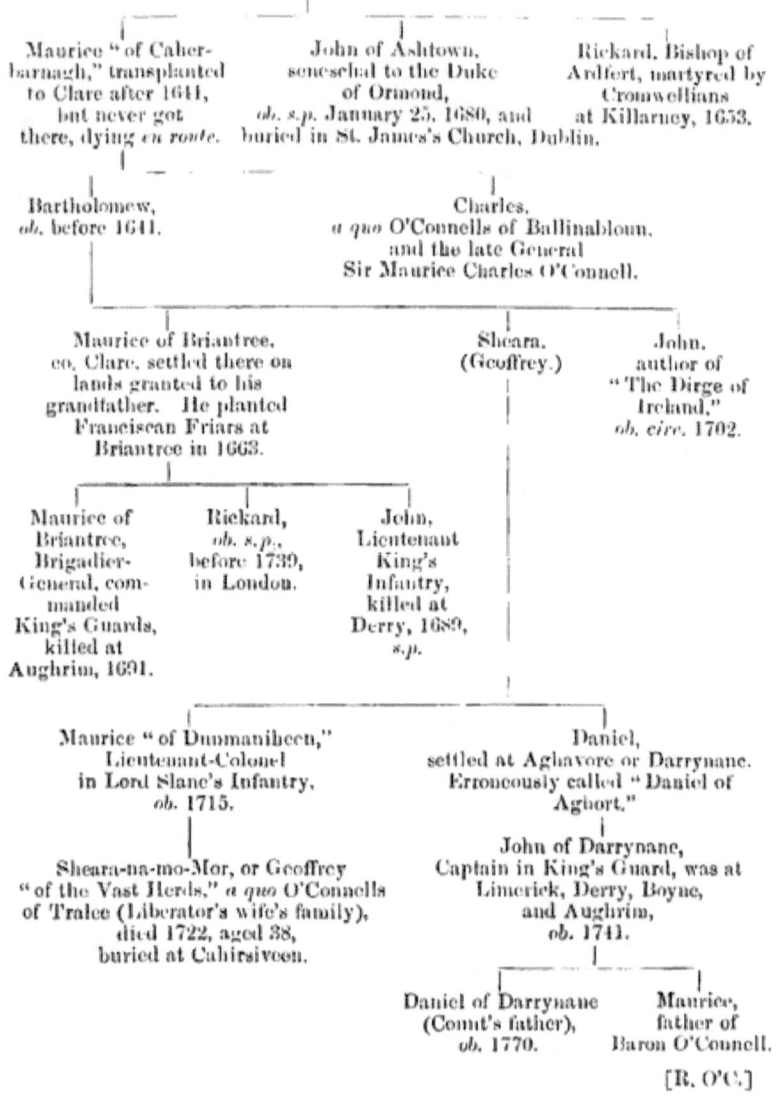

[R. O'C.]

Note B.

Fish in Kerry.

The *Kerry Magazine* for January 1, 1856, contains a "Report on the State of Kerry, A.D. 1673, May, 27, by Lord Herbert and others," taken from the 15th "Record Report," p. 670, MSS. vol. M, Birmingham Tower, Dublin Castle. This Lord Herbert was Edward, third Lord Herbert of Cherbury and Castle Island.

After dwelling on the remoteness of the district, the impassable state of the roads, the abject misery and complete lawlessness of the inhabitants, he says, "No kindes of manufactures or fishing, but of oysters at low water, even in this place, which before the discovery of Newfoundland was the fishery of Europe." In support of this statement the *Kerry Magazine* quotes "Carne de Regno Hib. Scotiæ Anacephalosis, 1666:" "Tertium promontorium vocatur Euragh [Ivreagh] inter Beantry et Baltimore situm. Hoc annuatim ingens nauclorum numerus non solum ex vicinis locis, sed etiam Hispania, Gallia, Hollandia, aliisq. locis ad capiendas scombros, halluca ac salpas, gerresque accurrit" (*Kerry Magazine*, vol. ii. p. 25). *Scombros* means mackerel;[1] *halluca*, evidently a misprint for *haleca*, herrings; *salpas gerresque*, cod and pilchard.

Arthur Young states that, in 1776, oysters cost 3*d*. per hundred in Tralee, a rise of 50 per cent. since 1756. My father has bought oysters there, in or about 1840, for 1*s*. 6*d*. the hundred.—[R. O'C.]

Note C.

I find it more convenient to group genealogical notices, old stories, and traditions of the "old stock" at the ends of chapters than to squeeze them into footnotes. Ross O'Connell has been my herald for the nonce, and has signed his contributions "R. O'C." Those which bear no signature are my own work. "I tell the tale as 'twas told to me" in every case, but I do not pledge myself to the accuracy of the statements made to me. Of the general accuracy of the old peasants and old ladies, whose depositions I have taken down, I have no manner of doubt. Many of the stories and traditions, the queer manners and formal customs recorded will be found very like Highland ones, related by dear old Sir

---

[1] Tunnies and mackerel are of the same family. The first are *Scomber thynnus*, the second, *Scomber scombrus* (Linnæus).

Walter Scott, in his copious and delightful notes to poems, novels, and the "Tales of a Grandfather."

O'MAHONY.

Quarterly, 1st and 4th, a lion rampant azure; 2nd, per pale ar. and gu., a lion ra. counterchanged; 3rd, arg., a chevron gu. between three snakes wavy in pale sa.

These arms are as borne by the Mahonys of Dromore, Dunloe, and Kilmorna, by Bartholomew, Count O'Mahony, and by James, Count O'Mahony. The Mahonys of Castlequin bear the snakes in 3rd quarter erect ppr. According to Sir William Betham, the common ancestor of the various houses of Mahony was Donogh "na Himerce" ("of the Pilgrimage") O'Mahony, Lord of Kinalmeaky, *circ.* 1180. The mere fact of the several branches bearing the same *quartered* coat is a strong proof that they did not separate from the parent stem until a far later period. It is unlikely that Donogh na Himerce bore any heraldic device, and it is absolutely impossible that he could have borne the elaborate coat given above, as arms quarterly were unknown to British heraldry till the reign of Edward III.

Ross O'Connell has supplied the armorial bearings and later ramifications of the family of O'Mahony. I abridge its ancient history from the "History of the Eugenians," by Richard F. Cronnelly, who gives the following extracts of the old topographical poems about them :—

> "The Clan Eochaidh without oppression,
> Magnificent their apparel."
> (Poem of Maelmurra, of Fahen.)

Their original territory was Ivaugh, or Iveagh, in South-West Cork, whence they subsequently migrated to Kerry.

> "Iveagh, the most westernly part of Banba,
> Is the extensive estate of O'Mahony,
> The fruitful land of fair fortresses;
> Extensive the brown nut-producing plains."
> (O'Heerin.)

The old poetical topographer also describes their territory in the same county in the barony of Kinelmeaky.

> "Kinelmeaky of the delightful fields,
> About Bandon of the charming groves,
> The warlike chief of glorious victories,
> Is O'Mahony of the foam-fringed coast."
> (Ibid.)

The district of Tubrad (Tubrid), in the barony of Iveragh, was also possessed by the O'Mahonys in Kerry. This branch is long extinct or sunk into obscurity.

The monastery of Timoleague was the burial-place of the O'Mahonys of Carbery.

A long pedigree of Donal O'Mahony, living A.D. 1600, is referred to as among genealogical manuscripts at Lambeth. Mr. Cronnelly gives as the principal O'Mahony castles: Rathlin, in Kinelmeaky; Ardnurran and Ringmahon, Dunbeacon, Dunmanus, Rosbrin, and Black Castle, in West Carbery; Ballydeolin, West Carbery; Dromdeedy in Lower Connelloe, County Limerick; Ballymodan, East Carbery.

THE MAHONYS OF DUNLOE.

John Mahony, of Dunloe, dying in 1706, left by his wife Honora, daughter of Maurice O'Connell, of Cahirbarnagh, two sons—Daniel, immortalized by Mr. Froude, as "Donell of Dunloe;" and Denis of Dromore, from whom descend the Mahonys of Dromore.

John's son, Donell of Dunloe, "the great and terrible Papist who ruled South Kerry with his four thousand followers" (Froude's "English in Ireland," vol. i. p. 452), left with other issue, a daughter, to whom, "as the only person in the barony worthy to wear them," he bequeathed his velvet breeches. This daughter was the wife of Donal O'Donoghue Dhuv, and the mother of Maur-ni-Dhuiv, Count O'Connell's mother.

Dunloe was, until the Desmond rebellion, one of the chief fortresses of O'Sullivan Mor. It was then razed by Ormond, who left standing only the north, west, and south walls of a flanking tower. These walls are of immense thickness, and probably defeated Ormond's hurried efforts to destroy them. O'Sullivan Mor removed to Dunkerron, and built the castle there in 1595.

Some seventy years later Dunloe passed to John Mahony as the marriage portion of Gillen, his second wife, daughter of a subsequent O'Sullivan Mor. He seems to have leased it from O'Sullivan before this marriage, as local tradition tells us that many of the splendid trees at Dunloe were planted by the care of his first wife, Honora O'Connell.

John Mahony rendered the tower habitable by building an east wall, and thus the fragment stands to this day, the wall of the seventeenth century very easily distinguishable from its companions of the thirteenth century.

James, eldest son of the first Count O'Mahony, by Cecilia, daughter and co-heiress of George, younger brother of Humphrey Weld, of Lulworth, married Lady Ann Clifford, daughter of the Countess of Newburgh, by her first husband, Hon. Thomas Clifford. The countess married, secondly, the fifth Earl of Derwentwater, who was beheaded 1746, and whose descendants, Earls of Newburgh, became extinct in 1814, when the title passed to Vincent, Prince Giustiniani, eldest son of Benedict, Prince Giustiniani, by his wife Cecilia, only child of Count O'Mahony and Lady Ann Clifford. Vincent, Prince Giustiniani, had an only child, Cecilia, in her own right Countess of Newburgh, who married the Marchese Bandini, and was mother of the present Marchese Bandini, now Earl of Newburgh, created Prince by Pius IX., and who assumed the name of Guistiniani.

Myles Mahony, of Castlequin, married Count O'Connell's aunt, the eldest daughter of John O'Connell, of Darrynane, and their grandson, Myles of Castlequin, whose brother Denis was Captain in the Irish Brigade, married (1788) Mary, daughter of Charles Jeffrey O'Connell, of Portmagee.

The arms of Mahony, as mentioned by Mr. Mahony, of Dromore, are quartered by the Lords Newburgh, who represent the Counts Mahony. The present Prince Giustiniani, though a Scotch earl, is an Italian gentleman, and therefore naturally knows something about an alliance of which his house has every reason to be proud. He quarters the arms of Mahony with those of Clifford and Livingstone.

Sugrue.

Arms: same as those of O'Sullivan.

Miss Hickson, in "Old Kerry Records," an admirable compilation, well worthy the study of any one interested in Irish history or Irish pedigree, expresses an opinion that Dunloe came to the Mahonys from the Sughrues by marriage of a Mahony with "a Sughrue widow."

I do not believe that Dunloe ever belonged to the Sughrues, or that such a marriage ever took place.

Miss Hickson quotes "tradition" as authority for both statements. Tradition is often an admirable, and always an amusing guide, but it can hardly be looked upon as proof of a marriage that, if it occurred at all, must have occurred two hundred and fifty years before the tradition was garnered into print.

Elizabeth, daughter of Robert FitzMaurice, of Ballyhealy, in Kerry, who married Timothy Sughrue, and was mother of Charles, born 1701, "prisoner of warr in Carlysle, and there unfortunately murthered by a French officer" in 1747, drew up, shortly after her son's murder, a genealogical catalogue of the glories and alliances of the Sughrues, for the benefit of her grandson Charles, then a minor, "in the hands of the Spanish Ambassador.'

Mrs. Sughrue, who unfortunately, and femininely, refrains from dating this diffuse document, makes no mention of Dunloe, and only gives one marriage between the Sughrues and Mahonys. Her father-in-law, Charles Sughrue, married, first, a daughter of Denis Mahony and Honora McCarthy, of Cosmaigne. This Denis was the father of John Mahony, who was, I believe, the first Mahony of Dunloe, and who married Honora, daughter of Maurice Connell, of Cahirbarnagh. Another daughter of this Maurice Connell was the second wife of Charles Sughrue, and the mother of his son Timothy, husband of Elizabeth FitzMaurice.

Mr. Sugrue, of Cork, lent me a copy of the informal pedigree drawn up by his ancestress.

The last O'Sullivan Mor died at Tomies in 1762. He left an illegitimate son, whose grandson is a fisherman at Killarney. This grandson told me that when a gossoon some thirty years ago, he went to see his grandfather lying dead at Tomies. He saw not only his departed ancestor, but also a great pile of old papers, "maybe three feet high, mostly written on skins in Latin and Irish; and faith I was in dread they might fall into the hands of the Mahonys or some other *new* people in the country, and they might get more of the old O'Sullivan estates, so I burned them all myself"!—[R. O'C.]

Note D.

The O'Falveys of Faha.

The Falveys bear vert a lion ra., crowned or; in chief two swords saltier ways ppr., hilted or. Crest: a ship under sail, ppr. Mr. Morrogh Bernard, of Faha, has kindly furnished me with a photograph of an interesting painting of these arms, in his possession. This escutcheon is rather an excuse for the elaborate framework as in book-plates of the Jacobean style (Warren, "Guide to the Study of Ex-Libris," p. 20), but natural flowers in the Chippendale manner show themselves "timidly and tentatively" in the neighbourhood of the motto. The whole is an admirable specimen of transitional style, and dates evidently 1735-1745.

Ross O'Connell has compiled the following note on the O'Falveys of Faha, from material placed at his disposal by Mr. Morrogh Bernard. An hereditary follower of the family, Sergeant Michael O'Connor, born in the now dismantled old home of Faha, of which his father was the tenant, drew up for me a short traditional account of the Falveys, and procured for me the poem blessing Honora O'Mahony, the charitable and beautiful wife of Hugh Falvey, whose sister married young John O'Connell, of Darrynane. Hugh Falvey was the conforming kinsman who saved the property of the O'Connells, and, I rather think, of other Catholic families in Kerry.

[When O'Heerin, who died in 1420, wrote his "Topography," the O'Falveys were persons of note and consideration in the south of Ireland.[1] It is not my intention to grope in the sombre night of remote antiquity. Skipping some two hundred years, I find, in 1617, one "Alive O'Falvey, a Desmond man," one of the few who were faithful to Florence McCarthy Mor, during his imprisonment in the Tower.

After 1641 Dermot O'Falvey, of Kilkeeveragh, was ordered to "transplant." His family and retainers numbered 115 persons. Hugh Falvey, of Faha, was also transplanted. His certificate is lost, but his name appears in the index ("Old Kerry Records," series ii. pp. 35–37).

The name of Falvey is found in King James's Irish Army List. Darby Falvey, of Faha, married Gobnett Galway, and, dying in 1711, was interred at Aghlish. The following is the epitaph on his tomb:—

> "Here lies interred the treasure of our ti[me]
> In vertue, with [wit], and in all parts sublime,
> Darby Falvey, whom God and man have blest
> From his craddle to his eternal rest."
> "He lived to the age of 68 years,
> And died on the 6th March, 1711."

His son, John of Faha (will dated October 5, 1742), left, with a daughter, Mary, wife of John, eldest son of Daniel O'Connell, of Darrynane, a son, Hugh of Faha, who married Honora, daughter of John Mahony, of Blackwater, County Kerry. This John Mahony, in his will, dated June 3, 1743, describes his mother as Mrs. Alice Mahony, of Dromore, and it is evident that he was eldest son (? *ob. v.p.*) of Donogh, *alias* Denis Mahony the first, of Dromore, by his wife Alice, daughter of Richard Pierse, of Ballinagard, County Kerry (will dated October 18, 1731).

Hugh Falvey and Honora Mahony left, with a son, John (*ob. s.p.* 1807), a daughter, Honora, who subsequently inherited Faha, and by her husband, John Bernard, of Ballinagard, Kerry, left two daughters, co-heiresses: (1) Martha, married Edward Morrogh, and was grandmother of the present Edward Morrogh Bernard, of Faha; (2) Mary, married Robert Netterville, and was mother of Arthur, eighth Viscount Netterville.—R. O'C.]

---

[1] The "Annals of the Four Masters" record that O'Falvey, Tanist of Corcaguiny (West Kerry), fell in the battle of Moy-Cobha, County Down, in 1103, with O'Muiray, Lord of Kerry; and that in 1158, O'Falvey, Lord of Corcaguiny, was slain by the O'Sheas of Ivreagh.—[S.]

Sergeant Michael O'Connor tells me the old white house of Faha was the first slated house erected in the district since Cromwell's time, and, as such, was a great object of wonder and admiration. The sergeant also gives me Darby Falvey's epitaph, and tells me his own ancestors repose close to Darby's grave. They rented the house and demesne when his posterity removed from it. Says the sergeant, "The mortar used in the old house of Faha was tempered with bullock's blood, mixed with hair, and so generous was Darby that he distributed the beef among the workmen. Not having sufficient blood to temper all the mortar required, he ordered some of his people to collect some of the wild cows from the mountains of Glancar and Glanbeigh. The gang was headed by a man named Ring Dow, Darby's poet. It had taken them some time to run ten head of these cattle into a defile, after which the men were attacked by two of the wild bulls, and had to run away, leaving bulls and cows behind them. On Ring Dow's return with his men to Faha, he informed Mr. Falvey of his ill success in an Irish verse, thus translated:—

> "'Iveragh, most stern and savage blue;
> Glancar, where corn never grew;
> Desmond mountain, high and blue;—
> Three parts that Patrick never gave his blessing to.'

"Darby Falvey soon after had a son John. He died after spending a good life, and was buried at Aghlish Church, close to the tomb of my ancestors. The following inscription was written on his tombstone:—

> "'Here lies Darby Falvey, whom God had blessed
> From his cradle to his eternal rest.'"—[M. O'C.]

Mr. Leahy, of South Hill, Killarney, gave me a better version of Ring Dow's poetry long in use in Kerry; and about ten years ago old Dan Sullivan, who had been the Liberator's steward, gave me the literal translation of the verse—

> "Rugged Iveragh, of evil deeds the bed;
> And stern Glancar, whose corn-fields never spread;
> These and the three hills dividing Desmond from the west,
> Are the three spots St. Patrick never blessed."

Dan Sullivan's translation is as follows:—

> "Nasty Iveragh, with the grey dragoons;[1]
> Glancar, that the oats never grew in it;
> All the ugly high mountains from that to the west,
> Were never blessed by St. Patrick."

---

[1] *A jeu de mot.* Grey dragoon is the name of a very bad weed; and Iveragh was full of outlaws clad in grey frieze, and riding rough ponies.

All these " nasty and ugly " spots are the beautiful mountain ranges we moderns rave about.

"Darby's son John," resumes the sergeant, "was succeeded by his grandson Hugh, who married Nora Mahony, of the Dromore family, who was deemed a great beauty, and equally good and virtuous. Her family have a time-honoured name in this county. She had one son and a daughter. The son became a Councillor, and the daughter, Nora Oge, was possessed of every quality that could adorn a woman.

"One night a party of men came to Faha House, and attempted to carry off the young and beautiful lady, but the ruffians were bravely repulsed by Mr. Falvey and his people. Miss Falvey afterwards married Mr. Bernard, of Ballinagard."

Sergeant O'Connor was too loyal to the old race under whom his forefathers had long prospered to give me any but the complimentary traditions. Mr. Morrogh Bernard, a venerable mason, a most intelligent old farmer, and some neighbouring gentlemen, told me the curious story of a curse.

In 1768 great pressure was brought to bear on Hugh Falvey by some of the iniquitous penal enactments. He tried to save his lands and spare his soul by the intervention of a friendly Protestant, one Samuel Windus, a Dublin hosier, whose name appears as pretended "discoverer," but really helper, in the O'Connell papers. Eventually, Hugh Falvey apostatized, and saved his lands. He and his eldest son John, who followed his example, became eminent barristers. Hugh Falvey constantly acted as trustee for his friends, Maurice and Morgan O'Connell, not merely as friendly "discoverer" of what they had, but as nominal purchaser of other lands Maurice bought from time to time.

On one occasion, at a dinner-party at the house of one of the Blennerhassetts, some of the born Protestants reproached Councillor Hugh with aiding a Papist to buy land, and threatened to swear Maurice O'Connell was the purchaser, and "discover" on him, and thereby seize the lands.

"Swear away, and be hanged to you!" replied Hugh Falvey. "I am ready to swear the print out of the Bible I bought them myself!"

This was technically, if not morally, true.

The old Councillor's house was broken into by robbers, who were repulsed by him and his son John, and in the scuffle the old man felt that one of his assailants had lost a certain finger. A man named Sullivan, maimed in a similar way, was arrested and hanged. His counsel raised the point of old Hugh Falvey's age, and probably defective vision.

His son replied, "If my father is too old to know, I am not."

Sullivan, who was innocent, was hanged; another man who had lost a finger having committed the burglary. Sullivan's sister cursed the two Councillors, but exempted the two Noras. The old man was found dead, and the young man was killed by a fall from his horse, as the curse had predicted.

It never occurred to the peasants that those who suffered innocent blood to be spilt rather than inform on the guilty man had a larger share of blood-guiltiness than the two gentlemen who honestly swore what they believed to be true.

Very shortly before the relaxation of the penal laws, when Hugh Falvey and Hunting Cap were both old men, Maurice wrote to ask him to purchase Tomies in the usual way. Councillor Falvey responded, "My dear Maurice, if I were a few years younger, I would be as ready to oblige a friend as ever. I regret that I am too near my end to perjure myself any more, even for so old and valued a friend as yourself."

Having given the curse on Hugh Falvey, I shall now append a free translation of "The Poor Scholar's Blessing" on Honora O'Mahony, Hugh Falvey's wife.

Note E.
"The Poor Scholar's Blessing,"

Taken down by Mr. O'Sullivan, Maylor Street, Cork, from the recitation of Sergeant O'Connor and a man in County Cork; literally translated by the Rev. Peter O'Leary, C.C., Doneraile; revised by Mrs. Morgan John O'Connell. This version does not profess to be metrical, but the general forms of the lines have been retained.

I.

"Long has been my weary wandering, without one living soul to bear me company.
  I have come from the distant North, from far Bananloch.
  I have journeyed thence on foot.
  I longed to reach the dwellings of the sages whose homes are in Killarney, by the waters of Lough Lein;[1]
  I longed to hear them utter the music of their verses;
  I longed to study with them—to be guided by their lore.

II.

"I had reached the land of Desmond, where the fair and noble mansions rise up without spot or stain,
  Where dwell the generous-hearted, where noble deeds are wrought.
  Then faint and weary-hearted on the greensward I sank;
  On the land of those generous people prone I lay.

[1] Killarney.

With tenderest compassion they helped me in my need ;
A noble beauteous lady then snatched me from the grave.

III.

"When I left my home in Galway high hopes surged within my breast ;
I reckoned on my talents, and on my learning too.
I brought this lore, these talents,
To the high-minded open-hearted sons of the Kerry land.
But I lost the sweet boon of health.
I made no friends by the way ;
I became an outcast far from kith and kin.

IV.

"Then I was guided by the grace of the Son of God
To the house of Falvey, where long I dwelt.
A ready welcome greeted me. Though long I tarried,
None would let me feel the burthen of a boon conferred.
Good friend, may thy race long flourish !
May it thrive among the nobles of the land,
And dwell for many a day in mansions fair and fine !

V.

"O Saviour of men, who knowest all our actions,
Who didst tarry in Egypt's land, seeking shelter from Thy foes,
Who wast scourged, who wast smitten and condemned to die,
Who wast crucified with bitterest intensity of hatred,
I pray Thee, and implore through the Holy Ghost,
To grant a place in heavenly glory
To the lady, beautiful and bounteous,
Who gave the suffering wanderer aid,
Who tended me within her spacious halls
From the day I lay down stricken
Until I could set forth again !

VI.

"Gracious and illustrious lady, whom the Son of God
Loveth for bounteous deeds,
Thy charity is not in vain.
The priest, the monk, the scholar, bless thee !
Thou hast the blessing of the maids
Who seek no earthly spouse.

VII.

"Truly thou art sprung from mighty Brian,
Who bore sway o'er the land,
Ruled it with fortress none might scale,
With buckler and with sword ;
From Brian, who drove the sons of Denmark
Far from the shores of Erin ;
Brian, whose kingly race traced back to Heber.

VIII.

"I must not pass in silence o'er the heroes
Whose home was in the sunny cleft among the hills.
Hugh, who is meet to preside over a gallant company,
He came to us from afar, followed by his swift hound.

He springs from the race of Falvè, who brought McCaurra
Back unto safety from the deck of the ship of Turgesius.[1]

IX.

"In recent times thy kindred
 Came hither from Iveragh,
 True sons of Milesius the Spaniard.
 Thy kindred were among the noblest
 Of the blood of the Gael.
 Through all the land of Erin there were none
 Who proved more worthy of their high descent.

X.

"Thy kindred were high pillars of the state,
 From the Knight of Dingle to the Lord of Lixnaw;
 O'Donoghue of the Glens, who smote his foes in battle;
 O'Sullivan Beare, of the long narrow meads; and he of Tomies, too.
 Akin to thee were lofty Geraldines,
 Their kindred, too, were thine.

XI.

"But lately came thy people from Dromore,
 Where heads of great old houses feasted,
 Quaffing healths from the costly bowl;
 Around the tables covered with fine white cloths
 Were gathered guests noble as any in Erin.

---

[1] The tradition referred to in the text is mentioned by Abbé McGeoghegan, in his history, under date 921, and in a paper on the O'Keefes by Father Yarlath Prendergast, in "Franciscan Annals," under date 944. It occurred in a sea-fight off Dundalk. Callaghan was the Christian name of McCarthy, King of Cashel. Father Prendergast thus tells it: "The Danes, having evacuated the city, marched to Dundalk, and embarked in their fleet, that then lay in the bay. O'Keefe pursued them, and sending a flag of truce, demanded the liberation of the two Irish kings. An answer was returned by the Danes that they would not give them up until they received an eric (indemnity) for the Danes who fell in fifteen battles with Callaghan and his forces. In the mean time Sitric ordered Callaghan to be bound to the mast of his own ship, and Dunchuan to be lashed up to the mast of the King of Norway's ship, in the sight of the whole Munster army. The Irish were enraged at this indignity offered to their king, but were powerless, as their land forces had no means of attacking the enemy, until O'Falvey, the Irish admiral, and his ships hovered in view. A dreadful naval fight began, and O'Falvey and his warriors very soon ran into the enemy's ships, which they grappled and boarded, releasing Callaghan, their king, and giving him one of his own swords. The Irish, seeing their prince at their head again, fought with renewed energy, and finally defeated the Danes and destroyed their fleet. The victory, however, was dearly bought, as the brave O'Falvey fell pierced with wounds. Fingal, the second in command, seeing himself surrounded by the enemy on every side, seized on Sitric, and leaped into the sea with him, and both were instantly drowned."

XII.

> "Ferriter of Boncashla was thy kinsman,
> In Dunboy and Dunlo long thy kindred
> Held prosperous sway.
> Should any one in future ask me,
> 'Who is this lady?' know ye
> She is Nora, O'Mahony's daughter,
> The bright compassionate lady
> Whose kindness saved my life.
> She lives in the land of Desmond;
> At Faha-na-Fiene
> Is her dwelling-place."

Regarding the name Desmond, Ross O'Connell appends the following correction:—

Desmond and Kerry were separate counties till the reign of James I., 1603, and remained distinct long after in popular parlance.—[R. O'C.]

The river Maine was the north boundary of Kerry and the south boundary of Desmond. By an inquisition taken at Tralee, August 20, 1606, the county of Desmond, containing the baronies of Dunkerron, Magunnihy, Iveragh, and half the barony of Glenarought, was the county palatine of Kerry, and both were obliged to be confirmed and known as the county of Kerry.

Note F.

Weather-slated Houses in Munster.

In describing Darrynane, I forgot to say it is weather-slated. The English reader may not quite understand this term. In old days, before Portland cement came much in vogue, people in the south of Ireland, where slates were cheap and plentiful, coated the walls of their houses with them. Many old houses in Cork still retain this protection against wet. When the present fine Court House in Cork, a classical structure with colonnades, was being "presented" for before a grand jury, an old grand juror proposed to weather-slate it. The opinion of the presiding judge, Chief Baron O'Grady, afterwards Lord Gillamore, was asked on the question. "Gentlemen of the grand jury," replied the judge, "in this country people would weather-slate a warming-pan."

This rebuke effectually reconciled the old gentleman and his brethren to stucco and classic art.

Note G.

Cantillon of Ballyheigue.

A branch of the great Norman house of Cantilupe; the see of Hereford still bears the arms of the Cantilupes, or Cantillons: gu, three leopards' heads reversed, jessant, de lys or, in honour of St. Thomas Cantilupe, Bishop of Hereford 1275–1282, and High Chancellor of England, son of William, Lord Cantilupe, Lord High Steward of England, and of Melicenta de Gournay, Countess Dowager of Evreux and Gloucester.

William de Cantelon came to England with William the Conqueror. An account of the family is given by the Duchess of Cleveland ("Roll of Battle Abbey," vol. i. p. 237, *et seq.*), who, however, errs in stating that the Wests, Earls Delawarr and Viscounts Cantelupe, are not connected with the family of Cantelupe. Lord Delawarr descends from Sir Thomas West, created Baron West 1342, and his wife Alainore, daughter and heir of Sir John Cantalupe, of Hempston Cantalupe, County Devon.

The Cantillons were among the earliest Norman settlers in Kerry. In 1306 David Fitzgerald was made Sheriff of Kerry, and Richard de Cauntelon was among his sureties. In 1307 John, son and heir of Richard de Cauntel, is described as "late Sheriff of Kerry."

The *Kerry Magazine* for August 1, 1855, publishes a "computation of the king's revenue from Kerry in 1254," taken from Carew MSS., v. 610, p. 49, Lambeth Library, wherein appears, "Howel de Cantilupe, Compot. de xvj^s viij^d pro vinis de wiscke."

The name, spelt in divers fashions, is of constant occurrence in all Kerry records from a very early period until 1688, when the Cantillons finally forfeited. In 1310 an action was brought before Sir John Wogan, Justice of Ireland, by Friar William of Bristol and other Franciscan friars of the "Convent of Ardfert," against Nicholas, Bishop of Ardfert, and four chaplains of the chapter, for forcibly taking from them the "corps" of John de Cantilupe, and burying it elsewhere; the bishop and chapter were all arrested (Ware's "Ireland," vol. i. p. 521, edit. Dublin: 1764). "At a gaol delivery held at Limerick in 1310, one William FitzRoger, being arraigned for feloniously slaying Roger de Cantelon, or Cantillon, pleaded that he could not commit felony by such killing, aforesaid Roger being an Irishman of the name of O'Hederiscal, or O'Driscoll, and not a Cantillon." The plea was valid, and the culprit was acquitted of felony, but the said Roger being an "Irishman of our Lord the King (*Hibernicus Domini Regi*), said William was fined five marks for the value of the aforesaid Irishman (*pro solutioni prædicti Hibernici*)" (Sir John Davies' "Historical Tracts," p. 25, quoted in O'Connell's "Memoir of Ireland," p. 53, and in John Burke's "Commoners of Great Britain," vol. ii. p. 569, art. "O'Connell of Darrinane").

Is it a proof of advancing civilization that the life of an Irishman is now more highly rated?

Thomas Cantylone died February 2, 1613, seised of "the three Ballyheigues" and other property in Kerry; by his wife, Honora Lalor, he left a son and heir, Richard, aged twelve years; this son, who died before May, 1654, forfeited Ballyheigue in 1641. Thomas Cantillon forfeited Ballyronan, and was transplanted to Connaught. His certificate, dated December 14, 1653, gives him eighty-six persons, twenty-two acres of summer corne, nine cowes, twenty-one garrons, and eighty-one sheep (Hickson's "Old Kerry Records," vol. ii. p. 34, *et seq.*).

In spite of forfeiture and duly authenticated banishment, the Cantillons managed to linger on in Kerry till 1688, when they followed exiled Majesty to France, and there proved themselves Irish of the Irish by speedily gaining in the strange land greater honour and greater wealth than they had ever acquired during the many centuries they dwelt in Erin's Ultima Thule, the kingdom of Kerry.

The Cantillons of Ballyheigue bore az. a lion ra. or, between two arrows in pale of the second, points in base ar. These arms were confirmed in 1710 to Richard Cantillon, banker, of Paris, descended from the County Kerry family, whose daughter and heiress, Henrietta, married, first (in 1743), William Howard, third Earl of Stafford; second (1769), Robert Maxwell, first Earl of Farnham. They were borne in 1850 by Antoine Sylvain de Cantillon, Baron de Ballyheigue and Chevalier de St. Louis, representative of the Kerry family, now extinct in the United Kingdom.

I have not succeeded in identifying the "subaltern Cantillon" to whom the great Napoleon left ten thousand francs for an attempt upon the life of Arthur Wellesley.

It is curious that many Norman families in Ireland bear arms utterly different from those of the houses from which they undoubtedly derive—Everard, FitzSimon, Cantillon, etc.—[R. O'C.]

The learned Dr. Smith, in 1756, was shown some rocks visible only at low tide, which the peasants say are the remains of an island that was formerly the burial-place of the family of Cantillon, who were the ancient proprietors of Ballyheigue. Crofton Croker, in his "Fairy Legends," thus describes it—

"The island was situated at no great distance from the shore, and at a remote period was overflowed in one of the encroachments which the Atlantic has made on that part of the coast of Kerry. The fishermen declare they have often seen the ruined walls of an old chapel beneath them in the water as they sailed over the clear green sea of a sunny afternoon. However this may be, it is well known that the Cantillons were, like most other Irish families, strongly attached to their ancient burial-place, and this attachment led to the custom, when any of the family died, of carrying the corpse to the sea-side, where the coffin was left on the shore within reach of the tide. In the morning it had disappeared, being, as was traditionally believed, conveyed away by the ancestors of the deceased to their family tomb" (p. 188).

Strange that so Irish a superstition should have grown up round a Norman race which one wave of invasion had brought into Kerry and another swept away. They fell with the other followers of the great houses of the Geraldines of Desmond and McCarthy Mor, and the English ancestors of the present popular Crosbies came in and settled at Ballyheigue and Ardfert. O'Callaghan, whose account I abridge, tells us how a son of that well-known valiant follower of King James, Viscount Bulkeley, married the daughter of Phillip de Cantillon, who had followed King James, and founded a great bank in Paris. Count Bulkeley and the Irish regiment of his name achieved high distinction in the long wars of Louis XIV. One of his sisters was married to the famous Marshal Duke of Berwick, another, first to Lord Clare, and secondly to Count Daniel O'Mahony, "le brave O'Mahony of Cremona." When the son of Sir Donogh O'Brien, of Dromoland, died in Paris early in the eighteenth century, his money matters were in the hands of Cantillon's bank. The son of Phillip de Cantillon's daughter, Count Henry Buckley, rose to be a general; but Marshal de Muy, no lover of the Irish, as may be seen in these letters, abolished "Bulkeley's," ninety-two years after it was raised for King James, and eighty-five years after its entrance into the French Service, namely, in 1789. Louis Philippe granted the title of Baron de Ballyheigue to Antoine Silvain de Cantillon, the representative of the family in France. A branch of the family who stayed at home settled at a place called Ballyphillip, near Limerick, and were wealthy and influential, but became extinct in the person of Mr. Cantillon, whose three well-dowered daughters married three of the finest and tallest gentlemen of the Munster Catholics—McWalter Burke, of Cornabulliagh, whose family is extinct; Mr. Phillip Blake, from the County Galway; and Mr. Maurice O'Connell, of Darrynane. I heard an old lady, descended from McWalter Burke's wife, one of the three Miss Cantillons, say that Mr. FitzGibbon, the father of the famous Lord Clare, was a poor boy from near their place, and that one of them taught him to read. He afterwards entered Trinity College as a sizar, and bartered faith for lore, embraced the legal profession, and was the distinguished father of a famous son.

Most honourable and interesting are the deeds of the uncle and cousin of these three damsels in foreign parts. I unearth them from O'Callaghan, whose book I can best compare to a marble quarry whence with toil and trouble come the precious blocks to be hewn into heroic effigies.

O'Callaghan gives the following interesting account of the valour of Mary Cantillon's uncle: "'A celebrated painter,' writes the Baron de Cantillon,[1] from Paris to Mr. [John] O'Connell, December, 1843, 'has reproduced a picture, which is at present my property, and which treats an historical subject concerning my family and yours. It treats of my great-grandfather, who was likewise uncle to Mary O'Connell, the wife of Maurice, your grand-uncle. The subject is drawn from the archives of the Minister of War in Paris. It represents Captain James Cantillon at the battle of Malplaquet, in 1709, charging, at the head of the Irish Grenadiers of Dorrington, the English troops commanded by the Duke of Marlborough.' The official documents explain it thus: 'When the left of the French Army, taken in flank by the right wing of the enemy's army under the orders of the Duke of Marlborough, began to recoil, the Maréchal de Villars brought up as quickly as possible the Irish Brigade, which was in the centre. It attacked the English troops furiously, and repulsed them. Cantillon, at the head of Dorrington's Grenadiers, got first at the enemy, shouting, "*Forward, brave Irishmen! Long live King James III. and the King of France!*" His sword was shattered, and he fell covered with wounds, having killed, before his death, an officer and several soldiers; only fifteen men of the company survived, the rest lay dead or wounded by their dead captain's side.'"

O'Callaghan also mentions that his son, the Chevalier Thomas de Cantillon, acted with distinguished bravery at the

---

[1] Le Baron Cantillon de Ballyheigue, Lieut.-Colonel 3rd Regiment of Hussars, President of the Council of War, Paris, in 1843.

battle of Laffeld, in 1747. He was an author as well as a soldier, and served under his kinsman, Count Bulkeley. He signalized himself in the attack on the disputed village in carrying at the head of his company the right of the entrenchment, defended by the English regiment of Pulteney" (O'Callaghan's "Irish Brigade," pp. 37, 38, 268, 269, 470).

In Fagan's "Life of O'Connell" the following letter is given as a correction. The Mr. Burke referred to was the father of the late Mr. Burke, of Lota Park, who descended from the Burkes of Cornabulliagh, whose hereditary title was McWalter:—

"You state that Hunting Cap never married. You have been misinformed. His wife was the daughter of Robert Cantillon, Esq., of the County Limerick, grandfather maternally of the late Robert Burke of this city. His son, Philip Cantillon, married my mother's eldest sister, but the family is now extinct. When 'Hunting Cap' came to Cork, in order to settle the marriage of his nephew John with Miss Coppinger, he frequently called on me, and entered into many family details, not forgetting this alliance of our families. His father-in-law, Robert Cantillon, was the near relative of two brothers, bankers in Paris, who had followed the fortunes of James II., and made large fortunes there, which the daughter of one of them inherited, and became the wife of the Earl of Stafford, the descendant of the unfortunate victim of the Popish Plot, Thomas Howard, Viscount Stafford, whose title of baron is now possessed by Sir George Jerningham, a descendant in the female line, the male being extinct. I have some letters written by the Parisian bankers between 1720 and 1730 to my grandfather."

BOOK II.

IRISH BOYS ABROAD.

1761-1769.

How the young cousins, Daniel O'Connell of Darrynane, and Morty of Tarmons, went to serve abroad—Maur-ni-Dhuiv's parting lament—English rhymed translation—How Chevalier Fagan got Daniel into the French Service and the Royal Swedish Regiment—Brief account of last campaign of the Seven Years' War, wherein the boys smelt powder on opposite sides—Chevalier Fagan's letter to Maurice O'Connell, describing Dan's admirable conduct during it, and prophesying his future eminence—Morty gets taken prisoner—Father Guardian O'Brien helps him, and writes to Maurice O'Connell, enclosing a letter from Morty, and consulting Maurice about the feasibility of making a match between Marshal Browne's son and Lord Kenmare's daughter—Dan's letter (Fort Louis-on-the-Rhine, February 12, 1764)—Answers to Maurice about his going into the Spanish Service—His reasons for not doing so—Money matters—Letter from brother Connell (1764) to Maurice—Satisfaction at Dan's conduct—Shelbourne leases—Irish pilots—Letter from Dan to Maurice (Schlestatt, in Alsace, April, 1765)—Friendship of Captain Fagan—Brother Connell's death—Notice of him—Some of his letters—Letter (Schlestatt, August 6, 1765) from Dan to Maurice—Wants help to accept colonel's offer of a place in Academy—Expectations of wars—Hopes of promotion—Kindness of his colonel—He expects to join the staff—Offer of place in Carabineers—His studies—Looking forward to serve his own king and country—Letter (Strasbourg, December 27, 1765) from Dan to his father, deprecating his displeasure—Death of the Dauphin—Loyalty of the French—School letter (Strasbourg, February 12, 1766)—Military School—Probable advancement—Some hopes of war—Letter (Schlestatt, June 16, 1766) from Dan to Maurice—Joins his regiment—Gets commission as first lieutenant—Sets out for Switzerland with his colonel—Anecdotes of Morty of Tarmons—Letter (Cambray, 1766) from Dan to Maurice—Marching with his regiment—Sister Abigail abroad—Cousin John FitzMaurice—Talks of wintering in Paris—Letter (Aire, August, 1767) from Dan to Maurice—Movements of the regiment—He acts as "Officier Major"—Meets relations—FitzMaurice—Mahony—His cousin the Abbé—Daniel Swiney—Robin Conway—Talks of a trip to Ireland—Orders to appear before the King—Cousin Maurice Jeffrey—Notice of Burkes of Cornabulliagh—Letter of Father Guardian O'Brien to Hunting Cap (Battevant, December, 1767)—Sir Walter Esmonde—Influenza—Chapter in Athlone—Blakes—Intends setting out for Spain—Mrs. Blake's visit to Darrynane—Rev. James Bland to Hunting Cap, on roads—Outlaws in Iveragh—Dangers to respectable Catholics—Smuggling—Letter from Dan to Hunting Cap (dated London, January, 1768)—Accompanies his colonel to London—Impressions of London roughs—A letter from Gravelines (March, 1768) to Hunting Cap—The post of "Sub-Aide Major"—Colonel's kindness—Letter (Gravelines, May, 1768) to Hunting Cap—Movements of the regiment—Indisposition of the Queen—Sister Nelly's marriage to Arthur O'Leary—Robin Conway—Penal law enforced against Tim McCarthy—First letter of 1769, dated from Manburge—The affairs of Corsica—Paoli—Regimental affairs—Armorial bearings—Matrimonial letter from Captain Robin Conway to Maurice O'Connell from Bergues (January, 1769)—The Sheriff goes smuggling—Letter from Dan to Maurice (dated Paris, August, 1769)—The camp—Captain Fagan—Paris and the gay world—Claims of preferment—Hopes of going home—Movements of the regiment—Stephen Fagan.

SOME time in the spring of 1761 Daniel Charles O'Connell, being then nearly sixteen years old, got his heart's desire, and entered the service of France. He was a tall, strong, handsome lad, with straight, fine, clear-cut features, blue-eyed, dark-haired, fair-skinned, as most handsome Irishmen are. He had also a very marked dimple in a very shapely chin. He was clean-limbed and muscular, without an ounce of superfluous flesh about him. As he was likewise endowed with the bright, winning look which accompanies a ready wit and perfect health, it was no wonder, with such good looks and the good manners so carefully inculcated in a well-disciplined home, that he soon found friends. By a letter of Connell's, written just before, it would seem that his fate was trembling in the balance, and Maurice had nearly started him in some other way of life. In the letter of congratulation, wherein Connell so quaintly styles Maurice "his Better half" (written from Hamburg on March 21, 1760 O.S., really, as we count now, 1761), "I am sorry," he says, "to think that poor Daniel is wasting away his time in that Idle Country. I request, my Dr. Brother, you may urge my Father to put him to some business, and that speedily. I shall Contribute, so far as my abilities can reach, to forward him in it. I highly approve of poor Daniel McCarthy's scheme of seeking bread abroad."

Dan, however, had not been idle. Before he left home he had acquired an excellent handwriting, considerable familiarity with English and Latin, and I hardly suppose, when the young servant-lad was taught to "read, write, and siffre," that the young son of the house did not make some way in figures and "ye spheres" and accompanying geographical explanations, in which poor John had himself drilled Maurice. All his life long my hero had a passion for study.

All the articles about him make him enter wrong regiments in wrong years, except a contemporary account in a Kerry newspaper, the *Kerry Chronicle*, preserved at Lake View, and lent me by his grand-nephew, Sir Maurice O'Connell. His own letters confirm it in every discrepant particular where it differs from the French "Biographie Universelle" the "Biographie Générale," and the hurriedly written account contributed to the *New Monthly Magazine* by the Liberator.

Tradition avers that Maur-ni-Dhuiv composed a lament on the departure of her son and sundry young kinsmen, who sailed from Darrynane Harbour. Two of her descendants gave me copies of a metrical translation by the late Father Charles O'Connor-Kerry. I am not disposed to think that all the eighteen lads embarked together. Irish verse was largely figurative, and eighteen was about the number of kinsmen then abroad; some, indeed, were already elderly colonels. I fancy that, in addition to the boys and actual children she beheld with her bodily eyes, she figuratively beheld their elders who had gone out as boys long before.

MAUR-NI-DHUIV'S FAREWELL TO HER BOY AND HIS KINSMEN.

[The lads were going to seek their fortunes in France and Austria.]

I.

"To your bark, brave boys, haste !
In our haven's deep strait is a sail !
On through the shallows, and o'er the watery waste
For France, with my blessing on the gale !

To the land of the Lily bear the Shamrock of our isle.
May they bloom above the blood-stained Rose!
Ye are safe upon the wide sea. The cruiser lags a mile.
God be praised! Ye have baffled your foes.

II.

"Let me weep; for we meet not again.
Never ship bore a goodlier freight—
Twice nine noble scions of the Soldier of Spain.
O'Donoghue's two gallant sons are climbing yonder mast,
To cast a last look on the land.
And my own five brave O'Connells are shedding tears so fast
They cannot see their mother kiss her hand.

III.

"There are three, there are three at the stern,
And three and three are leaning o'er the side.
Donal Cam's sable brows among them I discern,
And the fair locks of Mahony's pride.
In that galley are two more, but I cannot see their face;
Poor babes! are they laughing on the deck?
Oh, full soon they will be men, and prove worthy of their race!
Thy white shield, O McCartie, has no speck.

IV.

"My sons and my nephews, we are one;
One red stream is flowing in our veins.
My blessing, then, will follow you with the radiant sun,
And my fervent prayers when dark night reigns.
Ye go your ways. A greater chief from me shall yet be born
To triumph over ocean's haughty lord.
Remember in your heart of hearts the Sassenach's foul scorn;
In his breast find a sheath for your swords."[1]

When she saw the fleet little craft bearing away this band of boys, her own youngest son among them, the spirit of a bardic prophetess seized her. She followed them from her

---

[1] As I have already said, Maur-ni-Dhuiv's poem was translated by the late Father Charles O'Connor-Kerry, C.C. How accurate the version may be I know not. The ship only bore one of her sons—Daniel, her youngest; but four of the party were her nephews. The allusions to the shamrock, rose, and lily as symbolical of Ireland, England, and France, need no interpretation. "McCarthy's spotless shield" alludes to the well-known armorial bearings of that old clan—a snow-white shield, bearing a stag. Donal Cam was the last great chieftain of the O'Sullivan Beares, who defended Dunboy, and was finally driven to Spain. She metaphorically applies his name to some young scion of his race. The "Soldier of Spain" is a usual paraphrase for the mythical Milesius, whom many of the southern families of Ireland claimed as an ancestor.

lonely shore out to the wide thronged world beyond the sea, her fancy saw fame and fortune in store for them, and revealed a man, sprung from her race, who should burst the fetters and avenge the wrongs of his country. The proud heart of the woman who had gazed tearless on her dead firstborn craved an avenging hero, returning with fire and sword, to redress the wrongs of her race and creed. She did not dream of how this regeneration was to be achieved by the babe, yet unborn, destined to spring from her own race. Still less could she have dreamt of the peaceful triumphs of eloquence, of Emancipation won by a civil organization—by words and votes, not swords. The Tribune of the people always dutifully declared that his eloquence was inherited from his rhyming grandmother.

The passionate bitterness of the verses can be easily understood when we force ourselves to realize how education was contraband, and a career such as they sought forbidden in Ireland.

To the myriad perils of flood and field, which the cavalier of fortune must of necessity confront, was added the risk of capture at the very outset of the boy's career. The smuggling clipper with its freight has to run the gauntlet of pursuit. Superior speed and lightness of build will give it a lead, and suffer it to skim through the rocks and shallows of the perilous Smugglers' Sound, to race the heavier Revenue cruiser in the open seas. The mothers of the young lads had often to stand on the shore and watch the start of this perilous race at the very offset of the career of their boys.

The mother's parting cry to her boy gives us no details as to whither the fleet smuggling craft bore her precious burthen. Dunkirk was the great "smugglers' nest," and it was near the frontier where the Royal Swedes were generally stationed when not in the field. Caen was where the other boy, Connell, had been sent. Count O'Connell's own letters describe the arrival of sundry Irish lads, imported by himself and other kinsmen of the Brigade. The little wanderer, ranging from twelve to seventeen (the younger the better, so as to get schooling in France), was entrusted to a friendly smuggling skipper, and by him handed over, generally with from £20 to £30 in gold, and two suits of clothes and a good lot of Irish linen shirts—plain and ruffled—to the correspondent of the firm, who either entertained him himself or passed him on to some retired veteran of the Brigade, many of whom had married Frenchwomen and settled down as interpreters, or part instructors, part boarders, of Irish people; the lads learning certain branches of a military and polite education from the veterans, and attending classes for the rest. Others, again, had married rich wives, and lived at ease; but all were equally ready to take in a little boy from the old country, who came within the immense concatenations of a Kerry cousinship, where sixth cousins are quite countable. The new-comer was as a son of the house, until an officer returning to his garrison, a merchant visiting his foreign correspondent, a friar changing from one convent to another, or a batch of students going to some great college, took charge of the boy, and consigned him to the Irish officer who had got him into the regiment.

I am unable to find out to whom the boy Dan was consigned. Conways, FitzMaurices, and dear old Chevalier Fagan all appear as guides, philosophers, and friends in his early letters.

The old Kerry paper lent me by Sir Maurice O'Connell gives my hero's adventures on landing. I omit a few of its reflections and digressions here and there. It says—

"The following genuine account of so very respectable a character as Count O'Connell will, we hope, prove acceptable to our readers; more particularly when it is considered that this county gave birth to a man who, both as a gentleman and a soldier, would be an honour to any country.

"His father was celebrated for his hospitality, for which, as for the most unbounded benevolence and urbanity, the late ingenious Dr. Smith has paid him the highest compliments in his topographical 'History of Munster.' . . .

"At the age of fifteen, he [Daniel O'Connell] set out with the intention of joining the Imperial Army, where there were some of his relations, by whose interest he expected to get a commission. But having in his way through Flanders met Chevalier Fagan—then under cure from a bad wound, to whose generosity many of his fellow-countrymen were indebted for their advancement in life, and whose characteristic is beneficence—he was induced by his persuasion to join the regiment of Royal Suédois, to the colonel of which he was strongly recommended by the chevalier. In a few months he was promoted to a sub-lieutenancy. It was then near the close of the last Continental war, the termination of which put an end to further advancement, so that Mr. O'Connell remained a subaltern for seven or eight years."

The dear old Chevalier Fagan's actions, as alluded to in letters extending over forty years, prove the accuracy of this description of his fatherly heart towards young Irish lads. There was some sort of far-away cousinship between the families of Fagan and O'Connell, and a curious similarity in one point between the old soldier and the young one—each belonged to a family where twenty-two living children had been born to one father and mother. The quaint old Georgian grange of Darrynane, and the lofty, gabled town house of the Fagans in Cork, both exist—the one smothered in more spacious modern buildings; the other converted into a shop, as the tide of fashion has ebbed away from the hill which bears St. Mary's "North Cathedral" and the fine old town houses which have been long deserted by the upper classes.

The appellation "Chevalier" had a threefold meaning in eighteenth-century France. The cadets of great houses bore it as a title; Knights of Malta, as a matter of right; and the Military Knights of St. Louis, as a proud and hard-earned military distinction. Except in the case of princes, the admission to the Military Knighthood of St. Louis required distinguished services or some feat of personal bravery. I had the pleasure of examining a set of documents showing how Sir Charles McCarthy-Lyragh (descendant of McCarthy of Manche, who had followed King James to France) won it.

Chevalier Fagan does not seem to have seen much active service after this latter part of the Seven Years' War, but to have ended his days a half-pay captain of horse, while his *protegé* rose to be a general; but from first to last the same devoted friendship existed between them. A couple of centuries before a similar bond of almost paternal and filial affection and dutifulness had existed between two French gentlemen, soldiers of another King Louis. In the firm friendship of the two Irishmen, and the gratitude and respect of the younger, I like to recognize the same spirit which actuated Captain Louis d'Ars and his scholar, the Chevalier Bayard.

The very first letter in the precious book of bound Irish Brigade letters [1] referring to Count O'Connell and his comrades is endorsed, in his brother's hand, "Capitaine de Fagan, Bergue, 1762." It bears date, Bergue, January 2, 1762. It begins—

DEAR SIR,—I received the letter you have lately favoured me with but a few days ago. As Mr. Hennessy knew I was to come to this country, he kept it in his hands. I sent it off direct to Dan, as I know how proud he'll be of hearing from you, tho' you schold him to some purpose, and I dare say without the least fault on his side, as has constantly complained of your silence, and that he has show'd me a letter he writt to you last August. Had I the honour of being known to you, I should not be pleased with the needless Compliments you make me on my having been happy enough to serve him, for had I done infinitely more for him, I am daily more than sufficiently recompensed by the honour he does his country and all his friends.

I have Seen him very often in the months of 7bre, 8bre, and 9bre, and have received a letter from him yesterday. He is in very good health; and as to his conduct, its so prodigiously excellent that I give you my honour I never saw his fellow. His prudence, address, and singular knowledge of things have rendered him dear to Numbers of note, and his application, Master both of the french and dutch tongues; and what I think more surprising is that there are few subalterns of any age that know their trade half as well as he does. In short, Sir, if he lives, he'l certainly shine most brilliantly.

I can give you some little Advertisements as to his finances, which, I am shure, are actually low, as he was not a little embarrassed last winter for an equipage [outfit]. I prevailed on his cousin, Abbé FitzMaurice, to lend him wherewithall to enter the field. Which Money was to be paid his friends by you. I have heard nothing of that since, but have forwarded him a bill last summer, which Mr. Hennessy Remitted me. You must not be allarmed at what he actually costs you, for

---

[1] Lent me by my kinsman, Christopher FitzSimon, of Glancullen.

its so necessary for advancement's sake that it should be so, that I ashure you that one of my Brothers, who came to this Country at the same time with him, and who leads the same life, has already cost me forty pounds, and besides about thirty he brought with him from home. I still know the worth of Money, and my Means were not certainly equall to yours. I hope you'll be so good as to excuse my entering into this detale with you in favour of what has induced me to it, which can be nothing else than my friendship for your family and my love for my Country.

I consequently will be freer again with you, for as the present Moment seems criticall as to Changes and reformations in everything thats Regimentall, I think it would be prudent to Remitt something to this Dear Boy.

I repeat again, the Nerf of war is the Nerf of advancement. You'll probably enable him thereby to be, in a short time, able to do for himself. I'l forward with pleasure anything you chuse to send him. Adieu, Dear Sir, and believe me,

Sincerely attached to you and yours,
C. FAGAN.

The veteran was so much in the habit of speaking French that he comically gives "nerves" instead of "sinews of war."

From the letters and the notice in the old newspaper we can easily see exactly what befell the lad. I have not been able to make out who the acting Colonel of the Royal Swedes was. "The Count my Colonel" is what young Dan calls him. Dan must have joined the regiment as a cadet some time in the early spring, but after February 13. Probably his cousin Morty of Tarmons got a sudden call to Austria, and the same opportunity of transport was availed of to send out the two young kinsmen.

Joining the French Service in time for the two last campaigns of the Seven Years' War, the beardless boy, attached as a cadet to the foreign regiment, soon had a chance of learning practically "the soldier's glorious trade." The bold and sudden stroke of the allied commander, Prince Ferdinand, early in February, when military etiquette supposed all belligerents still comfortably settled in winter quarters, inflicted some damage on the French, though the eventual balance of honour and success lay with them at the close of the campaign of 1761. The decrees of kings and plans of field-marshals reacted on the fortunes of every gentleman bearing arms on any side. Doubtless the swift and sudden February attack, the early success of the Allies, and all the fighting that went on, led to the sudden calling out of scores of cadets who would not otherwise have been made into full-fledged officers so soon. For a long-headed, hard-working, strong lad like my hero, it was a wonderful chance. His natural aptitude for languages stood him in remarkable stead, as this facility is by no means common among French people. The stirring scenes among which he was thrown rapidly developed in him a precocious manliness and steadiness of character. All communications with home seem to have miscarried, but he had his father's nephew, the Abbé FitzMaurice, and the Chevalier Fagan to advise him. But for their timely aid he could not have accompanied the regiment, as campaigning implied a horse and various other requisites, uniforms, arms, etc., all comprised in the word "equipage," *i.e.* equipment, which a cadet was not possessed of, and for the price of which there was no time to write home.

The stout old captain of horse must have been wounded in the early hostilities of the campaign, and must have been lodging in some Flemish town when the boy Dan landed. He must have joined his regiment in the early autumn, as he mentions frequent meetings with Dan in September, October, and November, 1761, after which the armies retired to winter quarters.

At the close of the campaign of 1760 the French had all Hesse and the town of Gottingen, and good posts on the Lower Rhine. Prince Ferdinand, the allied commander, got his troops ready early in February, 1761, swooped down unexpectedly on Hesse, and drove the French beyond Cassel and Gottingen. The French lost Fritzlar on the 15th. The Allies proceeded to besiege Cassel on the one part, and to engage French and Saxons towards Gottingen, where the Prussians got the best of it on February 14 at Laganfalze, on the Unsbruk. The French withdrew then from a considerable extent of country. The Count de Vaux, Commander of Gottingen, then beat some Hanoverians and took Duderstadt.

Marshal de Broglie called up the army of the Lower Rhine,

and proceeded to relieve Cassel. He sent forward a splendid body of dragoons, who broke through the Hanoverian, Hessian, and Brunswick foot, and took two thousand of them prisoners. The siege of Cassel was raised after twenty-seven days of open trenches, and the Allies evacuated the whole country of Hesse. Both armies then retired to winter quarters.

All through the campaign of 1762 the two lads, who had left their kindred homes in Kerry, had plenty of hard fighting on opposite sides.

The rest of the united French armies retreated before Prince Ferdinand, and eventually fled behind the Lahne. There was a great deal of fighting outside Cassel until, in the words of the "Annual Register," "this capital of an unfortunate principality, which has been so often taken and retaken during the course of this war, despairing of relief, at length surrendered to the victorious arms of the Allies, after a siege of fifteen days of open trenches."

The signing of the preliminaries of peace at this time, notified in the two armies, put a happy conclusion to all military operations.

Such was the close of the Seven Years' War, in which young Dan O'Connell first smelt powder, was marched, countermarched, had his infinitesimal share of a series of reverses, and bore his small part in a couple of brilliant successes, serving against England, which he was afterwards to serve.

The first letter in the collection of Irish Brigade letters, as we have seen, concerns my special hero; the second relates to his cousin and lifelong friend, Morty of Tarmons, afterwards Baron Moritz O'Connell, of the Austrian Service. The writer, Father Guardian O'Brien, head of the famous old Irish Franciscan Monastery at Prague, was a cousin of Miss Molly Cantillon, who had recently espoused Maurice O'Connell, of Darrynane, young Morty's first cousin. The worthy father is such an amusing letter-writer, and so very much less dry and formal in style than the soldiers who fill most of the letter-book, that I shall quote any of his letters I can find.

I note a curious coincidence in three lives I have examined

into. Here we have Abbé FitzMaurice lending young Dan the price of the first "equipage," *i.e.* outfit; and Father Guardian O'Brien mounting and equipping young Morty when he was taken prisoner;—a clerical kinsman appearing at the turning-point of each boy's career. When Daniel O'Houny lands in Spain after the great Peace of Utrecht, and his way to all promotion in the British Navy is barred by the Test Act, Father John O'Houny, kindest, jolliest, and yet most devout of Irish friars, persuades the youth to enter the service of Spain. He endures horrible hardship and poverty at first, but dies an admiral. But for the three clerics, the pecuniary aid of the two first, the advice of the third, there would not have been three successful cavaliers of fortune, each would have been foiled on the threshold of a career of enterprise leading to an old age of honour and profit.

Young Morty O'Connell, of Tarmons, serving in the great Marshal Daun's own regiment of horse, can be easily traced, as history chronicles the movements of that distinguished commander, who was pitted against no less an antagonist than the great Frederick. The Austrian leader attempted to save Schwerdnitz, the key of Silesia, in July, but was caught between two Prussian armies and routed. The town held out till October, having resisted two months' siege with open trenches. Frederick turned his victorious arms on Saxony. At first the Austrians had some successes, but were badly beaten at Freyberg, and two hundred and forty officers were made prisoners on October 29.

The Prussians broke into Bohemia and pushed on almost to the gates of Prague; they entered that kingdom also from another quarter, and made destructive raids over Saxony, Franconia, and even Suabia.

Everywhere the Austrians were brave and unfortunate, though their Empress-queen saved her crown by their valour and devotion. Scores of brave Irishmen served in her ranks, from Marshal Ulick Browne down to the lads mentioned in this boy's letter a century and a quarter old.

He is in the Austrian corps garrisoning Bohemia, and comes into the capital to pay his respects to kind Father Guardian O'Brien. His writing is clear and legible, a small running foreign hand. The spelling is excellent. The only changes I make are filling in some of the abbreviations. His father was a younger brother of Daniel O'Connell, the builder of Darrynane, to whose eldest son, Maurice, he writes. That long-headed individual was brains-carrier, banker, and law adviser to his multitudinous kinsfolk.

Prague, April ye 12th, 1763.

DEAREST COUSIN,—Our regiment being within 4 Miles of this town, I came in here yesterday to Pay my Compliments to Father Guardian O'Brien, and return him thanks for his care in forwarding ye contents of ye bill to me, which he has effected 3 Weeks ago, at a very seasonable time when I had been in ye greatest Distress. This Money he has sent me intire, tho' had been indebted to him 4 Po^s since ye unfortunate time of my coming to Prague in September last, after ye loss of my baggage, when I had been in ye most grievous misfortune until relieved by this worthy Gentleman as being then destitute of all necessaries. So Expect, Dear Cousin, these 4 P^{ds} may be paid by my Father to his Orders without loss of time, as Civilities of this nature are not to be abused of. I know my poor Father will be surprised at my Embarrassing him so much, which he may be confident nothing but ye greatest Distress would oblige me too. I have lately received his Letter which gave me inconceavable Satisfaction to find that he, my poor Dearest Mother, and all my friends were well. Assure you both of an everlasting Duty at my Side which no change will make me forgett. I gott away from here in a hurry with Father O'Brien's horses to my regiment, as we afterwards march towards Vienna, where we remain in garrison.

Nothing at present could happen more lucky for me, as being there at ye fountain-head, all means will be tryed by Lt Colonel Pierce for placing me, if possible. Y^e Great God relieve me out of my present Station as being a very unprofitable and fatiguing one. No news here. Captain O'Connell is ransomed, and on March to his regiment, which comes in quarters to Colir, 7 miles from Prague. O'Sullivan likewise, who goes into Italy. My Dr Cousin and [your] Brother Dan O'Connell wrote to me lately. He is well, and greatly esteemed by his Colonel. Adieu, Dearest Cousin, and believe me to be with ye Sincerest Love,

Your ever Affectionate Kinsman and
most humble Servant,
M. O'CONNELL.

P.S.—Please to Present my best Compliments to Mrs. Connell, tho' unacquainted, also my Dr Uncle and Aunt and intire family of Darrinane, with all other friends in ye Country. My poor Dr Father and Mother, pray assure them that as soon as possible I'll go to see y^m [them], as they may be assured their Longing to see me can't be greater than mine to have one sight of y^m, as they occupy my thoughts continually. Dr Cousin, Excuse ye badness of my writing, as being in vast haste.

This epistle shows strong family feeling depicting Father Guardian O'Brien's kindness to this kinsman of his cousin's husband, whom he has as yet never seen, while Morty had never seen *his* cousin's wife. Each presents formal greetings to Mr. and Mrs. Maurice O'Connell, " tho' unacquainted" respectively with his own relative's spouse.

I can trace in the old "Annual Register" of 1762 the movements of the armies to which the young Dan and Morty were attached. The French had two armies in the summer campaign of 1762—one under the Prince de Soubise and Marshal d'Estrées on the Weser; the other under the Prince de Condé on the Lower Rhine. As the old "Annual Register" observes, the campaign began in very much the same place, and they contended for pretty much the same objects which they had struggled for in the two preceding years. In June they sustained heavy losses at Grakenstein, on the borders of Hesse, by the united arms of England and Austria, and were only saved from destruction by the heroism of M. de Stamville, with the flower of the infantry, who covered the retreat. In July they were obliged to evacuate Southern Hesse, and in August Gottingen and Northern Hesse. In the end of July they lost Munden, and the enemy crossed the Fulda. He sent message after message to Prince de Condé, to bring the army of the Lower Rhine to their aid. On August 30, however, the French, under Marshals de Soubise and d'Estrées, had a brilliant victory on the heights of Johansberg over the Prince of Brunswick, and garrisoned Cassel with ten thousand men.

Father Guardian Bonaventure O'Brien, of the Irish Franciscans at Prague, to Hunting Cap.

My Dear Cousin,—I received your letter with the bill for Mr. O'Connell of Daun's Regiment with a vast deal of pleasure, and without delay got that sum paid thro' the means of a friend of mine, a banker in this town, altho' the assignation was on Amsterdam. Since I had the pleasure of being acquainted with this young Gentleman, I neglected no occasion to render him all the service in my power, and without flattery he highly deserves the esteem and attention of every well-meaning man. Still, his being a near relation of yours shall urge me at all times to seek for fresh occasions of exerting my zeal and friendship in his favour. Pray make my humble respects agreable to my Cousin your spouse, whom I sincerely congratulate with, to have had the happiness of being join'd to a gentleman of your parts and happy character. If you are in Lord Kenmare's neighbourhood, you'd do me a singular favour in letting me know how old his daughter is, her humour and other qualities, also her fortune. This request will seem strange to you at the beginning, the case is—General Brown, only surviving Son and Heir to the late Marshal of that name, has spoke to me about that young Lady, and seems inclined to marry in Ireland. As he is extremely attatched to me, he confided this thought of his to me as a Secret, so that I wouldn't be glad any should know it but yourself alone. In case she would be to his purpose,[1] he intends setting of for Ireland in some time, and I am to accompany him. He has a charming Estate in this kingdom, and his Post besides brings him in a thousand a year. He speaks no English, so it is necessary to mention if the young Lady understands the french. I believe Lord Kenmare would willingly agree to the match. The Count told me he would write to him, but not till your answer arrives. So that I earnestly entreat you to loose no time in consideration. You'll pardon, I hope, this Liberty, which I do only on condition that you'll let me know when I can be serviceable to you or any of your friends in these parts, and you'll all find by experience that ye commands will be executed with the greatest readiness, candour and sincerity by him who has the honour to be, with the profoundest veneration and respect,

My Dearest Cousin,

Your Most Affec^{te} Mt Obedient and most humble Servant,

Bon. O'Brien.

Prague, June 1, 1763.

---

[1] Unhappily, she was only a child at this time, as the fourth Lord Kenmare was married in 1750.

P.S.—My being abroad in the country for several weeks with General O'Donnel has retarded this letter so long. Captains O'Connell and Macarthy, Colonel Mac Elygott and his brother the Major, who is actually here, make you and Lady their compliments, to which I pray yᵘ joyn mine, tho' unacquainted. I recommend Secrecy once more about what I mentioned. You'll be pleased to gett the four pounds mentioned on the other side paid to my father, John O'Brien, at Buttevant.

The letter had remained over from April to June before it was finally despatched.

General Browne did not marry Lord Kenmare's daughter, and the family of the heroic old marshal is extinct. Miss M. Agnes Hickson, on whose "Old Kerry Records" I have drawn so largely, sends me the following notice of the family. In trying to trace a connecting link between Limerick and Kerry O'Connells, Mr. J. G. Hewson, of Holywood, near Adare, "a very clever antiquarian and genealogist," sent her the memorandum. Miss Hickson writes me—

"Mr. Hewson says that in his youth, some forty-six years ago, there was living near him at Kilfinny, or near it, a Roman Catholic, Mr. Gerald FitzGerald, of Ballinvara, who married a Miss Brown, a member of the distinguished family of Browns of Camas Awney and Brown's Castle, near Ballylongford, between 1200 and 1584, when they forfeited for adherence to Desmond. One of them, however, Annabel Brown, married, first, a Captain Apsley, an officer in Elizabeth's army, by whom she had two daughters, co-heiresses of their maternal grandfather, John Brown of Awney's Estate at Hospital. One Apsley co-heiress married Lord Cork; the other, Captain Thomas Brown, and had by him a son, from whom Lord Kenmare descends in the *female* line, and who brought to him the Hospital Estates. After Apsley's death, Annabel Brown married Captain Spring, of Kerry, and by a network of marriages, of her father's kinsmen and her own descendants by Spring, she was ancestress of the Browns of Camas, in the last century. One of these, Ulick Brown, went into the Austrian Service in or about 1720, and became Field-marshal and Count under Maria Teresa and Joseph II., like his cousin Lacy. In or about 1840 Field-Marshal Brown's descendant in Austria died, and left a considerable sum of money to the Miss Brown, his cousin, who had married Gerald FitzGerald, of Ballinvara."

My hero's first preserved letter immediately follows Father Guardian O'Brien's in the letter-book. He is mentioned in a letter of Connell's. There is not a word of his campaigning or his adventures. Strange to say, in the long series of his letters, extending over sixty-six years, there is not a single description of any of his many escapes. The Chevalier Fagan writes of his first campaign. Count Bartholomew O'Mahony tells his family of his remarkable escape from what seemed certain death on board the floating batteries at the siege of Gibraltar, in 1782. In actual war-time it was very difficult to transmit letters. Still, just after, I am sure he must have written to his mother. He refers on several occasions to letters written to her and his various sisters, especially to Nancy, the youngest of all the family.

Doubtless he told his hairbreadth escapes to them. Curiously enough, the first letter preserved is about his leaving the French Service. The lad, with the eminent good sense which distinguished him, was strongly averse to forfeiting the advantages he had acquired by three years' hard work and steady application, and probably knew more about foreign soldiering being a very poor thing everywhere than did his brother at home, who might have fancied any young Irish soldier of fortune could live on a lieutenant's pay. That sagacious relative, however, had the good sense to yield to the boy's reasons, and suffer him to remain where he had already set foot on the lowest rung of the ladder of fortune.

The expectations entertained a year before by "Cousin Morty of Tarmons," that Lieut.-Colonel Pierce's good will and their residence at Vienna would have benefited his fortunes, were futile, though Marshal Daun's lieut.-colonel seems, by his name, to have been an Irishman. Dan's colonel was a foreigner. Irishmen, Swedes, and Germans served in the French Swedish, Irish, and German regiments, and probably there was no vacancy in an Irish regiment when the lad joined the Royal Swedes. "Officer in the Royal Swedish Regiment in his most Christian Majesty's service" is the invariable direction given until he became a captain. Cadets were not designated officers. Maurice Geoffrey and Maurice Charles were the sons of kinsmen. (The members of younger branches of Irish families generally used their father's Christian name. My husband was always "Morgan John," even a few years ago.) We trace them in many letters. "Abby" was the little niece, half reared at Darrynane, where her widowed mother and she went frequently on long visits.

The following is the first letter preserved of the future General Count O'Connell:—

Daniel Charles O'Connell, of the Royal Swedes, to his brother Maurice, of Darrynane.

Fort Louis-on-the-Rhine, February 12, 1764.

My Dear Brother,—I have just Recd. y^r Letter of the 20th December, Containing a Bill of thirteen £ Sterg., which has been punctually Discounted, and in Consequence of your Orders, Lose not an instant in answering you. It Does me the greatest Uneasiness to find me under a Necessity of troubling you, and the more so as I apprehend you suspect me of being ye Cause, by my Conduct, why it falls so heavy on you. Depend on't your Suspicions on that Head are very ill Grounded, as Well as the Unkind Conjectures of those that Insinuate that I never Write home but when I want money. I should be sorry to think you entertained so base an opinion of me, and I give you my honour no Sentiment so ungenerous, so unworthy, shall ever find a Place in my Breast.

With Regard to the Proposal you make me of quitting this Service and getting into that of Spain, I acknowledge myself too Deeply Indebted to my Dear Brother to Refuse Executing his will in any Degree, but at the same time, must observe to you how imprudent it appears to me to Relinquish a sure Establishment for an Uncertainty; but what ever be the consequence, I shan't hesitate to take the measures you Dictate.

I have communicated y^r L^r to my Colonel, who is vastly against my quitting, and whose Friendship I have Reason to Rely on. The Particular Distinction he makes between me and the other Officers of the Corps is a convincing proof on't. Captain Fagan also Disapproves ye scheme absolutely. So that, to be plain with you, nothing but a Certainty of meeting with some advantage in that service can justify such a proceeding. Let me know without Delay what you build on; and if you persist in my going to seek my fortune elsewhere.

Send me the Letters of Reccommendation necessary for a journey of 500 Leagues; and on the least prospect of pushing myself, I shall willingly concur with you, for make no doubt of my Readiness to Run every Risk on the lightest appearance of being Able to repay the favours of my friends. On the other hand, if you should Resolve to leave me as I am, Be good enough to let me know the Annual sum I can Reckon on. Whatever it be, I shan't murmur, and Rather than Importune you, I shall take some other Course of Life in hand if I find it impossible to maintain me decently in this.

Adieu, my Dear Brother. I shall ever Retain the warmest sense of y^r favours, and shall think me happy to occupy a place in y^r friendship and Esteem. Be good Enough to answer me without Delay, and Rely on't that I shall ever be, with unceasing tenderness, your most

Respectful and affectionate B^r,

DANL. O'CONNELL.

My Duty to father and mother, and affection to Sisters Connell and Brother Morgan, and My friendship to Mick Falvey, and compliments to Mr. and Mrs. Fagan. All friends in these parts are well. I lately had a L^r from C^{us} Maurice Geoffrey and Maurice Charles O'Connell; the former seems to be in distress. Let me hear some account from B^r Connell. My Love to all my Brothers and Sisters. Embrace Abby for me. My Duty to my Uncle and Aunt of Tarmons, and let em know that I expect soon to hear from $Cous^n$ Morty. I have wrote on that subject to Lt.-Colonel Pierce.

My address, A Monsieur D. O'Connell, Officier au Régiment de Royal Suédois.

The following letter from Connell O'Connell to his brother Maurice gives us the first mention of Daniel's soldiering in home letters.

This letter is of considerable interest, as it shows how, while one boy was gone to be a soldier in France, friends wanted another to enter the Spanish Navy. I append in a note[1] how well a naval pilot fared. From the letters of these Sullivans I fancy that was what made Dan's father and elder brother so desirous he should enter the Spanish Service. Says Connell—

[1] See Note A, p. 131.

London, July 25, 1764.

My Dr. Brothr.,—I have been duly favoured with y^r acceptable answer of ye 1st inst., by which I have ye satisfaction to find that absence does not in ye least diminish ye place I always flattered myself I held in your esteem, and which I ... and shall look upon my dear brother as my greatest happiness. Its with ye utmost satisfaction I hear of poor Daniel's conduct and advancement, but am greatly concerned att ye precarious situation of ye poor gentlemen of that country concerning Lord Shelbournes leases.[1] Mr. Owen O'Sullivan is att present in this town, but sets out for Cadiz next September, whence he immediately proceeds commander of a ship to Lima. Gyles is still here and goes out with him. He has been kind enough to make me an offer of his interest if inclined to goe that way, which I declined, as itt is very difficult to gett preferment in that service without great friends, and a person must qualify himself by serving ye King 18 months, and then, if he gets a voyage, lye idle a year or two before he can gett an other. Mr. Sullivan is a worthy honest man, and will, I am sure, serve me or any of our familys to ye utmost of his power.

I have not ye pleasure of being acquainted with Mr. McNamara, neither doe I know how he can be of any service to me, as we seldom touch so low as Malaga. I am att present going out ye same voyage in ye same ship, station, and employ I was before, and hope to be back in 5 or 6 months. B^r Morgan sent me Daniel's address. I have wrote to him some time agoe, but have received no answer. He likewise mentions a nephew of Father Morgan's, son to ye late Danl. Connell, who intends for ye sea; whom I should with pleasure serve if in my power, but can do no more for him than binding him to serve some of my acquaintance, except he chuses to wait till I am lucky enough to get a command. I have wrote by ye post to my Father. We have little or no news here. People in general imagine ye Peace won't be of long duration. Please to make my love to my Sister.

I am, my dear Brother,
Y^r most dutiful and loving
CONNELL O'CONNELL.

I shall here quote an earlier letter of poor young Connell's, and the letter referring to his death. He had spare cash and bills to over £70 on hand when he was killed. We thus perceive that seafaring was far more profitable, if less genteel,

[1] See p. 160.

than soldiering. At the same time, Dan was obliged to draw on unwilling supplies from home, and to practise the most penurious economy.

Connell had been serving on board a privateer, seeing the world, writing home most interesting accounts of foreign ports, tempests, hairbreadth escapes, and profitable ventures. He seemed on the road to fortune when he was lost at sea. There are a set of letters about him at Darrynane still, full of human interest. He had evidently intended to help on the young brother, who never trespassed more than he could help on friends at home, but who found it impossible to live without a fixed, though moderate, allowance.

The following letters were found by the present Daniel O'Connell in old Maurice O'Connell's *secrétaire*. Before the relaxation of the penal laws, the family did not put "O" on the outside of letters. Dan and Connell sign "O'Connell" inside their letters, and put "Connell," omitting the prefix, outside.

I extend contractions, but otherwise leave the spelling intact. The letter from the poor young sailor possesses considerable human interest.

Hamburgh, March 21, 1760 [O.S.].

My Dear Brother,—Your most acceptable favour of ye 15 Ultimo I with inexpressible comfort received, It being ye only one I had from y^t [that] Country since August, 1758, which I impute to ye reasons you assign in y^r letter, as I find by ye same that all my letters, both to my father and you, since my Departure from England till my arrival here, miscarried. I shall, according to your Directions, give ye an account of my Adventures since 20th January, 1759 [really 1760, as the old style legal year began on the 25th March], on which day we sailed from Falmouth, till ye 18th October, 1760, which was ye Date of ye letter you received.

I sailed from Falmouth on ye above Day, Second Mate in a Letter of Marque bound to Cape Breton and Rhode Island, to which place she belonged; but having ye misfortune to loose her Rudder on ye High Seas between ye 20 and 21 of March, in ye Lt. 28^d 31^m N., W. Lg. 46^d 15^m, bore away, with a kind of Rudder wee knocked up for New Providence, one of ye Bahama Islands, where we arrived ye 20th of April, with only 25 lbs. bread, half a Barrel of Beef, and one Cask of Water on board. Wee there remained till ye 2nd of May, when, having got a New Rudder and Everything else in proper repair, we Sailed for Cape Briton, where we arrived ye 3rd of June, after a Passage of 32 days, During which Nothing occurred. From Louisbourgh we sailed, a few days after Admiral Saunders sailed for Quebec, and arrived att New Port in Rhode Island ye 16th of ye following July, when, to Compleat ye Voyage, ye Merchants refused paying ye wages, which amounted to near £500. Wee, however, Libeled ye Vessel [technical phrase for seizing the ship for debt], which was ye most expeditious way to come by our money; but in spite of our Endeavours, the Merchants, through roguery, prolonged ye sale of ye Vessell for six weeks. When I discovered, being then there three weeks and unwilling to loose any more Time, I sold what was coming to me for £15, and immediately quitted ye Island for New Yorke. When I got there, I accidentally met Cousin Denis McGillicuddy, who was then fitting out in a Snow [species of brig]. I leave y^e to Judge our mutual pleasure at ye meeting. I remained 3 weeks after at New Yorke, and might, with ye recommendations of my friends, have gone Chief Mate of Several Vessals; but Cousin Denis being shipped chief mate of ye brigg wee both now belong to, and unwilling to part each other after so short an Interview, I concluded to come Second Mate with him. Wee are bound from here for Yorke, and shall, God willing, drop down ye river in a Day or two. Y^e Vessell belongs to Messrs. Stillwell & Keley, of York; ye latter of which gentlemen I was informed was a Limerick man. It's very much in his power to be of service to me. I request, my Dr. Brother, you may procure me Letters of recommendation from his friends in Limerick to that gentleman.

You can better conceive than I express ye satisfaction it gave me to hear of y^r being married in a creditable ffamily, and to ye satisfaction of my Parents and you. As to ye Unlimited Letter of Creditt you were good enough to Send me, as it Comes from y^r Hands, whom I always looked upon as my Better half, I shall only say that I expect, with ye Assistance of ye Almighty, never to be guilty of anything y^t may incur y^r Displeasure or in ye Least Alienate ye affection you always had and at present shew for me. It was vastly y^e . . . [illegible word] agreable as it happened to me. M. Bourouhes, who is ye Merchant we were consigned to here, he has been good enough to promise to recommend me to Mr. Stillwell, our owner. I have taken what you ordered, Namely, £25 stg., and you have two receipts of ye same date and for ye same. Y^r money I laid out as you'll see at foot of this letter. I am glad to hear that Brother Morgan is become attentive to his and my Father's business, but sorry to think that poor

Daniel is wasting away his time in that Idle Country. I request, my Dr. Brother, you may urge my Father to put him to some business, and that speedily. I shall Contribute, so far as my abilities can reach, to forward him in it. I highly approve of poor Daniel McCarthy's scheme of seeking bread abroad rather than . . . any time in them parts . . . He may depend, if ever it should lye in my way in anything that I can do by him, It is to be . . . the other will take ye Example by him. I could, in short, prolong this letter a twelvemonth; but as room grows scarce, and it would be putting you to needless expence to pay treble postage for a letter, I shall conclude with my Duty to my Parents, Love to y^r Spouse and my Sister, Brother Morgan and my other Brothers and Sisters, relations, and all Enquiring friends.

Y^r most Dutiful and Ever loving Brother,

CONNELL O'CONNELL.

P.S.—Let me once more remind y^e, my Dr. Brother, of the recommendation to Mr. Kelcy, and send it Enclosed to me to New Yorke. You may Depend I'll miss no oppertunity of writing either to my Father or you an account of my Venture.

	£	s.	d.
30 Cases Geneva, Falmouth, with all charges, on Board	21	10	4
100 lb. Bohea tea, at 2s. 6d., all Mixed	12	10	0
In all	£34	0	4

Connell was returning home in the spring of 1765, when he was washed overboard in a storm near Cape Clear. The ship must have been wrecked, as it eventually drifted off the north coast of Ireland, where it was washed ashore. The following letter simply refers to the poor lad's belongings. It is endorsed, "Messrs. Connor of London's letter of this Date."

London, June 11, 1765.

SIR,—We have yours of 30th April. Note what you say in regard to your Brother's affairs, in which we shall assist all in our power. As for what the People in the N. of Ireland write you, we can say little to that, for we had so many wrong accounts from them that we were glad to get clear at the expence of paying £500 and upwards before the ship could be got away. Your Brother's Chest is on board safe, but very little inside, we believe; nothing except an old coat or something of that kind, these very People in the North taking care to strip that with everything else. The Note you mention from the 2nd Mate for £8, we find, and shall be to your credit. There is also an other Note, of one Denis McGillycuddy, to your brother for £13 10s. 8d., dated 10th Day of April, 1760. As for money, we find only 3 gold crowns, and the Stock Buckle you mention never was his. His Shoe Buckles were in his shoes when lost. Can't be supposed he had two pairs. Them you mention were the Boatswain's, who was unfortunately Elsewhere Lost. The Silk and Velvet you mention is at the Custum House, and doe not apprehend any part except some trifle as belonging to him, and shall doe what we can for you. We find he had several things from people here on credit, which we suppose that money we paid Mr. Murphy long since was intended for, being £52, balance of his bill after paying the Hozier £14 10s. It is to oblige you that we interfere, as we can have no business with things of this nature, only great trouble. When affairs can be determined, we shall pay your order anything of your Brother's that may come into our Hands.

We are, Sir,
Your Umble Servs.,
Chars. & Ja. Connor.

The news of Connell's death naturally caused the most poignant grief to his young brother. The anguish he felt is discernible through all the stiff periods of his letter. Connell had evidently been the pet of all at home, where some coolness had supervened on Dan's refusal to give up the French Service. Connell must have been a man of most genial and lovable nature, and was the one of all the family whom Dan seems to have loved the best.

Selestatt, in Alsace, April 14, 1765.

My Dr. Brother,—I have rec[d] y[r] Letter of 4th february, wrote from Dublin, giving me the shocking account of the unfortunate fate of our Dear and Worthy brother Connell, for whose memory I shall ever cherish a tender regard, and should have been earlier in endeavouring to console you, my Dear Broth[r] and Parents had we not daily expected marching for Dunkerque, but our Reg[t] has been but yesterday countermanded. I am at a loss what to say. Laying my grief before you would be but aggravating yours, of which I apprehend the bad consequences, knowing your affection for Dear Connell, whose Virtues and happy Dispositions rendered him so justly Dear to all his friends. When I consider my Situation, just deprived of a Brother who discovered the greatest desire of forwarding me, whose Letter a Lasting Monument of his Fondness now between my hands, daily prescribes to me my Duty towards God and the World, at the same time that it puts me in mind of what I owe his soul. When I reflect on the Situation of my family, to whom I am but a useless burthen instead of helping 'em, as my dear Connell could have done, I am tempted to put an end to a Life now become Odious to me and importunate to my friends. Alas! my Resolution, I mean that Resignation we owe to the will of the Almighty, Resignation which ought to be Superior to all Wordly Accidents. This is sufficient to let you see the principles from which I endeavour to derive consolation, so true is it the only Source we can now render our Dear Connell is daily to fervently implore the Omnipotent's mercy for his soul. This certainly [would] be the proof he would desire of our Love, were he in condition to Desire one, besides we should Look on Death a seperation of a few years or perhaps but a few months, and a Motive so Laudable as expecting to rejoin a Dear one in the happy presence of our Maker should be an Additional [source] of satisfaction, not only during this Life, but also in the hour of Death. I am convinced you have already made the same reflections. I hope my Dear Brother will make use of 'em in all future occasions. I mean with me who am Daily in the way of meeting some Misfortune of a Different Nature, Misfortune with Regard to tenderhearted Parents, but a happiness with regard to me. Adieu, my dear Brother, grant me a share of your friendship proportionate to my affection for you, and be convinced I shall ever act . . . to the Sentiments of gratitude I owe to you and Dear Morgan and Parents, Accumulating favours of which I shall ever bear the deepest sence. May the Almighty grant you may one day find in me the Image and Virtues of Dear Connell!

I have according to your Directions Lacerated ye Last Bill, having already met with ye former and received the Contents, but my last letter undoubtedly Already come to hands will tell you so. Render, I pray you, my warmest Duty acceptable to my Dear Parents. I embrace most Lovingly my Dear Brother Morgan. May the Great God grant them and you a Long and happy Life, and render you, as hitherto, the love and delight of our Poor Afflicted Parents, who seem to have excluded me from all share in their friendship. I expected one day to make my dear Connell Mediator. Join that Good office to those you have already Done me, and you'll render more Cordial, if possible,

Your most respectful and affectionate B^r,

DANIEL O'CONNELL.

I once more Embrace my Dear Morgan, Sisters Connell,

all others my Brothers and Sisters. Write without loss of time, and Let me know what Arrangements you make with regard to me. My Dear Connell promised to share his last Guinea with me—a generous offer, which I shu⁴ never have abused. I am confident you'll continue, brother Morgan and you, to do for me whatever is in your power. Happy I am to have as yet two such worthy Brothers. The same will that Determines you to support me shall also Determine me to spare you as much as possible. The same friendship always did and shall ever subsist between Captain Fagan and me. My Complim^{ts} to his father and mother. Their sons in this country are all well. My next shall to brother Morgan in August or 7bre, with God's grace.

Address: à Monsieur Monsieur O'Connell, Officier au Régiment de Royal Suédois, en garnison à Schlestatt, Alsace.

The formal phraseology of the letter does not altogether conceal the lad's real heartfelt sorrow for the companion and protector of his earlier years. The natural grief of the survivor did not prevent his eager pursuit of a career of honour. His next letters tell us of a disappointment, followed by a well-deserved but unexpected piece of luck.

My hero passed seven uneventful years and more on the Alsatian borders, where the Royal Swedes were usually quartered—diversified, however, by a visit to London, to Switzerland, and to Paris. The winter of 1765-6, spent at the great Military Academy of Strasbourg, was of the utmost importance to his future career. Considering the remarkable profusion of tongues in Kerry, where Dr. Smith actually deplores the classic lore so diffused among the peasantry, added to the certainty that among the gentry every child grew up to speak English and Irish with equal fluency, Dan's turn for languages is not remarkable, such being the special aptitude of his native province. Chevalier Fagan describes him as able to speak French and Dutch before he had been a whole year abroad, and we find him engaging private masters for foreign tongues at Strasbourg. His English has begun to show considerable traces of foreign idiom; in fact, he did not write really good English until he had been a considerable time in England after 1792. "Tasted," literally, *goûté*, should of course be "appreciated." The Strasbourg letter of February 12, 1766, gives the key-note of the young fellow's character. He will work like a slave at the studies which prepare the way for future advancement; he requires a certain pittance, which it galls him to beg for, yet which he cannot do without. He is a favourite of his colonel, popular in the regiment, determined to make a respectable appearance, prepared to make any sacrifices of mere youthful enjoyments, but determined not to appear shabbily. What he wants with painting and music I can't quite make out, as the O'Connells, possessed generally of considerable literary and linguistic ability, were seldom known to evince any turn for these two arts.

Cousin Morty, of "Daun's," has evidently got a holiday, and gone to visit his people, for, instead of giving information about him, Dan asks it.

Dan was not only a very handsome young fellow, but remarkably tall, strong, and muscular. It was probably these personal advantages which led to his being offered a commission in one of the most brilliant of the French cavalry regiments—a flattering distinction he had the remarkably good sense to refuse, because he had not £60 to pay for the outfit, and had a horror of debt. He paid great attention to military horsemanship, probably with a view to the chance of entering the cavalry, but the chance did not again occur. "Aide Major" is adjutant, and, by the somewhat uncouth phrase, "I am getting into the Aide-majority," he evidently means he is getting into the adjutant's office. It is curious to see how long before Emancipation Catholics were looking forward to it, and the boy, who acts, as it were, as spokesman for scores of boys whose letters have perished, is hoping to enter the English Service without injury to his faith.

He writes, in 1765, full of the hope of entering the Military Academy, and begs assistance to be able to accept the colonel's offer of a place in the Academy.

Selestatt, August 6, 1765.

I have Last Month wrote to Brother Morgan, and requested you would not fail making me ye remittance you promise towards the beginning of October. The apprehension y^t said Letter might miscarry makes me Dispatch a Second and Entreat my Dear Brother to comply with my Desire. It's by so much the more necessary as the oppertunity my good Colonel affords me of accompanying a young brother of his this Winter at the Academy of Strasbourg. I say that such a fair offer I should never again meet with, as it's obtained not without ye greatest Interest, being destined for the young nobleman of the First Rank in the Kingdom, in so much that it would be doing me an Irreperable injustice to frustrate my scheme, as the Particular confidence and honour my Colonel does me should excite and animate your Efforts for me. You are without doubt surprized that, being so much in favour, I don't push forward; but have a little Patience, rely on't your money is not thrown away. In time of peace there is nothing to be done, but as three or four years will Infallibly bring on the war, I expect to be speedily and perhaps beyond your Expectation. Next Summer I hope getting into the Aide Majority,[1] which will open me a way to Advancement and increase my pay. My Colonel heartily Desires a Vacancy to give me, but you know we can't kill people without reason. It has been offered me several times to get into the Carabineers, the First Cavalry in the Kingdom, but, however, have refused it, because of the expence the first year. I should have at least £60 to put me in Equipage; but, on the other hand, the pay is so much better; however, I continue daily to perfect myself in Equitation and other Sciences. Adieu, my Dear Brother. Once more I request you won't fail for the 1st October, so that you must make the remittance on receipt hereof. In case you have proposed giving me nothing y^s year, let that rather be next year than to miss ye present oppertunity. My respectful Duty to my Father and Mother, Affectionate regards to my Dr Brother Morgan, Sisters Connell. You do me incomparable satisfaction by assuring my Father and Mother's regards for me. I hope in a year or two, if you obtain a passport to go to see you, and if possible to get into the English Service without Injury to my Religion. I hope you Endeavour to forget our Poor Connell's Misfortune. The Almighty grant him peace. I am and shall ever be, with unbounded gratitude and Fondness,

My Dr Brother's most respectful and tender

DANL. O'CONNELL.

Address: à Monsieur, etc., Officier au Régiment de Royal Suédois, en garnison à Schlestatt, en Alsace.

My best compliments to Mr. and Mistress Fagan. I hope Captain Fagan is well again. I have not heard from him these two or three months, as we are far asunder.

The fervent hope expressed by the young soldier of

[1] He means on the staff, and literally translates *état major*.

fortune of entering the British Army gives a shock to our preconceived notions; but the penal laws, though still disgracing the statute-book, were gradually softening in their application. Year after year Catholics hoped for that Emancipation to which a Daniel O'Connell of a younger generation was to contribute so largely, and which, but for the personal bigotry of George III., they would have received long before. In Kerry the old bitterness which had actuated the men whose broad lands were handed over to others, and whose homes had actually been uprooted, had passed away in the course of two or three generations; and the desire to serve at home was a natural one after all. The scores of Maurice O'Connell's letters which I have perused show very decided loyalty, and later on the two brothers, in their old age, wag their white heads in deprecation over "nephew Dan's" daring democracy. The next letter is to their father.

Strasbourg, December 27, 1765.

HONOURED FATHER,—The opinion I had of your being displeased with me is the only reason for which I so seldom addressed my letters to you, not but that I thought it my Duty to make you all possible submission, but believing your resentment somewhat violent, I thought it advisable to give it some time to cool. My Brother now assures me you have resumed the same tender and fatherly sentiments for me which always rendered you so justly Dear to us all, and particularly Distinguished you. Nothing can better prove your Indulgence and affection, and I should think me unworthy such a father, did I not take all imaginable pains to satisfy him and justify his tenderness. We have some Apprehensions of War in this part of the World, but I look upon it as improbable at this conjuncture for reasons well known to the World. I mean the want of money. The Dauphin[1] died the 21st, much regretted, and his second son, the Duke of Berry, succeeds him in his title and rights. The whole Court of Versailles is in the greatest concern and consternation, and the Army particularly bemoans his loss. No Nation are more notoriously attatched to their Princes than the French, and no Prince was more justly lamented than the Dauphin.

I return my dear Parents many thanks, as well for the generous Efforts you all make to support me, as for the

[1] See Note H, p. 145.

Desire you are good enough to show of my going to see you. I hope you make no doubt of my gratitude, nor of the satisfaction I should find in seeing you, but the present circumstances render it impossible, much more so if the War breaks out, as I must Endeavour to work my Way if possible, Without which I may long be a burthen on you. Remember me with all your usual fondness, and implore the Almighty's grace and protection for me. I shall be ever careful to avoid Every step that would cast a blemish or stain on the family, and remember that should it please the Omnipotent to carry me off, 'tis a tribute justly Due, and far from exciting your murmurs it should only serve to put you in mind of what you owe Him. Providence has destined me to a Life exposed to Accidents. All men can not live in security. I have voluntarily devoted myself to the military profession and with its pleasure I endure its fatigues and Dangers; besides, fortune has rendered it indispensable, so that Nature and Reason have been my guides.

My compliments to Morty of Tarmons. Let him know he has given me a great Deal of uneasiness. I wrote to Colonel Pierce to get an account of him. He has broke his leg some time ago by a fall from his horse at the Exercise of his Regiment. He received Morty's [letter] from Cork. All friends in this country are well. I mean my best of friends, Captain Fagan and Brother, Robin Conway, etc. As for FitzMaurice, I can give you no account of him. I believe 'im nevertheless well, but I never hear a syllable from him. My Duty to my Dear Mother. Love to Brothers and Sisters and friendship to all Relations, and believe me, with unceasing respect and unbounded tenderness,

My dear Father, Your Dutiful and Loving Son,
DANL. O'CONNELL.

Colonel Pierce now well. The following to Brother Maurice.

Written on same sheet of paper, below other letter—

I have recd. the contents bill 400.£ [French Livres],[1] which I entirely employ to my Education and support. Depend on't, not a farthing is misspent. 'Tis to spare Postage that I take the liberty of writing to my Dear Brother in this patched manner. I hope you'll not take it amiss. Address to me, Schlestatt. where the Regt. lies, but it's certain we are to Camp in 1767 before the King at Compiègne, which will be vastly expensive. Cousin Robin Conway received yours, in which you recommend to him the Care of the Linen sent me.

---

[1] In old accounts at Darrynane, French livres are valued as English shillings.

I am sorry you have sent it off, as the Expense will overpass its Value. I always supposed you could find an oppertunity for Dunkerque. I have prayed Cousin Conway to take it up and advertise me. I thank my Dear Brother for all the pains he is good enough to take. Be convinced not the Least Step escapes my attention. I shall never be happy enough to give you proofs on't. I Recd. in October a Letter from B^r Morgan. My next shall be to him. Assure him of my sincere and fond affection. My love to Sister Connell. I wish it were in my power to Embrace her and give her some proofs of my affection. How Do Sister Falvy and Abby do? You don't say a word of 'em in y^r Last. Adieu, my Dear Brother. It's 12 o'clock, and the School opens at 7 in the morning; after which, Manège, Peinture, Escrime et Musique ont chacun leur tour. I shall ever be, with due fondness and Gratitude,

My Dear Brother, sincere and affc^{ate},
DANL. O'CONNELL.

My next shall probably be in March or Aprill.
Except something unforeseen happens, my address as usual—Selestatt.

Old-fashioned etiquette prescribed to the young brother to call the wife of the future head of the family "Sister Connell." There were no less than three sisters, all Mary O'Connells—pretty blonde Mary O'Connell, his own real sister, who becomes Sister Baldwin; high-spirited Mary O'Connell, born Falvey; and Mary O'Connell, born Cantillon. He solves the puzzle of the three Maries by calling the second by her maiden name, and she becomes Sister Falvey. I am happy to state that her little daughter's hideous Irish pet name is transformed into its English equivalent, Abby. Her mother went to Cork when she was very young for her education. It was then the southern metropolis. Only people of great rank and wealth proceeded to Dublin, in those days, from the far south.

Dan's hard work at the Academy soon bore fruits—unless we are to attribute his promotion purely to favour. His appointment to be first lieutenant gave him a solid position in the regiment. We find him going to Switzerland, and later to England, to interpret for his patron the colonel. The reference to poor Connell's special friends, their sailor-kinsmen, MacGillicuddy and McCarthy, would seem to imply that they also had been lost at sea. Their deaths would thus seem more horrible to the young soldier than if they had been killed in following his own trade of war.

Two letters follow very close together for the old days of heavy postage. Young Dan's epistle to his "Honoured Father" and elder brother would have been tidings enough, had not Maurice sent him a long lecture with some reference to a previous gift of money, both requiring acknowledgment. On what principle this marvellously hard-working, self-denying lad was lectured to such a pitch, I fail to discover. He always stoutly stood up for his own good behaviour, and the unblemished state of the family honour in so far as he was concerned. He wrote from—

Strasbourg, February 12, 1766.

My Dear Brother,—I yesterday received your letter of the 15th December last, in which you reproach me with negligence and inattention towards you. You appear at a loss to fathom my motives, and seem to suspect that I have no other than the shortness of ye Sum you have been good enough to remitt me. Allow me the Liberty of assuring you your Conjecture is ill grounded, and the more so as I've had Long since the pleasure of returning you thanks and acknow-ledging the receipt of your Bill. You'll agree with me on the Injustice you do me when you consider not only the desire I have always testified of rendering my conduct agreab'e to you, but also ye constant and unbounded sense of gratitude I always expressed. I am sorry not to have it yet in my power to give you some convincing proof on't as may hereafter Shelter me from all Disadvantageous Imputations.

You are pleased to enquire after what I do in this town, and it's reasonable I should render you an account on't. I Duly frequent the Artillery and Mathematicks School, and the Academy. I have besides, private Masters for painting, Musick, and foreign tongues. The Latter I pay, and the Former cost me nothing, being received on favour. With regard to my Advancement, there's very Little to be expected as Long as the peace Continues. Nevertheless, I have the happiness of being tolerably well tasted in the Regiment, so that I flatter me my Colonel will let slip no occasion of pushing me, but you conceive he can't at present Lead me over many old Officers of Merit and Distinction, so that I must have patience till the war opens me a way to promotion, and endeavour in the mean time to found my pretentions on a reasonable knowledge of my trade, which shall become my sole occupation and study.

Colonel Murphy, to whom you'll pray recommend me, can let you know what's to be expected in the midst of inaction and peace, and inform you whether or no I am extravagant in my Demands, and if you find I am, restrain me—I am far from pretending you should do more for me, and could heartily wish I was able to dispense with your helping me, but it's really not in my power without renouncing the rank of officer, which I am persuaded would do you no small pain after the expences you have already been att.

Be so kind as to let me know, in your next, if you disapprove my manner of employing my time. I shall promptly follow the measures you think proper to dictate, and if yᵉ annuall sum I require strains you, retrench it as much as you think fit. I had rather refuse me all the pleasures of Life than put you to a stress above your means. I can't tell whether you do me the justice to believe me, as you appear a little diffident, but you may in all safety grant me your confidence, and be assured nothing could be more offensive nor Sensible than the reproaches you make me. I shu'd not have believed it some Days ago, and without prejudice to the respect and tenderness I owe you, I shall not so soon forget 'em. I have nothing new to tell you. We reckon camping at Compiègne in 1767. We may probably march into Flanders this spring. My regiment always lies at Schlestatt, where it passes the winter. Adieu, my Dear Brother. I hope you'll not be Displeased with your
     Respectful and fond Brother,
         Danl. O'Connell.

My Duty to my father and mother. Love to my Bʳ Morgan, Sisters, etc. What does Cousin Morty doe? Does he propose staying in the Country? No changes in our family; noe increase in yours. How does Abby doe? My Compliments to Mr. and Mrs. Fagan. Their friends are all well. The Captain is now at Paris. Let Brother Morgan know I've recd. his Letter a long time since. My next shall be to him. Adieu, my Dear Brother. Answer me speedily.

I purpose to join the regiment about the first of May. We are Closely applyed to the compleating of the Different Corps, and the Militia is already Drawn, or at least Marked. Some hopes of War. My compliments to Doctor Jeffrey Connell, of Cork.

This spirited letter of self-justification evidently produced the desired result. The pittance was not withdrawn, and the young soldier got promotion within four months—with an infinitesimal increment of pay, however.

The next letter joyously chronicles the first step on the ladder of promotion—Dan is a first lieutenant. He observes casually that his hard study has done him "noe trifling service," but attributes his luck wholly and solely to his colonel's favour. Considering the rank favouritism prevailing at the time, and the comfortable certainty of his own merits ever displayed by my hero, we have no reason to doubt him. I fancy he really deserved by merit what he obtained by favour. Even in extreme old age, he was singularly liked by every one who knew him intimately, so that I can imagine the tall, active, blue-eyed lad, with clear-cut features, fair skin, and dark brows, very popular with a colonel who liked to have agreeable, good-looking people under him. Size and looks are points strongly insisted on by my hero and by his kinsmen when they, in turn, are colonels and bringing out young cadets to serve King Louis. In letter after letter he bewails the pranks of the handsome, big, tall lads, and deplores the small stature of the two perfectly good little boys who came over. So a remarkably tall, muscular, good-looking, clever lad is indeed a joy for ever, to a colonel.

It is a pity we have no account of the projected Swiss tour. Dan evidently believes himself somewhat older than his baptismal certificate makes out; but as the aforesaid "baptisterium" appears sanctioned by all likely to know, he adhered to it until he discovered in his old age that he had been really born in 1745.

At Schlestatt, June ye 14th, 1766.

My Dear Brother,—I shu'd have wrote to you earlyer had I not daily expected an easier oppertunity, as we believed marching into the Netherlands in the beginning of the Fair Season, which project has miscarryed, and probably for a considerable time.

I have joined the regiment the beginning of Last month, after passing the winter at Strasbourg in the Closest Study and Application, which has done me noe trifling Service. I found on my Arrival at the Regiment the Commission of first Lieutenant, which my Worthy Colonel procured me preferably to ye Elder Officers—a mark of his friendship which leaves me no room to Doubt of his desire of promoting me on every Occasion, and assured me at the same time that, if he had it in his power to give me a Company instead of a Lieutenancy, he shu'd not hesitate an instant, but hoped in a Little time to be able to doe more for me. In Short, my Dear Brother, he carries friendship for me to the highest degree. When he is absent, During . . . I write to him twice a Week, and as confidently as to you. This advancement is worth me 5 Livres a Month, or 60 French Livres a year—a trifle as to the gain, but important for the rank. If you continue to support me four or five years, I hope with God's grace to be at the head of a Company, after which Providence will help me further. In short, you'll doe me the justice to agree with me that I make all imaginable efforts to rid you of a burthen which necessarily incumbers you. [Here follow a couple of broad jests, the only ones in the else prim and proper pages of the letter-book, concerning the want of heirs to Maurice and his rich wife.] Brother Morgan [he continues] is likely to become our *caput familiæ*. Pray how does he doe? Embrace him affectionately for me. When shall I be happy enough to see my Dear brothers and family? It's a question, as I am determined to await a fair oppertunity. . . . A few Lucky Campaigns can, please God, offer, the sooner the better. I sett off after to-morrow for Switzerland, where my Colonel makes a tour. He is good enough to take me with him, as I talk the Language. I can serve his curiosity, which is the sole motive of his journey. In a month it will be over. Toward that time I Expect hearing from you. Be exact, my Dear Brother, in answering me. I am on thorns when I spend some time without hearing from you and my dear aged Parents. I apprehend they have forgot me altogether, otherwise shu'd have wrote me a few Lines even in some of your Letters during four years that I am away. Pray be good enough to let me have Exactly my age in your next. I am quite at a loss to answer for it. I believe one or two and twenty, more or less. Adieu, my dear Brother. Let me know when you purpose making me your next remittance. You have long since received my acknowledgment for your last. I purpose spending next Winter at Strasbourg if we don't quitt the Province, where I shall recommence the thread of my study in order to Lay a firm foundation for my profession.

I have been touched to the quick at the news of my poor Dan[1] McCarthy's unfortunate end, as likewise Cousins McGillicuddy, etc. We are all Mortall, and consequently must go the same way late or early. In my way of thinking, the Difference is slight. We are, nevertheless, concerned for the loss of a friend. It's an Effort of human weakness common to all men, but we should endeavour to submitt it to our reason as much as possible. Once more Adieu, my Dear Brother. I Embrace you lovingly, and shall ever be your Respectful and fond Brother,

DANL. O'CONNELL.

The postscript contains the usual greetings to the family, and compliments to Mr. and Mrs. Fagan and Colonel Murphy. Dan hopes "Cousin Morty will take possession of his Ensigncy. Colonel Pierce is well, and lets him know the Emperor has conferred on him that rank by a vast recommendation and Interest."

The following anecdote concerning "Cousin Morty of Tarmons" was related to Ross O'Connell, of Lake View, by our cousin, Morgan O'Connell, the Liberator's son. As a young man serving in the Austrian Light Cavalry,[1] he had known that venerable man as Baron and General O'Connell. Miss Julianna tells the same story, only substituting a heavy purse of gold for the watch; but the moral is the same—the lad's steady demeanour and strict attention to discipline.

We shall see in a later letter of Captain Rickard O'Connell's how cadets in the French Service ate the coarse fare and did the hard work of privates, parading under a firelock eight hours at a time opposite a sentry-box. Young Morty was on some occasion placed on sentry duty on one of those corridors of some palace of Maria Theresa's, where that kind, motherly woman often had little friendly interviews with her Irish defenders and their wives. She noticed the tall, handsome Irish lad, and asked him to tell her the hour. He at once replied that he did not know, not having a watch. The Empress-queen smilingly dropped a fairy-godmother gift into the deep-flapped pocket of his uniform—according to one story, a watch; to another, the price of it. The young soldier never spoke a word, as she had not again addressed him, and remained in statue-like rigidity in the saluting attitude until she disappeared. This total absence of vulgar curiosity delighted her, and convinced her he was a true chip of an old block, such a real Irish gentleman as she loved to have in her service.

[1] In Baron Nugent's regiment—4th Chevaux Légers.

One of Maria Theresa's Irish officers soon after wedded a sister of my hero's, near him in age—Gobbinette, who in the keen of Arthur O'Leary, composed by her sister, Eileen the Raven-haired, is described as the lady of twenty-six summers, who has crossed the wide seas to dwell in the courts of kings. She was considered less attractive at home than blue-eyed, golden-haired Mary, or dark-browed Eileen, whose complexion was so fair that she was toasted as "the Lady of the Snowy Breast." She had the same delicate features, but was much freckled. When she went abroad, and used rouge and pearl-powder, she was considered strikingly handsome. As Lady Mary Wortley Montague pithily declares, the Vienna ladies used powder and paint to such excess that she could only compare them to "fair white sheep, freshly raddled." So a defective complexion did not matter much in Austria.

The venerable Miss Julianna O'Connell, with whom I spent delightful hours of old-world gossip in the summers of 1888 and 1889 and the spring of 1890, at Darrynane, told me that Major O'Sullivan's countenance was much disfigured by the slash of a sabre right across it, which scar was mightily displeasing to young Nancy, on whom he was disposed to fix his affections. Knowing what exceedingly autocratic notions the mother of the damsels had concerning their disposal in marriage, he cautiously sounded his way, and asked Abigail, or Gobbinette, as she was called in Irish, to try and find out secretly if he displeased her young sister, lest he should find himself wedded to an unwilling bride. Nancy expressed marked disapproval of the scarred soldier; and, in conveying her message back, the ambassadress betrayed a certain agitation, which led him to believe that she herself did not entertain a similar objection. He satisfied himself on the point, and then made a formal demand for her hand, which was acceded to with pleasure. He was sometimes on duty at court, and seemingly lodged in the palace. On one occasion Maria Theresa came upon young Mrs. O'Sullivan, sobbing bitterly in a lonely passage near the chapel of the palace. The Empress asked the young Irishwoman what ailed her, and was duly informed that she expected soon to become a mother, and could not help fretting when she remembered that her mother had borne twenty-two children, and she feared a similar destiny; and what would an officer's wife moving about the world do with such a family?

The good, motherly Maria Theresa was highly amused at this *naif* avowal, and offered to do what she could for the race of O'Sullivan by promising to stand godmother for the expected child. She fulfilled this gracious promise, and continued very kind to the family. Poor Gobbinette and all her children perished in the epidemic of small-pox which carried off several of Maria Theresa's own fair daughters. Major O'Sullivan did not marry again, and died Brigade-Major of Prague. He is only a captain, and just after bringing out his bride, when Dan mentions him in the following letter:—

Cambray, X^{ber} the 25, 1766.

My Dearest Brother,—I should have long since answered your letter containing Mr. Sexton of Limerick's draft on Mr. Woulfe at Paris for 400 Livres french, but have been the whole time on March with my Regiment, which is in a few days agoe arrived at Condé, some Leagues from here. Your letter came to hands on the road, so thought it needless answering it before our arrival. I alsoe had a Letter from our Brother, Captain O'Sullivan, of Konigcratz^r Re^t from Leibnitz, in Stiria, where his reg^t is now quartered. He and Gobby [Abigail] were well. He assures me she is vastly well pleased with the Military way of Living, and already begins to Learn the German tongue. He very civilly invites me to pass the winter with 'em, without considering that a young man obliged to forge his fortune himself can spare no time for visiting. Now the very unfavourable change in my Dear family's affairs render my application and labour more encumbent and needful than ever. And can assure you, my dear Brother, that, Exclusive of that motive, my own private Spirit and Ambition render me sufficiently anxious and attentive to every Event that may open me a way of pushing myself and disburthening you. My Cousin John FitzMaurice, with whom I am now, can tell you faithfully the daily efforts I make, and his uncommon good nature which makes him Desirous of helping his family renders him equally solicitous to procure me the means of making myself known and Laying an honourable foundation for my future, to which purpose he intends taking me with him this winter to Paris, to endeavour to get me some friends and protection, without which all personal merit is useless, or at Least very seldom recompensed. I have never had it in my power to go, but I have enough to Defray me, which I assure you is no trifle. I suppose he's known amongst you all, as he deserves, for the best hearted young man in the whole world, and can tell you he loves the last of us all beyond life. I shall spend ye greater part of the Winter with him, as well as all the time I can spare from Duty as long as the Regiment stays in Flanders, he being, after you, my dear Brother, the Closest relation and certainly the truest friend I have. I can't foresee when I may find myself in the way of being able to do without your help. I give you my honour it shall be the soonest possible, for fear you should think me Destitute enough of good nature and good sentiment to be capable of spending money, especially when I am acquainted with the State of your Affairs, wch certainly don't seem to afford you much. This very consideration should then have Determined me Long since to call no more, were I not persuaded you'ld rather strain a point for some few years to Establish me hereafter, otherwise should long ere now have taken some Resolution, as there's no maintaining the rank of an Officer with the pay we have, particularly now a Days, when every one is weighed in the Golden Scale; for short, my Dear Brother, you must Endeavour continuing your supplies Between my Father, Mother, Brother Morgan, and yourself, until fortune smiles on me, and then, rely on't, with the Almighty's Assistance you'll some Day have reason to be satisfied with the generous and good-natured Efforts you have made to support me. I hope the Almighty will put it in my power to be one Day useful to my family. This shall ever be my sole Desire and Ambition, for I shall neither spare my blood nor bones for that purpose, and should willingly go to the World's End for to push myself and prove to you the unbounded love and fondness with which I remain,

Dear Brother, Your Affectionate and
Respectful Brother,
Danl. O'Connell.

My Duty to my Dear Father and Mother; fond love to brother Morgan, Sisters Connell, etc.; and compliments to all enquiring friends.

Address: à Monsieur, Monsieur O'Connell, Officier au Régiment de Royal Suédois, en garnison à Condé, en Flandre.

Pray give me some account of the Linen which you were to send me. Let me know to whom you addressed it. Cousin FitzMaurice makes you his best affections. It's false that I have been made Aide Major. I only do the functions on't this considerable time, awaiting a vacancy, which you see comes slowly, but I can't reasonably kill him that occupies that post, much less tell him to give it up to me.

The next letter to be found describes how our hero came in contact with sundry kinsmen serving in the Irish Brigade, whose ranks he had not yet entered at that period of his career.

Aire, August, ye 20th, 1767.

I begin with imploring my Dear Brother's Indulgence, as having receiv'd his Letter a Long time since, and having delayed so long in Answering it; but the reason is that I was so much taken y^t by putting it off from one Day to Another I did not perceive how I differed it; and the more so, as when I purpose writing home, I commonly allow myself two or three days retreat, solely occupied with ye agreable project I have in head. Our Regt. came down here in the Latter end of June from Condé, to work in concert with many others at a Canal of Communication between two rivers, which scheme when carried into Execution, will be of infinite use and Conveniency for the transportation of every kind thro' all ye Different parts of Flanders and Artois, and Consequently favourable to trade. There's a Camp formed between Airo and St. Omers, where the troops imployed at the Works lodge. I have been sent off from our Regt. from the very Commencement to Act as Major Officer of a Détachement of three Hundred Men, wch are our Contingent. That gives me more work than the whole Regt. when together, as being obliged to reckon with the King and with the Regt. for every penny, besides the continual Changes occasioned either by Sickness or Desertion, wch is a Distemper pretty Common among the Private Men in all Countries at present. Three Regts. of the Irish Brigade work here also—Dillon's, Roscommon's formerly Rothe's, and Bulkeley's. I have met some relations in the two latter—FitzMaurice and two Mahonys, who received me with a great deal of friendship. Our Cousin the Abbé is well and now at Paris, but soon to come back. Tom [FitzMaurice] is lately become Aide Major, which renders his station very good. He is a young man of great worth and spirit. Captain Robin FitzMaurice has quitted ye service, and is retired at Cambray. Tim and Jerry Mahony are mighty worthy and good-natured men as any of our acquaintance, as is our Cousin and theirs, Danl Swiney. Robin Conway came to see me to Camp a day or two ago, and we agreed with each other to take a trip to Ireland next Winter twelvemonths, if please God we do well. We have recv^d our orders to appear before the King. I hope this Event will be favourable to me. I know our Colonel is determined to give retreats to old officers for to favour me. I am to be, conjointly with two others, Charged with Dressing and forming the Regt. this Winter. When once I have a foot in ye stirrup, I hope I'll rise. Our Garrison this Winter is not yet determined, but address to me at Aire. You'll do me Considerable Service and friendship, my dear Brother, to send me my next year's pension as Early as possible in the month of April or May at latest, as we have mighty considerable expences at ye Camp at Compiègne, where we are to appear in the most shining manner. I dare say there's no Regt. in France can show handsomer and better. I purpose setting away from the Camp to Calais. I shall Embark and Endeavour to spend some time among my Dear Parents and Relations. Your Delaying the allowance would render my scheme impracticable. There's no going without money, and that I shall never meet a fairer oppertunity than that will be, as the Regt. will certainly march up to the frontiers of Germany, our Usual Station.

I am sorry to acquaint you that our Cousin Maurice Jeffrey has Considerable debts in his Regt., which, if not paid, would throw indelible shame and blemish on me as of his . . . and all his other relations in the Brigade, and as I am persuaded he has too much spirit to Act in a low manner, I earnestly entreat, my dear Brother, you'll speak to him, and tell him to send over without delay the sum he owes, which I dare say is £30 sterling. Otherwise I must hide myself. I at the same time will tell you I believe his conduct was bad. He has a determined passion for gambling. Let him not come over any more, for I believe he has nothing to expect. Adieu, my dear Brother. I shall Expect your answer with impatience, and remain for ever

Your tender and obliged Brother,
DANL. O'CONNELL.

Here follow the usual "duty," "love," "tender affection," graduated to parents, sisters, and brothers, and the information that he is in constant correspondence with Cousin Morty, of Germany, who, as well as his sister "Gobby," are well. He reproachfully inquires why they never tell him of Nancy, and wants to know if she is married.

In the letter-book there is a very graphic letter of Father Guardian O'Brien's from Cork. This summer I met some of the denizens of old Broad Lane Friary, where he put up, and they explained his wanderings thus. It is the custom of the

Franciscans to have their houses inspected by a skilled ex-superior from a distance. The Father Guardian of Prague, having filled his period of office, was sent to inspect the Irish houses at home and in Spain. Inns were few and bad, and he stopped at the houses of Catholic gentlemen. Curiously enough, the great-granddaughter of the first host he mentions married Hunting Cap's nephew, John O'Connell, of Grenagh. They were my dear husband's parents. Sir Walter was a fine, jolly stout old gentleman, with heavy black brows, a purple velvet coat, and Addison's wig. His only child, the handsome Lucinda Esmonde (Mrs. McMahon, of Clenagh), obtained the portraits of her parents, so that the burly, jolly aspect of Sir Walter, whose portrait I possess, is even more familiar to me than the long straight face with regular features and pale blue eyes of the tall old man dressed in black, with a powdered wig of less ample proportions, which hangs on the walls of Lake View, the home of his grand-nephew.

Father Guardian O'Brien, in Ireland, thus relates his Irish adventures to Hunting Cap—

Buttevant, December 9, 1767.

DEAR COUSIN,—I arrived here yesterday after my tour, wch I ran thro', thank God, in passable good health, till the 11th 8bre, at wch time I was seiz'd with a violent cold, in the polite phrase call'd *influenza*. This confined me for some days at Cregg, the seat of Sir Walter Esmonde [1] near Carrick on Shure, but without applying to the Faculty I happily got rid on't. I set out from Cregg to hold my Chapter in Athlone; in my way was at Cornabolly, where I found McWalter [Burke], Biddy, and family in good health. They were kindly inquisitive about you, Molly, and friends at Darrinane, charm'd to hear you were well, and the more so as they had it from one who was there himself, and who reproached their indolence in not so doing themselves. The rocks of Iveragh are not so frightful as they imagine. I forced our friends into that persuasion, so that you are to expect a visit from them soon.

I can't omit a remarkable circumstance that happened at my arrival at Cornabolly. Miss Burke Martin, who accompanied the Drs Lady last summer to Bath, had a narrow escape of her life at her return. A violent fever had like

---

[1] His granddaughter, Jane McMahon, daughter of Lucinda Esmonde, was mother of Elizabeth Coppinger, my husband's mother, wife of Hunting Cap's nephew, John O'Connell, of Grenagh.

to dispatch her. McWalter was sent for. He conceal'd the cause of his errand to Limerick from Cousin Biddy. However, it unluckily transpir'd, and the Young Lady was given out dead. The story came to its maturity when I came on my visit to the Mother. McWalter was in Limerick. Everything seem'd to confirm the sad report. I was no sooner entered the house but Mrs. Burke flew to me, bawl'd and roar'd, clasp'd her hands about my neck, and kept me for near a ¼ of an hour in that position. She'd move the hardest heart. An old gentleman I had with me, pretty much of Mr. Leddy's disposition, fell into a flood of tears. I resisted, tho' softened within, consoled her, made use of all my Rhetoric to prove the story false; all to no purpose. The Lady ready to lie in was a delicate circumstance. I trembled for the consequences. McWalter arrives in an hour and a half after me, and chears up our drooping spirits. The girl was out of danger, and still he was obliged to swear it before Biddy would let him into the house. A sudden transition from grief to joy. Every thing had a gay face, and I pass'd some days with 'em merrily.

I was twice or thrice at Bridgetown, it being on my way to Ennis, as I now came from Athlone. They are very happy, at least I think so. They talk of going next Season to the West. Mrs. T. Blake and Biddy are not so great. Opposite characters can seldom hit.

Phill and family are well, jogging on *à l'ordinaire*. Blake and he are on the verge of being friends. The former bid me tell Phill to drop urging the bill he filed against him. I spoke enough to both, to drop animosity, renew friendship, and I hope it will be the case.

Now, tho' I have said a good Deal, I have much more to tell of my travels in the county Leitrim, the North, and I must reserve it for an evening conversation or another letter. I am well, and so are our friends here; [I] do intend setting out for Spain about March next, at or before that time I shall send my Mare to be an inhabitant of your Island. I am getting in the Collection from Phill and Messrs. Burke and Blake to buy a horse for our poor disabled Cousin James FitzGerald. When you have leisure to send your generous contingent, I can get it in Cork, Broad Lane.

A thousand affect. Compts. to Cousin Molly, The Worthy old Couple, Mrs. Connor, Miss N., and y^r Brother Morgan, and am very sincerely and affcly.,

My Dear Cousin,
Y^r most hb^e and most ob^t servant,
JNO. O'BRIEN.

All that's kind from me to the family of Tarmons. What news from Morty and O'Sullivan?

Father Guardian O'Brien's account of the possibility of travel did persuade Mrs. Blake to visit her sister, and I heard all about the visit from Miss Julianna O'Connell, who stayed at Darrynane during the last years of Hunting Cap's life. The blind old man was fond of his young kinswoman, and it amused him to chat to her of old times. A visit from beyond Ennis, in the County Clare, to forty miles beyond Killarney was a thing to be remembered, and during a good part of the way to be traversed in Kerry there were only beaten horse-tracks, such as exist now in the Alps, instead of roads.

Maurice O'Connell met his guests at his brother's house, of Carhen, about nineteen miles from Darrynane, and, having first despatched his confidential servant, Andrew Connell, to Killarney, to pilot them, sent on mountain ponies a considerable distance to meet them where roads ceased. Now, Mrs. Blake had heard much of the great hill of Drung, over which no road was made until 1782 or so, and anxiously inquired about it of Andrew Connell. It was at its base the visitors abandoned their hired horses for the ponies, and Andrew Connell begged the lady to condescend to ride on the pillion behind him, as he knew the hills and the ponies better than any of the party. No little mountain horse could have carried the tall Mr. Blake up such a hill, with a lady on a pillion behind him.

Seeing that Mrs. Blake's special terror was the hill of Drung, the sagacious servitor determined to ignore it as long as possible, and friendly mists and vapours shrouded its summit. Every time Mrs. Blake asked about it, he stoutly denied where they were; but at last the crest of the great hill became too tangible a fact for denial. The Irish Caleb Balderstone was equal to the occasion. Andrew Connell, who could speak good English, gravely responded, "Yes, madam, it is the hill of Drung, and if my master had got more notice of your coming he'd have levelled it before you"—a statement which the lady from the level land is said to have swallowed. They reached the hospitable house of Carhen before dark, and next day rode on to Darrynane.

It had long been a sore point with the poor childless, rather stupid lady, who found herself hemmed in between two such terribly keen, capable people as Maur-ni-Dhuiv and Hunting Cap, that her own people did not trouble to visit her. She probably also wished to show that she was nominal mistress of a wealthy and well-kept household. She had determined to accord her sister a formal, ceremonious reception, and mark her sense of neglect. So when her sister rode up she dropped a sweeping curtsey, and said, "You are heartily welcome to Darrynane, Mrs. Blake. It is good for sore eyes to see you." And then, at close sight of the long-unseen sister, pride and ceremony broke down, and she flung her arms round Mrs. Blake, and kissed and hugged her on the threshold.

Some one may say, "What has all this fiddle-faddle to do with the last Colonel of the Irish Brigade?" To which I respond—I want to make people understand the kind of life old people led at home as well as abroad, and to show the old-fashioned folk as they were—their foibles, their vanities, their sins and sorrows, and their high point of honour and careful courtesy.

Dr. Smith, while writing his famous "History of Kerry," visited Iveragh in 1751, and thus describes the hill of Drung and the mountain ponies—

"The road from the other parts of Kerry into this barony runs over very high and steep hills, that stand in this parish called Drung and Cahirsiveen, which road hangs in a tremendous manner over that part of the sea that forms the Bay of Castlemaine, and not unlike the mountains of Pemnaumaure, in North Wales, except that the road here is more stony and less secure for the travellers." Here the learned doctor proceeds to say that every one passing has to make verses in the mountain's honour, else who passes, neglecting this tribute, comes to grief—"the original of which notion must be that it will require a person's whole circumspection to preserve himself from falling off his horse."

"I have already observed," says the doctor, "that the horses in these baronies are naturally very sure-footed. They are small, but of an excellent breed. They climb over the most rugged rocks, and both ascend and descend the steepest precipices with great facility and safety, and are so light as to skim over waving bogs and morasses without sinking, and when heavier horses would certainly perish. They are strong and durable, and easily supported, and not ill-shaped, and so hardy as to stand abroad all winter, and will browse upon heath, furze, and other shrubs; added to this their gait is extremely easy."

The following extract from a letter written much later by the Rev. James Bland, of "The Rocks," *alias* Derryquin, gives a graphic picture of Kerry roads:—

Rev. J. Bland to Maurice O'Connell, of Darrynane.

Dr. Sir,—I rec^d your Le^r and did John Courcy's Business for him this day. With respect to the latter part of your L^r [letter], I do not think the Barony will be ever overloaded with roads from Darrynane to Corke. They are necessary, and therefore will never be granted liberally enough to hurt us. I have apprenhions, indeed, about a Road from Dunlo to Blackwater through the Mountains, which, as it never can be made, and would, if made, be of no sort of use, I do not doubt but the Grand Jury may present tremendously for it.

The year 1767 furnishes few letters from the young lieutenant, though doubtless some of those precise and formal epistles of his were duly despatched and received. On the other hand, the hoards of old papers in Hunting Cap's handsome brass-mounted bureau furnished me with some account of the risks the respectable Catholics ran from informers of the lowest class. We must bear in mind that Catholics were allowed no arms except fowling-pieces, and, I suppose, duelling-pistols.[1] I do not know if there was any limitation to the

---

[1] Catholics did not regain the right to carry arms for nearly thirty years later. In 1792 they were admitted to the outer Bar, and permitted to open school (without licence of a Protestant clergyman), to take apprentices, and even to intermarry with Protestants, provided the clergyman was a Protestant; if he were a Catholic priest, he was still liable to death, and the marriage was annulled. If a Protestant married a Catholic wife, he was disfranchised. Other disabilities remained. "Take the right of self-defence, for instance: the law forbade it to the Catholic. An Irish Catholic might rise abroad to be field-marshal (a rank which seven did attain in Austria); if he landed in Ireland he could not wear a sword—a Protestant beggar might pluck it from him in the street. The house in which he lived might be searched by day or by night. His Catholic host

numbers of either of these. About forty years earlier I find a letter from my dear husband's maternal ancestor, Stephen Coppinger, of Barry's Court, to his eldest son, then on a visit to the Earl of Barrymore in England, urging him to press " my very good Lord " for a licence for arms to protect his house. I infer blunderbusses to have been meant, as these, sometimes of gigantic bore, were what people specially relied on against housebreakers at close quarters. Possibly the possession of any firearms was a matter of personal favour, not of right. The old Catholics were noted as duellists and sportsmen, so pistols and fowling-pieces they must have had.[1]

Iveragh[2] was in an especial manner the happy hunting-ground of organized gangs of freebooters, who occasionally raided into the adjacent borders of the two Dunkerrons, in both which wild baronies the O'Connells held lands. Maurice and Morgan O'Connell, men of high spirit and personal courage, refused blackmail to a set of fellows named Connor, who were always known as "the Ladirs,"[3] or " Loders "—some

or hostess might be summoned to inform upon him ; if they refused, they were subject to £300 fine, or flogging, and the pillory if noble ; if not noble, to £50 fine and a year's imprisonment, if not flogged. For a second offence they were outlawed and their goods forfeited. Raids for arms were being continually made, in parts of the country, in consequence of this law, so that it was not obsolete [in 1792]" (Sigerson, "Two Centuries of Irish History," p. 127).

By the Emancipation Act of 1793 Catholics obtained "(1) the electoral franchise ; (2) the right of voting for civic magistrates ; (3) the privilege of becoming grand jurors ; (4) that sitting as petty jurors they should be no longer challenged for faith when a Protestant and Catholic were in litigation ; (5) the power to endow a college and schools ; (6) the right to carry arms when possessed of certain property ; the right to sit as magistrates, and to hold civil and military offices and places of trust under certain qualifications. They were enabled to take degrees in the university, and to occupy chairs in colleges yet to be founded" (Sigerson, "Two Centuries of Irish History," p. 129).

[1] By the Treaty of Limerick, 1691, noblemen and gentlemen were allowed to ride with a sword and a case of pistols, and to keep a gun for defence or fowling. In 1695, by the Act for disarming Papists, every Papist, though holding a licence, was ordered to deliver up all arms to a justice of peace ; any two justices might search for and seize their arms. Officers, covered by the Articles of Limerick, could keep a sword, gun, and pistols, on taking an oath of allegiance (Sullivan, "Two Centuries of Irish History," pp. 6, 19).

[2] *Glencar* is in Iveragh, and was full of freebooters. Dunkerron was only divided into North and South in 183–. The "Tirleachs," or "Treleachs" lived in Glencar. (See below, "Loders.")—[D. O'C.]

[3] *Laidir*, pronounced *Laudir*, means "strong" in Irish. Possibly, however, they got their name from being a remnant of what Mr. Froude

Irish nickname I am unable to construe. Miss Hickson, in her "Old Kerry Records," quotes a case from a contemporary Kerry newspaper. I quote it in full. Darrynane Beg is the next townland to Darrynane More, on which the mansion-house stands, but, owing to an intervening hill,[1] the people in the house could not see even if the tenants' cottages were set on fire.

The otherwise commonplace attack on young Mr. Mahony acquires a certain picturesqueness from having been committed with a scimitar. How such an Oriental weapon came over, deponent sayeth not.

"Old Kerry Records," as quoted from a Kerry evening paper, of an attempt to levy blackmail, in 1767 (from contemporary Law Reports).

"These Exts. duly sworn, and deposeth that on the 20th day of March last, Charles Connor, otherwise Ladir, and Daniel Connor, otherwise Ladir, son of said Charles, together with James Connor, otherwise Tirleach, and his five sons, James, John, Tim, Daniel, and Cornelius,[2] appeared on the lands of Baslicane, in said county, all except Charles and James Connor the elder, armed with Guns, Pistols, and Cutlasses, fired several Shotts to the terror of the inhabitants of the said place, said Persons being of very bad repute, notorious breakers of jails, and all professing the Pope's religion. From the above place they next marched to a place called Lohir, and from thence in a hostile manner thro' other villages to a place called Darrinanebeg, firing several Shotts by the way, and extorting from the inhabitants of the said places victuals and drink and all other necessaries; also frightening 'em to such a degree that they durst not follow their lawful occupation, but must give attendance to such vagrants, and when they arrived at Darrynanebeg afore said, declared that they would bring some of the gentlemen of the country under an annual contribution, particularly Messrs. Maurice and Morgan

---

(vol. i. bk. iii. s. iv.) calls "The Vicar-General's Gang," concerned in plundering the Danish treasure. This (Protestant) clergyman's name was the Rev. Francis Lawder, and his gang would be "the Lawders."

[1] Part of the demesne is in Darrynane Beg, and the Meadow Walk river is the boundary of the two townlands.

[2] These Connors lived in Glencar.

O'Connell, of Darrynane, whom on refusal they threatened to rob, murder, and do bodily harm to. This Ext. further deposeth that on Sunday, the 22nd of March last, on their return from Darrynanebeg, he had been told and verily believes it to be true, that Kean Mahoney, a young gentleman of the Parish of Drumod, in said county, on the high road, on his return from Divine Service, and that they assaulted him without any lawfull provocation, wounded him with Scymitars, cut two of his fingers, and laid open his head in several places, under which wounds he still languishes in extreme perill of his life, and further sayeth not.

"Daniel X Morane,
his mark.

"Francis X Meade,
his mark.

"Exts. [persons examined] bound in £20 each to prosecute at the next general assize and gaol delivery for this county. Taken and sworn before me, this 8th April, 1767.

"THOMAS ORPHEN."

"The foregoing is a true copy of the original information in the Crown Office of the County Kerry, attested by him the 6th of June, 1767.

"THOMAS HENLEY, D.C.C."

When the Loders, to the number of eleven or twelve desperate men, had actually harried his father's tenants, and attacked his kinsman, Kean Mahony, Maurice O'Connell used every exertion to assist in bringing them to justice. It was a dangerous act for a Catholic, and a specially dangerous act for a smuggling Catholic. The old gentlemen-smugglers, in proportion as they openly defied the Revenue enactments, professed the greatest abhorrence for all other sorts of law-breaking and law-breakers, especially for "Raps"—abbreviated form of "Rapparees." This name had been originally given to the gangs of disbanded Irish soldiers who preyed on Cromwellian and Williamite settlers, but it had got to mean any banded gangs of highwaymen. Murty Oge O'Sullivan Beare, beloved of Mr. Froude, actually put the following advertisement in the paper, to clear his outraged honour on the subject.

Under date of June 13, 1738, the *Cork Remembrancer* says, " Murtagh Oge O'Sullivan, of Eyres, in this county, published in a Cork newspaper an advertisement of this date, stating 'that he had been charged with the harbouring of Tories [1] and Rapparees,' and giving notice that he would stand his trial for the same at the next general assizes."

However, the smuggling South Kerry gentry had got a little too much ahead in 1767, even backed up as they were by the most powerful Protestants. To run a ship was one thing, but actually to rescue a smuggling-craft from its legal captors was too much of a good thing; and the Loders were ready to purchase pardon and gratify spite. However, their machinations were futile. The storm blew over, and the O'Connells remained unmolested in their wilds for seventeen years more, when a charge of conspiracy to murder was trumped up against them, to be triumphantly refuted.

I found the copy of an important letter in Hunting Cap's writing at Darrynane among his papers. I have since discovered its author. It agrees with his views, viz. an intense horror of the lower and meaner forms of law-breaking. As a Catholic, he violated laws in owning land, in having received a liberal education, in being deeply engaged in a smuggling-trade with a firm owning various ships and dealing with various ports; but his faith, his education, his property, and his business, though all illegal, were very unlike the lawbreakings of rogues and rapparees.

The Dennys, the great people of Tralee, and the Knights of Kerry always stood to the O'Connells. Ned and Barry Denny are frequently mentioned in the old letters in most friendly terms. The remarkable letter of protest against the violation of law and order in favour of a confirmed lawbreaker, who had, however, been aiding law and order in the matter of the assault case, was very probably addressed to one of the Kerry members. Maurice had also a great friend, a kinsman of his kinsmen, in Dominic Trant, a very eminent barrister, brother-in-law to Lord Clare, and the ancestor of

---

[1] " Tories " originally meant, as it does here, " robbers."—[D. O'C.]

the Trants of Dovea. Perhaps it may have been written to him. His cousin Rickard's epistle gives a most graphic account of the machinations of the informers, though I am unable to construe the Irish words.

This letter is endorsed, "10th August, 1767, Rick. Connell, of Tralee," and is addressed to "Mr. Mau. Connell at Darrynane," being seemingly sent by hand.

Dr. Cousn.,—I heard a rumour in this town that there was Information given against you, many of your ffamily, and several of your Ten^{ts} [tenants] by one of the Connors,[1] an associate of two fellows you lodged in this Goal, before Government, and in Consequence of such Informations and order issued to have you and many more of y^r ffamily and name taken for the Rescue of the Ship, and the order sent to the Dingle Revenue officers, to go round by water to surprize you, lest they sh^d be Discovered going thro' the Country. On hearing this report, I went to Pope the Goaler, and asked him what he knew of the matter. He told me that he discovered by some of the prisoners that the Connors had told them it was absolutely true; that the above Connor had gone to Dublin, by the persuasion (as every person supposes) of the Coll^r [Collector] Sealy, etc., who are endeavering, by what I can understand, to have desperate Informations given against your ffamily. Pope likewise told me about half an hour ago at his house that the Collector had come into him, and Demanded a copy of the Connor Committal, which he was obliged to give him, I believe to Bail the Connors. Its likewise said that there is an order from Government to Bail these fellows, by the interest of the Collector, etc., etc. If the whole of this is not true, you may depend a great part is. Some of the prisoners told Pope, who likewise heard it elsewhere, that Connor was guarded from Dublin to Cork, lest he should be Molested. I shall wait on Lord Brandon to-morrow in person, and will inform his Lordship of the Collector and Mr. Sealy's proceedings in favour of such raps—as you told me when last I had the pleasure of seeing you that his Lordship promised you his protection and Interest; therefore I think incombent on me, as you are not convenient to wait on his Lordship.

These gentlemen will only show their teeth when they can't bite, to take part with such Notorious Villans and Robbers. By what I could Learn from Dan Connell, you and ffamily are quite out of their power. I don't think you ought

[1] The gang of robbers already referred to.

to be asleep in their affair, but give fresh Informations as much in your power against all these fellows, and every gentleman in your and the adjacent Country ought to do the same if they can, and have ye others Taken if possible. Mr. Denny is hurrying me about some business, therefore have not time to write to Dan, but your showing him this letter will do. I have a close look out for them fellows, since I saw you, but could not discover their being in Town. If they show their nose, you may depend they shall be taken and Lodged in spite of our Collector and Sealy. Write me a few lines per Bearer. I told all this story to Barry Denny. He says and engages no Information they can give will be found;[1] if there were, no Cethy Ivvy [petty jury], I believe, would give a verdict on the Information of such raps. Pope, who seems to have your Interest at heart, tells me that the two fellows that's in Goal are steadfast men now whatever, and that they will doe nothing but what they ought. Compliments to Cousin Connell and ffamily of Darrinane.

RICKD. CONNELL.

Tralee, Sunday evening, 5 o'clock, August 16, 1767.

Extract of a letter dated from Tralee to a friend in Dublin. (Evidently a copy, in a neat round hand on a half-sheet of paper.)

October 17, 1767.

DEAR SIR,—No doubt you must have heard before this of our Goal Doors having been thrown open to four Convicts under sentence of Death, and of the apprehensions of this whole County in Consequence of the Escape of two of the *Lowders;* their being at this instant of time Eleven or Twelve desperate Fellows of that Family, who publickly lay Contributions upon the miserable inhabitants of a considerable Tract of this unhappy country; and who already proceed with redoubled audacity; elated, as they are, at the Recovery of two of their Associates from the Terrors of a Publick Execution.

It is true, my very good Friend, Goal Deliveries of this kind, and even the Escape of the Felons at the Foot of the Gallows and with the Halter about their Necks, are long since considered in this Country as *Things of Course,* and therefore what nobody can be surprised at. But in the present Case there is something of much more serious Concern to the Publick than either the corruption of Goalers or the Negligence of Sheriffs; and the People among whom a general Despondency seems to prevail, begin to attribute the

[1] *i.e.* the grand jury would refuse to find a true bill on their information.

non-Execution of the Laws to *Causes infinitely more Powerful*. There are even those who affirm that had not the Lowders broke goal they would have shortly obtained his *Majesty's* most *Gracious Pardon*, having been already reprieved at the Request of an EXCISEMAN, who suggested that they would make excellent Spies in the Business of the Revenue. It is said that this Reprieve was obtained without the recommendation of the *Grand Jury* who found the Bills of Indictment against them, or the *Judge* who tried and condemned them. For my own poor Part, I hold these Things are so improbable that I am resolved to suspend all Belief till I receive your answer, and if they should be confirmed by one so well informed as you must be, it will, I think, be high time for me to sell my Property in this Country, if any Body will be hardy enough to buy it, and retire with my Family to the NEW WORLD, rather than continue a Member of a Common Wealth where the Execution of the Wisest Laws can be suspended at the *Pleasure of the People*.

I am, Dear Sir,
Most sincerely aff., etc., etc.

Unsigned, but written in a neat, clerk-like hand.

Subsequent researches have shown this letter to be the composition of the Rev. James Bland, of "The Rocks," now called Derryquin. In the spring of 1890 Daniel O'Connell found a bundle of his letters, in which Mr. Bland encloses copies of letters like this, written for publication, but refused by the timorous press of that day. Both in the public and private epistles so long preserved, he expresses the greatest indignation at the outrage to which his Catholic friends have been subjected.[1]

---

[1] The commercial restrictions imposed upon Irish trade and manufactures by England for the advantage of her own, gradually compelled the Protestant colony to make common cause with the Catholic people. All manufacturers and their operatives were Protestants, Catholics being excluded. On these Protestants the laws made to discourage Irish woollen manufacture, the prohibitions against the exportation of woollen and glassware to any but English ports, fell heavily, and ruined many. The prohibition against the exportation of Irish wool bore directly on the Catholic (and Protestant) farmers. Hence all Irishmen were forced into a league of passive resistance, co-operating to defeat these hostile prohibitions by (among other means) "clandestine trading," which differed from modern smuggling in that the latter violates the laws made by a nation for its own benefit. This passive resistance threatened to change its character when the volunteers paraded with cannon labelled, " Free Trade or ——," in 1789. In 1780 free trade was granted.—[G. S.]

Dan's first letter of 1768 is from London, and full of horror and disgust at the roughness of the English lower classes. We must remember that the young soldier's experience of the lower orders was confined to France, where the most abject servility preceded the Revolution, and to Ireland, where a patriarchal friendliness prevailed in the remote Irish-speaking districts. Hogarth's "Gate of Calais" gives the key-note of this letter. The immortal caricature of Johnny Crapaud shows how the British Philistine regarded the foreigner. The German and Irish officers wearing King Louis's undress—for "mufti" was practically unknown in those days, unless for purposes of direct disguise—were "Frenchies" to the London rough, and if the tall young gentleman who interpreted, remonstrated in the soft southern speech with which they were familiar among Irish chairmen, a touch of Paddy on Johnny Frenchman rather made matters worse.

London, January 20, 1768.

My Dear Brother will be surprised to hear from me from London, where I arrived a few days ago with my Colonel, and am to go back next week to our Regt. quartered at Gravelines, in Flanders. Curiosity has led him here, and friendship induced him to take me with him, my real attatchment for his person, as well as the strong reasons I have for cultivating his good will, have obliged me to comply with his request, tho' attended with some expences. Notwithstanding that I am defrayed by him, yet cloathes cost, and I even laid in something in the fund made for our journey, that I should not seem quite a burthen or beholden to him—a delicacy of sentiments I dare say you'll approve. Considering the many advantages I probably will reap from the favour of my Colonel, Gratitude and Prudence suffice and lay me under the most absolute compliance with his will and orders. His views for advancing me, are, to make me at Compiègne Sous Aid Major, and then endeavour to push by my application and Labour. If Fortune be not very contrary, I hope I shall do something worthy of my Study and Ambition; if she proves unkind, not to say unjust, I must philosophically submit, but never cease a single moment to pursue every obligation that may render me capable of distinguishing myself in the career I am in. Such is the Duty, so is bound to act each man of honour. Reason condemns Ambition when pushed too far. I should be glad to chat with my Dear Brother about the Government of England. My eyes, unused to the Licentiousness that the English call Liberty, see with horror, nay, contempt for the Nation, their mistaken sense and notion of things. Royalty despised, subordination unknown, and unbounded pride and contempt for all other Nations. Inhumanity, ferocity—in a word, a barbourism unknown to the rest of Europe, renders the inhabitants, I mean the Lower sort of people of England, the most odious. I believe the better sort of people well-bred in all countries, so don't comprehend 'em in the above critick. Adieu, my Dear Brother. My Duty to my Dear Father and Mother, Love and Affections to my Dear Morgan. Tell him I wrote to him from Gravelines. I still ever remain, my Dear Brother, respectful and fond,

DANL. O'CONNELL.

If we had a month's *congé*, we should go to Darrinane—the Count, my Colonel, and I. I daresay the surprise would be agreable to you all.

In the following series of letters about everyday events, I shall for brevity omit the ceremonious beginnings and endings, and the minute details of payments made and requested, rates of exchange, delays of postage, and such like, but give in full all that relates to the inner life of the young soldiers abroad and the family at home. Lest the traces of excisions should suggest the idea of indelicate remarks, I shall state once for all, that I have not seen a single impure word under Count O'Connell's hand, and that the three or four jokes and observations I omitted were simply a little broader than our modern speech admits of. The worthy and precise young man's minute financial details and remembrances to everybody are too much for any nineteenth-century reader. A letter from "Gravelines, March ye 26th, 1768," begins with expressions of anxiety at being left long without news of home. He gives the following personal tidings:—

I mentioned in my last something of ye Expectations I had of soon getting into the State Major, but did not then foresee some circumstances that have been since the occasion of a more Early success. Now my hopes are accomplished for the present moment. The Post of Sub Aide Major is become Vacant, and given to me preferably to a great number of competitors, all much older in the Service. This I look upon as a great Advantage, because of the Career it Leads unto, and the Means it affords of reaping the fruits of a

Zealous Labour and making Talents known when Possessed; for the Pay is the same I had as first Lieutenant, but I have a fair prospect of soon becoming Ayde Major, which, besides a pay twice more considerable, may possibly lead to some honourable Advancement, so that I look upon my present promotion with an eye of satisfaction, the more so as its before the Camp. My Colonel, who bought four horses for 200 guineas when in England, lends me the use of one for that time, otherwise shu'd have been at a great stand where to have one. This Worthy Man is out of Measure my friend, and I wholly devoted to him. I hope you'll be punctual in remitting me my pension in the Month of April. I forsee I shan't have it in my power to step over this next winter, as I shall have the burthen of the Regiment's affairs upon my hands, as the Major and Ayde Majors will be absent, but the following winter shall, please God, see you.

He sends the usual "duty and fond love," "tender affections," to all the family circle, and concludes—

>My Dear Brother,
>   For Ever Yours,
>   DANL. O'CONNELL.

Address: à Mons. O'C., En garnison à Gravelines.

If you know anything of our cousin, the Abbé FitzMaurice, pray communicate it to me. Adieu, my Dear Brother. I shall expect a speedy answer.

I wish you'd have our armes painted on a bit of paper and enclose it to me. No man is without a seal in France—I mean men of Fashion. It's an affair of 2 shillings or half-a-crown. I don't know 'em exactly, so can't have 'em drawn.

>Gravelines, May 26, 1768.

I Duly rec^d my Dear brother's letter, dated at Tralee, containinge a bill upon Mr. George Wolfe at Paris, for the 400^{ll}, which bill has been acquitted upon sight. Receve my Warm thanks for your care in supplying me in so critical a moment when the Campaign rendered it particularly necessary. I mentioned in my last my having got into ye State Major, and the Expectations I conceive of a rapid advancement, tho' I always have in View and Don't omit anything that may give me a right thereto. Our Regiment is to March from this in the latter End of Next Month for the Camp. What may become of us after I can not yet tell, but shall take care to give you my address and a relation of anything worth your notice that might occur on that Occasion. I shall only observe that we might probably be comprehended in the body of troops that are to be sent to Corsica, which I should not be at all sorry for. The Indisposition of the Queen is, I suppose, well known to you. This Event may retard yᵉ Camp a month or two, and some people conjecture that, instead of being held at Compiègne, it may be held at a place called Trou d'Enfer, at 3 Leagues from Paris.

I am sorry to Learn the Low Sentiments of my former friend, yᵉ Abbé FitzMaurice. I shu'd have never thought him capable of a step of that nature, much less against Our Brother Tim McCarthy. But this only serves to prove the predominant power of money. Take care, my Dear Brother, that you shan't be within the reach of some one of these Apostates, for you have seen many Examples of yᵉ infamous Spirit that reigns in your Country, nor would I have you trust to any of them. I shu'd think my fortune, if I had any, as Safe in the hands of a Pandour or Prussian Black Hussard. Adieu, my Dear Brother. Let me duly hear from you, and believe me for ever, your loving and fond Brother,

DANL. O'CONNELL.

[Here follow the usual greetings.]

I twice wrote to Brother Morgan and have had no Answer. Tell him I am piqued at his neglect. I am sorry to Learn that our Sister Nelly has taken a step contrary to the Will of her Parents, but Love will not know nor hear reason.

I am here within four leagues of Cousin Robin Conway, and see him frequently. He and his wife are well. She is the best creature I know. Send me in your next the address of the Secularized Abbé FitzMaurice. I shall be glad to write to him about his Brother.

This letter of May, 1768, alludes to the runaway match of handsome Sister Nelly and the misfortunes of poor Sister Betty. "Dark Eileen," as popular tradition calls her, had been married, when under fifteen, to a rich old Mr. O'Connor, of Firies. When the young bride was being "hauled home," and lifted over the threshold by a shouting, cheering crowd, the strings of a harp, which hung in the hall, burst asunder. This was considered a very ill omen, and within six months she came home a girl-widow. No child was born to her, and though she neither entertained nor professed any special devotion for her husband, she regretted, on her return, the loss of the liberty and influence of the mistress of a household. While on a visit to her sister, Mrs. Baldwin, of Clohina, near Macroom, she met Arthur O'Leary, of Raleigh, better known as Arthur O'Leary the Outlaw. Though he was rich, high-born, and eminently attractive, her family refused their consent on account of his wildness and rash disposition. The wilful dame eloped with her golden-haired rider, whose melancholy fate she celebrated in Irish verse remembered to this day.[1]

It is sad to see the man to whom my hero was indebted for his first start in life falling away from his sacred calling, but the Abbé FitzMaurice not only apostatized, but put a penal enactment in force against Timothy McCarthy, of Oughtermoney, the husband of his cousin.[2] The venerable Miss Evelina McCarthy, granddaughter of this couple, wrote me about her grandmother as follows. Elizabeth, wife of Tim McCarthy, of Oughtermoney, was the eldest daughter of Daniel O'Connell and Maur-ni-Dhuiv. Writing to me about Count O'Connell, Miss Evelina McCarthy says—

"The sister Betty that he speaks of was my grandmother, married to Tim McCarthy, an only son and heir to a large property (he was done out of it—I had rather not say by whom or how). My father and mother were second cousins. My two grandfathers, Tim and Owen McCarthy, lived together for many years, and Owen lived till his death, at the age of eighty-one (your father-in-law, John O'Connell, remembered him well), with my grandmother Betty (O'Connell) McCarthy. She was a saint, tho' not a canonized one. In one of those dreadful famines that have visited Ireland since her soil has been polluted by the Norman and Saxon—I think it must have been the year after the Rebellion—Iveragh had not suffered like the rest of Ireland, and whole families came there seeking for food. For months my grandmother stood from early morning till night, a bag of potatoes and a bag of meal beside her, and distributed both to all comers, my mother and Uncle John taking care to renew the provisions as soon as the bags got empty. At last they began to feel uneasy, afraid their provision should fail and she be unable to continue her

---

[1] See p. 237.
[2] Under the Penal Code, if a Catholic became a Protestant, he could dispossess his father or kinsmen, and obtain their property.—[G. S.]

charities, but when they visited the bins they were always full. The more she gave, the more they had; and so it lasted till the famine ceased, and with it the calls on her charity."

Cousin Morty gets his first step much about the same time as Dan gets on the staff. Morty's lieut.-colonel, Colonel Pierce, seems to have been a personal friend and correspondent of young Dan's, as he occasionally mentions things he has heard from his kinsman's immediate commander.

In Dan's first letter of 1769 he begins those inquiries about armorial bearings and descents which form so large a portion of the correspondence of the Irishmen abroad with their relatives at home, who were frequently very hazy and remiss about coats-of-arms. In Ireland, the land of tribal pedigrees, like the genealogical books of Scripture, armorial bearings counted for less than anywhere else in Europe. I must say that when the family coat of the O'Connells had been duly registered by John O'Connell, of Ashtown, the Duke of Ormond's Seneschal, just after the Restoration, it was a shame for rich Maurice not to have sent it to the ambitious lad. The expenditure of a very few shillings would have procured it, but Maurice had seemingly a nervous dread of any pretensions or assertions which could possibly draw attention to the family, and the lad Daniel had to procure this information as best he could. Maurice may possibly have been ignorant of the registered coat. The old articles of plate belonging to his parents bear the device of a stag. Sir Bernard Burke's " General Armoury " gives : " Per fess argent and vert, a stag trippant between three trefoils, counterchanged ; crest : a stag's head erased proper, charged with a trefoil vert. Motto : ' Cial agus Neart,' or ' Virtute et Valore.' "

This letter begins about the long silence of the family. I skip all that part, and commence with the news it gives—

Maubeuge, January 1, 1769.

The affairs of Corsica make, I suppose, some noise among you, notwithstanding the inaction that the rigour of the Season obliges the troops in that Island to remain in. Everything seems to promise a stirring and troublesome Campaign. It's said forty Bataillions are to be Embarked for to reinforce the body of men already there, and notwithstanding these forces, it's very possible all our Efforts may prove Abortive, because of the inaccessible posts the Enemy occupies in the Mountains, and there's no doubt that if Paoli, their General, makes as vigorous a resistance as hitherto, it will cost France more men and money than the whole Island is Worth. An officer, a friend of mine, who is in that country, and with whom I keep up a regular Correspondance, assures me that the troops are prodigiously fatigued, the Enemy is much more numerous, and our Army apprehends being attacked, so that our advanced posts in the Mountains guard redoubts and other works where they are almost buried in the snow, and this hard Duty weakens us daily more and more, so that if their general knows anything of his trade, he'll lay hold of this favourable Conjunction and Push the handfull of men that lie there before the fresh troops. Our Regiment has hitherto been in Expectation of being sent there, but have just received fresh orders for preparing for the Camp de Plaisance at Compiègne. We're destined to appear there last summer, but the untimely death of the Queen put an Obstacle to itt. This almost ruins the Officers, because it puts us to double Expences. As for me, I hope to be made Ayde Major then, which will double my pay, and enable me to pay twenty pounds I owe. I give you my word there is not another Officer in the Regiment but owes more than twice that sum, and without some private arrangements I should have been as ill off as the others. You'll oblige me, my Dear Brother, to make me this year's remittance the beginning of May, for to be able to make fresh preperations. If I am [? not] employed in Corsica, and that I can obtain the Colonel's Concent, I shall undoubtedly take a trip to Ireland after the Camp, and think myself happy if I find all my family in good health. My truest pleasure would be to embrace you, my Dear Brother, and Brother Morgan, my dear Father and Mother, and Express to all my tenderness and gratitude. Adieu, Dear Brother. Pray write to me without loss of time, and believe me, y^r fond brother,

DANL. O'CONNELL.

Address: à Monsieur, Monsieur O'Connell, Officier Major au Régiment de Royal Suédois, à Maubeuge, en Heynault.

Pray do me the pleasure, my Dear Brother, to send me, by Cousin Robin Conways, the arms of the family. Nothing more ridiculous in this country than not to have the seal of the Family. Wishing you all a Merry Christmas and happy Year, I embrace all friends.

I cannot resist the temptation of inserting a letter from Captain Robin Conway. It contains one passing allusion to my hero. The marriage referred to turned out very happily, and Robin and his foreign wife were kindness itself to the multitudinous Kerry cousins. Several of the family were in excellent positions at home and abroad, but there was a brother of this good man in great poverty. I leave the account to show Robin's kindness. My chief object in this book being to show the old Catholic Munster gentlefolk painted by themselves, I insert this matrimonial epistle to Maurice O'Connell, of Darrynane—

Bergues, January the first, 1769.

My Dr. Cousin,—You must be certainly surprized that I did not answer your letters before now, which came to my hands in due time. The affair I had in hands at that moment hindered me, which was a Law Suite with the Magistrates of this town, and the same time was coming to a tryal—hindered me of proceeding further at that time.

Since the Reform [1] I courted a Lady in this town with the Concent of her Mother. Her nearest Relations opposed the Marriage, as the girl is an only child and well in her affairs, and my being a stranger without any fortune, upon which there was a Law Suite Commenced, which I have gained in spite of twenty-four Magistrates, and that thro' Means of a Lt.-General who commands the Province, whom I had the honour of knowing in Germany, and offer'd me his protection att his arrival in this Country. Now I am Marryed to the same Lady to the satisfaction of all my friends—no great fortune, but Means to live Decently independant. Would to God I had itt in that Country where I would relieve that Dear Brother that draws Drops of Blood from my heart to hear of his Wants. You'll tell me what would relieve him from this country. Yes, my dear Maurice, if I was master of the fortune, but as it comes by the Mother, she is Mistress while she lives. 'Tis certain I want for nothing, but cannot enjoy myself and knowing the Wants of my Dr. Brother; but for the present it is quite out of my power to relieve him, as I was something in Debt after the Reform, and that I pay it out of the poor pension the King makes me. These twelve months being over, I could allow him six pounds a year, which is all in my power till after the Death of my Mother-in-Law.

Oh, my Dear Cousin, what obligations I owe you and your

---

[1] Some regimental reductions and retrenchments.

family for your goodness to that Dear Brother, who is dearer to me than the rest of the World! Can I ever find Means to make you amends, be persuaded, Dr Maurice, that it will be my study Day and Night to find the Means to persuade you how much I am acknowledging, and Ever will, my Dr Cousin. Continue that which you Began, and procure that Dear Brother and his family, in sight of my letter, some Barrels of potatoes, with a hundred of Butter, and for May next you'll buy him two Milch Cows, which sum I will pay you on sight or to your orders. Let me have the satisfaction of your answering my Draught, which will be acknowledged as an Everlasting obligation. Embrace that Dear Brother for me, and tell him that this is all in my power at present. Oh, my Dear Cousin, if you could give my Mother a trifle to buy snuff with, what pleasure I would pay it along with the rest! You wanted to know the station of Maurice Charles [O'Connell] and Maurice Jeffrey [O'Connell]. The former is the Recruiting Officer of Rothe's [Irish Regiment], has nothing to say to the Regm^t, and has Double appointments [pay]; the Later is still Cadet in Bulkeley's [Irish Regiment], one of the best Lads that ever left his Country. I can assure you he is a credit to any Nation. They are now in garrison in Gravelines, three small Leagues from this town. It is but three days agoo since he and I cracked some Bottles of Wine. Next year the Royal Sweades are coming to Flanders. Then I may have the pleasure of seeing Daniel att my house. He was perfectly well when I saw his letter two days agone to Mr. Fagan. Be pleased to accept the compliments of an approaching year from him who is ever your Sincere and aff^te Kinsman,

ROBERT CONWAY.

And be pleased to make the same compliments to your worthy family, Timm McCarthy and his family, Kean, Miles and family [Mahonys], the families of Kinsmen James and John Segerson and families. By this Post I'll write to my brother.

I turn from the lad in his garrison, and the happy Benedict, who send their New Year's greetings, to the gem of the Darrynane smuggling papers. The sheriff, who will be of the smuggling party, and the loyal Protestant gentleman who transmits by a sure hand the epistle of one smuggling Papist to another, should have figured in "The Two Chiefs of Dunboy." If my reader will look back to the portion of our history referring to 1767, he will see informations against the highwaymen, the Loders, sworn before Thomas Orphen, as the local Justice of the Peace. The Blennerhassetts were frequently colloquially spoken of as Hassetts. I fancy the "Villens" are the informing pardoned marauders.

The letter is addressed, "Mr. Mau. Connel, Darranane," no postmark, seemingly sent by hand.

Saturday, Feb. $\frac{11}{2}$, 1769.

Dr. Sir,—All parties at last have agreed to our former scheme, and Wednesday next we all sett out in the night for Glancare; the Sherrif will be of our partie. Rich^d and Arthur Hassett are dooing what they can to sett or find out particularly where those Villens are. This is sent by express to you by Mr. Orphen, to whom I've enclosed it. I hope we may have success, and have great hopes we will not fail in our attempt. When we meet we shall talk of the matter. I rec^d both y^r le^{rs} [letters].

I am y^{rs} affectly.,
Dens. Mahony.

Young Dan's next letter is of considerable interest and importance. He has at last visited Paris, but, ever full of the pressing business of pushing his fortunes, he spares not a word to describe its sights and wonders. His studies, the slowly and surely laid foundations of future eminence, are all he mentions. He does not give any details about the king, whom he must then have seen for the first time. Says my fellow-worker, Ross O'Connell—

Maria Leszinska, wife of his Most Christian Majesty Louis XV. and daughter of Stanislaus King of Poland, died June 25, 1768; she was mother of Louis le Dauphin, and of the four princesses known to history as Loque, Graille, Chiffe, and Coche. It was this lady's "bonnet de nuit de dentelles avec de grandes girandoles de diamants" that so electrified Madame de Genlis, when that future nursery governess to princes was presented ("Memoires," ch. ix.). Some two years after the queen's death, a certain young soldier, Dumouriez by name, returning from Corsica, sees "with sorrow at Compiègne the old King of France on foot, with doffed hat, in sight of his army, at the side of a magnificent phaeton, doing homage to the —— Dubarry" ("Memoires du Gen. Dumouriez," quoted by Carlyle, "Revolution," vol. i. p. 3). Young O'Connell probably saw this and many other things with a semi-prophetic sorrow equal to Dumouriez's—things it was not safe to trust to the post, and he unhappily wrote no memoirs.

St. Simon says that, under Louis XIV., every letter that passed through the post was opened, extracts were made of anything likely to interest or amuse the king, and these were read to his Majesty. Innumerable *lettres de cachet* were one of the results. The system obtained for years before an intelligent public suspected that le Roi Soleil, and after him Louis le Bien-aimé, enjoyed the firstfruits of its correspondence. Louis XVI. was too honest to profit by stolen confidences, but his police were far too conservative and far too wise to abandon a plan that answered so exceedingly well, although the letter-writing folk had grown somewhat cautious by this time, which accounts for the absence of many things one would expect to find in letters of the period.—[R. O'C.]

This letter of my hero's is in my possession, having been given me by the present Daniel O'Connell, of Darrynane. Some words are illegible, as something was spilt over the paper.

Paris, August 7, 1769.

I apprehend my Dear Brother may disapprove of my deffering to acknowledge the rec' of his letter and bill, but as it came to hands only a few days before the departure of my Regiment for the Camp of Compiègne, and that I had formed the resolution of taking a trip to Ireland, directly after postponed . . .

. . . Of the Camp which held a month . . . Capitaine Fagan, my worthy friend, came from Paris to see his brothers and me, and thought it absolutely necessary I should come down here for the oppertunity of making acquaintances and appearing in the World. He took me with him, and gives me Lodging and every other Conveniency I could expect of you in his place. I have taken some masters that I have not had an oppertunity of finding Elsewhere; that motive, joined to a strong appearance of a speedy advancement, induces me to make a longer stay than I at first intended, nor can I well determine what shall become of me this Winter. The trouble and expences the Camp laid me under, and the success with which the Regt. appeared there, gives me from the share I had in it the most solid Claims to preferment. I daily see my Colonel here; there's nothing in his power but I can firmly rely on, but if in his Regt. it fails, I think it Cannot Elsewhere, at least it shall not thro' my fault. I can justly say I paid it dear whenever it comes, tho' . . . of my country I have (thank God) been more happy. Adieu. I hope, before the latter end of the winter, I shall, if possible, go spend a month with you. My tender duty to my father and mother. I hope they will receive me with friendship and pleasure. With love to Brother Morgan, Sisters Connell, and compliments to all. I shall remain, with the truest affection, my Dear Brother,

Yours most respectfully,
Danl. O'Connell.

My warm compliments to Mr. and Mrs. Fagan and family. Captain Fagan sends you his, and Entreats you'll be so good as to say to Mrs. Fagan, his mother, that he with impatience expects a letter from her. All friends here are well. The German Fagans are very well. Address to me as underneath. Our Regt. is to march to Phallzbourgh, in Alsace.

Address: à Monsieur O'C., Chez Mons. de Fagan, rue de Richelieu, vis-à-vis la fontaine à Paris.

Stephen Fagan is now butter-merchant in Cork. Gratitude, I think, my dear brother, obliges all our family to deal with him preferably to any other person, considering the obligations conferred on me by his brother.

I shall close my second chapter with this Compiègne letter. My hero, during this sojourn in Paris, prepared the way for entering the famous old Irish Brigade with which his name is identified, though it was in the Royal Swedes that he won his first honours as a boy-cadet in the Seven Years' War. He again distinguished himself in that regiment when, sent back to his old comrades as their lieut.-colonel, he led them on board the floating batteries before Gibraltar in 1782.

The third book of this history relates to the Irish Brigade, which my hero now entered, in Clare's famous regiment.

NOTES TO BOOK II.

I shall begin the Notes to Book II. with a brief account of Irish pilots and their gains in Spain.

I also append to this second portion of my chronicle some notes on the O'Sullivan race, many of whose offshoots figure in these pages. Two of the most typical instances of the survival of the old pride of power among women of chiefly race came under my notice among kinswomen of Maur-ni-Dhuiv. Horrible and grotesque as are some of the details, I think they are too valuable, as illustrations of old manners and customs, to be forgotten. I purposely disguise the persons and places mentioned in "The Two Red Roquelaures," as the descendants of the thrifty couple might not care to have their homely ancestors paraded with full name and address.

Note A.

Irish Pilots and Seamen.

A letter of Gyles[1] O'Sullivan to his cousin, Maurice O'Connell, of Darrynane, dated Cadiz, October 10, 1758, gives an interesting account of Irish pilots. Owing to the great influx of foreign pilots, those of Spain petitioned the king against their employment. The Irish pilots are alone admitted to the West Indian ports, and they must first serve two campaigns, or eighteen months before the mast. Gyles could find no other chance than joining one of their men-of-war, which were here in this post continually to cruise after the Moors, in the station of a foremast man. At the end of fourteen, instead of eighteen, months he was appointed "in ye Quality of Pilot," and released from menial work.

"In Sep^r, 1756, began my Campaign, at which time my Uncle was on his passage from ye South Seas, and suffered so much fatigue comeing round Cape Horn in ye dead of ye winter, that after his arrival here he was in a very bad state of health for 6 months afterwards. In May following, 1757, there came an order here from the Court to fitt oute a fregitt

---

[1] *Gyles*, here, is modified from *Giolla-Iosa* ("Servant of Jesus"), whence *Gillies* and *Gyles*.—[S.]

of War with 307 guns, to carry a Million of Hard Dollars to ye Bank in Amsterdam, as likewise to get two of ye best navagators that was well acquainted with the Channell, for ye more security of ye King's ship and money, which was immediately put in execution, and all ye dilligence possible made to get Pilots, but could get none to their satisfaction. At ye same time, ye ship i belonged to arrived from a Cruise, and ye Captain, hearing ye search they were making for Pilots to goe in ye fregitt, he instantly went to ye Major General of ye Marine, who was ye Person that first sent me aboard, and by ye large description he and his officers were pleased to give of my capacity and Knowledge I had of ye Channell, He immediately ordered me aboard of a fregitt, as one of ye two of those before mentioned. At ye same time was informed that my Uncle was ye only man they could find fittest for this purpose, if they could prevail on him to goe, upon which he was sent for by the Captain General of ye Marine, who told him if he chused to goe, he would get him liscence from Court to sail to ye Indies. My Uncle told him, provided he did so, with giving him ye Captain's table and a Cabin as well as ye rest of ye officers, he was ready to obey the commands, which he granted Him."

In another letter he mentions that his uncle, Owen Sullivan, the pilot, is worth £2000, "which I assure you he has need for, as there is not a year that passes but he spends £300, which is what gets him great esteem and credit he has. As for me, I am making all the Interest I can to get into one of the Flota Ships that goes out Next year for Vera Cruz, in the Bay of Mexico."

Note B.

O'Sullivan.

Arms: per pale vert and arg.; on the first a buck pas. ppr.; on the second a boar pas. per pale sa. and ppr.; on a chief or. two lions ramp. comb. gu., supporting with fore paws a sword entwined with a serpent. O'Sullivan Beare: Per pale sa. and ar., a fesse between two boars pas.; that in chief to the dexter, that in base to sin.; all counterchanged. Many versions of these two coats have been borne by different branches of the O'Sullivans and Sullivans. MacGillicuddy bears gu., a wivern or.

The following quaint rhymed description of the arms of O'Sullivan is preserved by the Ardea branch of the O'Sullivan family:—

> "A robin redbreast perched upon a crown;
> Two lions rampant, with a dreadful frown;
> A stately stag and a grisly boar do stand
> Beneath a nervous and unconquered hand,
> That grasps a sword, around whose blade
> A shining, sparkling evet is displayed."

Motto: "Lamh foistenach an uachtar."

The O'Sullivans of the Eugenian race were formerly princes of Cnoc-Graffan, a territory in the barony of Middlethird, in County Tipperary, thus mentioned by O'Heerin—

> "O'Sullivan, who delights not in violence,
> Rules over the extensive Eoghanacht[1] of Munster,
> About Knockgraffan broad lands he obtained,
> Won by his victorious arms in conflicts and battles."

The O'Sullivans were, however, dispossessed of this territory by the McCarthys and Buadach, and the chiefs of the sept removed into the Counties of Cork and Kerry, where they became possessed of extensive estates. About this period the family of O'Sullivan appears divided into two great branches, viz. the O'Sullivan Mor, Lords of Dunkerron, in the County Kerry, and the O'Sullivan Beare, Chiefs of Beare and Bantry, in the County of Cork. O'Sullivan Mor's country contained two hundred ploughlands, and he found McCarthy Mor in fifty gallowglasses in time of war and £20 yearly, or value to that amount. In a document addressed by Sir Warham St. Leger to Lord Burleigh, preserved in the State Papers Office, the O'Sullivan Mor of their time is described as "Lord of a great country, the Earl's (Donal McCarty) seneschal and marshal, married to Florence MacCarthy's sister, and able to make a hundred swords."

Donal, who married Mary, daughter of Cormac Og, Lord Muskerry, died A.D. 1548, left issue Dermod, Tanist of Dunkerron, who married the daughter of Sir Owen McCarthy Reagh-Boghe (Buadac in Irish, "Victorious in battle"), who married the daughter of O'Donovan of Carberry; Connor, who married Winifred (or Honoria), the daughter of Edmond FitzGerald, Knight of the Valley; Donal, who married the daughter of O'Leyne, widow of MacGillicuddy; Ellen married Donal O'Sullivan (the heroic Donal Cam, the defender of Dunboy); Beara, a daughter who espoused John, Knight of Kerry, and his son and successor; Eoghan of Dunkerron, who married Julia McCarthy (living in 1603).

In this castle of Dunkerron, near Kenmare, was an inscribed stone legible early in this century, "I.H.S.,

---

[1] i.e. Eugenians—descendants of Eoghan Mor, one of Olioll Ollum's sons.

Maria Deo Gratias †. This work was made the xx. of April, 1596, by Owen O'Sullivan Mor and Shyly Ny Donogh McCarthy Reagh," Shyly, or Sheela[1] (Julia) was daughter of McCarthy Reagh, Prince of Carberry. Donal, the last O'Sullivan Mor, died at Tomies, near Killarney, in 1762, and was buried in Mucross Abbey. He left no lawful issue.

Charles Edward's distinguished companion of "The '45," Sir John O'Sullivan, was the son of a cadet of the family, and has a descendant now living, the Hon. John Sullivan, formerly American Minister to the courts of St. James and Lisbon.

The O'Sullivan Beares were the second branch of the O'Sullivan race, and were even more powerful than the O'Sullivan Mors. It became customary to call the one, Lord of Dunkerron; the other, O'Sullivan Beare, or Lord of Beare. There is an old Irish saying, "O'Sullivan is lord from Beare to Dhous" (Dhous is a distant hill far beyond Bantry town).

"O'Sullivan Beare,"[2] says Mr. Windele, "by his tenure was obliged to aid McCarthy Mor with all his strength, and to be marshal of his army. He was to pay, for every arable ploughland, five gallowglasses or kerns, or six shillings and eightpence, or a beef for each, at the option of McCarthy. McCarthy was to receive half a crown for every ship that came to fish or trade in O'Sullivan's harbours. O'Sullivan was to give McCarthy merchandise at the rate he purchased it. He was to entertain McCarthy and all his train two nights at Dunboy, and whenever they travelled that way. He was to send horse meat to Paillice for McCarthy's saddle horses, and pay the groom three shillings and fourpence out of every arable ploughland. He was to find hounds, greyhounds, and spaniels for McCarthy when he came, and one shilling and eightpence annually to his huntsman, out of every ploughland."

The third branch of the O'Sullivan sept takes the name of MacGillicuddy, deriving their descent and surname from Gilla Mochuda, of the race of Donal Mor O'Sullivan. The chief representative of the family still retains the title of "MacGillicuddy of the Reeks," and holds a portion of the lands of his ancestors. Tradition avers that he holds these lands on Dame Nature's own patent until the Reeks be a winter without snow.

The fourth branch of the O'Sullivans became "McFineen Dhuv" ("the sons of Dark Florence"). The epithet "Dark"

---

[1] Correctly Sighle.
[2] Mr. Cronnelly says, "O'Sullivan Mor," which is clearly a mistake, as Dunboy was O'Sullivan Beare's stronghold on Beare Haven.

was much needed, as a branch of the McCarthys were styled "McFineen" ("sons of Florence"). Several families whose names have been variously anglicized are branches of the O'Sullivan clan, such as the Sugrues of Fermoyle and Cork, who have continued to bear the O'Sullivan arms.

Note C.

Conway of Bodrhyddan.

Arms: sa. on a bend cotised ar, a rose between two annulets gu. The Kerry Conways seem to have borne the annulets of the field instead of gu., as does Conway, Marquess of Hertford.

The Conways.

Much information anent the Conways and their kinsfolk is given in the Blennerhassett pedigree in "Old Kerry Records." Jenkin, younger son of Sir John Conway, of Ragely, and great-grandson of John Conway, of Bodrythan, Flint, and of Janetta Stanley, of Hooton, settled in Kerry in the reign of Elizabeth. He left one son, Jenkin, and two daughters. Elizabeth married Robert Blennerhassett, of Ballyseedy; and Alice married Edmund Roe. The line of Jenkin the younger terminated with his granddaughters Avice and Alice Conway, co-heiresses of Killorglin, of whom the elder married her second cousin, Robert Blennerhassett, of Ballyseedy. Elizabeth, daughter of Edmund Roe and Alice Conway, married her fourth cousin, Captain James Conway, son of Christopher Conway, of Rathmines, by his second wife, Mary, daughter of Sir James Ware;[1] said Christopher being great-great-grandson of John Conway, of Bodrythan, who was great-grandfather of the elder Jenkin, and head of this branch of the house of Conway. Captain James had a son Christopher, of Claghane, County Kerry, who married Joan Roche, and had, with a daughter, Elizabeth, wife of John O'Connell, of Darrynane, seven sons, of whom the two elder alone have any interest for us.

James went to France with the brigade, and had two sons, officers in the French Service.

Thomas, the second, had three sons.

1. Christopher (*ob. s.p.*).

---

[1] Sir James Ware, Auditor-General, M.P. for Mallow 1613, ob. 1632, descended from Roger de Ware, a Baron of Parliament, *temp.* Edward I. By his wife Mary, daughter of Sir Ambrose Briden, of Maidstone, Kent, Sir James was father of Sir James Ware, Auditor-General, P.C., M.P. for Trinity College, 1639, the famous antiquarian.

2. James, Count Conway, the "old Colonel James" of the letters, married Julia Mahony, and had two sons.

(1) Thomas, General Count Conway, Governor of the Mauritius before 1783.

(2) James, "Vicomte" Conway, served in Dillon's Regiment.

3. Edward, married Ellen Mahony, and had James, Colonel 53rd Regiment, whose son Thomas was Colonel of the Grenadier Guards, and C.B.

Sheara-na-mo-Mor O'Connell, of Iveragh (*ob.* 1722, *æt.* 38), married Elizabeth, daughter of Edmund Conway, of Glenbeigh, Kerry; and their eldest son, Maurice, married Jane, daughter of Thomas Blennerhassett, of Killorglin, who was younger son of Robert Blennerhassett, of Ballyseedy, and Avice Conway, co-heiress of Killorglin. This Maurice was, by his wife Jane, grandfather of the Liberator's wife.— [R. O'C.]

Note D.

Shevaun-ni-Dhuiv's Vengeance.

In my mission of chronicler to the old, real Irish, I gladly step a little aside among the "cousins and the aunts" of my hero to collect any picturesque episodes. I cannot resist the temptation of this especial digression. We might think it concerned some mediæval lady out of Scott's "Border Minstrelsy," instead of a comparatively modern eighteenth-century gentlewoman.

The old folk have many stories about three ladies of the Dark O'Donoghues: Maur-ni-Dhuiv, my hero's mother; Nor-ni-Dhuiv (Honora O'Donoghue Dhuiv); and Shevaun[1]-ni-Dhuiv (Joan O'Donoghue Dhuiv). These two latter were either sisters or aunts of Maur-ni-Dhuiv — the greater number of old people say aunts. This redoubtable Joan was familiarly known by an Irish phrase which means, "A bite out of the devil's belt," meaning that she was fierce and strong and daring enough to have committed such an outrage on Satan's personal trappings. She was married to a McCarthy, "out west," of whose home, lands, or male posterity no trace now exists. Like all the other lands of Catholics, theirs lay at the mercy of a Protestant discoverer. Shevaun-ni-Dhuiv was left a widow with several daughters and one handsome son, the "apple of her eye." Near her house was a mill, originally a feudal appendage to the property, and

[1] Recte Sjobhan, or *Siobhan.*

occupied by tenants. The young folk of the mill were orphans. Shevaun-ni-Dhuiv had always been exceedingly kind to them. When the young miller grew up, the return he made was to lodge preliminary informations against his benefactress. These, however, required a little more "hard swearing" to dispossess the McCarthy family. Shevaun-ni-Dhuiv got a timely warning, and sent a trusty messenger to Glanlesk, where the wildest of wild men defied law and order, but were as docile as sheep to O'Donoghue behests. The O'Donoghue Dhuvs, however, were only a younger offshoot of the chiefly family of the Glens—chieftains of Glanflesk. The lady's messenger bore a very oddly worded message. The faithless follower of her children's house was on no account to be killed; but he was to be prevented swearing away their birthright. Her bidding was carried out to the letter. A great gang of O'Donoghue peasants came down from the wild glens, surrounded the mill, seized and overpowered the miller, and cut out his tongue. They did not inflict any other injuries on him, and Shevaun-ni-Dhuiv's brutal expedient perfectly succeeded.

However, the handsome lad, whose lands she had preserved by such a desperate expedient, was snatched away from her by an early death. Sergeant O'Connor, R.I.C., to whom I am so largely indebted for Irish verse, remembers one verse of the keen she made over her son. Every keen described the dead, generally invited different classes of mourners, in different stanzas, to swell the burst of tuneful sorrow above the bier, and in other verses recited the ancient lineage of the dead. In the verse my staunch and zealous helper remembers she appeals to her daughters, the fair maidens whose dowries were to have been provided by their brother. The Irish was kindly written down by Mr. O'Sullivan, of Maylor Street, Cork, to whom also I am so much indebted.

A iṅṅa oᵹa ꝼeaꞃꞇa ᵹabaꞃó uaiṅ amac,
Aᵹuꞃ ꝼeucaꞃó a' b-ꝼeicꝼió ꞃib m' Aꞃꞇ oᵹ a' ꞇeacꞇ
Aᵹuꞃ a' cloiḋeaṁ ceaṅṅ óiꞃ 'ṅa ᵹlac
Iꞃ é ꞇo ᵹlacꝼaó ꞃᵹiṁ ᵹo maꞇ
Cuṁ ṅa m-baṅ ꞇo ᵹleuꞃ 'ꞃ ꞇo cuꞃ amac

Shevaun-ni-Dhuiv's words, addressed to her daughters, run thus in English—

> "O young maidens, speed quick from me forth,
> And watch: can you see my young Art approach,
> And his sword with gold hilt in his hand?
> 'Tis he would take care, well-equipped,
> To speed young maidens fittingly forth."

Note E.

The Two Red Roquelaures.

Now, the following veracious history is known to many people, and the descendants of the two wearers of the red mantles it commemorates still exist. Not to hurt any one's feelings, I shall conceal, as far as possible, time, place, and personal identity, merely observing that the proud lady's people were akin to Count O'Connell's relatives, which is not giving a very clear clue to their identity.

A Catholic gentleman of one of the old Celtic families along the Cork and Kerry borders rented from a Protestant a large tract, once the estate of his own ancestors. At that time "Papists" were restricted to thirty-two-year leases, but renewals on payment of a fine were so customary that the old people were generally pretty safe, and if any unforfeited lands remained to them, their landlords would help them to screen these from the discoverer. A respectable peasant farmer of the same clan, but by no means of the same family, who had a good farm and a thrifty wife, lived near this gentleman. These folk had made a good deal of money without in any way attempting to overstep social distinctions or compete with their namesakes. The gentleman's wife belonged to an exceedingly ancient and haughty family, and had a proportionate amount of pride. One Sunday she came to Mass in the little thatched country chapel, in a beautiful and costly new-fashioned garment made of fine scarlet broadcloth. It was called a roquelaure, and resembled Red Riding Hood's historic mantle.

On the following Sunday the farmer's wife discarded the dark blue cloth cloak of a Munster peasant, which even the richest farming women wore, with satin lining to the great hood, and the audacious milker of many cows appeared in a precisely similar scarlet roquelaure to the high-born lady.

The haughty dame rushed out of her seat, tore the offending mantle off the other woman's back, dragged it outside the chapel door, and trampled it underfoot in the chapel-yard.

The following Sunday she rode to Mass in a different mantle, while a large pig, attired in her own discarded scarlet roquelaure, was solemnly driven up through the gaping congregation to the chapel door—"through all the flock," as the peasants say.

The farmer's wife swore to be revenged, and her vow of vengeance was that she would set her keelers in the proud lady's drawing-room. She incited her husband to go to Dublin, see the head landlord, offer him a large sum for the reversion of the farm at the expiration of the lease, and the rent during several years the lease had yet to run.

The landlord outraged all customary methods of dealing among gentlemen by accepting these terms. His point of honour was not proof against two rents for one farm. When in the course of time the proud lady's husband rode to Dublin, with plenty of gold pieces in his saddle-bags to pay the fine and renew the lease, he learned, to his cost, that he had been forestalled. He and his wife had to surrender the place, and go and live in quite a small, unpretending residence, while the drawing-room was converted into a dairy, and instead of spindle-legged chairs, china bowls, and beau-pots, great wooden keelers, ranged on lengthy stands, held the milk of the outraged dame's many fine cows.

Note F.

Penal Papers. 1775.

A Friendly Bill of Discovery: its Bill of Costs.

Bills of discovery were the machinery by which Catholics could be deprived of those estates which had escaped confiscation. If danger threatened, a friendly Protestant would file one. Of course, if he or his heirs liked, they could hold the lands for ever. Hugh Falvey, of Faha, brother to the widow of John O'Connell, of Darrynane, acted as Hunting Cap's perpetual shield until, in extreme old age, he got a scruple of conscience about it. I am sorry to say the faithful friend was of necessity a renegade from the ancient faith, else he could not have done this good service to friends whose faith was firmer than his own. Mr. Attorney Francks's bill of costs is duly put away among Hunting Cap's papers. Observe that he omits the name of who paid him.

Samuel Windes *against* Maurice Connell *and others.* } Hugh Falvey, Esq., Dr., Easter and Trinity, 1775.

	£	s.	d.
Taking instructions at Corke for a Bill	0	6	8
Search in Dublin for, but could not find any Prior Bill	0	6	8
Drawing Draft of Bill 36 Sheets	0	18	0
Copy in Wide lines to be perused by Counsel	0	6	0
Paid fee to Counsel for perusing	1	9	3
Instructions and attendances	0	13	4
To engrossing the Bill	0	18	0
Parchment and Stamps	0	5	0
Signing and filing	0	4	0

	£	s.	d.
Drawing affidavit of Plaintiff's Religion, and Stamp	0	3	0
Paid swearing and filing	0	3	7½
Sub pœna in 4 copies	0	6	0
Drawing and engrossing Declaration of Trust	0	6	8
Stamps and Paper	0	14	0
Paid Consideration to the Plaintiffs	0	11	4½
Entering appearances for 3 of the Defendants	0	10	6
Attatchment and Clk. to stamp	0	7	0
Alias and pluris Clk. and stamp	0	14	0
Proclamation of Rebellion, and stamp and Clk.	0	10	2½
Commission of Rebellion	1	4	8½
Term fees and sollicitations	0	15	0
Ingrossing a second Bill in the name of Martin Dell against Maurice Connell, Hugh Falvey, and Alexander Carthy only	0	18	0
Parchment and stamps	0	15	0
Signing and fyling	0	5	0
Declaration of Trust and stamp	0	5	0
Affidavit of Plaintiff's Religion, and stamp	0	3	0
Swearing and fyling	0	3	0
Sub pœna	0	4	0
Appearance thereto	0	10	6
Postage of letters to Trinity, 1775	0	1	4
Michaelmas Term, 1775—			
Attatchment to the Sergt.-at-Arms	0	16	10½
Paid the Sergt. for his Return	1	2	7
Brief for Counsel for Sequestration	0	3	4
Counsel on motion and attendance	0	12	6
Paid for the Order and Clke	0	11	6
Writ of sequestration	0	17	6
Return	0	3	4
Paid for the Cert. of Bill and no answer	0	3	3
Order for hearing fee and Clk. and stamp	0	7	0
Copy and service	0	1	1
Setting down the cause for hearing	0	3	6
Drawing affidavit and service of order for a hearing, stamp and swearing	0	4	7½
Drawing Brief for a hearing	0	10	0
One Copy 5 Sheets	0	10	0
To Counsel therewith	2	5	6
Attending Counsel therewith	0	5	0
Attending on the hearing	0	5	0
Paid Cryer, Court Keeper, and Tipstaff	0	4	10½
Paid Ushers	0	2	2
Drawing Draft Decree, 24 sheets at 4 p. sheet	0	8	0
To Counsel for perusing and signing	1	2	9
Two copies	0	8	0
Stamps	0	2	0
Signing Decree and attending	0	2	6
Paid office fees for fyling and engrossing Decree	4	19	8½
Fee on Enrollment	0	6	8
Paid for the Injunction to get the Possession, fee and Clke	0	13	8
To Sheriff for giving Possession	2	10	0
Drawing Conveyance to the Discoverer	0	13	4
Ingrossing the same	0	13	4
Parchment and stamp	0	3	0
Paid Consideration to the Discoverer	1	2	9

						£	s.	d.
Attending the Execution of Deed	...	...	...	...	0	6	8
Memorial and Registering ...	...	...	...	...	1	0	0
Postage	...	...	...	...	0	3	0
1775—August 30—							
Received yr Rect on account	...	...	...	...	£37	4	2
						4	7	6

Received the contents in full of all demands this 10th of September, 1776.

Tho' Franks, Junr.

Note G.

Extracts from a Diary of a Journey from Dublin to London in 1765, by Maurice O'Connell, of Darrynane, being his Impressions of Inns, Royalty, and the British Museum.

I obtained the manuscript journal of a trip to London in Hunting Cap's handwriting from the Rev. Matthew Russell, S.J., who received from the Liberator's son Morgan, late Registrar of Deeds, the bulk of the papers borrowed by his sister Ellen, Mrs. FitzSimon, of Glancullen, for a Life of the Liberator. Several older family papers were in the collection. I fancy a few extracts from the journal may amuse the reader.

Hunting Cap begins thus—

"Sent my horses to the Cross Keys, the 28th January, 1765. My Servt to Dublin ye 1st February, 1765, att 4s 4d per week."

He and party slept on board the packet, and "lay at Poolbegg to Sunday," and were two days and two nights crossing to Holyhead.

There is nothing of special interest in the brief records of the journey, except that the young mountaineer seems to have had some eye for scenery—a rare quality in those days. He says—

"Between Bangor and Conway is the Inaccesible and Extraordinary Mountain Pen Man Mawr, Projecting into ye Sea; on ye edge of which is ye High Road wch is cover'd from ye Edge of ye stupendous Cliff by a six foot Wall, the Country at ye same time being Romantick and Agreable."

He notices the magnificent Castle of Conway, considers St. Winifred's Well "well worth a traveller's view." The Irish gentlemen seem to have ridden to Chester, for the item occurs, "Discharged and paid our Holyhead guides, which, between Mr. Dillon and me, came to £1 10s., including 3s we gave the guide gratuity."

"*Mine Host's Discourse in Chester.*

"Our Landlord [in Chester], one Church, an intelligent Man, was amazed at ye Conduct of ye Irish Landlords, and told a passage of a Townsman of his, a Mercer, who had some years before made a purchase in ye neighbourhood, and made a Lease of it for 16 years, at ye Expiration of wch another Man bid him £30 more for the Land, wch he refused wth indignation, said ye Tenant paid Him Honestly, and should always be continued at ye old rent, and y^t ye Bidder must be Bad Man and a Rogue. This Landlord mentioned ye taxes he paid yearly—his rent for House and Land was £150, Exclusive of a small Estate wch may be worth £60 yearly, his Window Tax was £40 yearly; Malt Liquor Liscences, £27; Duty on every Barrell of D^o. 32 q^{ns}, 7^s 6^d; but on ye whole his Tax yearly, including Land Tax, amounted to £80 yearly—an amazing sum, and yet the Man was Rich and Easy in life."

The comfort and wealth of the great old posting inns impress the Irish travellers, who are now proceeding in post-chaises. Hunting Cap distributes his adjectives as judiciously as a guide-book; passes through what he describes as "agreeable," "fertile," "picturesque," "barren," or "pastoral scenes," and visits the noble buildings in old cities.

Eight miles from Castle Bromwich, where they dined the day they left Birmingham, they came to an inn worth recording—the great inn of Meriton.

"We halted at the Great Inn, a noble Building, fit for ye Residence of any Nobleman in England, wth suitable Offices, Cellars, and very elegant Gardens, Decorated wth a pond and Canall, gravel walks, and all done by ye ffather of ye present Occupier, who alsoe holds Lands to the amount of £450 yearly. His Ale was remarkably Good, and a vast variety of itt. I have drunk of 3 kinds, very fine and palatable. Hence we travelled 8 Miles to Coventry."

He next records his first sight of London. The party slept at St. Albans,

"21 miles of London, in Herefordshire. This day we Ran 39 Miles, p^d 6 Turnpikes, and passed thro' 4 Different Shires.

"On Tuesday morning ye 12 set out, travelled thro' a pleasant Country to Barnett, where we breakfasted, and within a mile of wch is a House of ye Late Admiral Byng's —a very fine Seat, and Close by the Road. Hence thro' ffinchley Common to Highgate, on a Hill within 2 Miles of

London, commanding a Beautiful prospect of this Great City. Between yᵉ towns of Highgate and Barnett the Country is beautifully interspersed with handsome Houses. Not far from the Road at High Gate yᵉ Captain was sworn very Regularly, and thence we got to London at 10 O'Clock, on the whole 21 Miles, and put up at yᵉ Axe in Aldermanbury."

"*Impressions of the Royal Family.*

"On Sunday, the 17th, after hearing Mass at Moorfields, Messrs. Dillon and Cantwell and I went to St. James's to se the Royall ffamily. We gott into the Antichamber, thro' wᶜʰ all the Company pass to gett into the Drawing Room, and where the Gentleman Usher attends, and some of the Guards. Here we saw the nobility of both sexes as they went thro' most Magnificently and Brilliantly decked out, and in some time came the Royall ffamily in their way from Chapell. Fforemost was the King, a Tall, Ruddy, fair Haired, sandy complexioned, smooth faced, but soft countenanced man, inclined to be fleshy, Discurcive and Harmless, good humoured, but [of a] weak, injudicious Turn. Next after him was the Queene, a Low, pale faced, mean Looking Woman, large Mouth, and nose a little turned up, brown Hair, and on the whole rather ordinary, and not the Least Majestick. After came the Dukes of York and Gloucester, both in Complexion and Countenance like the King, York's only a Little more Lively, but neither soe tall, and York's yᵉ lowest of the three. After them yᵉ princes Henry Frederick and Frederick William; the former very like yᵉ rest of the Brothers, but the Latter Dark Complexion and hair, and eyes, and more Snug, sensible Look and Aspect than any of the Brothers. After came the two Princesses—yᵉ elder, Louise, Extremely Low, pale, sickly Countenanced, and puny, but Caroline Matilda, the younger, very tall for her age, fresh Complexioned, and Comely. I should not from seeing them goe by yᵉ day be able to give soe minute a description. Where I had a full oppertunity of viewing them attentively was on Wednesday Night after, at Covent Garden, at the play of Coriolanus. The King and Queen in one box, Decorated with Scarlet and Silver, and opposite to it yᵉ 2 youngest princes in a box decorated wᵗʰ Green and Gold. Yᵉ Queen's Dress yᵗ light Blew and Silver, yᵉ King's Brown Cloath wᵗʰ Broad Gold Lace, and yᵉ Insignia of yᵉ Garter, wᶜʰ he always wears. The Two Dukes I often saw in the House of Lords and Park; the latter of which, Gloucester, is soe much in love wᵗʰ Lady Dowager Waldegrave, yᵗ she has this Week been ordered not to appear at Court, from apprehension that he would feign marry her. The King Extremely weak, and unfitt for G⁣ᵗ passes.

"Soe much for yᵉ ffamily. Now for remarkable places."

Hunting Cap makes just the proper remarks about Westminster Abbey ("a prodigious, large, ancient, but noble pile"), St. Paul's, the Tower, and their contents. "Innumerable," he exclaims, "are the magnificent Buildings of yˢ very Great City. I shall, therefore, only Touch on some of the most remarkable."

He begins his list with the British Museum, then housed in a different edifice from the present pile. Says Hunting Cap—

"*The Old British Museum.*

"First the British Museum exposed to view in Montague House. This was the Chief Mansion House of the Montague ffamily, built and Decorated at a most Immoderate expence, and purchased at only . . . 000 pᵈˢ, the ffamily being extinct, for laying out and Exposing the Museum. You go up a Grand Hall cover'd all over Wall and Ceiling with Noble paintings by the best hands, ascend a noble staircase wᵗʰ these Decorations still growing on you, and among other noble paintings you see the Sun in two opposite Corners of the Hall, shining on yᵉ ceiling, and reflecting all down it soe naturally and strongly to yᵉ Eye, as to cause an Astonishing Deception. Thence you lead into a suite of rooms Most Magnificent in themselves, where you see an Innumerable fund of curiosities Antient and Modern, Two Egyptian Mummies, Two Pillars of Agate and Amber, a vast Collection of Antient Roman Curiosities, Dresses, Arms, Medals, Tools, Sacrificing Implements, Coins, Statues, Paintings and Carvings, A noble and numerous Collection of Paintings by the first Hands of Every Country; all Foreign Fishes and Fowls, Insects and Animalls, Fossils and Minerals and Shells; with a variety of the forementioned rings, jewels, Arms, etc., etc., of foreign Countries, Antient and Modern; vast, Large, and Numerous Librarys in all Languages, with, in short, everything the whole World almost yᵗ is Rare and Curious. Whole sets of Agate and Amber Tea things and Spoons, an Agate Draget Box, etc., etc., mostly collected by the Late Sir Hans Sloane at a vast expence, and reckoned among the compleatest and best assorted Museum in Europe, and purchased from his Heirs att £25,000. You have here an Indian Scalp with the Hair on. You gett in here by Tickett, and pay noe Money. The time allowed to any one company is only 3 hours."

Note H.

Louis de France.

Louis de France, Dauphin de Viennois, only son of Louis XV., born September 4, 1729, died December 20, 1765. By his second wife, Maria of Saxony, he left three sons—Louis, Duc de Berri (Louis XVI.), Louis Comte de Provence (Louis XVIII.), and Charles Comte d'Artois (Charles X.). The Count has made an extraordinary mistake in describing the Duc de Berri, who succeeded his father as Dauphin, as the *second* son.—[R. O'C.]

BOOK III.

IN THE IRISH BRIGADE.

1769-1779.

Daniel Charles O'Connell joins as aide-major to "Clare's" (October, 1769)—*Kerry Chronicle* on Dan—Colonel Meade—Royal Swedes—First letter from Dan on entering Brigade—No promotion in Royal Suédois Regiment—Succeeds Conway as aide-major in "Clare's"—Regimental affairs—Debts—Chevalier Fagan helps—Lord Kenmare's advice—Chevalier Fagan to Hunting Cap—Dan's sense of honour—Series of letters to Maurice O'Connell: from Dan, Rochefort (December, 1770)—Sailing for East Indies—Captain aide-major—His father's death—Letter from Chevalier Fagan—From Dan (the Road of Rochefort, January, 1771)—Farewell letter—Dan's first letter from Mauritius (July, 1771)—Six months' voyage—Hopes for war—Provisions scarce—Hard times—Chevalier Fagan again—Hunting Cap at home—Morgan O'Connell of Carhen's marriage—Catherine O'Mullane—Morgan of Carhen—Maur-ni-Dhuiv again—Romantic anecdotes—Arthur O'Leary, "the Outlaw"—Fair Mary Baldwin's love-story—Niece Abby—1772: James Gould writes to congratulate Maurice on the major's return—Smuggling—Hugh Falvey, of Faha, the friendly "discoverer"—From Daniel (Clonakilty, April, 1773)—Tralee—Cork—Finds a ship for Dunkirk—Hopes to march in June for Poland or Italy—Jerry McCrohan—Ample sea stores—Dunkirk (April, 1773)—After a passage of four days—Military acquaintances—Alliance with England—Military movements—Setting out for Bethune—Jerry Falvey—Family affairs—Bethune (April, 1773)—McCarthy Mor, the real chief of the family—Charles McCarthy—Margaret McMahon—Lawsuit with Herberts—Lord Clare—No war at present—South Sea discovery—Late for Indian promotion—Arthur O'Leary, "the Outlaw," shot—Eileen's grief—Vengeance—Bethune (June, 1773)—Poor Arthur—His widow and orphans—Preparations for war laid aside—Military gossip—Tom Conway—Bethune (September, 1773)—McCarthy Mor—Irish Parliament—Certificate in favour of a rebel—Nancy's marriage—Hunting Cap's wife—Leaving for Rocroi—Eugene McCarthy—Affairs of the nation—Chevalier O'Mahony—Count O'Mahony—Lord Clare—Rocroi (February, 1774)

—The Duke d'Aiguillon and military affairs—Mighty changes expected—Miss Browne's marriage—Talk of visiting Ireland again—Rocroi (July, 1774)—Death of the king—Duke d'Aiguillon—A well-wisher to Ireland—Military gossip—Fears a dissolution of the Brigade—Hopes of going to court—Eugene McCarthy—Colonel Meade—Lord Thomond—Rocroi (August, 1774)—Visit to Ireland in October—Colonel Meade—Clohina—Death of Colonel Meade—Rocroi (October, 1774)—Going home—Regimental movements—Death of Mrs. Fitz-Maurice—Major Sullivan—Paris (October, 1774)—Trip to Ireland postponed—Military affairs—Friendship of Doctor Mahony—Administration in France—Mr. Crosbie, of Ardfert—Lord Shelbourne—Colonel James Conway—Abbé Connell—Episcopacy of Kerry—Doctor Mahony and the chevalier—Paris (December, 1774)—Money matters—Mr. Hickson—Military constitution—Changes in the Brigade—"Bulkeley's"—"Clare's"—"Dillon's"—Major Conway—The Marquis of FitzJames—Gloomy forebodings—Lord Kenmare—Marquis de Syvrac—Paris (January, 1775)—The critical situation of the Brigade—Courtly acquaintances—Evil forecasts—Bishopric of Kerry—Abbé Connell—The prince at Rome—Obligations to Doctor Mahony—The last of "Clare's"—Dan pays a visit to his family—He hopes to serve his country—The Count de Maillebois—Sir John O'Sullivan—Cork (March, 1776)—Clohina—Abby Gould—Passage in the Havre packet—Troops marching—Cork the rendezvous for troops bound for America—Dr. Connell—Jemmy Baldwin—Letter from Robin Conway—Morgan in Cork—Mr. Wise—Havre (March, 1776)—Passage takes six days—Denis McCrohan—Going to Paris—Cambray (June, 1776)—Expectation of military changes—Formation of regiments, etc.—McCarthy Mor—Walsh's regiment—Dan on other people's small boys—Introduced to the Ministers—Studies—Calais (July, 1776)—Family affection—Bad health—Eugene McCarthy in Count Walsh de Serrant's regiment—Jeffrey Maurice O'Connell's boy—Death of Daniel O'Connell, of Ballinablown—Intercedes for Arthur O'Leary's widow—Calais (September, 1776)—Quite well—Regimental movements—Talks of a trip to Paris—Le Comte de Maillebois in command—His kindness—Young Falvey—Mick Falvey—Birth of Morgan's second son—Gravelines (December, 1776)—Military preparations—Flattering offers of the American Congress—Major Conway—A tour to Paris next month—Jeffrey Maurice's boy—Abbé Moriarty—James Baldwin—Notice of "Berwick's"—Paris (January, 1777)—Forms a design of going to America—He is refused permission to go—M. de Maillebois presents him to the Ministers—Faction and intrigue—Chevalier O'Mahony—Rickard O'Connell—Gambling—Tom FitzMaurice—Cousin Morty in Germany—Paris (March, 1777)—Roguery of Dan's servant—Presented at court by M. de Maillebois—Difficulties of promotion—American plan—American War—Chevalier O'Mahony—Mr. Trench—Mrs. Mahony—Mr. Mahony, lieut.-colonel in the Spanish Service—Count Mahony, ambassador at Vienna—Burses founded by Dr. Connell—Certificate of baptism—Arms—Pedigree—Gravelines (May, 1777)—Where to send a boy (in reply to Hugh Falvey)—Dijon—Jerry Falvey—Major Conway—Florence—James Mahony—Captain Rick O'Connell—Paris (October, 1778)—Pleasing news of laws in favour of Roman Catholics—Sighing for the liberty of spilling his blood in defence of the English king—Friends and distinguished acquaintances—Some advantages offered in the East—Refused—His sister's illness—The pedigree—Paris (October, 1778)—Rick Connell arrives—Linen and genealogy required—Rumoured death of Tom Conway of desperate wounds—His recovery—Campaign in Bohemia—Military talents of Lacy—General Dalton—Army gossip—Sister Nancy—Captain Rickard O'Connell takes up the pen—His personality—His flirtations—Captain Rickard on Dan—Rickard's relations, etc.—Plot to murder him—His letter to Maurice Leyne—Waits on the Earl of Inchiquin—His friendship—Religion a bar—Daniel Charles O'Connell a major in "Berwick's"—Major O'Connell's advice—Hunting Cap lends money for Rickard's advancement—"Alps of difficulties"—Gratitude—His adored patron (our hero)—Camp near St. Malo (September, 1778)—Captain Rickard to Maurice Leyne—Joins the Brigade—Regimental duties—Colonel O'Connell—Chevalier O'Mahony—Colonel Conway—The drum beats!—March, 1779: Captain Rickard writes to Colonel O'Connell in Paris—Rickard to Maurice Leyne—Illness—Rickard sentimental—Approbation of the Colonel—A letter from Colonel O'Connell to Rickard, telling him of Count Walsh de Serrant's favour—Captain FitzMaurice—Offer of a commission in "Dillon's"—Going to Martinico—Wants Colonel O'Connell's approval—Colonel O'Connell says No—Rickard's commission in "Walsh's"—Captain O'Connor—August, 1779: Captain Rickard writes again to Maurice Leyne—Rickard a rebel—French war news—Cousin Conway—Dr. Sheehy—Père Felix O'Dempsey.

In the autumn of 1769 Count O'Connell entered the famous old Irish Brigade. His letters depict much of its inner life, but are incomparably less graphic than those of his cousin Rickard O'Connell, from which I shall also quote. Owing to his transfer to the German Legion, my hero was not with the Brigade on the dark day when it was disbanded. A separate chapter, by many degrees the most historically important in this book, describes his successful negotiations with the British Government about the creation of an Irish Brigade in the service of England, led by the late officers of dead Louis XVI., and with no conditions contrary to the faith or honour of Irish Catholics. The account of my hero in the *Kerry Chronicle* of March 9, 1785, gives a brief summary of his career, which is exactly borne out by the old letters except in one particular. It states that Lord Clare appointed him his adjutant, but young Lord Clare had not yet joined, and it was the managers of the regiment who received him into the Irish ranks. It states also that the peace following the Seven Years' War had stopped all promotion except by seniority and routine, and that of necessity Mr. O'Connell remained a subaltern for seven or eight years.

Young Dan O'Connell owed the superior training which first advanced his fortunes to his own steadiness of conduct. He was exceedingly strong and healthy, tall, spare, and muscular, with great powers of enduring fatigue and hunger, and no craving whatsoever for drink. He frequently observes incidentally, à propos of privations and illnesses, that a scanty supply of meat or drink is no great trial to him. He was likewise quite free from any tendency to gambling. His foreign colonel pitched on this singularly constituted youth to be guide, philosopher, and friend to his own young brother, and, to keep them together, had procured him an order of admission to the famous Military College of Strasbourg, whose portals seldom opened to our countrymen. Doubtless the abstemiousness and the power of sustained application were partly due to an honourable ambition, but they were to a considerable extent natural idiosyncrasies, idleness and drink being actually distasteful to my hero.

Daniel O'Connell's sojourn in Paris in 1769 was attended with the most solid advantages. As "sous-aide-major" (assistant-adjutant) he reaped some honour from the fine show made by the Royal Swedish Regiment. Nothing could exceed the friendship and good will of his colonel. His cousin Conway, who was resigning the "aide-major"-ship of "Clare's" on being made major, doubtless used his influence with Colonel Meade, who had the practical control of the regiment while its boy-colonel, young Lord Clare, was yet being educated (this was the young orphan son of the veteran of Fontenoy). If we substitute "Colonel Meade" for "Lord Clare," the account given in the old Kerry paper of 1785 exactly tallies with the letters. It is important to mark the date on which the last colonel of the Irish Brigade first entered its honoured ranks, viz. in October, 1769. All his modern biographers make him enter in 1757—twelve years before.

The contemporary account is correct as to dates and as to facts, saving Lord Clare's personal intervention. Having stated that Count O'Connell joined the Royal Swedes at the close of the Seven Years' War, the *Kerry Chronicle* says—

"He was promoted after a few months to a sub-lieutenancy. It was then near the close of the last continental war [the Seven Years' War], the termination of which first put an end to further advancement out of the ordinary routine, so that Mr. O'Connell remained a subaltern for seven or eight years. Unlike the generality of the young officers of the French Army, of whom it is no libel to say that dissipation has not anywhere more fervent votaries, he applied himself wholly to the study of his profession, both in theory and practice. His industry was not employed in vain. He acquired such a complete knowledge of discipline that, contrary to the general practice, Lord Clare [it should be Colonel Meade who was commanding the regiment] selected him in preference to all his own officers for aid-major in his regiment —an appointment which, as it gives the rank of captain and opens out a sure road to higher promotion, is usually bestowed by the colonel on his own relations or favourites in the corps. In this capacity he continued to serve both in the Indies and at home, till the death of Lord Clare furnished the Minister with a pretext to reduce that regiment, or, what was equally injurious to the officers, to incorporate it with that of the Duke of Berwick."

The long series of letters describes all this. Again the kindest of friends, Chevalier Fagan, came to the young soldier's aid. He supplied the funds which bought the outfit, including the famous red uniform so conspicuous at Fontenoy. It was not merely a matter of a change of coat, but of the purchase of a complete Indian outfit; hence the loan of sixty guineas, which weighed so heavily on my hero's mind, lest he should die without its being repaid. General Sir Martin Dillon lent me an old French coloured plate of an officer of "Clare's" in 1770, and a more becoming or picturesque garb no good-looking youth need desire. The scarlet coat is shaped much like the brown coats worn at Dublin Castle Drawing-rooms a few years ago. The facings are of the O'Brien colours—green and yellow, yellow plastron and cuffs, and the coat-tails turned back with green. The breeches and gaiters are white, with dark garters outside the gaiter. The hat is a most picturesque and becoming small three-cornered beaver, bearing the famous white cockade, and bound with silver. Silver epaulettes, a gilt gorget, with a silver star and falling lace ruffles, add great elegance to the dress. In the print the officer of "Clare's" is armed with both sword and musket—the latter small, short, and furnished with a short bayonet.

The young man had to sail almost immediately for India. The three following letters of Chevalier Fagan's and Dan's are in the letter-book; the two next were lent me by the present Daniel O'Connell, who found them in old Maurice O'Connell's *escritoire*.

Paris, the 15 9bre, 1769.

My Last to you, my Dear Brother, from this Town acknowledged the Receipt of your Bill on Mr. Woulfe, which has been duly acquitted, and do apprehend it will appear extraordinary to you to have me Apply to you so Soon for money, after receiving my usual remittance; but shall in a few words explain things so as to justify the necessity I am under to induse y^e at the same time to speak your mind freely with respect to futurity. Among many reasons that made me desirous of spending some time at Paris, the most important was that of my Advancement to become Aid-Major in some regiment. I drew near Court for to look out in the method of succeeding, and seeing no appearance of a vacancy in Royal Suédois Regiment, I bethought me it would be prudent to Accept the offer made me by M. Meade, Colonel of Clare's Regiment, of the Aid-Majority, vacant by the advancement of Conway, our Cousin, to the Majority. This proposal has been so much the more agreable to me, as I may rely on M. Meade's friendship and the pleasure of having so close a connection with Conway, for whom I have a real friendship and regard. Nothing could be more obliging than the extream desire Colonel Meade shows of having me in his Regt., and as there has been no example of an Aid-Major's having been drawn from out of a foreign corps such as the German and Irish, not even out of one Regt. into an other, he had a good deal of trouble to succeed, tho' one of the officers of ye nation the best befriended. You can Easily conceive that three months of indispensable stay in Paris, besides a total change of Regimentals and Equipage, lays me under a great deal of expence. Every stitch of my former Equipage is useless. Add to this the debts I had been obliged to contract for the Camp; but I already mentioned to you such have been the unavoidable circumstances that threw me into distress of money, for which I have and had recourse to my friends, ye warmest of whom is Fagan. Had he not given me a lodging, I should have come to the ground. In regard to futurity, my Dear Brother, the point is this—My application to my trade and the facility God has been pleased to give me, put me in the way of pushing in the service. Now I am on the high road, so consult yourself and see if Ambition and the love of your family will engage you to forward me in my pursuits. I never shall be extravagant nor lay out a penny but for my advancement, less upon my honour for my own sake than for that of my friends and family. Now, it's necessary I should form a plan, and must found it on what I can expect from you. I had a strong desire of stepping over, but on my Lord Kenmare's advice laid aside that notion because of the troubles among y^e. Besides, I am persuaded by Cousin Robin Conway ye have no eager desire of seeing me, so I defer. Till then I heartily wish my Dear Brother MAY *conceive* things in the light I do. If not shall always comply with his will, and shall ever be y^r fond and respectful Brother,

DANL. O'CONNELL.

My fond duty to my father and mother, and love to brother Morgan, Sister Connell, and all relations. My kind comp^{ts} to Mr. and Mrs. Fagan. Let me entreat you'll give Stephen Fagan, of Cork, the preference of your Butter. I owe many obligations to his worthy brother. My address: A mons. O'C., Aide-Major du Régiment de Clare, Irlandois, chez Mons. Fagan, rue de Richelieu, vis-à-vis la fontaine, à Paris.

We have no letters for several months, but just as my hero is sailing for India he writes, and a month before, his truest and best of friends, Chevalier Fagan, writes too. The young kinsman, who was like a son to him, has left, and the veteran writes from the now lonely lodgings, where his beloved "Dan, the best behaved and most brilliant" of Irish lads, had sojourned for months with him. But for that timely shelter, my hero emphatically declares he could never have pushed his fortunes in Paris. Maurice was deaf to the young brother's entreaties for an Indian outfit, and the kind old captain advances the money, risking it willingly, yet at the same time pretty sure he won't be let lose it. I have seldom read more touching letters than the old captain's and the young adjutant's (so I suppose we are to construe "Ayde-Major").

Chevalier Fagan to Hunting Cap.

Paris, 9bre ye 30th, 1770.

Sir,—I lent 1200 Livres to a young gentleman of your acquaintance, which, from the opinion I have of his Parents, I expected would have been remitted to me before now, and as my circumstances are not equal to the pleasure I have always had in obliging a friend, I am sure you'll prevail on them to acquitt themselves of a debt of honour if you think it such. If otherwise (which I can hardly suppose) I beg you may convince them I shall think myself sufficiently repaid by the service my money has been to the best behaved and most brilliant young man I have ever met with.

As I presume they may depend on my veracity, I give them my word of honour he knows nothing of this letter, and that I chiefly write it because I am informed his not being able to pay me preys on him, notwithstanding all I have done to make him easy thereabout. As I intend leaving this about the middle of next January, if you favour me with an answer, I beg it may be speedily, if possible, and desire you may think me happy in ever in power to be of the least use to you in this country, who am, Sir,

Your most obedient servant,

C. FAGAN.

Address: à Monsieur, Monsieur Fagan, ancien officier de Dragons, vis-à-vis la fontaine, Rue de Richelieu, à Paris.

Rochefort, 8bre [1] 20, 1770.

My Dear Brother,—I have at length recd. a letter of yours dated Novembre 22d, by which you tell me that you have answered very punctually my several letters. This appears to me very extraordinary. I see no moral possibility of their miscarrying all. I recd. no bill nor note of any kind these 13 months, so believe you'ld do well to write to your Correspondent on whom you drew to know if said bill has been presented to him for payment, and if not to stop it. I entreat, my Dear Brother, you'll acquit my debt to Captain Fagan, to whom I owe 60gs. I very probably pay you an age after, perhaps never. Let me request you'll do honour to this.

When you receive my letter I shall be no more in Europe. My regiment is just ready to embark for the East Indies. If

[1] It must be December.

I come back from that country, you may depend my first desire shall be to see my family. I part Captain Aid-Major. Adieu, my Dear Brother. I have been a long time since informed of my poor father's death. Comfort my Dr Mother, and tell her I hope to see her well on my return to Europe. I Embrace my Dr Morgan and Sisters. Adieu once more, and Believe me Eternally, your fond Brother,

DANL. O'CONNELL.

Send a bill to Captain Fagan, payable to his order. All friends here are well. This letter Captain Fagan will enclose to you in one of his own.

The kind old father had died, and in his will had left £20 to his young son. This sum he does not seem to have received at the period of writing.

The probable rescinding of the sailing orders to "Clare's," which the Chevalier Fagan anticipated, did not occur; so in the very first days of 1771 he sends Captain Daniel's farewell letter to his people, with a brief and dignified note. Dan evidently sent on the letter to his friend, and then wrote a second letter direct home as the ship was about sailing, on January 15.

Paris, Jan' ye 9th, 1771.

SIR,—As I expected from the change made in our ministry that your Brother's Regt. might have had counter orders, I postponed sending you the enclosed before now. He is actually at sea, and it is not yet known whereunto bound. I flattered myself you'd have favoured me with an answer to my last before now, and rather suppose a miscarriage than that you decline a civility I am entitled to,

Who am, Sir,
Your most humble and obedient Servant,

C. FAGAN.

From the Road of Rochefort, January the 15th, 1771.

MY DEAR BROTHER,—I am this day come aboard with all my regiment, and await only the first favourable wind for to sail. Our destination is supposed to be the East Indies. The calls I am under on this occasion have obliged me to have recourse to the purse of my friends, the more so as I have not received a penny from you near two years past. I have drawn upon you for two bills, one of thirty-five and the other of twenty-five guineas, for to clear myself entirely before my departure on an Expedition which will probably become perilous. I hope and Entreat you'll do honour to my Draft. It shall be in all appearance the Last. Adieu, Dr Dear Brother. I received the letter ye sent me by the way of Bordeaux, mentioning my D^r father's Death. May the Almighty be merciful to his Soul! Comfort my poor Mother. Reckon little on me, as my fate is hazardous. If I live and Come back, I shall be happy to see you all again. If not, Look upon me as a tender and loved fond child and Brother.

DANL. CONNELL.

I embrace B^r Morgan, Sisters O'C. Console my Dr Mother. If possible to let you hear from me, I shall. I am Captain Ayde-Major, and hope I shall soon be better. If war is declared at least hope to deserve more.

Daniel Charles O'Connell to his brother Maurice, from the Mauritius.

At the Island of France, the 25 July, 1771.

MY DR. BROTHER,—I arriv'd here the 10th Instant, after six months' voyage. I wrote to you from Gorea and from the Cape of Good Hope, where we put in. I can't well tell you my further destination, whether to remain here or go to Pondicherry, whether war or peace, having left France when everything was in a hubbub. I am, thank God, perfectly well in health, tho' a little weary of the turbulent life I lead these 18 months, but a happy and glorious Campaign would console me of All my trouble and hardships. It's with the utmost trouble that we support life here. We are a numerous corps of troops, and provisions very scarce. No money at all. War alone can make our lot better; worse it can't be. I am glad my Dr Brother can form no idea of this misery. I am nowise Struck Down. Adversity has a term as well as prosperity. Our Soldiers are good and willing, tho' poor; the greater the misery, the more intrepid when question of plunder. I shall lay hold of every oppertunity of writing to you. I apprehend, however, I shall meet with few. My fond Duty to my Dr Mother. I hope she is healthy. May God preserve her, and give me the pleasure of seeing her one day! Love to Dr Brother Morgan, Sisters, etc.

Adieu, my Dr Brother. I request you will Let me hear from you if possible. I hope to see you in some years. Adieu. I shall ever remain y^r fond and tender Brother,

DANL. O'CONNELL.

Cousin Conway desires his best comp^ts to you and family.

I hope you have paid my debts. It's the only pecuniary request I purpose ever making you.

Chevalier Fagan writes under this—

Sir,—I have forwarded this letter on receipt, convinced it must be pleasing to you to hear from so worthy a Brother. I most probably will be in Kerry next Spring. Shall be proud of the pleasure of meeting you there, and expect that, when personally known to you, you'll thank me about reminding you of an obligation, tho' I hate to refer to any, I have ever conferred, even the pecuniary ones, if not directed to do so, as necessitated by circumstances.

Your Humble and Obedient Servant,
C. Fagan.

When opportunity offers, I beg you may Let my Father know that I intend parting hence for London on the beginning of next month.

Paris, Jan. ye 5.

I do not see any letter of Captain Daniel O'Connell's acknowledging the trifling legacy of £20 left him in his father's will, but I have no reason to suppose it was withheld.

The next letter of the young captain's to be found after the one announcing his arrival in the Mauritius is written as he was about sailing from Ireland in the April of 1773. From a later letter he seems to have served in the East Indies also during the interval of a year and three quarters which remains unchronicled in the letters. All officers in the French Service could easily get leave in winter, so that we may suppose five or six of the eighteen months to have been passed at home, then the voyage from the East Indies took six months. The present Daniel O'Connell thinks his distinguished namesake, who was too used to the sea to feel either fear or illness, got conveyed on some semi-scientific sailing trip round the world. Shortly after he got back to France, in 1773, he wrote to his brother—

"The officer of the Navy with whom I made the South Sea Discovery, is gone out a second time to that part of the world with three ships, the one of which is a 64. He wrote to me to propose me that Journey. He was gone before I arrived here, where I found his letter."

What did they discover? Was it treasure, territory, some strange bird or beast, some tidal or atmospheric phenomenon? Whatever it was, Dan had described it to Maurice by word of mouth, and unless some further hoard of letters be discovered, we shall never know.

De Bougainville discovered two archipelagos in the South Seas, which he named Les Navigateurs and La Louisiade. He returned *viâ* the Mauritius, in 1769. Our hero consequently did not accompany him, but he most probably obtained Colonel Meade's leave to go on some subsequent cruise. He would have had time for this between the dates of this letter and the next, which chronicles his departure after leave. Six months seems to have been the longest leave. Dr. Sigerson gives me the following information about "Gorea," extracted from an old French school-book:—

"*Gorée* was a French colony on the Island of Gorée, which lies south-west of the French colony on the Isle of St. Louis, at the mouth of the Senegal, on the West Coast of Africa." "This," he remarks, "was on the way to or from the Cape of Good Hope. The expedition in which O'Connell took part probably helped to found or augment French colonies."

There is a wonderful difference in the tone of the letters henceforth. The boyish habit of deference and dependence vanishes, to be replaced by the most affectionate familiarity. Maurice also is ready with generous aid, more than once pressed on the full-grown man in a manner very different to the small supplies grudgingly doled out to the high-spirited boy, who underwent a perfect purgatory between pinching and scraping to pay for the masters and fine clothes that were necessary for the pushing of his fortunes, and forcing his pride to sue for the small doles so grudgingly administered from home. At the same time, the later letters are so full of the wildness and extravagance of the young Irish lads, especially the handsome ones, that one can hardly blame Maurice for suspecting the boy to have spent on personal luxuries what he really spent on education and appearance. Any sort of show was eminently distasteful to Maurice O'Connell, or Hunting Cap, as he was always called. He refused to pay the tax imposed on the beaver hat, which was always worn in dress by the old-fashioned gentry. He adopted instead a hunting-cap, whence his nickname, "Hunting Cap" ("Murrish-a-Cauppeen"), is the hero of many an anecdote.

When Captain Daniel, of the Irish Brigade, came home after an absence of eleven years, he found many changes. Kindly Donal Mor had gone to his long rest, and was buried in the ruined church of the Abbey Island, where he, Maur-ni-Dhuiv, and Maurice sleep in the one large tomb. The lady-like nonentity, Maurice's "Molly," was nominal lady of the house, and of her kindness Dan always retained a warm recollection. His brother Morgan had also married. His "Kitty," Miss Catherine O'Mullane, of Whitechurch, County Cork, was a charming, bright little woman, clever, capable, and lady-like. She was not a bit pretty, and the sin is laid to her charge that she introduced cock-noses, bad teeth, bad hair, and common sense into the family, though, indeed, of the latter her mother-in-law had introduced more than enough. She was the mother of ten fine children, and, when left a comparatively young widow, brought them up admirably. Sir James, her youngest son, was supposed to most resemble the older generation. The Liberator and most of the others were of quite a different type. The pictures of Hunting Cap and Count O'Connell show long, oval faces and long, straight features. The three brothers of that generation were so far like their three nephews in being tall, powerful, blue-eyed, dark-haired men. I knew old Sir James well. He used to speak of his mother with devoted affection and respect, as wise, witty, and kindly, and one whose children rose up and called her blessed.

Daniel O'Connell, of Darrynane, has supplied the following notice of her husband, whose grandson and namesake I married. My husband was a very handsome, jolly, tall, stout, fresh-looking man, and the old folk of the family always said that Morgan John reminded them of Morgan of Carhen.

Mr. V. J. Coppinger, B.L., of Pembroke Road, discovered the Protestant marriage licence of Morgan and Catherine O'Mullane in the Record Office, Dublin. All Catholics who expected to inherit landed property took out these Protestant licences, but were married by their own priests. On April 16, 1771, the Protestant Bishop of Cork grants his licence to Morgan O'Connell, of Darrynane, esquire, and Catherine O'Mullane, of the parish of Holy Trinity, Cork, spinster;

surety, John O'Mullane. Her sister Ellen got a similar licence to marry Francis Ryan, merchant, Cork (surety, Morgan Connell, Darrynane), in December of the same year.

They had another sister, Mrs. Nagle, said to have been a very charming woman, who lived until 1830.

Kate O'Mullane's brother and nephew were both very extravagant, and the Liberator purchased from the latter a fragment of property called Brittas, near Mallow, worth about £300 a year. Count O'Connell presented him with the purchase money. He settled it on his second son, Morgan.

I shall now insert his representative's account of Morgan of Carhen. The O'Mullanes being extinct, and the old house of Carhen being dismantled, I have failed to find any account of the O'Mullanes. The papers at Darrynane all refer to its own inhabitants of different generations.

[Mrs. M. J. O'Connell has given a full account of the Count O'Connell's elder brothers, John and Maurice ("Hunting Cap"), but has left it to me to furnish a few notes on the third, Morgan, my great-grandfather.

The most remarkable fact about him is that he was the father of "the Liberator," but for which circumstance his career would be quite devoid of interest.

He was left some small means by his father, and, marrying a lady of an old family, Miss Catherine O'Mullane, of Whitechurch, County Cork, settled at Carhen, about a mile from the present market town of Cahirsiveen; the ruins of the house he built there still remain, and are pointed out to strangers as the birthplace of his famous son.

Besides the Liberator, his wife bore him three other sons and six daughters. Their rich and childless uncle at Darrynane looked on the boys almost as his own children, and, besides paying for their education, left all his means to the three survivors of them—one, the second son, having died young, an officer in Walsh's regiment of the (English) Irish Brigade.

Morgan O'Connell, like his brother, Hunting Cap, was a keen, shrewd man of business, and took an active part in the smuggling-trade; he also kept a kind of general store where

Cahirsiveen now stands, in which he seems to have dealt in pretty nearly everything, "from a needle to an anchor." This was not, in the middle of the last century, looked on as derogatory to a gentleman in the way it would now be. My readers will recall Pope's lines, in the "Essay on Man"—

> "Boastful and rough, your first son is a squire;
> The next a tradesman, meek, and much a liar."

Besides his trading and farming, which he carried on extensively, my ancestor established salt-pans at Carhen, which is close to an inlet of Valentia harbour. When the chief products of the country were salted butter and provisions, this was not only a means of profit to himself, but a benefit to his neighbours.

He gradually acquired a considerable landed estate, part held under Trinity College, Dublin, and part under Lord Lansdowne, until 1806, when he purchased the fee of the latter. The lease of the college lands expired in 1865,[1] the lease also containing a covenant for perpetual renewal on the expiration of each life, by the insertion of a new one and payment of a fine. Donal Mahony took this lease as trustee for a number of his neighbours, to each of whom he subsequently made a sub-lease for his own term with *toties-quoties* covenants. These came to be known as "Shelbourne leases." In 1803-6 the fee of the lands was sold by the Lansdownes to the various tenants, who held them under the renewed leases. Many parts of the lands had been sub-let on *toties-quoties* leases, nearly all of which have been converted into fee-farm grants, under the Renewable Leaseholds Conversion Act. He also held other lands by terminable leases from sundry landlords.

Personally, Morgan O'Connell seems to have been a big, jolly man, popular with his neighbours, an inveterate snuff-

---

[1] The college lands were held by lease for twenty-one years, renewable by custom every seven years, on payment of certain fines; owing to these not being paid when due just after the great famine, the lease expired as stated. The Lansdowne property was held by what are known in Kerry as "Shelbourne leases." An enormous tract of country was leased about the year 1700 by Lord Shelbourne to Donal Mahony, of Dunloe, for ninety-six years, provided three lives named in the lease should so long last.

taker, and a remarkably good hand at a game of backgammon, of his prowess in which more than one legend still exists.

He died in 1807, long before which date he had given up his shop and smuggling business, and become a simple country gentleman.—D. O'C.]

Morgan and Catherine proceeded to Darrynane soon after their marriage, and I fancy a daughter or two were born there. The childless wife got jealous of the "fruitful mother of children," so they settled at what is now the ivied and ruined house of Carhen, near Cahirsiveen, where their famous son was born. Maur-ni-Dhuiv, if no longer nominally the mistress of Darrynane, still ruled in all essentials. Her husband had besought her and Maurice to remain together, and they carried out his behest. The bright-coloured silks opening over a satin petticoat, and fine lace caps and ruffles for dress, and the dimity and calamanco—the former like white twill bed-curtains, the latter like furniture chintz—that she used to wear in the mornings, were put aside, and for the rest of her long life the old lady is described as dressed in black silk, with white coif and kerchief, and plain cambric ruffles, without a particle of lace or coloured stuff. She is still spoken of as thus differently attired, and her appearance is traditionally remembered. The old smuggling-bills year after year set forth for her use a piece of rich black silk, and the French cambric for frills, coif, and kerchief, black silk stockings, and fine French shoes. The quaint old massive silver, the rare and beautiful Oriental china, the rococo mirrors she had smuggled in the "fifties," and the handsome massive furniture she and Maurice had caused to be built in Ireland, were as Dan had left them, and as they are to-day, not a split in the dark mahogany or a crack in its joinings, the beautiful brass scutcheons round the key-holes intact. Intact was the huge china punch-bowl used for christenings, too, likewise the perforated blue-and-white fruit-baskets, which, with the long-handled silver spoon that is about to stir the jam of a sixth generation, seem exempt from the mutabilities of time and fate.

His father's empty chair, his mother's black gown, and

the occasional genial presence of sister Kitty, were the chief changes, save, of course, the absence of some sisters, and all gentle maids had to marry young in those days.

When Dan came back at last, Nancy was the only sister at home, and she married soon after he left. During this visit, my hero met for the first time two of his brothers-in-law. In spite of the feud between Hunting Cap and Arthur O'Leary, he made the acquaintance of that handsome and charming outlaw, whom he found very agreeable, but whose imperious rashness filled the prudent soldier with apprehension for his fate—apprehensions very soon fulfilled. On this occasion he saw a good deal of his sister Mary and " Brother Baldwin,"[1] as he in future always styles that excellent, upright, and highly cultivated gentleman, evidently his favourite brother-in-law. Mary was married very soon after Dan went to France. She was the flower of the flock, blue-eyed and golden-haired. She had had a little romance of her own, sternly repressed by her redoubtable mother. The small trading-ships, which alone visited the wild south-west coast, conveyed such rare travellers as business brought over. One of these brigs was driven in on the rocks at Darrynane, and crew and passengers hospitably entertained for several days, until whatever could be saved was saved. I found many letters of thanks from persons so rescued and sheltered, among Maurice O'Connell's papers.

Among the rescued wayfarers was a very elegant young English gentleman, named Herbert, a near relative of the Earl of Powis, who had come over to visit some Irish estates. He profited by his sojourn to whisper his vows in fair Mary's not unwilling ears, and proceeded to address her mother. The stern old dame gave him a very bad reception. He vowed and swore he would obtain the formal consent of his parents, but she was obdurate, deeming that if he was an adventurer, of whom one knew nothing, he was no fit mate for her daughter, and that if he was the near relative of a great nobleman, he was not likely to be allowed to marry a simple gentlewoman of no great means, and the old lady was too proud to allow her daughter to enter any family on

[1] See Note E. p. 246.

sufferance; so the young man departed, with many vows and promises, and for several months nothing was heard of him. Golden-haired Mary might fret in secret, but her mother arranged her marriage with Mr. Baldwin, of Clohina, near Macroom, who made her a most excellent husband, but who by no means struck her fancy, as he was not young, and was a tall, gaunt, long-limbed personage, whose ungraceful stature was doubly conspicuous in an age of silk stockings and buckled shoes.

Mr. Baldwin, curiously enough, was a convert in penal days. His family had come over in Elizabeth's time, with their kinsmen, the Herberts, and had settled on Irish forfeitures, intermarrying with other Protestant families for a couple of centuries. James Baldwin and his younger brother secretly embraced the ancient faith, through the efforts of a Catholic tutor. On avowing it, they were turned out, and the elder brother suffered positive persecution from his father for a long time. At last the old gentleman relented, and he was enabled to marry. In 1762 he brought home Mary O'Connell, and with her a hundred and twenty head of black cattle, some mares and garrons, her foster-sister, Cathy Sullivan, a riding-mare, and a small sum in cash. At the wedding breakfast a letter came from Mr. Herbert, announcing that he had at last extorted the consent of his parents, and of his kinsman, the Earl of Powis. However, the ring was on fair Mary's finger, and she had a good husband and a happy home. In after-years, when even the best of husbands are apt to be a little tiresome sometimes, she could always put down her spouse by observing, "But for you, Mr. Baldwin, I might have been Countess of Powis." Old Miss Julianna O'Connell remembers old people telling her, when she was young, what a pretty creature Mrs. Baldwin was, and how beautifully dressed she used to be, particularly on some special occasion. She rather thought it was to Nancy's wedding that she came with her pretty little daughter. Mother and child were both dressed in open, long-waisted silk gowns over blue satin quilted petticoats, and the loveliest lace cap was partly covering the golden hair she wisely did not powder. When her brother Dan saw the six children, he immediately claimed this little damsel and three of the prettiest as real O'Connells, whereat poor brother Baldwin laughingly observed he was only giving him the plain ones for Baldwins. We must bear in mind that these were the O'Connells of the elder type, before wise and witty Kate O'Mullane had brought in cock-noses or scanty locks.

Dan and Nancy were the only unwedded ones, for their niece Abby had been married some time. She was a handsome, wilful, petted girl, whose mother let her have a good deal of her own way. She had point-blank refused two eligible suitors of her uncle Maurice's providing. He lost his temper in the end, and told her she should forfeit his friendship the next time she refused a good match. The next good match which offered, and which she feared to refuse, was a Mr. James Gould, a member of a very ancient family, in the County Cork, settled near Clonakilty, and much mixed up with the smuggling-trade. His temper was as violent and impetuous as her own, and they eventually separated, without any stain on her character. When her uncle and ex-playmate returned, she had only been married a short time, and she and her husband and Dan were all on the most affectionate terms. In a letter, only dated "Friday," but evidently written in the early winter of 1772, James Gould writes to Maurice O'Connell, congratulating him on the major's safe return. "Major" is a mistake for "aide-major," *i.e.* adjutant.

"With the greatest pleasure I was last night informed of the Major's safe arrival at Darrinane after a prosperous voyage. I sincerely congratulate him thereon. He was fortunate in Meeting so good an oppertunity, and it seems others were as Fortunate in meeting with him. Please to assure him of my warmest regard and affection, and, had I been at all prepared at present for so Long a Journey, would go from hence to see him, but I intend having that Pleasure speedily."

Abigail Gould's first cousin, young Jerry Falvey, of Faha, went out with her uncle the following April. Messrs. Deasy and O'Brien, James Gould, and Maurice O'Connell had all been concerned in a smuggling venture, carried out by the vessel of the former. Such contraband goods as the aide-major and the cadet were going out to King Louis in the return ship.¹ James Gould writes—

"I have the pleasure to inform you that I saw the major embark at the Galley head last Thursday, on board the Clonakilty Vessell, returning to Dunquerque, and that the wind has been as fair as possibly could be ever since. I make no doubt, as the Vessel is a prime Sailor, that he will be safe arrived this day. It happened very fortunately, as it was very uncertain when an oppertunity would offer from Cork. Besides, will save him vast trouble and Expence, the Owner having very civilly declined receiving any payment either for him or Hugh Falvy's son, who went with them. God conduct them safe!"

Mr. Gould suggests that, in return for this civility, they should be as favourably treated as relatives were in settling the accounts of the previous venture.

He writes on the 18th; on the 14th the aide-major himself writes, announcing his immediate departure for a voyage, which only took one day longer than Mr. Gould had anticipated. The parting gifts of Irish broadcloth and sea stores strangely suggest the gifts a modern emigrant receives at departure.

Daniel Charles O'Connell took out with him a young lad, who did not seem particularly promising material for the Brigade, but who turned out very well after all. His share in the matter merely consisted in getting him a cadetship and exercising a general supervision over the son of that Hugh Falvey to whose theological laxity and friendliness the O'Connells owed the preservation of their property. He had turned Protestant to save his property, but had no theological reasons for so doing. His elder sons followed his example, but there was no reason why this young boy's faith should be sacrificed to mammon. The lad's mother was the holy lady, Honora O'Mahony, whose heroic charity is remembered to this day in the quaint rhyme of the grateful poor scholar,² whom she had

---

¹ It was penal for any Papist to go or send any one for education abroad, to send money in aid of educational or religious purposes, and death to enlist in foreign service. Hence this contraband commerce was carried on at considerable risk. At one period, however, foreign enlistment was connived at.—[S.]

² See p. 57.

nursed in a malignant fever. The Mahonys and O'Connells were many times related besides their connection with Hugh Falvey through the marriage of his sister, Mary Falvey, with John O'Connell, of Darrynane. To my hero his faith was not merely the spiritual element by which he hoped to save his soul in the next world; it was indissolubly wedded to his honour here below: a successful career to be pursued with no stain to faith or honour was Daniel O'Connell's great object in life. Such a career was most certain to be met with in the service of France. My hero brought out two nephews, and, besides, helped on young kinsmen whose parents were unable to provide for them respectably at home. He suffered many things from these lads. The strong, handsome ones were as wild and unmanageable as young colts; the good boys were either delicate or small of stature. Young Falvey was neither poor nor nearly related to him, but friendship, consanguinity, and religious principle all made him wish to start this son of Honora's in an honourable career without loss of his creed. All the other boys came from near the sea, and were too much accustomed to that element to feel either fear or illness, as inland-bred Jerry Falvey did. No wonder the poor lad was very sea-sick and very frightened in a storm, encountered in a trading-ship, probably not of very great size. From this unheroic beginning his protector did not draw very favourable auguries; but the pages of M. de la Ponce's list of officers of the Irish Brigade show that he persevered and got on, and we find him and other Falveys entering the English Irish Brigade with Count O'Connell.

Clonakilty, April ye 15th, 1773.

My Dr. Brother,—I recd. y^r letter p. Mr. Falvey, wch removed my uneasiness, tho' not my jealousy, at not hearing from you during my stay in Tralee, wch I think the more unkind as you was indebted to me for a Letter. I've been at Corke, and finding no Ship there ready to sail, came back here, where I fortunately find a passage for Dunkerque on board a brigg, 170 tons, belong to Mr. Deasy and Comp., who have been mighty obliging and have refused taking a penny from me. I was, till then, extreamly uneasy to see my term approach and no possibility of getting off, otherwise than by Dublin, so cruel is it to be stinted to time when the Sea must be crossed and Expense avoided. I hope this oppertunity will answer every end.

To be revenged for your unfriendly Silence, I shall not acquaint you with my arrival at the other Side. Don't expect to hear from me before the End of June. I hope then to inform you that we are marching away to Poland or to Italy, and that this Event is likely to produce me some advantage in the way of promotion. If this should happen, God knows when we meet again.

I am glad to hear our friend Arthur arrived safe. Adieu, Dr Brother. My fond affections to my Sister. You'll not forget the promice you made of carrying her to the county Limerick this Summer. Had I remained I should have certainly attended her. It will give me great pleasure to hear you have gratified her. My love and Duty to my Mother. I hope she has no return of the gout since I left. How is poor Nancy? Remember me most tenderly to her. Remember me also to Dr Brother Morgan and his Catherine. A great many assurances of friendship to Keane and Joanney, and our friends at Tarmons. I am exceedingly obliged to my dear Brother for the kind part he has acted for my friend Copinger. I am sure I need not reccommend the little boy to your care. Your friendship to him I will Consider as conferred on myself. Farewell, my Dear and Darling Brother, and Believe me most unalterably,

Your loving and much obliged Brother,
Danl. O'Connell.

Brother and Sister Baldwin left this but last Saturday. Jerry McCrohen is now here. I lay at his house while in Corke. He'll find you the memorandum of the cloathes, 3 yards cloth at 23^s & 4½ yds. white serge. I've taken no trimmings nor Buttons.

Jemmy Goulde and Abby and my Sister desire their love to all. They have provided me with so ample a sea store that I think I shall sell to the amount of some pounds thereof at the other side. I have experienced a great deal of friendship and good nature both here and at Clohinah.

After all, Dan did announce his arrival in foreign parts. He writes, on reaching " The Smuggler's Nest "—

Dunkerque, April ye 19th, 1773.

My Dr. Brother,—Notwithstanding my jealousy to you, I lose not a moment in informing you of my arrival here after an agreable passage of four days, as you'll see by my last from Clonakilty, dated the 15th, so that I've full time to join my Regiment. I've met here some of my Military Acquaintances, who tell me that the rumours of an approaching war seem highly probable. An Alliance with England is spoke of as a matter of Certainty, and it is assured that some French troops are to be Embarked in English Ships for the Baltick. This last circumstance I have reason to doubt of. If, however, they come to a rupture, we shall not be Idle. I hope to have it in my power to give you a more authentick account in a Little time hence. Till then, I refer you to the *Hibernian Chronicle*.

I shall set out to-morrow for Bethune, where I shall arrive ye Second Day. I've a fellow traveller, Jerry Falvey, who does not Seem to have a relish for war. All he has seen hitherto cannot please him so much as Faha. He has been mighty Sick on the passage, and mightily terrified Yesterday at a Gale of Six Hours we had in the Channell. We Shipped some Seas, and he thought himself undoubtedly lost.

I shall be impatient to hear from you, my dear Brother, and must beg leave once more to trouble you with expressions of my most thorough sence of your friendship and favour. As gratitude is probably the only return I shall ever have it in my power to make, it shall be my constant study to act agreably to your desires, and shall flatter me, with the Assistance of the Almighty, never to give any material room for reproach to my friends or acquaintances. I shall attend to my profession with redoubled Efforts, and if they prove fruitless, I shall derive consolation from my consciousness of having done my Duty. Give Nancy my address, and let her know I shall be glad to hear from her. How is my poor Mother? Assure her of my Duty and Love. I believe you would do right, my Dear Brother, to pay her Dower, exactly what my father's will cuts out for her. A community of purse, which I know you have adhered to from a principle of generosity, does not suit her delicacy. She does not know how to ask, and I perceived it made her unhappy not to offer me some money at parting, which I certainly would have refused. I do assure you she has not mentioned it to me, but always shewed herself thoroughly sensible of the happiness of having so good a Son. I am convinced any indifference from you would shorten her days; therefore be careful, my Dear Brother, to show her none. I must also reccommend Nancy to your care. She has been left to your Charge, and it is incumbent on you to provide for her by removing any obstacles arising from her want of fortune—at least so far as £300. You have been hitherto the support of your family, and it's no small proof of my confidence in you to take this liberty with you, but remember, my Dr Brother, you have made it a point I should, and I've too good an opinion of you not to Comply.

Farewell, my own Dr Brother. My most warm affections to my Sister, and Believe me, most unalterably,

Your respectful and loving Brother,

D. O'C.

À Monsieur, Monsieur O'Connell, Capitaine Ayde-Major, au Régiment de Clare, en garnison à Bethune. My affections to Brother Morgan and Catty. Best compliments to the family of Cummanahorna, and all other friends.

The majority of Pondicherry's Regt has been filled. It's worth £300 p. an. I am sorry I did not accept it.

It is impossible not to feel touched by the portrait of the high-spirited Maur-ni-Dhuiv, who knows not how to ask, and her struggle between love and pride. Her husband's will leaves her her own belongings—her horse, pillion, and horse furniture, certain cattle and sheep, and pasturage for them, a share of plate, linen, and furniture, but a miserably small pittance of hard cash, unless she leaves Darrynane and gives up part of her other provision. Now, Dan's idea evidently was, that, with his brother's increased wealth, the old lady should enjoy both the jointure provided for her if she left, and the share willed her if she remained in her old home. Sheep or cattle seem to have been sold only once or twice a year, if the testimony of old account-books be conclusive, so that would account for her having no ready money at the precise moment of her youngest son's departure. Mistress of the house that had been built for her she always remained, and dispenser and organizer of the most open-handed hospitality. On one point only she was ever stingy—she did not permit the reckless and lavish consumption of eggs by her household—they should be brought to her to count out and dispense; and the Liberator told his dear eldest daughter, who told me, that the queer Irish nickname sometimes bestowed on this otherwise lavish old lady was Pinnath-na-ove ("She who is stingy of eggs").[1]

Dan's next letter refers to McCarthy Mor, about whose claim I have seen many letters and documents. My fellow-

[1] Recte pjaijca ija úba, "the Afflicted of Eggs," or "the Egg-tormented."

worker, Ross O'Connell, has drafted a very interesting and elaborate note,[1] which will be found at the end of this chapter, as also a letter from Counsellor Murphy to Madam O'Donoghue, in which this landless foreign tanist is flatteringly referred to. Those curious in family histories can read Donal McCarthy Glas's great pedigree-book and his "Florence McCarthy."

Ross O'Connell is the direct descendant of The McCarthy Mors and The O'Donoghues, which accounts for these letters being at Lake View. His father, Sir Maurice, is the son of Jane O'Donoghue, aunt to The late O'Donoghue of the Glens, and great-great-granddaughter to that Madam O'Donoghue to whom the letter was addressed about her nephew's death. That lady was the sister of the second last McCarthy Mor, about whose style and title there was no doubt, but on his death by a fall from his horse several claimants cropped up. The Madam's[2] legal adviser, Counsellor Murphy, enters into an elaborate statement of business matters, and announces McCarthy Mor's death to her. The letter bears date March 18, 1770. The postscript says—

"P.S.—Charles, the son of Florence, the elder brother of Justin McCarthy, is now McCarthy More, and a prettier fellow has not been a McCarthy More this age past. He is a Captn in Clare's Regim^t."

Notwithstanding the lawyer's dictum, we find the dashing young soldier still unable to substantiate his claim three years after. He was doubtless on the high seas to Mauritius when the Chief died.

The next letter refers to Arthur O'Leary's death. As I have procured a copy and translation of the keen composed by poor Nelly herself, I shall not spoil an article I have written for publication by any long account here of their loves and the desperate adventures which led to his death. Suffice it to say that Arthur O'Leary, who had been in the Austrian Service, and was a remarkable athlete, sportsman, and marksman, had a desperate rivalry with a rich Protestant, a Mr.

---

[1] See Note A, p. 225.
[2] "Madam" is the title of a Chief's wife.

Morris, who was mean enough to offer him £5[1] for a famous race mare, described by dark Eileen as "the dark-brown steed, the peerless, whose forehead bore a snow-white star." O'Leary challenged and struck Morris, who refused to fight a Papist. He got O'Leary outlawed. The high-spirited young couple were actually besieged in Raleigh, near Macroom, which they rented from one of the Mynheer family, who afterwards married a niece of dark Eileen and of my hero—a Miss Baldwin, of Clohina. They beat off the soldiery, Eileen Dhuv loading the guns for her husband.

He was shot down on the night of May 4, 1773, and the mare galloped home riderless and struck the bolted door of Raleigh with her heels, until Eileen rushed down and flung it open, to see the mare standing riderless, with long reins trailing in the dust, and the saddle splashed with blood. She sprang on that blood-stained saddle, as she describes in passionate verse. The mare flew on with her for miles, and on the green meads of Carrigaminma, beneath a great bush of golden gorse, she saw Arthur dead, with an aged crone keening over him.

Eileen spared no efforts to bring the murderers to justice. A couple of soldiers who were of the party were sent off to Barbados. Mr. Morris's complicity was not proved, but Arthur's brother, largely incited, I fear, by the widow, shot Morris in Cork, and fled to France.

Eileen had married in spite of the warnings of her family. She tells us in the keen that she eloped with her blue-eyed, bright-haired rider of the dark-brown mare. Dan would have Maurice let bygones be bygones and make friends, but he had a very hot-headed woman and a very hard-headed man to deal with, and it was years before a real reconciliation was effected. Old Maur-ni-Dhuiv forgave her, however, according to Miss Julianna, on the plea that no woman could have been expected to resist the pleadings of so handsome and attractive a suitor. That a widow of full age should have been supposed incapable of bestowing her hand where she pleased is a curious instance of the patriarchal tyranny of old family life.

[1] No Papist being by law allowed to have a horse of greater value than £5.—[D. O'C.]

Bethune, the 29th April, 1773.

My Dear Brother,—I trouble you thus early in favour of a friend whom I've the most earnest desire of obliging. McCarthy More, Captain in this Regiment, for whom I've the most warm wishes, is carrying on an affair of the last importance to him; which makes it indispensably necessary to prove himself in the most authentick and undeniable manner, the real Chief of that family. From the conversations I've had with you concerning him, and the genealogy you have given me, y⁰ can have no Doubt of his being the person. The Certificate, signed by the principal officers of the Regt., both in age and rank, was given in the year '65. He was then in London, where he thought it might have become necessary. This Certificate proves him most incontestably the Son and representative of Florence McCarthy, Elder Brother of Justin McCarthy, of Begnis. This point cleared up leaves no room to dispute his quality of McCarthy More. I therefore make it a particular request to my Dr Brother that you transmit me as soon as possible an attestation in the most Authentic form, Signed and Certified by Lord Crosbie, Colonel Hasset, Barry or Ned Denny, and the other principal gentlemen of your County, setting forth that Charles McCarthy, Esqrs, Captain of Clare's Regment, in the service of his Most Christian Majesty, has by birth an undoubted right to the title and quality of MacCarthy Mor, the Elder branch of that Family being Extinct by the Death of the Late McCarthy Mor, Officer in the Guards. The Bishop of our Church is also to sign this Attestation. Let me Entreat you'll not put it off. Any considerable delay may make his Scheme miscarry. Any expence attending it will be reimbursed me here. I hope I need say no more to Ensure my Dear Brother's Attention to an object which I have so much at heart. His mother is Margaret McMahon, daughter of Bernard McMahon, of the County Clare, who Died a Captain in this Service. I mention this, tho' I believe it foreign to the affair I urge. Don't wait for the August Assizes for the Execution of our Scheme if you can avoid it, but if waiting till then will make it more perfect, you can put it off. Let the attestation be made before a Notary Publick. That form is important here.

I arrived here the 22 inst, and have been since confined to my room by an Eruption, which I look upon to proceed from the Small Pox. I've taken and am to take more medicines, and already find a good of 'em. My right arm, in which I was cut for the inoculation, is covered with a breaking out. It's now withering. I hope soon to hear from you, my Dear Brother, and to learn that all our friends are well. Our

Colonel is now to join us. Young Lord Clare is also to make his first Entry as Ensign this Season. No appearance of War at present, tho' for a considerable time past Everything seemed to tend thereto. We are in a state of Lethargie here.

I have, unfortunately, been too late for the Majority in the East Indies. The appointment is £300 p. an. I am sorry to have missed it. Our present Minister pays no attention to Merit or Military Capacity. Seniority alone leads to advancement. Adieu, my Dear Brother; the hopes of War give us spirits. We were dejected. Conway, Falvey, and all desire to be remembered.

Believe me, Dr Brother, with the greatest tenderness and Respect,

Y^{rs}

D. O'CONNELL.

My Love and Duty to my Mother, Sister, and Nancy. Affections to Morgan. Comp^{ts} to all friends.

The officer of the Navy with whom I made the South Sea Discovery, is gone out a second time to that part of the world with three ships, the one of which is a 64. He wrote to me to propose me that Journey. He was gone before I arrived here, where I found his letter. I am become so fat that my regimentals were all too narrow, but Conway tells me he has reserved business for me which will bring me down.

Address: à Mons. Mons. O'Connell, Capitaine Ayde-Major, au Régiment de Clare, en Garnison à Bethune.

We see by this letter that Dan's Irish sojourn lost him two chances, as he was late in receiving the invitation to start on the naval voyage of discovery, and too late to accept the Indian promotion with its large increase of pay.

The next letter refers to Arthur O'Leary's death.

Bethune, June ye 20th, 1773.

MY DR. BROTHER,—I recd. your favour of the 23rd last Month, by wch I learn the unhappy fate of poor Arthur Leary. I can't express how much I've been shocked at it. The short acquaintance I had with him gave me a more favourable opinion than I had at first conceived of him. I still foresaw that his violence and ungovernable temper would infallibly lead him into misfortune. Brother Baldwin has given me a full account of the circumstances that preceeded and attended his last moments. It's, however, no small comfort to be assured there remains some Livelihood for his Orphans and Widow. Her Situation, my Dr Brother, when she considers her own imprudence in the disregard she showed for your advice at the time of her marriage with that unfortunate man, wou'd be distracting were she not encouraged by the goodness of your mind. You are too generous to add to her misfortunes. I am sure you've ere now forgot that she Ever offended you, and let you exert your friendship for her and children. The ingratitude of M—— is a discouraging circumstance, but be assured, my Dear Maurice, you'll not Every where meet with the same return. You'll find in your family hearts as feeling as your own, and more suited for friendship. I speak from my own private experience. My attatchment for my Dr Brother makes life dear to me, and the happiness of Seeing him again the first Desire of my Soul. All preparations for War are laid aside here. Things seemed to promise a speedy rupture on my arrival at the Regt. Foreign troops in this Service were to be sent to Sweden to assist that Crown against Denmark. We were to Embark at Dunkerque. I am sorry to think this Nation in a very declining situation. No man of capacity at the Head of the Ministry. No Encouragement for Merit and Ability. Favour still gaining, and Seniority the only other title for promotion. This throws a damp on every Mind, and has already made a very great and unfavourable alteration in the Army. Tho' no profession requires greater powers of mind than ours, Still there's none where they are so utterly thrown away. You may judge, my Dr Brother, whether I partake of the general dissatisfaction. You know I have rather too much Ambition, if a Military Man can be said to have too great a share of what is the spring of all great actions. However, I must bite my Nails and have patience. Let friendship fill the room of Ambition. Its enjoyments are more sure and within my reach, while you, my Dr Brother, continue to share my sentiments. Remember me tenderly to our Mother. It gives me infinite pleasure to hear she is well. My fond Duty to my Dr Mother, and most tender affections to poor Nancy. Tell her I recd. her Letter, and shall answer it in some time hence. I fear I bodder you with Letters. If that should be so, I'll not write so often. It's an unexpressible satisfaction for me to tell my Dr Brother with what tenderness and respect shall ever be, his loving and obliged Brother,

D. O'C.

Remember me to our friends at Tarmons and Coomanahorna. My next Shall be to my Mother or Nancy. I hope I shall soon hear from you—at least every month. If my sister will give me leave I will sometimes trouble her with an Epistle.

Let poor Tom Conway know I think he has very little to expect from this quarter. I can't prevail in his favour, nor in favour of Denis Falvey's son. I find very little feeling for their misery among the Brothers here. Good God! dear Brother, how base and ungenerous is the greater part of mankind! Florence, our Cousin-German, is here, but I fear will make no hand of this trade. He is awkward, and his unworthy Monster of a Father has not even given him a Common Education. He can scarce write his name. I fear he will be obliged to go back to your Country.

We must bear in mind that Dan was a highly educated man, with an unspeakable contempt for ignorance. A father who sent out his son into the world an illiterate country bumpkin was, in his eyes, an odious monster; so was a father who did not at once discharge a son's debts to the regiment, or his debts of honour.

Bethune, September the 16th, 1773.

I recd. my Dr Brother's letter of ye 27th last month, and am extreamly obliged to him for the trouble he has been at about the affair of McCarthy More, who desires I should express his gratitude in the strongest terms. Nothing can be more authentick. I heartily wish it may contribute to Establish him in this part of the World. It certainly was an Extraordinary instance to find an Irish Member of Parliament deliver a certificate in favour of a Rebel. The account you give of my Mother's good state of health, as well as Nancy's Marriage, affords me the greatest satisfaction. My Dear Brother's prudence and his good nature towards his family leave no room to doubt of a prospect of doing well. I have very much at heart poor Nancy's happiness, and must Envy my Dear Brother the many favours and acts of friendship he has done his family. Wou'd to Heaven I had it in my power to afford me that Enjoyment! no doubt the sweetest and most pure that mortal can taste. You've not mentioned a Syllable concerning my Sister, which makes me uneasy. No member of the family, after you, can claim a more just right to my tenderness. I beg you'll assure her of my most invariable attatchment, and never more forget her in yr letters to me.

I am sorry to inform you that we are to leave this town on the 23rd inst. for Rocroy, in Champagne. It's one of the worst garrisons in France, distant from here about 150 miles. We arrive the 1st October. I could wish Eugene [son to his sister Betty, Mrs. McCarthy] arrived before that time. His joining his Regt. will be attended with a great deal of trouble and Expence. I shall, however, take measures for that purpose. I am now to spend a Winter very differently from the last. The Sweets of Friendship are not to be Excelled. I shall remember with pleasure our *tric trac*. I hope you will not forget.

No news in this Country. The Ministry seems inclined to adopt some new plans of Œconomy. The King has given orders to Demolish and sell some houses where he never set a foot in his life, and whose repairs cost him annually 5 or 6 Millions. The Farmers General's lease being expired, they were raised 15 Millions. That Company will take care to have the rise paid by the poor. These two objects and some others make 45 Millions yearly, which is nearly what the army costs. Never was a better harvest or a more plentiful crop. This Province is the Granary of France; still, from the Exportation of Corn, I strongly infer that before the End of the Year, Bread will bear an exhorbitant price. Adieu, my Dr Brother. I hope soon to hear from you.

I remain, most unalterably Yours,

DANL. O'CONNELL.

My Fond Duty to my Mother. Comp^{ts} to all friends.

"Sister Nancy" married her cousin, Captain Maurice O'Connell, of the French Service, and Ballinablown family. They had no children, and eventually settled in Killarney. When married, he owned a property called Lative, which he was subsequently obliged to sell.

I shall group the letters of 1774 and 1775, as they relate to the last days of one of the most famous of the Irish regiments—"Clare's," so renowned at Fontenoy. Old Lord Clare was known in France as Marshal Thomond, having claimed the higher title on the death of the head of the family without issue. My hero speaks of his son indifferently as "young Lord Clare," or "young Lord Thomond." The poor lad died young and unknown to fame, after a few months' garrison service in "piping times of peace" with the regiment.

These letters are very interesting, as they contain an account of the wise reforms which inaugurated the reign of Louis XVI., which was to end so disastrously within less than twenty years.

We find mention made of an honourable and accomplished Irish gentleman who was a valuable friend of my hero's, and came, I know not quite how, into the wide meshes of the net of a Kerry cousinship. Ross O'Connell sets it all forth in a note of much interest. Chevalier, afterwards Count, Bartholomew O'Mahony, entered the English Service with his friend as colonel of an Irish regiment, and, with a similarity of fortune, received the great cross of St. Louis and the rank of general at the Restoration. He was well received in court circles many years before my hero was permitted to make his bow to lovely Marie Antoinette, though, curiously enough, he did not attain to "les honneurs du Louvre" until the same occasion as my hero. The chevalier was a near kinsman of "le brave O'Mahony," that famous Count O'Mahony, sung by Davis, who saved Cremona, and who was most distinguished in Spain under the Duke of Berwick.[1] He and several others of the family were among those French officers whom Louis XIV. sent to prop up his grandson's new throne with their good swords, and who settled in Spain. This young man was nearly related to "le brave O'Mahony's" son, the Spanish ambassador to the court of Vienna, who, from his high position, much helped his kinsman at the court presided over by the beautiful daughter of Austria. Chevalier O'Mahony, who owed his title to being a Knight of Malta, had had nearer, if humbler, protection and access to the great. His uncle was one of the royal physicians. With kindly old Dr. Mahony the two young men boarded during their bachelorhood.

Rocroi, February the 26th, 1774.

My Dear Brother,—I've been a long time in expectation of hearing from you, and cannot help feeling some uneasiness from your unusual silence. I hope, however, it proceeds from some extraordinary occupations that leave you no leisure. The busy scene of this World, my Dr Brother, affords nothing comparable in my eyes to the enjoyment of that tender friendship I feel for you; and I should think myself highly condemnable if anything should divert me from expressing it. This I do not mean as reproach. Perhaps I have caus'd your silence myself by not answering

[1] See p. 320.

your last, but then I wrote two letters at a time, one to my mother and the other to my Sister. The fear of putting you to a useless expence prevented me from writing to you at the same time. I am more anxious to know how you are than jealous with you. I would not have you think that I resent your silence, but my uneasiness for you is at present the Dominant Sentiment. I suppose the Publick Papers have ere now given you an account of the change of the Ministry of France. The Duke d'Aiguillon is now at the head of the Military and Foreign Affairs, and on the Highest favour at Court. He is looked upon as a man of extraordinary Capacity, and indeed the places he occupies require uncommon Abilities and Application to fill 'em well. Mighty changes are expected, and very sanguine expectations formed from his Administration. He is the most Assiduous man in the Kingdom, and since his succession he is at work Night and Day; immense is the Career, if not boundless. When anything material shall appear, I'll give you an account of it. The Marquis de Monteynard, late Minister of War, is not Exiled. His Retreat is 120 thousand livres, wch makes £5000 pounds.

Miss Brown is married to the Marquis de Syvrac, a young gentleman of a very good reputation, rich and 25 years old. Her fortune was 500,000 livres in hands, and 200,000 more p. an. during ten years. In all, Seven hundred thousand Livres, about 35 Thousand pounds. Adieu, my dear Brother. My Tender Duty to my Mother, and affections to my Sister Molly, Nancy, etc. Best Comp^{ts} to all friends, particularly to the Coomanahorna family. Tell Sister Betty that Eugene is well, and a very good boy. I remain for ever, my Dr Brother,

Your most loving and affectionate,
DANL. O'CONNELL.

Our young Colonel is to come to the Reg^t next May. I may possibly spend the next winter with, perhaps sooner. My Compts. to the Carhen friends.

The Miss Browne referred to in this letter is Lord Kenmare's daughter, the damsel about whom Father Guardian O'Brien had written, at the request of her unseen and elderly kinsman Count Browne of Austria, so many years before she had attained a marriageable age.

"Our young Colonel," as I said before, is the son of Lord Clare, who is to take his place at the head of the regiment with which his brave old father had won the marshal's baton. As Marshal Thomond, old Lord Clare appears in French papers.

Rocroi, July the 6th, 1774.

My Dr. Brother,—I this day recd. your very agreable favour of the 15 last month, and am exceedingly sorry to have given you room to make any charges on me, the more so as you have been uneasy lest my silence might have proceeded from Sickness. The revolution caused in this Country by the Death of the late King kept my mind in suspence, and Expecting daily changes and considerable Events, I deffered writing from day to Day. Your papers will acquaint you, before you receive my letter, of the Duke d'Aiguillon's Retreat. M^r le Comte de Mouy, who commanded in Lille, has reimplaced him in the Military Department. This gentleman, by the way, is not looked on as a well-wisher of the Irish, and it's much to be feared he may give us a fatal blow. This being perhaps a groundless fear we all hide [it], and I request, my Dr Brother, you'll keep a profound Secret. Our unfortunate Nation is fallen into utter contempt among the French since the Death of Lord Clare, whose favour with the King, and the then recent memory of Fontenoy and Lansfeld, still supported us. It is impossible our Brigade can last much longer. With respect to me, my Dr Brother, is a matter pretty indifferent to me. I shall obtain in any Reg^t in France the same place I here occupy, but if our dissolution should take place while the war holds between Russia and the Turks, I am resolved to try how far Fortune may be favourable to me among them. My sole regret would be to have spent my youth, and risked my life so often, to so little purpose. By what I mention you'll conceive how precarious our fortune is. Where I to go to Ireland this winter, I may be absent at the most critical moment. This perplexes me so much that I cannot determine, with any degree of certainty, what is to become of me. Colonel Meade's opinion will probably fix my resolution. Most of my friends are of opinion I should go to Paris to be introduced and known, but the unavoidable necessity of running into Debt makes me quite averse to that. Such, my Dear Brother, is my present situation. You may depend no consideration less weighty could balance the pleasure I should feel in spending the winter with you. Whatever be my fate, Believe me to be for ever,

My Dear, Dear, Brother's most loving and affectionate,
D. O'C.

Let my letter be a Secret to the World, as our apprehension may possibly prove groundless. I would not for any consideration be the author of spreading 'em. I shall write to you again towards the middle of August.

My Duty to my Mother. Tender love to my Sister, and best wishes to all friends. Eugene [McCarthy, Betty O'Connell's son] is well, and desires his duty to you. Colonel Meade not yet home, but Daily expected. Young Lord Thomond is with us. He is now 17 years old, and promices so so. I wrote to Jemmy Baldwin by this post.

Rocroi, August the 8th, 1774.

MY DR. BROTHER,—It's with the greatest satisfaction I acquaint you that I shall soon set out for Ireland, and hope to Embrace you early in October or perhaps sooner. 'Tis needless to tell you how happy I shall be when with you. I was afraid it would have been out of my power to gratify my wishes that way this Winter, but circumstances proved more favourable than I expected. Colonel Meade is just set out for the Waters of Aix la Chapelle. His constitution is prodigiously shattered from our long voyages, and I greatly fear he'll not get the better of it. It would be the greatest loss I cu'd suffer in this part of the World. His friendship I can rely on, and few men are men more deserving of the Esteem of his acquaintance than he. I shall set out the latter end of this month for Dunkerque, where I expect to meet a ship. If not, shall go by the way of England. When in Cork I shall immediately go to Clohinah, where I shall acquaint you of my arrival.

Adieu, my Dr Brother. My Duty to my Mother. Best love to my Sister. I shall soon embrace you all.

D. O'CONNELL.

Brave Colonel Meade died soon after, exhausted by hardships, long voyages, and unwholesome climates. O'Callaghan tells us that Colonel Meade succeeded Chevalier de Betagh as second colonel of "Clare's" in 1770, and was "the representative of a name respectable in Munster to our own times. This gentleman," continues O'Callaghan, at p. 46 of "The Irish Brigade," "who had previously served in the regiment of Lally, continued to be colonel-in-second to the regiment of Clare, as long as it was kept up, or until 1775. For the young comte, or Earl of Thomond and Lord Clare, dying under age and unmarried at Paris, December 29, 1774, and the united titles of Thomond and Clare ceasing in his person, according to the new arrangement of the French Army already spoken of as having occurred in June, 1775, the regiment of Clare, about eighty-six years from its first formation in Ireland, and eighty-five years from its arrival in France, was incorporated with the Irish infantry regiment of Berwick."

Rocroi, the 9th 8bre, 1774.

My Dr. Brother,—I just recd. y^r letter dated Limerick, ye 22^d last Month, by wch you express your surprise at my long silence. It gives me inexpressible concern to have been the innocent occasion of y^r uneasiness. I give you my word I wrote you three times, and have still the copies of my Letters, and am wholly at a loss what to attribute their miscarriage to. Jemmy Baldwin, in a Letter I had from him some time ago, also reproaches me with Unkindness. To prevent my Dr Brother's further anxiety, I send this to Paris, to be put into the Post Office. I hope to have the pleasure of Embracing you before the latter end of October. The Regt. parts from here the 22nd for Bethune, our last quarters. I go along with my Lord Thomond to Paris, where I shall remain a few days only, and then steer for Hâvre, where I expect to meet a ship for Cork. Perhaps I may meet Arthur Ferris, which wo'd do me great pleasure. I mentioned my resolution thus far to you in a letter I lately wrote to you. I had no account before your's of the Death of Mrs. FitzMaurice of Belleville. I fear poor Jack will more than ever repent what he has done.

Adieu, my dear Brother. Be convinced that nothing on earth can be more dear to me than your friendship, and judge whether I w'd omitt writing to you so long. I am exceedingly impatient to Embrace you, and assure you by word of mouth of my most unalterable love and Friendship.

D. O'Connell.

My tender Duty to my mother and most warm affections to my Sister. Comp^{ts} to all friends. I had lately a Letter from Morty. He is well, and tells me that Major Sullivan is to pass the Winter in Ireland.

Paris, 8bre ye 6th, 1774.

My Dr. Brother,—A few days before my Departure from Rocroi I had the pleasure of hearing from you, and immediately answered y^r Letter. I then Expected to see you in a short time, but as some affairs, too tedious to mention, tho' relating to my Advancement, require a longer stay here than

I at first could presume or foresee, the displeasure I feel from being deprived of the happiness of embracing you, and the fears of your being uneasy at my Delay, determine me to write a Second Letter. I fear I shall not have it in my power to go to Ireland this Winter, as the bad Season is soon to set in, and most probably before I shall be able to form any judgement on my Expectation. As the Work is only done in December, if I can possibly terminate my affairs should they even prove unsuccesful, my most warm wishes are to spend a Month or two with you. Rely on't, my Dr Brother, nothing on Earth could give me greater pleasure than being with you, but as my Station in Life, though honourable, wants bettering, I am forced to Submit my wishes to my interest. The friendship of Doctor Mahony enables me to pursue it. I lodge here with him, nor does he make the least difference between me and his nephew. I shall say more if I can hope to succeed. It's principally thro' the Channel of his friendship. I need not reccommend to my Dr Brother to make no mention of all this. I suppose your publick papers speak very favourably of this commencement of Administration in France. I shall not descend into any particulars on that head. I had the favour of seeing young Mr. Crosbie of Ardfert here. Lord Shelburne is also arrived in Paris. I have taken, conjointly with Colonel James Conway, what steps lay in my power towards procuring for the Abbé Connell the Episcopacy of Kerry. His nomination meets with strong opposition from the Clergy of the Diocese. I am sorry for his own sake that he won't reconcile himself the friendship of these people. I fear he may have cause to repent it.

Adieu, my Ever Dr Brother. My tender Duty to my Mother, and most warm affections to my Sister. Kind comp^{ts} to all friends. Believe me for Ever,

Y^r fond and loving Brother,

D. O'CONNELL.

Doctor Mahony and the Chevalier his nephew, my bosom friend, desire their best compliments to you and family.

During the penal times the priests were so largely dependent on the gentry that these latter meddled in Church matters to an extent which would not be tolerated now. I have a copy of a curious letter of one of the old Lord Cahirs to my husband's great-grandfather, William Coppinger, of Barry's Court, full of indignation that his bishop would not promote a priest he favoured, and asking him to get the protection of the Bishop of Cloyne for his *protégé*. Whatever the merits of the Abbé O'Connell, the diocese of Kerry was lucky in rejecting him, as they got in Dr. Moylan one of the ablest and most energetic prelates of the age.

There was a Father Morgan O'Connell, uncle to Captain Rickard O'Connell and to Dr. Maurice Leyne, frequently mentioned in the Leyne family papers as the erudite, eccentric, and proud parish priest of Killarney in 1782. I fancy I identify him with the young cousin of that name, who was a clerical student in Paris in 1744, and with this Abbé O'Connell. He was nearly related to the Conways, and in a subsequent letter Dan mentions that they are to bring influence to bear on the prince in Rome. By "the prince" I fancy they mean Cardinal York, brother to the Young Pretender. The late Mrs. McCartie, of Headford, County Kerry, a grand-niece of Count O'Connell, in a family memorandum, states of this O'Connell, "He was a wit and a holy priest."

Paris, December 18, 1774.

My Dr. Brother,—I recd. your letter of the 18th last Month, enclosing Mr. George Gould of Corke's Draught for 600ll, the payment of which is to be fulfilled the 2nd next Month. I feel to the last degree this new instance of your delicacy and good nature. You not only prevent my wants, but also my calls, and Sacrifice your own interest to forward mine. Be persuaded, my Dr Brother, that I am highly sensible of your Innumerable Acts of friendship, for which I shall be ever acknowledging. A young Mr. Hixon has also forwarded me a letter of yours, in which you reccommend him to my friendship. A most unfavourable change in our Military Constitution disables me from rendering him as immediate services as otherwise I should have endeavoured to do at your reccomendation. The young gentleman's own behaviour is vastly deserving, and reccommends him very much to all his acquaintances. Our five Regts are now reduced to three in the following manner: Bulkeley receives Serrant's Regt., formerly Rothe's; Berwick's is to be incorporated with Clare's and Dillon's, to raise a second Bataillon. After this change the Brigade will consist of but 3 Regts., viz.—

Bulkeley's, Clare's, and Dillon's, of two Bataillons each, instead of five Regiments of one Bataillon as heretofore. The approaching and unavoidable Death of Lord Clare will assure his Regiment to the Marquis of FitzJames, Eldest son to the Duke and Colonel of Berwick's, incorporated with ours, of which ten Attendant he remains Colonel Commandant in the room of Meade, who probably will gett, as well as Serrant,[1] a French Regiment. After which the Regiment now called Clare's will take the name of Berwick's. This destroys all my expectations, which I thought shure this winter. Major Conway had called for an other Station, which was to be granted, and I was to be Major in his place. Now the two reduced Lt Colonels and Majors will get the first vacancies that shall offer, and I loose Meade, on whose regard and friendship I cu'd for ever rely.

The Marquis of FitzJames, wth whom I have but a slender acquaintance, will noe doubt always prefer the officers of his own Reg^t, and promote them preferably, so that after all my Services and Expectations, wth a Capacity allowed equal to any Station, I may possibly spend the rest of my life a Captain. This, my Dr Brother, is indeed very hard, and, I must confess, damps my spirits. At the Eve of Advancement an uncounted change thwarts and crushes me. Patience is a distressing remedy, and still the only one that remains.

I most carefully attend and cultivate the best acquaintance, in hopes hereafter some oppertunity more favourable may offer. Lord Kenmare and his son shew me a great deal of politeness. They are to go to Ireland next spring. I told his Lordship you would be very glad to waitt on him, and requested he would give you leave, to wch he answered in the most oblidging manner. I think you'll do well to see him. I am little acquainted wth M. de Syvrac.[1] His wife is brought to bed of a son. Adieu, my Dr Brother. I wish you and my Sister and Mother happy new years, and am for ever,

Your most obliged and most tender brother,

D. O'CONNELL.

My worthy friends, Doctor Mahony and his nephew, wth whom I live as if a Brother, desire a thousand comp^{ts} to y^r and family. I owe 'em vast obligations. I fear entre nous Major Conway made an indifferent match. Adieu, plains moi. Our present minister grants nothing, and particularly to young men. No advancement, says he, to be Expected without twenty-five years' Service; so I am still far remote. Adieu, my Dr Maurice. Perhaps fortune may be more favourable.

The year 1775 opened gloomily enough for the old officers of "Clare's," but our hero's motto, though not expressed in words, was "Never say die;" and he remained on in Paris

---

[1] Walsh, Count de Serrant.
[2] The Marquis de Syvrac, married to Lord Kenmare's daughter.

in the winters, with the exception of a visit to Ireland. He had the company of his similarly circumstanced friends, Chevalier O'Mahony and Colonel Conway, all living close together in the rue de Tournon. He studied hard; cultivated many fine people, native and foreign, whose interest was to be of use to him; and at the very moment when he thought his fortunes near the lowest ebb, had the good luck, by a military critique, to excite the interest of the Minister of War. I shall give the anecdote in full from a contemporary newspaper when I have quoted his letters.

In a letter of 1776 he mentions his luck in attracting the notice of the Count de Maillebois, but speaks as if he had just attracted his attention in the ordinary performance of duty.

Paris, January the 30th, 1775.

My Dr. Brother,—You've, I suppose, ere now received my last, by which I acknowledged the reception of Mr. George Goold's Draft on Messrs. Arnould, of Paris, for the Sum of 30^{ll}, the Amount of wch I recd. the 2nd Inst., and beg leave to express a new my gratitude and Thanks.

I believe I made some mention of the critical situation of our Brigade, the fate of which is still in agitation, and will probably not be decided before the Month of April. Whatever be the event, it must be unfavourable to me, as it deprives me of Advancement, which I looked upon as certain this winter. The number of our Regts. will most probably be diminished, and consequently some Majors and Lt.-Colonels reduced.

For all this I know no other remedy than patience. Many people of the first rank are good enough to express a good deal of kindness and friendship for me, but such is the inflexible character of our minister that neither friends nor capacity weigh with him without twenty-five years' Service, nor indeed is promotion much better than Show in this country; for what ever be the Rank of a Military Man, the mediocrity of his pay keeps him in continual distress and makes him very little more happy than before. Such is, my dear Brother, the prospect I have before my eyes. Had I but adopted any other course of life and applied with as much assiduity and labour as in this, most certainly I should acquire, without the dangers and hardships I have already undergone, a comfortable and easy livelihood, whereas now I am but at the commencement of my toils. However, my Dr. Brother, I shall not sink into low Spirits. This life is so short that at best it's little worth repining at.

James Conway has some expectations of obtaining ye Bishoprick of Kerry for Abbé Connell thro' ye Channel of ye Prince at Rome.¹ Still, the Abbé has no time to lose in sending him the postulation signed. If he can't procure himself that, let him send the Authority of the Primate, in consequence of which he Acts as Vicar General *ad interim*. The address of J. Conway is underneath. Adieu, my Dr. Brother, adieu. Remember me most respectfully to my Mother and most fondly to my Sister, and best friendships to all friends. Doctor Mahony and his nephew desire to be most kindly remembered to y^e and family. Make mention of 'em all in y^r Letters to me. I have the greatest obligations to the Doctor and his nephew, my bosom friend. How does Br. Morgan? Has he got many Daughters? I should be glad to hear he had a boy. When shall I hear from my Dr. Brother? Adieu. I wrote several times to Jemmy Baldwin, and got no answer.

D. O'Connell.

My address: chez M. de Mahony, Medicin du Roi, rue de Tournon, à Paris.

T. Conway's address: à Monsieur, Monsieur de Conway, Colonel d'Infantèrie, rue de Tournon, Paris.

Colonel Tom FitzMaurice—not yet a colonel, however—in sending Maurice O'Connell, of Darrynane, some money for a widowed sister of his, writes thus in 1776 (February 2). He incidentally mentions that his pay "is scarce sufficient for me or any one in my station to keep Buckle and Tongue together." He seems to infer that my hero is at home, for he says, "Cousin Daniel, I suppose, gave you my address, which is Libourne," etc., and also mentions that cousin Daniel gave him an account of the poor circumstances of a relative in Ireland. He gloomily proceeds to say—

"You have no doubt been informed of what happened me last year in common with a great number of others of our country. I probably shall soon undergo a worse Event. The only comfort I shall expect by it is that Cousin Daniel and I will probably join, and by that means live in Society together for the future. This arrangement will be in one shape detrimental both for his and my future fortune."

¹ We presume Cardinal York.

From this it would seem that there was considerable risk that my hero might have had to go on half-pay. As it was, instead of being full captain and adjutant (aide-major) he deemed himself lucky to go as second captain under his friend McCarthy Mor. They had, however, the honour of being appointed to the chasseurs, formed of the picked men made into one company and chosen of the pick of the two regiments of "Berwick's" and "Clare's." Clare's grand old regiment ends sadly and prosaically enough—not cut to pieces in such a rush as broke the English ranks at Fontenoy, but sinking into a state of inefficiency and finally losing its identity in mingling with "Berwick's." The brilliant verse of Davis contrasts strangely with the very prosaic version of the adjutant—for so I conceive "aide-major" to mean. Drinking, gambling, and running into debt, according to his later letters, had attained a great pitch among the Irish-French officers. Davis's beautiful song about "Clare's Dragoons" has given rise to a wrong impression that "Clare's" were horse-soldiers. In point of fact, "Clare's" was the infantry regiment raised, clothed, and armed for the service of King James by Daniel O'Brien, third Viscount Clare, early in 1689. The accurate and laborious O'Callaghan begins his formal account of "the Infantry Regiment of O'Brien, or Clare," at p. 38 of his "History of the Irish Brigades in the Service of France."

There is no letter discoverable from Daniel O'Connell between January, 1775, and March, 1776. A visit to his family will account for some part of the second winter. The *Kerry Chronicle* of 1782, happily preserved at Lake View, thus fills in the narrative—

"The death of Lord Clare furnished the Minister with a pretext to reduce that regiment, or, what was equally injurious to the officers, to incorporate it with the Duke of Berwick's.

"Being at this time free from professional engagements, he [Daniel O'Connell] made a visit to his family. It was about this time rumoured that Government would accept the offer which the Catholic nobility in Ireland made of raising regiments at their own expense to serve in America. Had the proposal been acceded to, Lord Kenmare, who was at the head of the measure, and who, during his residence in France, had known Mr. O'Connell's merits, proposed to give him the command of one."

I omit a long dissertation on the refusal of the Government to accept this offer, and go on to the next narrative portion.

"Disappointed in the hope of acquiring laurels in the service of his country, Mr. O'Connell returned to Paris, where, instead of indulging in the pleasures to which a handsome person adorned with the most elegant accomplishments would have unquestionably introduced him, he devoted his time to the University. He lost sight for a while of his profession, and for two winters thought of nothing but science. Being already acquainted with the mathematics, he made chemistry and the *belles lettres* his chief pursuits. The course of his studies was interrupted by a chance circumstance.

"An ordinance for the regulation of discipline was issued from the War Office, upon which he drew up some strictures, which fell into the hands of the Comte de Maillebois. This deservedly admired general was so much struck with the ingenuity and spirit of these remarks that he desired to see the author, for whom, on acquaintance, he conceived the warmest friendship, equally honourable to both these distinguished characters, that, although M. de Maillebois did not then stand well at court, still his recommendation immediately procured for Mr. O'Connell the brevet rank of colonel and a pension of 2000 livres (*i.e.* about £80), no very great sum to the parr of the London Stock Exchange, but a vast affair in the ideas of a Frenchman, who estimates these 'graces' not according to their intrinsic value, but as honorary marks of distinction, which imply merit in the person on whom they are conferred. Shortly after, he was appointed Lieut.-Colonel of the Royal Suédois, where his former comrades were still simple lieutenants. With this regiment he was at the taking of Minorca."

Now, "Clare's" was dissolved in January, 1775, and Minorca was not attacked until 1781. The events of six years are compressed into this paragraph. The letters relating to

M. de Maillebois's favour and his appointment to his first regiment and cordial reception by his German family, as he calls them, will follow; but unfortunately, there is not a single letter during war-time. Whether all communication had become impossible, or that he wrote to his mother instead of to his brother on these occasions, it is now impossible to say. Instead of a moving chronicle of perils by flood and field, we have the inner life of a soldier of fortune laid bare. It was a mighty rugged ladder the Irish gentleman had to climb to attain to fortune. The Count de Maillebois may have been favourably disposed to this handsome, clever, agreeable Kerry man because in his own boyhood he had himself been the pupil of another handsome, clever, agreeable Kerry man, Sir John O'Sullivan, Charles Edward's comrade of "the '45," his military mentor and devoted follower.[1] O'Sullivan had early discarded the ferule for the sword, and in the intermediate capacity of military secretary to the famous old Marshal de Maillebois, the conqueror of Corsica, was credited with no inconsiderable share in that achievement, the stout old toper, his commander, having made the wisest possible dispositions every morning, and invariably drunk himself out of all recollection of them every night, leaving his subordinate to remember all details. Whether influenced by agreeable recollections of his Irish tutor or by a more unprejudiced view of men and things than was usual among French folk dealing with foreigners, M. de Maillebois showed the greatest interest in our hero, and promoted his fortunes by all the means in his power.

The first two letters of 1776 merely contain an account of our hero's preparations for leaving Ireland and an account of civilities received. The third contains an account of his journey over. The fourth is of considerable interest, as it contains an account of the remodelling of the Irish Brigade.

Corke, March the 2^d, 1776.

MY DR. BROTHER,—I arrived here in the afternoon on Wednesday, and found to my great Satisfaction y^r letter from

---

[1] O'Sullivan, who was one of the O'Sullivan Mor family, had begun to study for the Church, and adopted the dress and style of Abbé. Finding he had no religious vocation, he accepted the post of tutor in the marshal's family.

Killarney. I am glad to find you have taken yᵉ lands, tho' dear, as they are a conveniency. I remained at Clohinah until Sunday last, then came to Clonakilty, where I remained 3 nights. Abby [his niece, Mrs. Goulde] had been delivered of a fair Daughter but six days before. She is as well as can be expected. All friends here are well, and desire their best wishes to you. There are now in this Port four ships bound to Hâvre. I believe I shall take my passage on board the Havre Packet belonging to Mr. Connor. She is a very stout Vessell, well laid out for accomodation, and commanded by an excellent seaman, who has been some years past on that trade, and therefore well acquainted with the French Coast on the Channel. She is to fall down the River in 2 or 3 days, and to have no delay at Cove. Let me beseech my Dr. Brother to be under no sort of uneasiness. There's now every appearance of good weather for some time; the wind as fair as can blow and very moderate. Be assured I shan't lose a moment in acquainting you of my arrival at Hâvre. Troops are daily marching in here. All those destined for America are to rendezvous at Corke, and to take in provisions there, so that both Beef and Butter will sell at high rate. England seems determined to crush them next Campaign. 15,000 Hessians are taken into pay.

Adieu, my Dr. Brother, Farewell. I shall write to you by post when ready to sail. My most tender affections to my Mother and Sister, and best wishes to all friends. Be ever assured of the heart of yʳ own

D. O'CONNELL.

I am much obliged to my Dr. Brother for the orders he sent of taking up here any thing I may want. I shall take up 3 gallons of the best rum to be found, and nothing else, for nothing is wanting to me. Charles is to be this night at Clohinah, to-morrow at Dromore. He carries Compliments to Mr. Mahony from me. He also carries back yʳ hussard Coat. Doctor Connell and all friends here desire their best wishes to you all. Adieu, my Dr. Dr. Brother.

I met here and everywhere since we parted with the most friendly reception. Jemmy Baldwin has accompanied me hither.

Corke, March the 7ᵗʰ, 1776.

MY DEAREST BROTHER,—I am still here, tho' I every Day expected to Sail. The Vessell is at Length ready, and nothing but yᵉ wind now detains us. I hope it will offer to-morrow, and give us a quick and agreable passage to Havre. I reᵈ here a Letter from Robin Conway, of Bergues. He gives me many accounts of changes to take place, but as none is hitherto confirmed, I shall not trouble you with the details of them. I have [met] many persons of y^r acquaintance in this Town, and recd. a very many civilities everywhere. The Reverend Robert Conway and family have been particularly attentive and polite, and introduced me into some of the Protestant families. I flatter myself I have reconciled some of their fair to the French gallantry. Jerry McCrohan has procured the Rum. It is of an exceeding good quality; I believe the best to be found in Corke. The 3 gallons have produced 15 bottles. I have also taken a bottle of Port and 6 of Porter on your account, contrary to my intention; for I c'uld not prevail on Jerry, who procured them, to receive from me the amount, so that I must daily lay you under new burthens. Farewell, my Dearest Brother, farewell. Be assured that no expressions can equal the under feelings of your most respectful and obliged brother,

D. O'CONNELL.

Morgan is here since Saturday. Mr. Wise has agreed to take his farm off his hands. My fond Duty to my Mother, and Love to my Sister. Let her know that I visited Mrs. Sheehy. She is well, and a pleasant, agreable woman. I don't know whether I informed you in my *last I gave 3 guineas for my passage* and am to be found in ship's provisions. All y^r acquaintance here, particularly the family I live in and the worthy Dr. Connell, desire their most affectionate Compliments to you. My arm is still threatening, and I fear will be worse before I've leisure to go thro' poor Doctor Mahony's prescription. Doctor Connell makes nothing of it. Remember me to Cousin Charles.

Havre, Thursday, the 14th March, 1776.

MY DEAR BROTHER,—I thank God that I can so easily inform you of my safe arrival here, and remove any uneasiness you may be under on my account. On Saturday last, in the afternoon, we fell down the river to Cove, and sailed at break of day. We made this land this morning at 6, and came in with the afternoon tide. I never had a more agreable passage. The weather was so remarkably fair that I might with safety come over in your boat.

I had very good accomodation, and an honest, good, and good-humoured Captain; so that every thing answered beyond my most sanguine expectations. To make the arrival more pleasant, I met on the Quay with Mr. Denis McCrohan, Philadelphia. He is now over a bottle with me, and we just now drank our friends at Darinane. To-morrow, at 4 in the morning, I set out for Rouen by the publick coach, and shall arrive at Paris on Monday or Tuesday, whence I shall write to my dear brother, after a fortnight or three weeks. I have now no other uneasiness than that which must needs arise on reflecting that the seas now seperate me from you; but, however, the pleasing thought of meeting again feeds and comforts my soul.

Farewell, my dear Brother Maurice. Farewell, my own dear brother. I can never express what I feel for you, nor feel more than you deserve.

My Duty and Love to my Dear Mother and Sister, and best compliments to all friends, not forgetting Charles FitzM.

D. O'CONNELL.

Mr. McCrohan wishes I may recommend him to your friendship. He intends going to that country on some business. I think he needs but show himself to please; and I well know your good wishes for his family. Let Mr. John Mahony, of Killarney, know that I have seen Mr. Stuart and settled to have the linen, which I found still in his hands, part to-morrow for Calais, to the address of his brother Jerry.

The following letter is one of the most valuable in an historical point of view, as it details the reorganization of the Irish Brigade. The kindly Duke de FitzJames was to lead back its officers to the British Service, and he and his "Capitaine en Second," as colonels of the first and fourth regiments of King George's Irish Brigade, were destined to fare especially badly in their new capacity, some twenty years after this letter was written:—

Cambray, June ye 10th, 1776.

MY DR. BROTHER,—I wrote you two letters, one on my landing and the other in about 3 weeks after, as we agreed. The latter I entrusted to the care of an Irish Clergyman just setting out for Corke by the way of Hâvre. I fear he neglected forwarding it, as I've had no answer to it or the former. Ever since my arrival on the Continent we have been in anxious expectation of the mighty changes in our Military Constitution. They have at length taken place as follows:— Ever since 1762 the Infantry in France was divided into Regiments of 4, 3, 2, and 1 Bataillons. Last year [1775] the Marshal de Mouy put each Reg^t to 2 Bataillons, except the 12 first, which from some private considerations he left at 4. These the present Minister has also put to two Each, by means of which these 12 1st Regts. now make 24. Each Bataillon consisted till now of 9 Companies, one of which grenadeers, which made 18 companies to a Reg^t. A Captain, Lieutenant, and Sub-Lieutenant, to Each Company; an Aide-Major and Sub-Aide-Major to each Bataillon; a Colonel, Lt.-Colonel, and Major to each Regt. Such was the composition of a Regt., till now the present formation is as follows: Each Regiment is now composed of 2 Bataillons; each Bataillon of 4 Companies of foot—1 of Grenadeers, or of Chasseurs, wch among you is called Light infantry. Therefore 6 Officers to each company, viz. a Captain, Captain en Second, Lieutenant, Lieut. en Second, and 2 Sub-Lieutenants. The Aide-Majors and Sub-Aide-Majors, Chiefs of Bataillons [the chiefs of battalion were created by the late Minister], and two Colour Bearers, are reformed and rank according to Seniority—the Aide-Majors among the Captains, and the Sub-Aide-Majors among the Lieu^{ts}. The 10 1st Captains take Companies; the 10 youngest are Captains en Second; the Lieutenants in like manner, according to their Seniority. The Officers of Light Infantry are to be chosen by their Colonels among the most active, vigilant, etc., in each grade. McCarthy Mhor is Captain of this company, I Captain en Second. The pay of a Captain of a Company is 2400 livres clear, without any stoppage in the pay. The pay of Captain en Second is 1560, also without any stoppage. The 1st Lieut. has 900 livres, the 2nd Lieut. 800, the Sub-Lieut. 720; a Cadet to each Company at 12^{sols} a Day. There's also a Colonel en Second to each Regt. Walsh's Regt. is to be raised again and a 2nd Bataillon added to it. The reformed and à la suite officers are to compose the new Bataillon, and are more than sufficient in number. Besides this advantage, we have a District of French Flanders to recruit in, so that the Irish Brigade is on a much more respectable and solid footing than those many years past. The centre of the French Army is formed into Divisions, to each of which are attached a certain number of General Officers, the same only to be employed in the field in case of war, and are to keep the troops under their inspection in the strict exercise of military discipline, and to form them to the Evolutions, according to the principles established. There are various other changes relative to this system too long to be explained in such a manner as to make 'em intelligible to you. The Soldiers' pay is increased by a Sol a Day. I had a few days since a letter from FitzMaurice, who informs me of his receiving from you a letter, dated the 30th April, wch has removed my uneasiness. He tells me he sent some [money], or a bill, thro' the Commander of a Ship, addressed to a Mr. King, Merchant, in Corke, to be remitted you for the use of his Sister. I suppose he acquainted yᵉ thereof in due time. I have some expection of getting a Commission for Eugene in "Walsh's." I would wish to be rid of him, for between us I fear he'll prove Daddy's own child, particularly if he should remain in this Regt., where there's the very worst example for young men. He discovers the strongest propensity to gambling and not averse to the bottle. It's but by the dint of enquiry that I've discovered debts he contracted during my absence in Coffee houses, etc. I should have him in a Dungeon on bread and water to pay them, was I not apprehensive that it may prevent Serrant [Walsh, Count de Serrant] from giving him an Employment in that Regt. In short, my Dr. Brother, this Boy has given me a surfeit of bringing over any others, nor, indeed, could I expect much from his Strain. May God grant he'll alter, but I fear that when abandoned to himself he'll plunge headlong into the vices he shews so strong an inclination for. Adieu, my Dear Brother. Let me hear from you immediately; and present my most tender Love and Duty to my mother. Most cordial affections to my Sister, to Nancy, etc. I've been almost constantly sick since I came on the Continent with an Ulcer, Called in French Dàrtre farineux,[1] which broke out near the Elbow, and which affected me in Ireland. I am going thro' a course of Medicine and so strict a Diet that in 3 months I am not to taste a bit of Meat nor a drop of wine or any other liquor. It's much to be dreaded I shan't succeed to remove it compleatly. These kind of Eruptions proceed from an acrimonious quality of the blood seldom to be entirely cured. I've been busy while in Paris in seeing my acquaintance. Was introduced to the Ministers with great encomiums on my talents, but confined to our . . . little possibility of advancing. I've now leisure to read, and do apply with unrelaxed zeal to acquire everything that may prove useful hereafter in my profession. The Regt. is indeed on a mighty indifferent footing, and our Duke [FitzJames], who is very friendly to me, is not a man to feel nor think. He was vastly pleased with your present of Rum, and desires me to return yᵉ thanks.

D. O'CONNELL.

My best Wishes to Brother Morgan and Catty, and to our Tarmon friends. I write to James Baldwin of this. . . . Remember me to Maurice Charles.

The wild boy Eugene, of whom his terribly sober uncle predicted such sad things, turned out very well, and died a British colonel.

[1] Eczema.—[S.]

My hero was quite consistent in "damning vices he had no mind to." He had a positively morbid horror of drink, the besetting sin, indeed, of our countrymen. His poor brother-in-law, Tim McCarthy, was a worthy, good sort of man in every way except a propensity for punch, which was not supposed at all shameful by his friends in general. At that time, of course, the tendency, if not checked, would have ruined Eugene, and I think his uncle contrived very well to keep it in check. I let the lecture stand, with this qualifying adjunct as to Eugene's future bravery and success, and will add that his poor father is not to be supposed a gambler and a scapegrace because the boy was such for a time.

Calais, July the 6th, 1776.

MY DEAREST BROTHER,—Robin Conway has just sent me inclosed y^r most feeling letter of ye 15th of last Month, w^h tore my heart to pieces. How shall I atone for the uneasiness I caused the tenderest of brothers by assuring you, as mentioned in my last from Cambray, that I had wrote by a Mr. Tully, of the County Wexford, a clergyman bound for Dublin or Corke, as an oppertunity should offer at Hâvre? My telling you in that letter that you shu'd hear no more from me until I was able to inform you of the changes likely to take place, and my being foolishly confidant that gentleman wu'd not fail forwarding it, is but a slender apology, and Satisfies me but little; however clearly it must prove to my dear Brother that I did not mean to be neglectfull, and most unworthy, no Doubt, must I be, if capable of not feeling in the most lively manner the obliging solicitude and the melting expressions of his Letter. Believe, then, my D^r, Dr Maurice, that it's from the bottom of the fondest heart I . . . in your Anxiety and most solemnly protest to you it now makes me as miserable as you cu'd have been, nor shall my mind be at rest till you assure me you're perfectly satisfied I am no further blamable than for not having wrote by Post rather than by any other Channel—a fault which hereafter I shall most carefully avoid, if my dearest Brother will but forgive the Present.

The Regiment arrived here on the 26th ultimo. When I wrote my last we were as yet ignorant that we shu'd change garrisons. However, this has turned out pretty favourably for me, the bad state of my health making it absolutely necessary that I should take the Sea Baths. I am now, thank God, some days past much better, my breast stronger, my appetite recovering, still bound to a Vegetable Diet, and total abstinence from Wine, which you know to be no hardship on me. My daily bathing and slender food, joined to a good deal of exercise, has Emaciated me a good deal, but that's soon made up when the Constitution is settled. I shall have much to do to exterpate the Levain which has corrupted my blood, and which is to be attributed to my East India sufferings, and my daily wasting myself in the practise and functions of my employment, for which I've been but ill rewarded. Experience makes me wise. *Nunquam sera est ad bonos mores ria*, which I construe thus: "Better late than never." I was never so near home in garrison as now, but the vicinity avails little when not Master to make use of it, as I can wish. Was I as free as you, and unrestrained, how briskly shu'd I skip along the watery surface to Embrace my friends at Darrinane! Give 'em all my most warm love— all, that is, my Mother and Sister. Love to B^r Morgan and wife, Nancy, etc. Tell Betty her son[1] is well and Officer in Walsh's Regiment, with an appointment of 60^{ll}, 3 pound st., a month, which will make him hereafter ever independent of the World if an unhappy propensity to *family failings* does not destroy him, and get the better of Admonitions and Example, wch I venture to say I have always given him, but I am not further accountable for his future welfare, nor bound to be for ever his slave. He is still here with me, as his Reg^t is at Libourne, near Bordeaux, and a likelihood of its coming down to this Country. I wrote to [Walsh] Count de Serrant for leave to keep him here till then, in order to save me the vast Expences of sending him 240 or 250 Leagues, which, besides Equipping him, falls indeed too heavy on my purse. When next I go to Ireland, if Jeffrey Maurice's son promice well, I shall make an Effort to bring him out, and then think I've paid my tribute till better times enable me to do more. The Death of Cousin Daniel Connell, of Ballinabloun, tho' expected some time past, still call'd forth from me the tribute of concern due to a relation and an honest man, the last almost of my poor Father's contemporaries. Let me know in your next how he disposed of his affairs, and whether he has bequeathed anything to Charles Phillip, for whom I form many sanguine wishes. How does our brother-in-law mean to settle? and where? Many good wishes to him and Dan Connell, Tom Conway and Cousin Maur. Charles. Farewell, Dearest, Dearest Brother, farewell. Love me as I love you.

D. O'CONNELL.

Were it possible you'd bring your heart to forget the faults of the unfortunate Widow Leary, charity and her

---

[1] This is the handsome wild boy, Eugene McCarthy.

misery and misfortunes call upon you for mercy. I wish it
may be, cu'd be, but dare not urge it from a sence of her
offences; however, from my Dr Maurice's good heart anything may be expected. Follow but its dictates, and I'll
venture to affirm you'll forgive.

It was many a day yet before this high-spirited, wilful
woman and Maurice made friends. Her offence was marrying
in opposition to her family when she was first a widow. Her
" misery " was of the heart, not of the pocket; for she was left
well off.

Calais, Sep^{bre} ye 26th, 1776.

MY DR. BROTHER,—I recd. in due time both your letters,
and rejoiced to hear you are all well. It's happy my Mother's
Accident has been attended with no bad consequence.

I am now perfectly recovered, and live as freely as you
reccommend. Your opinion of diet and the Medical tribe was
also mine till experience proved to me the use of both. I
am persuaded Diet is a sovereign remedy in most disorders,
and perhaps the only, or at least the chief, one that nature
intended for the use of man, most disorders proceeding from
an irregular unabstimious mode of living. The Regt. parts
on Sunday next, the 29th, for Douay, where I shall pass the
winter. I, however, purpose taking a tour to Paris towards
the New Year. I have had some invitations to pass the
Winter, but have no Semestre, so am under a necessity of
remaining with the Reg^t. M. le Comte de Maillebois, son to
the famous Marshal of that name, and himself the man of
the highest Military repute among us, commanded here this
summer. Upon some acquaintance he was pleased to distinguish me, and gave me a memorial, demanding a Majority
for me. What the result may be I know not. There's none
vacant in our Brigade, and I fear my quality of a foreigner
will prove an obstacle in a French Reg^t, but whatever be the
result, it's vastly flattering to have been proposed by an
Officer of that rank and merit. It's principally on that
account that I intend making an Excursion to Paris. This
you'll keep to yourself. Young Falvey was near being carried
off here by a putrid fever, brought on thro' his own imprudence. He had at first but a Tertian Ague, which is very
common on the Sea Coast of Flanders, and particularly in
this town. No arguments cu'd prevail on him to observe a
Diet till he relapsed in a most violent manner, and was for
many Days in the highest danger. He is recovering, but I
fear will not be able to march off with us, and must remain

here until he gathers strength. Give his father my best Compliments, and let him know this fit of sickness has cost the boy £10, which the Reg^t advanced him, and it's absolutely necessary he shu'd add this sum Extraordinary to the next remittance to be made him, otherwise it would be impossible he should acquit them. Now, my Dr Brother, between you and me, I fear this young man will never be prudent, nor prove any great matter. He seems now somewhat more sensible of his past misconduct, but I can't depend much on his promices. I think for the present you will do better not to tell his father so, but rather urge him to send the £10 Extraordinary, as they are really indispensible. Let my friend Mick Falvey know I've been always waiting to see and obtain a Commission for his son in Royal Suédois, but it's now impossible—none but Sweeds or Germans can be admitted. He must, therefore, drop all hopes that way, and strike out some other plan. If he intends him for the Service, he had better send him for a year to the Barbets of St. Omer's, and then to Walshe's Reg^t as a Cadet, if he can be admitted. There is a Cadet to each company, and with 12 Sols pay. They are regularly to be promoted by seniority, except misconduct should cause one or the other to be passed by. No young man whatsoever can be made an Officer offhand as heretofore; he must go thro' the devoirs of Cadet. I request you'll give Mick Falvey this detail, and assure him that I shu'd be happy to have it in my power to comply with his request.

    I am glad to hear Morgan has given you a namesake [his second son, who died in the West Indies]. He may now hang up his Armour like a gladiator who has given ample proofs of military prowess. This, however, with due submission to my mother, and with proper restrictions in favour of his Wife. Farewell, my Dear Brother. My Duty and Love to my Mother, and most tender Affections to my Sister, not forgetting our friends at Carhen, Tarmons, etc. Eugene is with his reg^t at Baupaume, near Arras. He is well, and Count de Serrant has given me a favourable account of him. I wish he may continue to deserve it. FitzMaurice and Barry are his friends as much as I cu'd be; so is Chevalier Mahony, who is Captain en Second. Farewell. No news here. Some hopes of war, and an anxious Expectation of the result of the . . . I shall write once a month, and request you'll be exact . . . I am as usual,

                    Your most affectionate Brother,
                              D. O'CONNELL.

    The next letter refers to our hero's desire to serve in

America. To tell the truth, he does not seem to have been specially interested in the rights of the war, but to have had a purely professional desire to see service.

Gravelines, X^{bre} 6th, 1776.

My Dear Brother,—Having nothing Material to inform you of, I deferred writing to you this time past, and now lay hold of the conveniency that offers to avoid you unnecessary expence. This part of the World affords nothing new, except many military preparations, which are common all over Europe, and portend a War before long. In the Interim we here remain in anxious expectations till the trumpet sounds and calls us forth. Among other considerations, the great appearance of war at home has determined me to decline offers seemingly very advantageous made me by the Emissary of the American Congress, and which Major Conway has accepted, and is now parted. I must add, my Dr Brother, that I wished your approbation before I took that step. If, therefore, the prospect of War shu'd vanish at home, be not surprised, my Dr Brother, to see me undertake a Foreign Enterprise, the rather than spend the remaining part of my youth in inaction. If fortune should prove favourable, I may have it in my power to help my family, and at worse I run no other risk than what's common to every military man. I hope soon to hear from you, my Dr Brother, and heartily wish the bearer may arrive safe and without accident. The Reg^t is come here about a fortnight since. How long we remain I can not say. I purpose making a tour to Paris next month to see my friends and acquaintances, and to examine what's brewing. I shall also have some Conversation with the American Envoy. From there you'll receive my next. Morgan wrote to me some time since from Corke, to acquaint me of the *pleasing circumstance* (his own words) of a young Son. The bearer carries my congratulatory answer. My Sister has no doubt ere now recd. my letter from Douay. I hope the want of any material subject will be a sufficient apology for my writing so seldom to her and to my Mother. It's with the deepest concern I've learned that your measures in favour of our Cousin Jeffrey Maurice have proved fruitless. My heart bleeds for the poor man's sad and pityable situation. I wish, my Dr Brother, you may bring his Eldest boy to Darrinane, and take some care of his Education for a year or two, and then send him over to me, if you judge him qualified, either from his parts or figure, for a soldier. I hope with the divine assistance to be able to put him in the way of decent bread. If you find it convenient to comply with this request,

I shall expect you'll keep him as much as possible under your own eyes, and from every example of vice or low beheaviour. Farewell, my Dear Brother. Your approved good dispositions make me confident that my application on this occasion will not be disagreable. Besides the pleasure produced by a good action, [which] is the purest enjoyment of life, Nature and humanity call upon you to help the poor man's distressed young family. Adieu, my D^r, Dr Brother. No words can convey the warm emotions of a heart for ever your own.

D. O'CONNELL.

I wrote by this hand to my Mother. Remember me most kindly to all friends, not forgetting Ma^r Charles. Tell Abbé Moriarty I beg to be remembered in his prayers. Jemmy Baldwin charged me to see the Honble Mr Southwell, and to make some Enquiry concerning his Estate. I did, and mentioned since what I learned of it. I hope my letter came to hand.

It seems a great pity that my hero did not, after all, get a chance of serving under Washington, whose genius he early recognized. All his life he seems to have had a hankering after the Russian Service, whence doubtless the fame of the brave deeds and brilliant success of the Lacys came to inflame the Irish cavaliers of fortune all over Europe; but he never succeeded in carrying out this notion.

I cannot better close the record of 1776 than with the following notice of "Berwick's."

O'Callaghan (p. 603) quotes thus the English traveller, Mr. Thicknesse's, description of the Irish officers of "Berwick's" quartered in Calais ("Journey through France and Part of Spain"). Under the head of "Calais, November 4, 1776," he observes—

"I found Berwick's Regiment on duty in this town. It is commanded by Mons. le Duc de FitzJames, and a number of Irish gentlemen, my countrymen (for so I will call them). You can easily imagine that men who possess the natural hospitality of their own country, with the politeness and good breeding of this, must be very agreable acquaintances in general; but I am bound to go further, and to say that I am endeared to them by marks of true friendship. The King of France nor any prince in Europe cannot boast of troops better disciplined; nor is the king insensible of their merits, for I have lately seen a letter written by the king's command, from Comte de St. Germain, addressed to the officers of one of these corps, whereby it appears the king is truly sensible of their distinguished merit, for braver men there are not in any service. What an acquisition to France! What a loss to Britain!"

Paris, January the 25, 1777.

Some days before my departure from Gravelines, where the regiment now lies, I rec^d my Dr Brother's Letter of 9^{be} Last, to which, according to his desire, I deffered announcing untill I had seen my friends here. I had formed a design of going to America, but on such advantageous terms only as might justify my taking that step. Everything promised me the greatest success, when on a Sudden our Court came to the resolution to deny them any help, at least openly. I was to be made a Colonel here, and to be employed in that Country as *Major General*, *i.e.* Quarter Master General of the foot, but being refused the confirmation of the rank of Colonel in consequence of the above resolution, I thought it prudent, and so have my friends, to lay aside all thoughts of going over merely on the promices of Emissaries vested with powers vastly limited. If hereafter our Court shu'd alter its plan, I shall willingly jump at every oppertunity of promotion and glory.

M. de Maillebois honours me with a continuance of his favour, and has presented me to both Ministers with the highest encomiums. Many fair promices have been made me, and assurances that my talents shu'd not remain unrewarded, but such is the Sun of Courts, and so predominant is faction and intrigue, in time of peace particularly, that the nobility invade every post of honour or profit, and leave us private officers but the dangers, labour, and fatigues. Scarse is a place vacant when obtained by a Person at Court for some needy relation, and when we make our application it always comes too late. Nothing, in truth, but the invincible passion for glory and military honours can urge a man to labour against such difficulties. However, in my case I hope at length to overcome them. I shall remain here until April in close attendance on Count de Maillebois—happy I can make him my patron. I lodge with Chev. Mahony, whose friendship and attention for me none but yours can equal. His friends, who are numerous and of the first rank, become also mine. No young man of his country this century more esteem'd and beloved, and there's every prospect of his making a handsome fortune, if promotion and favour without much money can be so called. His Revenue is about £200 English a year, which is but short for the company he sees. He has been introduced to the royal family, and has the strongest reccommendations from Vienna thro' Count Mahony's[1] care and interest. I wish from the bottom of my heart they may not prove fruitless.

I am sorry to inform Cousin Rick Connell that there's no sort of encouragement to be expected here, nor, I believe, in Germany. As he is determined to try fortune, I think America is now the only theatre where bravery and Conduct can open a road for a young man destitute of money or friends in power. Was there the least chance of his doing anything here, I shu'd warmly press him to come over, and shu'd with pleasure share my Slender means with him; but in truth I see no hopes. If, however, he wishes otherwise, I shall not attempt to dissuade him from it. He may rely on finding a true friend in me. Mr. . . . has played a new trick. He shut himself up with a boy of sixteen, officer in his Reg^t, and played till he won of him 500 Livres. I have had him put into prison. He shall there remain 3 months. I fear he will never be reformed, and will be at length turned out of his Reg^t. Poor Tom FitzMaurice does every thing he can to correct him, but to no purpose. Farewell, my D^r, Dr Brother. My Duty to my mother, and most tender affections to my Sister, etc. Believe me for ever,

Most unalterably your own fond brother,
D. O'CONNELL.

Tom FitzMaurice has not a shilling besides his pay that I know off. Address to me at Gravelines. Chev. Mahony salutes you most kindly. I yesterday had a letter from Cousin Morty, from Germany. Many kind Comp^{ts} to my Aunt, Dan, etc.

The next letter contains a brief notice of our hero's first appearance at court, attaining merely, however, to the outer circles. The innermost circle was only to be approached through the Heralds' Office, and was yet beyond his reach.

Paris, March the 10th, 1777.

I recd. some days since my Dr Brother's letter of the 2nd february, and am glad to hear the conveyance which carried my Packet from Gravelines arrived safe. I can't but feel with the deepest sense of gratitude your kind anxiety with respect to the loss I suffered thro' the roguery of my servant. It's true he robbed me of almost the whole of my wearing

---

[1] Count O'Mahony, son of "le brave O'Mahony," of Cremona renown (see p. 320), was Spanish Ambassador at Vienna.

apparell, Linen, stockings, and every thing he thought worth carrying off, among which my sword gave me particular concern, but, tho' considerable the loss, I've still repaired it without incurring any Debts, and am now sufficiently stocked with every thing necessary. It's true I was obliged to lay out in that way the money I had brought with me from Darinane, which might doubtless have been better employed, but I cu'd not have foreseen nor prevented that Accident. Our lives and fortunes are always in the power of those that no consideration of honour nor fear of God restrains. To some we needs must trust, and all that we can do is to be guided by prudence in our choice. The fellow who so basely betrayed me deceived every one. No man bore the appearance of honesty and fidelity more than him. I was indeed unwilling to let you know it, well knowing it would give you more trouble than it gave me, and determined not to trouble you so soon, after all the favours you had just heaped on me. Economy is a never-failing resource. My expences I immediately reduced by one half. That way I've continued till my arrival here. I assure you on my honour I don't owe a penny, and have no sort of calls for the present. If my affairs require, I shall come here for a part of next winter (as probably will be the case). I shall then receive, with my usual sentiments, what you can, without inconveniency to yourself, be able to spare me, and most earnestly request you do no more. By remaining with the Corps I have no wants, and my sole motive in coming here is the pursuit of promotion. It's but just to sacrifice that end to your more immediate calls. M. de Maillebois honours me with a particular friendship. He carried me to Court, introduced me to both Ministers with such praises as give me room to expect may have some effect when they come from an Officer of his Weight and Distinction. There's no Majority vacant in the Brigade, and it's a matter of the greatest difficulty to obtain it in the French Regiments for a Stranger. It's nevertheless my aim. Places more honourable I cu'd obtain, but as they require a vast expence, and give little or no pay, I can't think of accepting them. In this unhappy country nothing can be done but thro' intrigue and importunity. The young men of the Court engross everything. Before we can be apprized of the vacancy they have already the promice. Shu'd I from a disgust relinquish my demands, why then I must sit down all my life and die a Captain, or at most a Lieut.-Colonel, like the man who can scarse sign his name—a circumstance truly hard to be borne with. Patience alone and perseverance can overcome these Difficulties.

I shall think no more of my American plan, as my D\ Brother wishes; but I differ quite in opinion with him with regard to the event of the War. Tho' feeble and unsoldierly the efforts they have hitherto made, still, if Washington pursues the plan he hitherto seems to have adopted, and that the inhabitants of that country do not fall off, it's almost impossible that England can support the enormous expence attending that War. The late check received by the Hessians proves that there's still a degree of spirit, and some notion of discipline, in the Rebel army.

Chev. Mahony gives you his best compliments, and requests you'll be so kind as to see Mr. French, Merchant, in Corke, and know from him whether Mr. George Woulfe, of Paris, remitted him 2000 Livres, French, to be paid to Messrs. Mahony, of Tranlanloe, heirs to Mr. Mahony who died a Lieut.-Colonel in the Spanish Service. This gentleman appointed Count Mahony, the Ambassador at Vienna, his Executor, and the Ambassador charged Chev. Mahony to remit the heirs' said sum of 2000 Livres, which remained in his hands. This money Mr. Woulfe remitted Mr. French . . . months ago for that purpose, and has no account from him as yet. I request, my D\ Brother, you'll loose no time in making the necessary enquiries about this Matter, and let me know it.

I am sorry to tell you there's nothing to be done about the Burse founded by D\ Connell, of St. Denis, untill there's a Certainty of the Death of his Nephew, to whom he left his fortune. Doctor Connell, of Corke, was charg'd to make the proper enquiries at home, and those who may be concerned hereafter wu'd do well to take every step to obtain a certainty of his Death. Till then there's no chance for their children. Farewell, my D\ Brother. Be so kind as to send my complete Baptisterium, and let it be dated for the year 1747, January, February, or March. I also beg you may send, out of the Herald's office, our Arms, correctly drawn out, and be prepared one of these days to send me our Genealogy. It's a thing very necessary in this country. Adieu, my D\ Brother. I shall be at Gravelines towards the 1st of April, and hope soon to hear from you. My tender affect. wishes to my Mother, Sister, etc. Believe me, as usual,

Your fond and obliged brother,

D. O'CONNELL.

Gravelines, May 17th, 1777.

I receiv^d my Dr Brother's letter of the 27th March, and have made, in consequence, every possible enquiry to be able to answer with a degree of certainty to Mr Hugh Falvey's desire of my pointing out the most Eligible place for the instruction of his Son. Blois is by no means to be thought of, tho' it might have some reputation in the former periods of the French Monarchy. It's now but a poor contemptible Country Town, altogether unprovided with any means of information. Angers, Dijon, and Caen, in Normandy, are flourishing cities, well inhabited, and the residence of many people of fashion. Each of 'em the Seat of a University; but Dijon is, in my opinion, preferable to either, and indeed to most places in the Kingdom, or any other, for a person whom I suppose to have already made a proficiency in the study both of Law and the Belles Lettres. 'Tis a Bishoprick, the Seat of a Parliament, the place of assembly of the provincial States, an University, and besides is possessed of an Academy of Belles Lettres, which makes no despicable figure in the republick of Letters. It contains, besides, many curious remains of Antiquity, having been in former ages the residence of the Sovereigns of Burgundy.

With respect to polite Education, he will find out every oppertunity of good company, which he can, provided he makes himself agreable by modesty, affability, and delicate attention to the Ladies. He must avoid with particular care excesses in Drinking, or any low Debauchery, which, tho' overlooked in our country, begets a lasting contempt amongst the French. Many English he must expect to meet there, but if he desires to reap a benefit from his Séjour in this Country, and to become conversant with the spirit and manners of the Nation, he must avoid any connection which may tend to divert him from that purpose. I make no doubt but his own good sense and penetration will point out the proper course to be followed that way, and make any further observations of mine quite unnecessary. Pray let him know that I'll be very happy if you and he will correspond with me, and afford me every oppertunity of shewing him the sincere regard I bear his father and family. Jerry[1] is perfectly well, and Expects as well as I to have the pleasure of seeing him when he comes over. This town is but 4 leagues from Calais, and a proper place to rest himself for a few days.

I have, methinks, Dwelt sufficiently on the subject. No change amongst us since my last. Major Conway is arrived safe at his destination, and will, I hope, soon be known in an honourable light. I can't help wishing som'times to be along with him. Florence James Mahony is come over here, and

---

[1] Poor Jerry Falvey, after his various misfortunes, turned out very well, and persevered in his military career.

no man can behave with greater prudence and reserve than he does hitherto; whether or no he may continue is the question, but the state of his Affairs affords him no means of Extravagance. His situation at his present age is really moving. It's impossible to deny him some slender acts of friendship while his behaviour reccommends him. His brother-in-law, Florence Mahony, who was also amongst us here, has been made a Sergeant in the Service of the English East India Company. This thro' the interposition of Captain Fagan, who spent the last winter in London. Farewell, my Dr Brother. My most Dutiful Love to my Mother, and fond affections to my Sister.

Your most affectionate
D. O'CONNELL.

I entreat you may take one of Jeffrey Maurice's sons, the most promicing for parts and figure. Make him learn to write and cipher, and read English and Geography.

An interval of seventeen months in the letter-book is followed by two letters in one month. Letters have lately turned up in so many unexpected ways and places that I am disposed to consider that the letter-book does not contain nearly all the correspondence. It probably consists of such letters as my dear old friend and cousin, Mrs. FitzSimon, found and borrowed, with other papers, from her brother Maurice O'Connell, of Darrynane, for a life of their father she began, but put aside, many years ago.

The letter here quoted of October 5, 1778, is one of the most important in the series, as it embodies the sentiments of a representative Irish French officer, and they are so different from what we should suppose them to have been. Against France, their foster-mother, these men would never bear arms. They were only too ready and willing to serve against all the rest of the world in the armies of the British king if their faith were recognized. Neither bigotry nor disloyalty is discernible in their sentiments. At the same time, when the sovereign of their native land refuses to receive them, they are quite ready and willing to bear arms against him. In a few months we find them serving against England, simply because they are denied a sphere for their energies at home.

The future Captain Rick incidentally mentions our hero in March, May, and September, 1778, March and June, 1779, and January, 1780, in a manner which leads me to infer that he did not share in any foreign expedition in those years.

Paris, the 5 8bre, 1778.

I in due course, my Dr Brother, answered y^r letter of the 3rd June last, since which I've not been favoured with a Line from you, and have not rec^d, directly or indirectly, the least account from my friends at Darinane. You can easily conceive how unpleasing a circumstance this must be, and how uneasy it needs must make me. I am inclined to believe my letter to you has miscarryed; therefore I address this inclosed to my friend Fagan, who is now in London, and send it by hand in order he should put it in the Post Office of that City, by which means it cannot possibly fail to come to hands.

Your publick Papers have transmitted here the pleasing account of the New Laws in favour of the Roman Catholicks. A Revolution so unexpected and so long wished for must needs procure, in course of some years, an accession to the power and prosperity of the Kingdom of Ireland, and unite in one common Sentiment of loyalty the hearts of that long-oppos'd and long unfortunate Nation. One step more still remains to be made—I mean the Liberty of spilling their blood in defence of their King and Country. I doubt not 'twill soon be granted, tho' no motive cu'd ever induce me to bear arms against France, where I early found an Asylum when refused one at home. I still wish the prosperity of the country, and at the same time that I pursue with inviolable fidelity that of my adopted King, Nature, stronger than reason or principle, still attaches my heart to Ireland.

No change in my situation as yet. I hope, however, time will make it better. I've indeed great reasons to expect it. Many friends and numerous and distinguished acquaintances, and, I thank God, a well-established character. It's time. I am hard sett to weather it out, till better times come on, but the sweets of ease will appear the more savourable after some distress. Some advantages have been lately offer'd me in the East, but my friend Count de Maillebois, to whom I am so much indebted, and to whom I have sworn an everlasting attatchment, wu'd by no means permit me to Accept. The circumstances for and against are too long to be enter'd into here. Efforts will be made this winter to procure some Accession to my appointment; till then I must own I shan't be happy in mind. I've a great deal to do to keep out of Debt and support the decency suitable to my Station and necessary to keep up an intercourse with my friends, tho' I assure you that I've the utmost modesty in every respect, and carry parsimony as far as ever decency can admit. I with impatience await the remittance you've been so kind as to promice me in the course of September, and pray you previously to accept my warm acknowledgements. Would to God, my Dear Brother, I cu'd at length be no more a burthen on your good nature! I feel and am conscious this has been too long the case; but then, what can I do? I am equally conscious I've not the least reproach to make myself. You know the world too well to impute to me what is but the effect of chance and insurmountable circumstances. Farewell, my D{^{r}}, D{^{r}} Brother. My Duty to my Mother, Affections to my Sister, etc. Believe me during Life,

Your much obliged and most loving Brother,

D. O'C.

My friend, Chev. Mahony, desires his affectionate Comp{^{ts}} to you and family. I hope my Sister's indisposition is *long since over*. I request you'll endeavour to forward to Mr. Nowlan, of London, by some safe hand, the Pedigree. Capt. Fagan will take care to have it faithfully delivered here.

Paris, October the 15th, 1778.

My Dr. Brother,—Yesterday I rec{^{d}} yours of the 25th Ultimo, containing Mr. George Goold's Draft on Messrs. Dupont and Comp. for the sum of 800{^{ll}}. I immediately presented said bill, which was duly accepted, payable the 20th next month. According to your desire, I lose no time to give you the most early notice thereof, and return you my most grateful acknowledgements for this very necessary supply. You'll see by my last how much it was wanting. This winter new Efforts shall be made, thro' the Channel of my friend M——, to obtain some accession to my finances, the success of which you shall be immediately informed of, and with the greatest exactness. You ask me whether he cu'd not, thro' his reecomendations, have me employed by others; but the nature of his connections, and many other circumstances which I cannot here mention, made it hitherto impossible. I have nothing to add to what I mentioned in my last. Rick Connell is arriv'd a long time since, and is perfectly well and much pleased with his new Station. I hope it will be made still more agreable to him. If a sure oppertunity cu'd be met with, either from Cork or Dublin, for London, by which the Linen and Geneaology prepared for me cu'd be transmitted to London, Captain Fagan, who is there at present, wu'd find several oppertunities to forward them here. I suppose his mother has his address, which I've not as yet. Mr. Nowlan is well acquainted with him, and wu'd do that business with pleasure, as he several times assured me by letter.

Your papers have no doubt mentioned the death of poor Tom Conway; but tho' desperate the wound he received, he is recovered. The ball got in under his ear, and come out a little above the temple on the opposite side. He was despaired of for a long time, but there's a certainty of his being now perfectly well.

The Campaign in Bohemia is, I suppose, by now at an end, and the success ou't on the side of his Imperial Majesty due to the Military talents of Lacy, who took so good a camp at Koniggratz that he cu'd not be dislodged, and at the same time cover'd Prague, while Loudon at the other side intercepted Prince Henry. L^t.-General D'Alton, our countryman, commanded at Arnau, and repulsed with the greatest valour and capacity several attacks. The possession of this important pass made the Junction of the two brothers impossible, so that our two Countrymen have shined this Campaign. Farewell my Dear, Dear Brother. All friends here are well, and desire to be remembered to you. Pray remember me to M^r and Mrs Willow when next you've an oppertunity. My Love and Duty to my Mother. Fond affections to my Sister, etc. Be always persuaded of my deep sense of gratitude and most unalterable tenderness and love for you.

D. O'CONNELL.

Have you seen Lord Kenmare? I wrote to Sister Nancy, but got no answer. Is she removed to her new place?

The letters which have reached us are few in number for the period from 1777 to 1783, and this is the very time during which Rickard O'Connell's fluent pen fills up sundry missing links.

The young soldier and the young physician, who figure therein, both learning their trades in France, seem to have kept up a very lively intercourse. The wonderful biographical letter which my feminine prudery has caused me to condense very considerably, was evidently written as a confession and a justification for the edification of old Colonel James Conway and my hero, for he distinctly states that, had he not confided all his troubles to his dear Cousin, Maurice Leyne, he would not have been in France earning the bread of a gentleman. The future doctor, clever, studious, and well-conducted, was a young man after my hero's own heart, and he was at hand to urge Rick's claims of friendship and kindred. It was no small effort to a man to go and serve among small boys as a cadet, as Rick did.

To Rick's fluent pen and close observation we owe the three line sketches of my hero, which depict him at intervals all through the else almost unrecorded years of his life, while he was waiting for promotion, watching opportunities and trying to help his friends.

This Rickard figures so often in the letters, both as writing and as written about, that I feel disposed to dwell at some length on his very interesting personality. By many degrees the most amusing letters of a somewhat formal series are written by this officer of the Irish Brigade to a kinsman, then a young medical student in Paris, who was afterwards Dr. Maurice Leyne, of Tralee,[1] a famous physician, some of whose letters of advice to Hunting Cap I had already perused. To his grandson, Mr. J. Leyne, of the Registry of Deeds Office, Dublin, I am indebted for the loan of the book of copied letters, on which I shall freely draw. Would that I could recopy them in full! But though Count O'Connell's letters are written so that any Christian gentlewoman can quote nearly every word, other eighteenth-century gentlemen were not so guarded in the expression, or so high-minded in the conception, of their ideas. Captain Rick was an appalling flirt, and he suffered from some asthmatic disorder for which he habitually swallowed the queerest herbal decoctions. He discourses to his cousin with great frankness of both his expectorations and his flirtations.

> "The light that lies
> In woman's eyes"

was a perpetual and perilous Will-o'-the-wisp to Captain Rickard.

More valuable far than formal panegyrics written to Hunting Cap are the young man's accounts of his kind patron to the other young man, who was the depository of his confidences amatory and medical. He gives us precisely those graphic, unconscious touches which Count O'Connell omits. We hear the everyday details of foreign soldiering

[1] See Note F, p. 246.

from a man who has joined sufficiently late in life to note them, whereas to a boy of fifteen or sixteen all such things seem matters of course, unworthy of being recorded.

Colonel Newcome was never kinder to a lad than Count O'Connell to this engaging scamp. "Captain Rick," as he is always styled, describes his kind patron in the full-blown glories of his first command, just as he gives us the most graphic descriptions of the hardships of the drill-ground and the march. He belongs to the family of Sir Lucius O'Trigger and Charley O'Malley. He possesses every attractive Celtic foible from which my hero was free. I was going to credit the formal, long-headed excellence of the brothers Maurice and Daniel to their drop of English blood, but Captain Rick also descends from the honest Williamite, Captain Jenkin Conway. Alice and two Elizabeth Conways convey exactly the same amount of Saxon ichor to their posterity, but it fails to influence the captain.

His real circumstances are like those of a hero of Lever's. He is as poor as a church mouse, but he counts kith and kin with the finest of people, and is constantly going among them. His grandfather was a rich man, Geoffrey of the Great Herds (Sheaira-na-mo-Mor). His mother descended maternally from the O'Briens of Ballycorrig, a family sprung from a younger son of the famous Earl of Inchiquin, "Red Murrough the Burner." My Lord of Inchiquin acknowledged Captain Rick as a connection, and would have helped him had not his faith debarred him from any post within the range of his cousin's influence. He was a welcome guest with the O'Briens, at stately Ennystymon, in Clare, with the Knight of Glin, in Limerick, and with a score of lesser gentry in Clare and Kerry. Yet he tells us his father was steeped in poverty, had had the narrowest escape of losing the farm, the "sole subsistence of a decayed family." He tells Hunting Cap, whom he seems to want to watch over his parents, that his ancestor, Maurice the Transplanted, put his Cromwellian grant of Briantree into Lord Inchiquin's patent, and took from him a lease of ninety-nine years.

There was a promise of renewal to Maurice's heirs, and a fine promised, but never paid. The descendants sold their interest to persons named England, and some others. The lease fell out just as Rick joined at Cambray. The Englands threatened to turn out his father, who seems to have been under-tenant to the representatives of his grandfather. Luckily, in the litigation which followed, Lord Inchiquin prevailed against the middlemen, owing to non-payment of fine, and at once acceded to Rick's pathetic appeal, as he says—

"Thereupon his Lordship generously gave my brother a lease of 3 Lives of the Farm on which my Father always lived since his Marriage, and of 3 others. . . . It is enough for me that bountiful Providence has been pleased to make me in some Degree the instrument for obtaining a poor subsistence for my decayed family."

In 1777 Rickard O'Connell, then a full-grown man, entered the Brigade. In his letters he shows a considerable acquaintance with both English and Latin authors, and was a person of no small intelligence. He seems to have led an idle life, rambling and sporting about. Probably the poor circumstances into which his family had fallen precluded their collecting the means to send him abroad at the usual age—from thirteen to sixteen. He, however, had to fly from Ireland, where he had got himself into a very serious scrape. It arose out of an unlucky love affair, and the vengeance he incurred nearly led to his being murdered in 1777. The Knight of Glin, Mr. O'Brien, of Ennistymon, and Mrs. McMahon, of Clonina, all tendered varying advice. Captain Rick was guided by the lady. No stone of either the ancient castle or more modern house of Clonina, where she dwelt, is now to be seen, but the most vivid tradition of " Fair Mary " still exists in West Clare. My Clare home is about ten miles from hers, in the McMahon country. She was the daughter of important people—Charles McDonnell, of Kilkee, and Isabel O'Brien, of the great house of Ennistymon. Tiege McMahon, of Clonina, who loved her, had only a long pedigree, a dismantled castle, and an impoverished estate. She was a famous rider, and he once saved her life out hunting when her horse bungled at a great leap; and soon after discovered his love to her. Her parents refused his suit; the lovers eloped, and not only lived happily evermore, like lovers in a story, but Fair Mary was renowned for her piety, charity, and noble life. Old people will repeat uncouth rhymes, wherein this golden-haired, pearl-breasted lady is celebrated for her beauty, charity to the friars and the blind poor. The O'Donoghue of the Glens and Sir Maurice O'Connell, of Lake View, represent the extinct family of McMahon of Clonina in the female line. To her Rickard O'Connell confided his troubles.

"Next day I halted," he says, "at Clonina, every one of whose respectable inhabitants I allways had, and still have, reason to believe my real friends. Tom McMahon's mother, to whom I now communicated every particular from the Beginning, with that unlimited Confidence due to her truly respectable Character and Generous Friendship, told me without Reserve she did not like I should cross the Shannon."

"Fair Mary," who may be aptly styled "Wise Mary" in this case, did not merely ground her advice on the possible dangers of assassination; it was on the dangers of the peccant Clare man being offered up "on the shrine of Kerry acquaintance," and hurried into an undesirable marriage.

The following December (1777) the Knight of Glin sent him word that a plot to murder him was set on foot.

It now became imperatively necessary to seek a living out of his own country. To young Maurice Leyne, student of medicine, in Paris, he writes, in March, the long story which I have abridged, and in it he gives the following most graphic account of the adventures of a poor gentleman in search of a patron :—

Extract of Rickard O'Connell's letter to Maurice Leyne.

Chez Monsieur Jacquelin,
Vis-à-Vis L'enfoncement, Rue la Hachette, à Paris.

Mahery, March 1st, 1778.

The only pleasing account I can give of myself is that I have been to wait on ye Earl of Inchiquin last 7ber, in Ennis, and met with a very favourable Reception. I had ye honor of being acquainted with this Nobleman, both in England and Ireland, before his Accession to his Title. I was introduced and recommended in Ennis by two of his most respectable Relations and Friends in this Country, in whose presence he assured me of his Patronage and Friendship. But there are two *Bars* in my way. One is, I fear, insurmountable—my Religion, which I shall not change; yᵉ other very hard to be got over—*Poverty*, the worst of all recommendations to yᵉ Great. Unhappy Poverty! yᵉ only cause which has hindered me these four months of going to his Lordship, for I have found it entirely impossible to raise as much money as would bear my expences to London, and yᵉ few Friends who would assist me if they could are, by Extravagance, yᵉ too constant attendant on landed Property in this Country, reduced to almost as low an ebb of Cash and Credit as myself, tho' they have Estates. [Would not this do for our portrait, O landlords of a century later? It was the thrifty Hunting Cap who eventually supplied Rick with some ready cash to bear him to France.]

Every night I have to keep a Sentinel on my Father's house, every Day I am in arms. Wherever I go that meagre Friend Distress still stalks in view, Danger lurks in wait, and care is the Constant Companion of my Pillow. Such must be my helpless, almost hopeless, Situation while I must remain under the misfortune of remaining in my native country, from which you pretty well know it has not been hitherto in my power to transport myself. [Now my hero makes his first appearance in the letters as "Major Connell," being still only a major in "Berwick's," and these Irish kinsmen only producing their O's when abroad, until the remissions of 1782 enabled them to produce them at home.] To be remembered by Major Connell, for whom I shall ever entertain yᵉ sincerest affection and esteem, is an honor I shall ever gratefully acknowledge. My Father, who had yᵉ honor of being acquainted with Colonel Conway, presents affectionate Respects to him and to yᵉ Major, to which I beg leave to add mine, tho' I have not yᵉ honor of being known to yᵉ Colonel. I know not what you will think of an Idea that presents itself to me. You never were a stranger to my thoughts. I will make you acquainted with it. You who have yᵉ happiness of seeing both these gentlemen, may suggest to them to use their Influence for procuring me some Employment, civil, Military, etc., by which I might procure yᵉ means of Subsistence, and be in some degree a useful member of Society. It is true I already mentioned my inclination for yᵉ Military state to Major Connell, who thought me far too advanced in life for a Cadet, nor am I ignorant of the Difficulty of obtaining even to that. Yet if anything could be done in that or any other way, I shᵈ have yᵉ firmest Reliance on yᵉ Generosity and Good Nature of both these gentlemen, for with yᵉ Colonel's Character I am well acquainted. It is needless to tell you that my views are not aspiring. The growth of Ambition is a plant that thrives beneath ye Genial Influence of prosperous fortune, is checked by the bleak chill aspect of Adversity and Disappointment.

I am not quite such a stranger to the world as to rely implicitly on a great Man's Promices. I may happen to be left to feed, or rather to perish, on Expectations to the last hour of my Life. Moreover, I fear ye great Obstacle of my Religion must interfere with any interest made for me in England. I trust in Providence that I shall be able in May to make up a little Sum that will enable me to quit a country where I have met with nothing but misfortune and Disappointment, which I am resolutely determined on. Could I meet any encouragement to direct my steps to France, perhaps I may even yet be happy. You required a long letter. This is unconsionably so. I hope soon to hear from you again, but never so long a letter as this. Adieu, my dear Friend. While I exist I must be unalterably

Y^r most affectionate,
RICKD. CONNELL.

In May, when Rickard O'Connell had some chance of getting a little money, he sent his faithful henchman into Kerry, where he himself dared not venture. How he sped with his reverend kinsman is mentioned. Hunting Cap either lent or gave him twenty guineas—from the brief endorsement on the letter I cannot say which.

The "Alps of Difficulties" he had surmounted are partially described. In a letter I need not quote in full he says—

Approbation of my intended Expedition, and generous Assistance towards carrying it on, have made Impressions that neither Time nor Chance can eraze. I will not trouble you with attempting to express my gratitude to you and my dear Colonel.[1] Words cannot do it. The Hope of being hereafter able to shew it by Action rouses my drooping Spirits.

I am sorry to write anything that I know will not be agreable, but it is impossible for me to bring my Brother along with me; blame me not for this. If I can work my own Way, If I can surmount the Alps of Difficulties I have to encounter, all circumstances consider'd, and comparing small

---

[1] I should infer he refers to my hero as his colonel, but M. de la Ponce gives a later date for the commission—September, 1779. Perhaps he had heard some premature reports of his friend's promotion.

Things with great, it shall be a Passage equal to Hannibal's; and I solemnly assure you it is what a Mind less ambitious than mine to seek the Paths of Honour under the Auspices of an almost Adored Patron would give up all Thoughts of, deter'd by the Difficulties I labour under, which, without the immediate Interposition of Providence, are insurmountable.

If ever you speak to Father Morgan, he will let you know the only Notice he took of your Letter was to tell the bearer it required no Answer. Neither the Charity becoming a Clergyman, nor the Hospitality esteemed hereditary to a Connell, inclined him to direct my poor faithful Fellow to a Resting Place where he may be refreshed, even for an Hour, from the Fatigues of a long Journey undertaken merely from his Affection to me. His Reverence, indeed, by a Verbal Message, recommended to me to commit Matrimony; were I obliged in Honour to return to Kerry, his Recommendation were needless. In spite of my Veneration for the Religion of which they are Ministers, I abhor the selfishness of his ungenerous, hypocritical Tribe. Their nasty lazy Lives are employ'd in preaching brotherly Love and Charity, yet, tho' they live on the Fat of the Land, the Man who carries his Fortune by his Side, whose Inheritance is his Sword, owns more Benevolence than a whole Convocation.

I never knew a Priest posses'd of a manly spirit but one (Owen Sullivan), and, to show how constant my old Sweetheart Misfortune has been to me, He died poor, last November.

I write by the Bearer to recommend him to Cousin Morgan for a Night's Lodging, and entreat you will do the same at his Return; to you I submit whether you will be pleased to write any Thing more to him.

If ever I am prepared, I hope to get a ship from Limerick; from whence I will write to you. Adieu, my Dear Cousin and much Respected Friend. I hope you will believe no Man except one is so high in the Esteem of

Your much obliged and most affect. Cousin,
RICHD. CONNELL.

Fenloe, May 25th, 1778.

My affec' Respects to all Friends, and tell Cousin Dan I will write to him.

Rick is now happily landed in the Brigade, where he finds Kerry men in the proportion of three to one of any other country. According to my hero, that was not wonderful.

To Maurice Leyne, in Paris.

Camp near St. Malo, Sep. 23, 1778.

I deny every syllable of it. Tho' I am here strutting in Scarlet, a Candidate for a Regiment, I am not grown conceited, nor am I become such a Rascal as to forget the Friend of my Bosom, nor was it possible for me to write sooner with Propriety. [Words are illegible here and there; but it seems Rick sits on his straw bed, on which couch he has been studying French grammar, is expecting a Review in two hours, and begins his epistle before it. He goes on to say], I was never healthier or happier, or in higher Spirits except with him. Such is the hurry here [he continues] that I could not get a Tent for many Days after I joined the Regiment, nor was I able to procure a Soldier's coat and Firelock before last Friday, yet I assure you that of four Cadets who have all spent some Time with ye Regiment, none of them promises better than I do. Were you to see ... House and Furniture, you would think it ... to live here. I assure you I find none, but am happier here than in the best apartments I have ever been in. O cruel Fortune, that did not suffer me to embrace this life earlier!

In a few days we shall decamp. When we get into a Garrison I shall be more at Leisure, and will fill the sheet as usual. But here such continual bustle—from dressing to exercise, from exercise to Review, from Review to exercise, from thence to Ceremonial Visits—that I am mostly on my Legs except whilst I sleep. Colonel O'Connell ... that I intend to write a Novel ... amusement. I wrote to him, to Chevalier Mahony, and to Colonel Conway. I request you will present my affectionate respects to them. The Drum beats. Adieu, my Friend. O! that you were a soldier and in this Regiment! Good God! I should be happier than falls to the lot of Mortal.

R. O'C.

25th, 6 o'clock in the evening.

O Hal, Turk Gregory never did such Deeds in Arms as I have done. This morning at Dawn we left our Camp and march'd to a Harbour 8 miles off. We were divided into two parties. One represented the English, who were supposed to make Descent; the other was to beat them back to their Ships. Tho' I do not think the Victory gained by the French will be recorded in the Annals of Fame, yet I am sure the affair made a great Noise in the World. You must know that tho' I have been only five Days learning the Excercise, Captain O'Connor permits me to march in ye Ranks and carry a gun. I fired 70 Cartridges, and the next most dexterous member of my Party fired but 50, upon my Honour. I dined with the Colonel . . .'s Brother, our second Colonel, who happened to pass by our Party and saw me charge, fire, and jump over Hedges and Ditches, and was told by Barry, my officer, how many cartridges I had fired, talked with admiration of the dexterity of so fresh a soldier. I request that you will go immediately and tell this to Colonel O'Connell and Chevalier Mahony, and also to Colonel Conway.

À Monsieur, Monsieur Leyne, Étudent en Medecine, Hotel d'Angleterre, Rue des Anglois, à Paris.

De present chez Mr. Bondel Avocel, Rue Guinégaud vis-à-vis la dernière porte de la Monnaie.

Monsieur de la Ponce, in his valuable manuscript notes for a work on the Irish Brigade, preserved in the Royal Irish Academy, gives us my hero's appointment as Lieut.-Colonel of the Royal Swedes on September 19, 1779; and here is Rick talking of "the colonel" a full year before. Could he have got the rank of colonel when he had intended going to America? In the January letter of 1777 he says—

"I was to be made a Colonel here, and to be employed in that Country as Major General, *i.e.* Quarter Master General of the foot, but being refused the confirmation of the rank of Colonel in consequence of the above resolution, I thought it prudent . . . to lay aside all thoughts of going over."

Perhaps he may have got confirmation of the rank. He seems to have been in Paris all through the years 1778 and 1779—at least, the new recruit sends him messages to Paris.

For the whole of 1779 the letter-book is a blank. In March, 1779, Rick O'Connell, writing to Maurice Leyne from Quimper, says he wrote him in a letter of January to Colonel O'Connell. Consequently, my hero was in Paris.

Rick fills two doleful pages with the medical symptoms of a chest attack, which he fears is the beginning of an hereditary asthma to which his father was liable, and which he fears may disable him from a military career—

"The Service," he says, "is my only Amusement. When Exercise is over, I betake myself to study the Ordonnance, and thus my life passes without any Variety except some short morning visits to the old officers, and mounting Guard once a Fortnight. I fancy a fellow so fond of Ease as you could find no great amusement in stalking under a Firelock Opposite to a Sentry Box for Eight hours in the 24. I who have spent a youth of dissipation have not spoke to a woman since I came to France. The spirit of Intrigue, which once solely seemed to Animate me, is fairly laid."

Here Rick plunges into a sentimental disquisition. On Sundays, when he can get away from the pleasure-parties proposed by the young officers, he bends his solitary steps to some stream, where fancy recalls past adventures on the banks of the Shannon, Fergus, Inagh, Lough Lane, Lough Lee, Blackwater, Feale, and the strand of Tralee, and the various protestations and declarations of "lips that sweetly were foresworn." Mira, Clio, Eloisa, and Rosetta are the fanciful names he bestows on these damsels. How well Davis divined the sentiments when, in the "Battle Eve of the Brigade," he made the officers drink—

"Good luck to the girls whom we woo'd long ago,
  Where Shannon and Barrow and Avondhu flow!"

"But the Drum rouses me from my Reverie. Away, y̆ᵉ soft Illusions, idle dreams of my feverish youth! Henceforth the tender sighs, the softened accents, the melting Murmurs of Love, must give place to the loud Music of that 'spirit-stirring' Instrument. The laborious ardious paths of my profession must be Trodden. It is certainly a great encouragement to me that my Endeavours and good Conduct meet with the Approbation of the Colonel, and gain the good will of the officers and soldiers.

"I lately got a letter from Colonel O'Connell, wherein he mentioned that Count Serrant [Walsh de Serrant, Colonel-Proprietor of 'Walsh's'], who, when absent, knows everything that passes in the Regiment, has been pleased to say very handsome things of me, wishes for the oppertunity of placing me, and hopes there may be a vacancy next month. I find myself on the most pleasing terms with the Corps, amongst whom there are some really worthy Men, and as for the Soldiers, for the last two months they have anticipated my future *great Consequence* by calling me nothing but *Mon Lieutenant*. All this staggers my Brother Cadets, who tell me they must lead the Van for promotion, for that I have no Occasion for a Commission."

Rick O'Connell is one of the very few eighteenth-century

folk who seems to love Dame Nature as we do, and he gives a pretty description of the clear streams, meandering rivers, green fields, and woodland steeps of the country near Quimper, bursting out into all the beauties of a luxuriant spring. Towards the end he says—

"Colonel O'Connell has told you that I had good news from Ireland a Day or two after I wrote you last."

Extracts from Richard O'Connell's letter to Maurice Leyne, March 26, 1779. This second letter, following so soon on its predecessor, is full of Rick's symptoms—rather like chronic bronchitis. All the duty he is doing is looking on while the corporals are teaching the recruits the first principles of the exercise. He then goes on to tell his friend of a promising opening. As the negotiations are to be conducted by Colonel O'Connell, it is evident he continued in or near Paris.

"Captain FitzMaurice [the kind Colonel Tom of later letters] sent for me," he writes. "He had a letter before him from Paul Sweeny, who desired him to let me know that Count Dillon offer'd to give me a Commission in his Regiment. The Count, an ambitious, high-spirited, fine young fellow, is going to Martinico with 900 pick'd men of the Regiment, which compose as fine a Battalion as any perhaps carrying arms. Changing uniform and some other Preperations are attended with some Difficulty; but to encounter Difficulties is the business of my life. It was with Difficulty I came here. God is all-sufficient, and will assist me.

"If I return, Maurice, I shall return a good officer, probably with a good rank, as military operations will be carried on briskly. The warmth suits me, so that I hope I shall soon shake off this cough.

"You may, perhaps, hear of this affair before you receive this letter, as I am determined never to take a step without Colonel O'Connell's Advice and Appropation. I wrote to him by the post which went off at 3 o'clock, about an hour after my conference with Captain FitzMaurice. The Colonel will see Count Dillon, who is now in Paris, where they will settle about what is to be done. Not having time to write to you before this Day's Post went out, this Letter must wait until Monday, by which means the Colonel will hear from me 3 days before you. I much wish to hear from you. But our Regiment marches from here on the 6th of April."

Our friend Rickard's dream of glory was deferred by my hero's cold common sense. He made him stay on in "Walsh's," which was full of Kerry kinsmen, whose colonel was an old friend, and whose uniform could be easily managed. I can perceive a little disappointment in his tone, but no faltering in his loyalty to the friend he looked on as only a shade less infallible than the Pope.

From Croisic, June 17, 1779, he writes—

I am sure Colonel O'Connell has told you that Count Serrant has been pleased to name me, last April, to succeed one of our officers who has resigned. I expect my commission by every post. I would have been ordered to Paimbœuf, to join the first Batallion, to which I shall belong when my Commission arrives. But here we have a great many English Recruits, whom we have got about the beginning of May. I have been appointed to teach them the Exercise, and, as they are already pretty forward, I believe I shall soon go to Paimbœuf. [Here comes a delicious bit. I have transcribed growls galore from my hero over the iniquities and enormities of the boy-cadets he and sundry kinsmen kept importing, but here is an imp who surpasses them all.] This employment of Exercise Master, which I am obliged to stick very close to, and in which I am likely to Continue, is of the tiresome sort. It requires a great deal of Patience, and very much application, both rough and smooth, to transform a peasant, as dull as the clod he treads on into a smart Soldier, and that in the time. But the most grievous Task ever imposed on me was to Lick that bear's cub I brought with me from Ireland into a soldier. Captain O'Connor, our treasurer, my particular Friend for some months past, and my captain when I was a Chasseur, who is in many Respects a father to our boys, took him away from his Cousin at Quimper, and requested me to take the ungracious burthen on my shoulders. Captain O'Connor's request, together with my great regard and Esteem for his respectable family, induced me to spare no pains. I endeavoured to work on his Temper by soothing, together with a show of Confidence and reward; then severity, when milder means proved unsuccessful to keep him out of harm's Way. But on the route hither he gave full scope to his Temper, and one day at dinner, consisting of more than 12 persons, before we finished our Soupe, according to our rules I took him on my back, and, for want of a sufficient number of Cadets, got 9 sub lieutenants to thrash him while he was able to roar. When the Discipline was over, and he recovered breath enough to curse, he became worse than ever, and swore the most ex'crable oaths—he would Murder every one of us. Some of those who had been insulted complained to his cousin, who dragged him on the guard. But I made a shift to get him out by assuring the Major that if he was not put to bed he would not be able to march with us. On our arrival here Captain O'Connor begged I would teach him at least as much of the Exercises as would give him the Gait and Air of a Soldier. Before we were many days at this work, Harry took the sulk, and refused to obey my command, and that to in the same Rank with my English men, the most of whom are as wicked Dogs as ever trod the deck of a Privateer. Tho' under Arms, they laughed aloud, and "damned their eyes, but the lad had spirit." Lest the contagion should spread amongst fellows so apt to catch it, I ordered Harry to Prison, but upon his peremptory refusal was obliged to seize him and clap him into the dungeon, where, lest he should fret himself into a fever, I prescribed for him the cool Regimen of Bread and Water. Captain O'Connor, despairing to get any good of him, at least until he gets a little more sence, wrote to Doctor MacMahon to send him to school for 2 or 3 years to Nantes. Having played the devil after his enlargement from the Dungeon, he is now, thank God! gone, and I am rid of him.

 Croisic, as you may see by the map, is a Peninsula within a few leagues of the mouth of ye Loire. Y^e town, which is neither large nor handsome, stands not far from the isthmus, along the Shore, where is scarcely any sign of summer but ye heat. Not a Shrub grows on the whole peninsula, except a few in ye Town, which are sheltered by houses from ye Atlantic winds. The dulcet notes of Philomel, or any of the inferior choiresters of the grove, were never herd here. Even the Cuckhow does not deign to pay us a visit; but my ears are forever grieved with the screaming of sea Fowl. In a solitary mood, lost in depths of thought on a primrose bank by the murmuring brooks of Quimper, could I enjoy my thoughts. When tired of stuffing my head with the ordonnance, I retire to the breezy shore and listen to the hollow murmurs of Ocean. Fancy imperceptibly transports me to the strand of Tralee or the cliffs of Liscannor, where my old acquaintants would hardly believe that I pass here for a woman hater! As I ne'er ventured to speak French yet to ladies, the Flirts will have it that I have no tongue except for exercise, where they find my English commands so boisterous that they think I could never Attune my voice to the soft accents of Love. Oh woman! in spite of all I have suffered, my heart owns that this world without you were insipid. In the name of Friendship, my Dear Maurice, lose no time to let me hear from you. Adieu.

R. O'C.

Maurice Leyne is now addressed, "Etudiant en Medicine au Collège des Lombards."

From Paimbœuf, on August 20, 1779, Lieutenant Rickard writes again to Maurice Leyne. There is a bitter anti-English tone in this, wanting in all the other Irish Brigade letters I have seen.

Would to God, my Dear Maurice, that we were at this moment 200,000 strong in Ireland, and that I had the command of our single company of Oak Park! I would kick the Members and their Volunteers and their unions and their Societies to the Devil! I would make the Rascally spawn of Damned Cromwell curse the hour of his Birth! Oh, Heaven! can there be such Brutes in human form? But my dear Country swarms with them.

I am astonished that a Parisian should ask an Inhabitant of Brittany for News. All we know here is that the combined Fleets of the House of Bourbon were many Days ago near the Channell's mouth. This is certain. We have reason to believe that many of the Troops are embarked before this time. It is said they are to Beard the Brittish Lion in his Den. It is also said that his Friend the Russian Bear begins to grumble about this Proceeding, and offers his clumsy mediation at Versailles. Should it be rejected, I still fear that the other Lordly Savage, tho' he seems grown old and dozed, will at length give himself a savage shake, tho' it is a good while since his Roarings have shook the shores of the world.

It is certain the West India Fleet [the Jamaica Fleet, etc.] are safely arrived in England. They bring an Accession of 10,000 Sailors. They will have at least 45 Ships of the line in the Channell. My own opinion is that 45 well manned English ships are equal—I mean only in the narrow Seas—to any force that ever floated. [A very touching bit follows about kind Robin Conway and his Flemish wife, who were always so kind to the young Irish boys coming to the Brigade.]

Cousin Conway desired I should open any Letters that may come for him, and send him such as may be of consequence. The last Post brought 3—one from Dr. Sheehy, which I did not send, because I believe they may be just going to dine together; and one from Père Felix O'Dempsey, an Irish Capucin. It seems His Reverence has a stronger vocation for Fighting than praying. He writes to Mr. Conway to desire he will instantaneously write to "Sartine," as he calls him familiarly, to make him a Chaplain of a French man of War, and Provide such another place for Père Alexander. The other was from Mme. Conway, which, tho' she will soon tell him the contents of it, I could not find it in my heart to keep from him. I had rather get such a Letter from a wife, were that wife Mira, and I able to support her, than a Colonel's Brevet. . . . [He desires to be remembered to Colonels O'Connell and Mahony, Dr. Sheehy, and Abbé Leyne, and ends.] Adieu, My Dear Friend,

R. O'C.

NOTES TO BOOK III.

NOTE A.

McCarthy Mor and O'Donoghue of the Glens.

Arms: a stag trippant gu., attired and unguled or.

[From Burke's "General Armoury"—

McCarthy (chiefs of Carbery and Muskerry, County Cork, a powerful Irish sept, descended from Cartach, King of Desmond, prior to the English invasion, the chief of which was styled, MacCarthy More). Arms: a stag trippant gu., attired and unguled or.

McCarthy (*Earl of Glancare and Viscount Valentia*, extinct. *Donogh MacCarthy More*, seventh in descent from *Cormac More McCarthy*, was so created 1556, died *s.p. m.*). Arms: a stag trippant gu, attired and unguled or.]

Donal McCarthy Mor, created by Elizabeth, in 1566, Viscount Valentia and Earl Clan Carthia—generally but erroneously written "Glencar." "It is quasi Earl of the family of the Carthys, as in England Earl Rivers is of no place" (Crosley, "Peerage of Ireland," 1724, under "Glencar")—titles that he afterwards resigned to reassume his more glorious hereditary designation of McCarthy Mor, was the descendant of a long line of McCarthy Mors, Kings of the two Munsters, Kings of Desmond, and Lords of Muskerry; the family of which he was the chief, illustrious in descent, illustrious in achievement, illustrious in its alliances and in its possessions, could well bear comparison with any noble, nay, more, with any royal, house in Europe.

Donal died, as even the anointed of the Lord, with the exception of Frederick Barbarossa and Don Sebastian of Portugal, must; and by his wife and niece Honora, daughter of the sixteenth Earl of Desmond, left issue one daughter, Ellen, wife of Florence McCarthy "Reagh," Prince of Carbery, a distant kinsman of the McCarthy Mor, and chief of a younger branch of the widespreading house of McCarthy; his ancestor, Donal Oge, was a younger son of Donal McCarthy

Mor, King of Desmond in 1195, of whose eldest son the Earl of Glencar was the direct descendant.

On the death of the earl, in 1596, the clan Carthy, according to the ancient Irish custom, "the lewd and barbarous usage of Tanistry," elected as chief him whom they deemed the most worthy member of the clan. The choice fell upon Florence McCarthy Reagh, the earl's son-in-law, who, if we are to believe those who knew him in the flesh, possessed in a superlative degree all the qualities of mind and body that win the love of man and woman. His fortunes and misfortunes, the wondrous story of his feverish life, cannot be exemplified in a note, any more than the glories of his pedigree; on both volumes have been written—well-meaning volumes, that have, perhaps, left matters more involved than they found them. It is my immediate mission to treat of his descendants. Florence—whose brother Dermod, it is perhaps worth mentioning, married Helen, daughter of Tady O'Donoghue, of Glauflesk—had by his wife, Lady Ellen McCarthy, with other issue, three sons: Tadg, the first, who died a boy-prisoner in the Tower; Florence, the third, of whom later; and Donal, the second, who succeeded his father as McCarthy Mor, and left by his wife, Lady Sara McDonnell or McConnell (as it was then indifferently spelt and spoken), daughter of the Earl and sister of the Marquess of Antrim, two sons, Florence McCarthy Mor, who died without issue, and Charles McCarthy Mor, father, by his wife, Honora Burke, daughter of Lord Brittas, of one son, Randal, and two daughters, Elizabeth Madame O'Donoghue, and Ellen Mrs. Conway.

The son, Randal McCarthy Mor, married Agnes, daughter of Edward Herbert, of Muckross, and had an only child, Charles McCarthy Mor, commonly called the last McCarthy Mor, who died unmarried at Putney, March 13, 1770, an officer of the first regiment of Foot Guards (commission as ensign dated June 1, 1761), of whom presently. The daughter Elizabeth married Jeffray, The O'Donoghue of the Glens (he died 1758), and had issue Daniel, The O'Donoghue, who married Margaret, only child of Murtogh McMahon, of Clonina, in Clare (by his wife, Mary, daughter of Charles James McDonnell, of Kilkee), and had issue, Charles, The O'Donoghue, who, dying in 1808, left, with a daughter, Jane, wife of Sir James O'Connell, Bart., of Lake View, a son Charles, The O'Donoghue, who, dying at Florence in 1833, left by his wife, Jane, daughter of John O'Connell, of Grenagh, an only child, Daniel, The O'Donoghue, who married Mary, daughter and subsequently co-heiress of Sir John Ennis, Bart., and, dying in 1889, left, with other issue, a son,

Jeffray, now The O'Donoghue of the Glens. Charles McCarthy
Mor, who died in 1770, left the remnant of a once territorial
estate, by a somewhat iniquitous will, to his maternal grandfather, Edward Herbert, of Muckross. The Herberts, previous
to 1770, rented [1] Muckross from the McCarthy Mor for £20
per annum, as I discovered from an old but, strange to say,
dateless deed in the possession of Sir Maurice O'Connell, and
are therefore styled "of Muckross" before they acquired
that estate. The lands left by McCarthy Mor comprised Pallas,
Muckross, Cahirnane, Castlelough, Caragh, and "several
other denominations of land," being the estates settled upon
Lady Sara McDonnell on her marriage with Donal McCarthy
Mor, and restored to her by an act of grace of the Court of
Claims, July 28, 1663, after her husband's death.

The O'Donoghues, next of kin and natural heirs, being
Papists and "mere Irish," were not likely to prosper in a lawsuit; yet such a glaring injustice could not be entirely glossed
over, and, legal proceedings being instituted, the Herberts,
somewhat frightened, were glad to enter into a compromise; [2]
they retained possession of the fattest portion of the heritage,
and certain barren tracts in Glencar were ceded to the
O'Donoghues as the price of their silence. This property is
still in The O'Donoghue's possession. Thus did the ancient
acres of the McCarthy Mors pass into the possession of a
family in whose veins runs no drop of McCarthy Mor blood.
Captain Charles McCarthy, Count O'Connell's friend and
brother officer—the "pretty fellow" of Counsellor Murphy's
letter, given below—seems to have had a perfect right to call
himself McCarthy Mor, if he cared to assume a barren and
landless title. Florence McCarthy Mor had by his wife, Lady
Ellen, daughter of the Earl of Glencar, an elder son, Donal
McCarthy Mor, whose descendants have been already given,
and a younger son, Florence McCarthy, who married Mary
O'Donovan, and had issue, Denis of Castlelough [3]—an estate
granted to him by his first cousin, Charles McCarthy Mor.
Denis married Margaret Finch, and had two sons. Florence,
the elder, followed James II. to France, and, marrying Mary,
daughter of Bernard McMahon, had, with several other
children, an eldest son, Charles, "the pretty fellow," who, on

---

[1] The rent paid by Herbert of Muckross is frequently mentioned
in later deeds relating to the Herbert-O'Donoghue quarrel anent the
McCarthy Mor estate. Some of the deeds are in Sir Maurice O'Connell's
possession.

[2] By an agreement, entered into as late as 1802, the original of which,
together with McCarthy Mor's will, is in The O'Donoghue's possession.

[3] Of Castlelough; also called "of Begnis."

the death, in 1770, of his third cousin once removed, Charles
McCarthy Mor, became *de jure* McCarthy Mor. Justin, the
second son of Denis of Castlelough, married Catherine,
daughter of Colonel Maurice Hussey, and had a son, Randal,
who sold Castlelough, married, and had several children, " all
uneducated paupers" ("Life of Florence McCarthy," by Daniel
McCarthy, p. 448, *et seq*., quoted from Egerton MSS. 116).
Florence, the "pretty fellow's" father, is described as elder
brother to Justin of Castlelough, because the O'Donoghues
and O'Connells would naturally know Justin, who lived near
Killarney, though they might have forgotten the existence of
his expatriated elder brother.

The present recognized head of the house of McCarthy,
in the male line in Ireland, is Mr. McCarthy, of Carrignavar,
in the County Cork, who descends from Dermod (born 1310,
died 1367), second son of Cormac McCarthy Mor and Honora
FitzMaurice, daughter of Maurice, sixth Lord of Kerry. The
Saxon has been kind enough to ennoble this branch as Lords
Muskerry in 1495, as Barons of Blarney in 1578, and Viscounts Muskerry and Earls of Clancarthy in 1660. The
third son of the first earl of this creation was created Viscount
Mountcashel and Baron Castletuohy, June 3, 1689. The
proud old race lives on, honoured in the land, though its
lands, and even its titles (a Trench is Lord Clancarthy, a
Morgan is Lord Muskerry), are the prey of the invader.

From the middle of the sixteenth century, and I know not
for how long previously, the chief residence of the McCarthy
Mors was at Pallice, some five miles from Killarney. Close
by, at Grenagh, now the home of their descendant, Donal
O'Connell, great-grand-nephew of the count, the curious in
such matters may still see, in what is even now called the
"Gallows Field," the high green mound whereon the old
chieftains held their open-air court, and laid down life-and-death laws of their own making; "criminals passing to death
shuddered away at their feet;" a few gigantic ash trees—and
every year, alas! they grow fewer—mark the course of the old
avenue; but every vestige of McCarthy Mor's house has long
since vanished. On the high road from Killarney to Killorglin,
between the gates of Lake View and Grenagh, stand the ruins
of the church of Killalla. Here runs the legend : A certain
McCarthy Mor was wont to hear his weekly Mass. It was his
execrable habit to be behind time; but the docile priest never
dreamed of beginning the Mass until the chieftain arrived.
One unhappy Sunday there was a strange priest, who happened to be in a hurry, and who had not that respect for a
McCarthy Mor innate in the heart of every Kerry man; he

waited, indeed, but he did not wait long enough. At the most solemn moment of the holy sacrifice the McCarthy entered the church. Outraged at the insult offered him, he strode to the altar, drew his sword, and with one blow cleft in twain the officiant's skull. He wiped his blade on the vestments of the prostrate priest, returned quietly to Pallice, and, being McCarthy Mor, never heard any more about such a trifling matter. The church was, not unnaturally, disused from that day; and, the legend adds, the McCarthy Mor never again heard Mass.

One more old-world story. The O'Connells held Ballycarbery as hereditary constables to the McCarthy Mor (see deposition of Teigue Hurly, March 28, 1617, quoted in Daniel McCarthy's "Life of Florence McCarthy," p. 404, *et seq.*).[1] The McCarthy of Henry VIII.'s day sent a cradle to the O'Connell of the period—a shorthand order to O'Connell to send for a child of McCarthy's to foster. The vassal, who, after the unhappy manner of his race, had probably children enough of his own, declined to take the hint, and declined somewhat forcibly by cutting off the messenger's head and sending it back in the cradle. McCarthy naturally hanged the bearer, and found some more tractable retainer to nourish his offspring.

The following letter of Counsellor Murphy, referred to above, gives an account of the death, burial, and will of "the last" McCarthy Mor. The original is at Lake View. I have been unable to trace "the pretty fellow." A Count McCarthy figures among those admitted *aux honneurs de la cour de France*, in 1777, and a Vicomte McCarthy in 1788; but they were probably descendants of Donal-na-Pipi McCarthy (ob. 1612), first cousin of Florence McCarthy Mor, Lord Glencar's son-in-law, some of whom settled in France before 1776.—[R. O'C.]

Counsellor Murphy to Madam O'Donoghue.

London, March 18th, 1770.

DEAR MADAM,—I gave my bro' W'm the melancholy account of McCarthy More's death the very day he died, that he may communicate it to you and the friends of his father's family. I was one of six who went in two mourning-coaches to fetch his corpse from Putney to town, and saw him buried in the parish church of St Giles's. The next day I was

[1] This book is a remarkable exception to the generality of Irish histories and histories of Irishmen. It is lucid, accurate, and interesting, and has been of great service to me in the compiling of this brief note.

desired by the grandf' and his brother Tom to be present at the reading of the will, which Owen McCarthy, the son of Florence McCarthy, who lived once with your father, produced, saying that the servant who lived with McCarthy More before he came to live with him, had robbed him and broke open his trunks, and that upon his coming to live with him he had examined these trunks, and that, seeing several papers in them, he carefully carried them to McCarthy, and that amongst them there appeared a will, w'ch he gave his master, who read it, and desired him to lock it up in a bureau, where it has remained *ever since open* until he then produced it. You must know this was but one of four parts of this will, w'ch M'r Herbert got made by his attorney, one Palmer; and the Herbert family kept one part of it, Palmer one part, and M'r George Brian a third part, so that this differed in nothing from their parts, and therefore they knew, and M'r Herbert talked to me about the contents of it before Charles was buried. I understood from him that you had 5 or 600£ legacy left you; but upon hearing it read, I found y'u had not one shilling left y'u, but that 500£ had been left to your younger children, and same to Mrs. Conway's children. I think 200£ to Sam McCarthy, the eldest son of the late Randal McCarthy, and, as I can recollect, this is all left to y'r family. Old M'r Herbert has by this will *McCarthy estate for life*, w'th 1000£ legacy, and so on to his family, and after the death of the old gentleman the whole estate was devised for ever to Tom and Ned Herbert, and to their heirs, so that none of y'r family was ever to have a foot of it. 200£ were devised to *Mr. Palmer* the attorney, and 200£ to *Mr. George Brien*—for what I know not. It is very odd that M'r Owen McCarthy and the woman and boy, tho' this will lay always open before them (by which they saw they were left totally unprovided), should not have attempted to prevail on him to make another later will! It is hardly credible, but they did, and they are both very silent. She wears a wedding-ring, as if married to Charles, and is called Mrs. McCarthy in the family; but all this is nothing unless she can prove her marriage, w'ch she has not yet pretended to do, and M'r Owen affects a silence w'h to me appears misterious. The woman has had 10 or 15 guineas given her for mourning and support, and I suppose Owen is to be taken care of. I asked him some questions w'h puzeled him, and he said *it did not belong to him to say anything*. I imagine, was you here, you c'ld prevail with Owen to speak out, and I believe the pore woman w'ld confide herself and her child more to you than to them. I own, tho' I have not been at all well treated by any of you since the late poor McCarthy More's time, it grieves and shockes me for what has passed, and therefore I will, on account of our old intimacy and the regard I bear to the memories of y^r Brother and Father, serve y^u all I am able, and therefore I write y^u this letter, and only conjure y^u not to let anybody living know what I write to y^u, or that I write to y^u at all, as y^u tender y^r own interest. First, then, I engage, suppose even there should not appear any other will, that half the estate in point of law shall be rescued out of their hands. I have allready given them a hint of my opinion by making them read one clause of the will twice over for me; but I s^d not a word to them, tho', this morning, as it might do good and no prejudice. I told their lawyer, tho' they did everything they c^ld to preserve the whole estate to themselves, they overacted their part, and Providence w^ld rescue a moiety from them. When I have a power of attorney from you and Mr. Conway's children, I will then act openly for you, for I care not whether they are pleased or displeased. But let me be the first to say I will see justice done you; but let not a word come from you; beware of *Supple* and all *Killarney clerks*. Set out for Corke, and there get a ginerall power of attorney drawn and executed by you, and by as many of y^r children as are of age, and a power from y^u as guardian to those who are not, to impower me to call for a coppy or coppies of all the wills Charles has made, to demand in due time their legacies if no will appears but this I have seen, and in all things to act for y^r interests, and for y^u all. A Notary or any Council will draw this for you [one word illegible], a like one for Mr. Conway and his daughters (for I hear he has no sons), and send to me as soon as you can; but do not delay sending me y^r own on account of that. Both you and Mr. Conway may be guardians to y^r children under age, tho' Papists, as legacies are only in question *at present*. This will they got made soon after Charles came of age.

I could wish for many reasons you would come over directly. The voyage is nothing, and you will be well paid for y^r journey, even under this will, but you will open the mouths of Owen and of Madam. Be sure you secure the possession. The tenants won't, I fancy . . . [illegible] . . . to them against y^r family. I have lately wrote to Dr. Ankettle to Limerick. I hope to be able to assist his brother; but of this hereafter. If the Doctor or his brother have any papers to send me, and you sh^ld come over as I w^ld advise you, bring me what they may want to send me. Write to me directly, and send y^r pacquet under cover to Edmund Burke, Esqre, in Fludyer S^t, Westm^r. This only on the outside cover; the inside directed to me. Remember me affectionately to the few worth remembering amongst my neighbours.

I am, y^r still sincerely affect. friend,
DAVID MURPHY.

P.S.—Charles, the son of Florence, the elder brother of Justin McCarthy, is now *McCarthy More*, and a prettier fellow has not been a McCarthy More this age past. He is a Captn in Clare's Regim^t.

[Indorsed, " Councillor Murphy's letter."]

Mrs. Conway was Ellen, younger sister of Madam O'Donoghue; she, together with her children, Ellice wife of Florence McCarthy, Catherine wife of John Mahony, Anne widow of — Mahony, Joan wife of Justin McCarthy, Ellen wife of William Godfrey, Mary wife of Denis McCarthy, and Alice, spinster, ceded to O'Donoghue all claim to the McCarthy Mor succession, in consideration of £1500, April 23, 1776.—[R. O'C.]

NOTE B.

O'DONOGHUE OF THE GLENS AND O'DONOGHUE DHUV.

[Arms: vert, two foxes ramp. combatant ar., on a chief of the last an eagle volant sa. Crest: an arm in armour, embowed, holding a sword, the blade entwined with a serpent, all ppr.

The O'Donoghue of the Glens bears the same arms with a different crest. A pelican on per pale, ppr.]

The O'Donoghues were of the great Eugenian race, *i.e.* of that group of "chiefly" houses traced to Eoghan Mor, one of Oilliol Olum's sons.

The pedigree, sung by the poet Cathan O'Dunin on the inauguration of Tieg-an-Enig, chief of his race, in 1320, gives twelve descents back from that hero. Four more are recorded in a subsequent pedigree, and the achievements of chiefs and their adventures can be followed in the local chronicles, in the Four Masters, in Don Phillip O'Sullivan's " Catholic History," etc., to the time of James I. The adventures, forfeitures, and attainders of future chiefs are easily traced during the Cromwellian and Williamite wars of the seventeenth century. Burke gives considerably over two hundred years of the modern descent of the second branch —that of the now existing O'Donoghue of the Glens—who branched off at the thirteenth generation of O'Donoghues at Amhlaoibh, fifth in descent from Donnchad, from whom the O'Donoghues took their clan-name. Some cadet of the family of the Glens was called as a nickname "Dhuv" ("Dark"), and his family retained the name. They were settled in Glanflesk at a place called Anees, and of this family was Donal O'Donoghue Dhuv, father of Maur-ni-Dhuiv. The O'Donoghue Dhuvs seem to be extinct. Maur-ni-Dhuiv had a brother Geoffrey; but no one appears to know if he ever married, nor is there any trace of his posterity. One of her brothers did marry and had a daughter Joan, who married Denis McCartie, of Churchhill; but the family pedigree is the only possession she seems to have brought her husband. There is no one in Glanflesk claiming in any way to represent this third family of O'Donoghue. The late O'Donoghue of the Glens married Mary, daughter and eventual heiress of Sir John Ennis, Bart., of Ballinahown Court, Athlone. This fine property is entailed on her second son, so that we shall probably see an especially prosperous branch of an ancient Munster "chiefly" house established on the Leinster and Connaught border. The O'Donoghue retains the unsold and unforfeited ancestral lands and a portion of the McCarthy Mor heritage in Glancar.

FEMALE DESCENTS OF THE O'DONOGHUE DHUVS.

The descendants of the O'Donoghue Dhuvs in the female line are the O'Connells and their kindred. A great-granddaughter of Maur-ni-Dhuiv, Catherine O'Connell (daughter of Ellen of Carhen, and her cousin Daniel, of the Tralee family) married Denis McCartie, of Headfort, County Kerry, who descended from a younger branch of the McCarthys of Muskerry, as follows (see Cronnelly's "History of the Clan Eoghan," *i.e.* the Eugenian families, to which stem most of the Cork and Kerry families trace back):—

Dermot Mor McCarthy, first Lord of Muskerry, born 1310, and slain by the O'Mahonys 1367. He left, with other issue,

Cormac, Lord Muskerry, born 1346, slain by the Barrys in Cork, and buried in Gill Abbey, on May 14, 1374. He left, with other issue,

Tadg, Lord Muskerry, born 1380, governed Muskerry for thirty years, and died 1448, leaving issue, Dermot, ancestor of the McCarthys of Drishane, and the founder of the Castle of Carrigafooka, near Macroom, and Ellen, who married Dermot McCarthy, Prince of Carbery, Eoghan of Rathduane, and his successors.

From this Eoghan of Rathduane descended Donagh

McCartie, who lived *temp.* James II., and who married Eva O'Donoghue of Glanflesk, by whom he had issue,

Charles, who married a daughter of Barrett of Barrett's Country, by whom he had issue a son,

Charles, who married Mary O'Leary, daughter of Arthur O'Leary of Iveleary, and niece of Colonel McCarthy of Drishane. Their son,

Denis, married Johanna O'Donoghue Dhuiv, niece to Maur-ni-Dhuiv. Their son,

Charles, married Mary O'Donoghue, of Killaha, niece to The O'Donoghue of the Glens. Their son,

Denis, married Catherine O'Connell, daughter of Daniel O'Connell, of Tralee, and the Liberator's sister, Ellen of Carhen.

Their son, Daniel McCartie, of Headfort, married the Liberator's granddaughter, Mary, daughter of Maurice O'Connell, M.P., of Darrynane. These latter are living, and have nine children.

The branch of McCarties who had settled at Rathduane, the confiscated estate of their ancestors, held it, like most Catholics, on a middle interest—a lease of lives renewable about every thirty years. These leases frequently went on thus for a couple of centuries, but during the lifetime of Denis McCartie, husband of Joan O'Donoghue, the lease was not renewed. Their son Charles settled at a small place called Churchhill, near Millstreet. His son was left Headfort by an old childless relative.

About the middle of the last century, or rather later, David Haly wrote to Mr. Kean Mahony, to inform The O'Donoghue that he had found a patent granted by King Charles I. to Thady O'Donoghue, of Killaghey (Killaha, in Glanflesk, The O'Donoghue Glen country) in the County of Kerry, in an office in which he was writing. He quietly annexed it, and offered it for sale for £2 2s. The original is at Lake View.

O'DONOGHUE ANECDOTES.

There are many stories and traditions about the O'Donoghues of the Glens. The curse which is said to have prevailed for seven generations is accounted for in various ways. It is certain that The late O'Donoghue (Daniel, long M.P. for Tralee), who saw several of his sons come of age, succeeded seven generations of chiefs who had died during the minority of their heirs. My husband, the late Morgan John O'Connell, whose sister married [Charles,] The O'Donoghue who was the seventh on whom the weird fell, believed that, among the conflicting stories of its origin, the following was the best authenticated.

Geoffrey O'Donoghue—probably the poet-chieftain whose verses are still extant—took the Irish Catholic side in the wars of the seventeenth century, while his younger brother espoused the English cause, to the great indignation of all of his name and creed. In some battle the chieftain killed his brother in a hand-to-hand conflict. Their aged mother, when the corpse of her recreant son was brought home to her, fell on her knees and cursed the "seed, breed, and generation" of Geoffrey unto the seventh generation. The curse she specially invoked was that the son who slew her son was not to see his son of age, and that it should endure for seven generations.

Some quaint O'Donoghue stories were told me by Mr. Marshall, of Callinaferey, the High Sheriff for Kerry in 1890, whose great-great-grandmother was an O'Donoghue. His grandmother knew her grandmother, who had told her the stories she told him.

Towards the middle of the last century The O'Donoghue of the Glens, Geoffrey by name (like The O'Donoghue of to-day), had a beautiful daughter, Elizabeth, the aforesaid ancestress. I fancy he must have died when she was very young, but not until he had raised a considerable sum of money on Killaha, part of his Glanflesk property, round a ruined castle. The lender was Mr. Markham, a gentleman of English descent, living at Brewsterfield, near at hand, which had been granted to ancestral English relatives. In course of time, Mr. Markham wooed and won the beautiful Elizabeth O'Donoghue, and, instead of a dowry or repayment of the loan, received Killaha.

The O'Donoghue living in the seventies of the eighteenth century was a very wild, extravagant, powerfully strong man named Donal, or Daniel, whose mother was McCarthy Mor's sister. After long years of litigation with the Herberts, they recovered some of the McCarthy Mor property. Geoffrey, the present O'Donoghue, has some remnants of it in Glancar.

The O'Donoghue one day sent an unusually fine salmon as a present to his sister. Mr. Markham very kindly brought in the rugged retainer, bearing the huge fish, to his wife, who happened to be in the dining-room. The wild clansman had never been further than the kitchen in any gentleman's house, and was much interested in looking about him. There was a flower-knot outside the principal window, and some fowls flew into it while the lady was engaged in getting out the whiskey for him. He at once shouted at the birds, and, clutching up a sod from the turf-basket, hurled it at them. Glass flew in all directions, showering on the peasant's head and face. He dropped on his knees, and began to pray hard and fast in Irish; for he was ignorant of the properties of glass, or how a sharp shower of splinters could rain from what seemed a wide open space, and deemed himself the victim of some enchantment.

In a few years, this wild retainer, whom Mr. Markham begged from the chief, became quite an accomplished footman, and attended his lady to Dublin about the time of the Rebellion. There was a sort of curfew law, and people out late without a pass were arrested. My O'Donoghue clansman was taken up, and, instead of giving a civil answer, threatened the chief and all the O'Donoghues of Glanflesk on those who had presumed to touch O'Donoghue's clansman. I need hardly say the plea was ineffectual, and the retainer was led to a dark cell, already tenanted by one other person. His fellow-prisoner happened to be a negro servant similarly entrapped. They went to sleep without any light, and at break of day the sun's rays aroused them. The horror and terror of the mountaineer at seeing the black man can be imagined. He thought it was the foul fiend incarnate. He immediately began to roar, curse, and pray, and when the sentry fetched the turnkey to see what was amiss, he bounded past the soldier, through the half-open door, dashed past the sentinels, and gained the open streets. He never went near his employers, but ran like the wind towards the open country. Day by day he tramped on until he gained Glanflesk, and never left it more.

I fancy the following refers to his old master.

An odd trait of rough-and-ready old ways appears in the petition for compensation of a bailiff whom The O'Donoghue of 1776 had flogged within an inch of his life. The chieftain, notwithstanding a legacy from his cousin, McCarthy Mor, was extremely hard up, and it was of great consequence to him that his creditors should not serve him with writs. A valiant bailiff, Dennis Houlahan, had the pluck to serve him. On November 25, The O'Donoghue came up "in a most furious and outrageous manner, armed with a weighty whip, seized deponent by the breast, and dragged deponent out of the street of Killarney aforesaid into an orchard outside the town, the door of which he, the defendant, locked. Defendant then ordered deponent to strip off what clothes he had on, which deponent refusing to do, defendant severely flogged him with the heavy end of said whip." I spare the reader the minute description of the subsequent condition of skin and shirt of the outraged myrmidon of the law, and of the language applied to him. He was also obliged to have "the close attendance of a chirurgeon."

Notwithstanding these precautionary measures, a number of writs were served.

Note C.

The Strong Chieftain and the Smith.

The son of McCarthy Mor's daughter was a man of gigantic strength and stature, and the following story was told to Mr. Marshall by his grandmother, whose grandmother had told it to her.

The brawny chieftain was the strongest gentleman in Kerry, but there was a smith near Killarney who was the strongest peasant. The smiter of the anvil could not challenge a person of such consequence to a trial of strength, but he frequently and loudly bewailed that he did not know if he were indeed the strongest man in the whole kingdom of Kerry. The O'Donoghue heard of the other strong man's standing grievance, and determined to gratify him. He disguised himself like a farmer, rode up on a rough country garron, and requested to have a missing shoe supplied. While the smith was forging one, he took up a cool shoe which was hung ready, and snapped it in two with his hands. "I don't think much of your shoe," said he. The smith finished his task, and the chief tossed him a crown piece. "I don't think much of your crown," said the other strong man, snapping it between two fingers. O'Donoghue mounted and rode away, and though the smith was much gratified that he had been given an opportunity of testing their respective strengths, it always remained a moot point whether the chief or the peasant was the strongest man in Kerry.—[Communicated by Mr. Markham Marshall, Callinafercy, County Kerry.]

Note D.

Dirge of Arthur O'Leary.

[The greater part of Arthur O'Leary's pedigree will be found in the keen. I shall give the family arms here. I cannot be sure which coat he bore, but am inclined to think it was the ship.

Burke's "General Armoury" gives three sets of armorial bearings borne by the O'Learys. The McCarthy O'Leary's, of Coomlagane, bear the first mentioned.

O'Learie. Arms: a lion pass. in base, gu.; in chief, a ship of three masts sa.; sails set ppr.; from the stern the flag of

St. George flotant. Crest: out of a ducal coronet or, an arm in armour, embowed, holding a sword ppr., pommel and hilt gold.

Motto: " Ladir isé lear Righ " (" Strong is the King of the Sea," or " Leari is powerful "). Another motto : " Fortis undis et armis."

O'LEARY (Drumcar, County Cork, Fun. Ent. Ulster's Office, 1637, Donogh O'Leary, gent.). Per fess ar. and vert.; in chief a talbot pass. gu., and in base a boar pass. of the first. Crest: an arm erect, couped below the elbow, vested az., the hand holding an evet or lizard, all ppr.

O'LEAURY. Arms: a falcon, rising within an ivy branch, moile, all ppr. Crest: an arm in armour, couped below the elbow and erect, grasping a dagger, all ppr.]

I cannot resist the temptation of quoting my hero's sister's lament. Eileen Dhuv, in her wild and passionate outburst, seems to belong to an earlier age than any one called by so homely and prosaic a style and title as " Sister Nellie." But we must bear in mind that these old native Irish people, like Walter Scott's Highlanders, had a sort of dual existence. They spoke English, wore clothes of English fashion, and conformed more or less to English customs in everyday life; but they hankered in their hearts after the lost lands, the old tribal rights and privileges, and in moments of excitement used the Irish speech they had first learned. The curious custom of fosterage, by which the children of the gentry were always suckled by peasant women, who remained about them during childhood, and by which their foster brothers or sisters constantly remained with them as personal attendants through life, made Irish as familiar to them as English. The far more flexible language lent itself to emotional improvisation. All that was poetical and picturesque, all that appealed to pride or fancy, was enshrined in musical Gaelic metre. Miss Evelina McCarthy tells me she remembers her venerable grand-uncle, Count O'Connell, in his old age in Paris, reciting and expounding to her long passages in Irish verse; and surely he was one of the most prosaically sensible of men. Though I don't know ten words of Irish (" And more shame for Morgan John's wife," as blind old Tiege McMahon said to me), I confess to a certain sympathetic stirring of the pulses when I have heard passionate Irish verses recited. I am indebted to Sergeant Michael O'Connor, an old follower of the extinct Falveys of Faha, for this poem, and to Michael Houlahan (since dead), an old follower of the O'Learys, a car-driver in Cork, for telling me the retired sergeant of the R.I.C. possessed the precious manuscript. I hope some time or other to publish my long account of the tragedies of Murty Oge O'Sullivan Beare and Arthur O'Leary, and meanwhile secure this opportunity of preserving the keen by a prose version.

It seems to me these wild verses and fireside stories, though often full of trivial details, are what really throw light on the life of the old native Irish gentry—by no means a specially faultless set of people, but whose brave men and chaste women we gladly claim as the kinsfolk of our children.

This fierce and passionate poetess, and this stately and sensible veteran, were great-grand-aunt and great-grand-uncle to my own young son.

I visited Darrynane in the April of 1890, and, a hundred and seventeen years all but seven days from the date of Arthur O'Leary's death, recovered three of the missing verses. They were recited to me by Mary O'Sullivan Liah, a tenant's daughter, who had picked them up, with many verses already preserved, from the recitation of an old woman, now dead, named Kate Murphy. She was much helped by a tenant, John James Galavan, both in reciting and translating. The Rev. John Martin, C.C., wrote down the verses from the young girl's recitation, and translated them, J. J. Gallavan often making valuable suggestions.

The Dirge of Arthur O'Leary,

Shot, May 4, 1773.

By his Widow, Eileen O'Connell, the Raven-haired.

[This keen was copied by Mr. O'Sullivan, Maylor Street, Cork, from a manuscript of Edward de Wall, a hedge schoolmaster, living in the beginning of this century, who took it down *circa* 1800 from the recitation of Norry Singleton, a famous keener. Dark Eileen improvised it over her husband's corpse. Portions are missing, and Mr. O'Sullivan states that verses have been interpolated. The Rev. Peter O'Leary, C.C., Doneraile, kindly made me a literal translation, which I have rendered into freer language. I retain more or less the form of the lines, but do not profess to have executed a metrical translation.]

I.

" Beloved of my steadfast heart ! loved with the fondest love from the day I first beheld you ride past the gable of the market-house,[1]
 Eagerly my glances sought you ; then I gave the deep love of my heart to you.
 I stole away from my kindred with you ; I fled from my home with you. Yet never did I rue that day.
 I found chambers gay with tinted hangings, parlours brightly decked for me.

---

[1] She first saw him riding into the square of Macroom. She was visiting a lady whose house looked out towards the corner of the market-house, by which he rode in. His formal offer of marriage having been refused by her family. Dark Eileen eloped with him.

Beeves were slaughtered, spits revolving, loaves fresh kneaded, ovens heated, red wine flowing from the cask for me.
I might sleep on downy pillows, past the morning till the noontide, past the time the maids went milking,[1] did I will it so.

II.

" Beloved of my steadfast heart ! well your beaver did become you, with the golden band around it ; well your silver-hilted sword,
Thus equipped for deeds of daring, on your dark-brown steed and peerless, whose forehead bore the snow-white star,
You made the Saxons quail before you, bowing down to the very ground,
Not for any love they bore you, but for sheer dread of you—
And yet it was through them you fell,
O darling of my soul . . .

[The rest of this verse is lost.]

III.

" O my snowy-handed rider ! well your jewelled brooch became you, fastened in the cambric ruffle, and your beaver laced with gold.
When you returned from beyond the seas, all the street was cleared before you, not through any love they bore you, for deadly was their hate.
Beloved of my steadfast heart ! when little Connor and the younger Fiach O'Leary, children of our love, shall ask me where I left their father !
I must answer them with anguish—
' 'Twas in Cil-na-martyr[2] that I left him.'
Loudly they will call their father, who will not now be there to answer to their call.

IV.

" My love and my darling ! kinsman of the mighty Earls, Barrys, Lords of Barrymore !
Well your slender sword became you, and your beaver laced with gold ; fine small shoe of foreign fashion, and broadcloth woven beyond the seas !
Beloved of my steadfast heart ! No ! I could never credit that you lay dead,
Not till your mare came back to me, the long reins trailing in the dust, and your heart's blood on her forehead.
Blood-splashed the splendid saddle, too, where you were wont to sit and stand.
I made but one bound to the threshold ; I made but one bound to the gate ; I gained the saddle in one bound more ;
With clapping hands and cries I urged her onward ; at utmost speed the good mare flew,

---

[1] "Milking-time" in Munster Irish is synonymous with 11 a.m. Dark Eileen does not mean that she was a sluggard, but that, in her rich young husband's house, she was not obliged to go and rouse the dairymaids herself.

[2] The family burial-place of the O'Learys is in Kilcrea Abbey, but it was several years before Dark Eileen was suffered to bury her husband there, and the animosity of the Morrises forced her to bury him in an alien grave just outside the old churchyard of Kilnamartyr, near Raleigh.

Nor paused till where you lay, till where I found you dead before my eyes.
There was neither pope nor bishop, there was neither priest nor cleric, to chant the holy psalm above my dead ;
Only an aged crone, withered and lean and grey, who spread her mantle's ample folds above you, my love and my all !

v.

[Father Peter O'Leary says there was here a beautiful verse he heard recited by old people, describing the scenes through which dark Eileen sped. As she did not know where Arthur lay, she let the mare go on, trusting to the noble animal's sagacity to find her master, and merely urged her to her fullest speed.]

VI.

" Beloved of my steadfast heart ! arise and come with me, come back to our home with me !
Then we shall gather a goodly company ;
Then beeves shall be slaughtered, music shall echo through our halls ;
Then I will spread our marriage-bed with sheets of linen wide and fine, and coverings dark and warm ;
Then the deadly chill which numbs your every limb will pass away.

[The next verse is imperfect. Eileen seems to be indignantly repudiating a charge of having left her dead to seek sleep.]

VII.

" Beloved of my steadfast heart ! oh, do not hearken to the false, lying words of hatred that have been said !
They said I left your side in search of slumber.
Alas ! there is no deep dreamless sleep for me evermore.
I left your side because our babes were weeping ; I left your side to hush them to their rest . . .

VIII.

" Good people, do not listen to the word of any woman in all Erin, nor where'er the sun shines down.
Who is the woman, wedded to my Arthur, and mother of his children, Who would not go forth maddened among the dark woods for Arthur O'Leary's loss ?—
He who now lies stretched out dead before me since the morn of yesterday.
O fell Morris ! may every curse befall you ! May your heart's blood curdle in death within your veins !
May the sight leave your eyes, your limbs be stricken powerless, you slayer of my darling !
And there breathes no man in Erin to let a bullet fly at you !

IX.

" Beloved of my steadfast heart ! rise up, my Arthur, spring on your fleet steed.
Go, ride through Macroom and far into Inshigeela[1] with the wine-cup in your hand, as it flowed in the halls of your sires.
Endless my woe, and bitterest my sorrow, that I was not there beside you when the fatal ball was fired ;
O rider of the smooth white hands !

---

[1] Iɲɼe Ʒɩle, bright isles ; the old O'Leary territory and castle.

X.

"Keen, heart-piercing is my grieving that I was not close behind you [1] when the fatal shot was fired.
Would I had been there to get it!
Would that it had struck my garments, or haply my right side!
Would it were I that was stricken, and that you went scatheless on,
O my blue-eyed rider, and lived to aim avenging shots again!

XI.

"Beloved of my steadfast heart! vile the treatment of my hero, of the treasure of my heart.
Nought is left him but a coffin and a coffin lid; nought else for my knight of the generous heart—
He who was wont to angle in crystal streams, and quaff the red wine in halls, and toast me as the Lady of the snowy bosom.
Woe is me a thousand times, who am bereft of his sweet company!

XII.

"Torture and destruction seize you, Morris, vile and treacherous wretch,
Who robbed me of the head of my household, slew the father of my babes of tender age!
Two are just playing through my dwelling; the third yet slumbers beneath my breast.
Alas! I fear I may not give it birth.

XIII.

"My love you are, and the light of my heart!
When you passed out the gate, you turned quickly back, you kissed your children once again, and, smiling, kissed your hand to me;
You said, 'Arise, Eileen; be quick, and set all gear in order with all your care and skill!
I go from home this day; perchance I shall never return.'
I thought he spoke the words in playful jesting, as he had often jested thus with me before.

XIV.

"My loved one and my treasure, my knight of the bright sword!
Arise, and don your garb of broadcloth fine and smooth;
Throw on your beaver, draw on your gloves, take your whip from its crook.
The mare stands saddled without the door; go, hasten by yon narrow track to the east;
The very boughs will bend down low to greet you; the streams will narrow their waters to let you pass;
The men and the women will greet you respectfully,
Unless, as I fear much, the old gentle manners are lost to them now.

XV.

O my beloved, sole treasure of my bosom! I weep not for my kindred dead and gone,
Nor were our children dead would I bewail them so.

---

[1] She means on the pillion, in which case her arm would be passed round his waist, and might have received the fire.

I wail not Donal Mor O'Connell, nor young Connell drowned in the
    raging sea,
Nor the lady of twenty-six summers who has crossed the wide ocean to
    dwell in the courts of kings.¹
No pangs such loss could cause would rend my bosom as the sight I
    witness now.
I gaze upon my Arthur, my horseman of great prowess, the rider of the
    dark-brown mare,
Who was stricken on the green plain of Carriganimma.
Accursed be the spot! accursed be its name!

XVI.

"Oh my dear one, my true love!
    Still your wailing, O ye kindly women of the streaming eyes,
    Till my Arthur quaffs to you ere he sets forth to school.
    Not for verse or lore is it he goes there, but he goes where earth and
        stones shall lie heavy on his dust.

XVII.

"Beloved of my steadfast heart!
    Could my voice but reach the shores of Darrynane Mor or Carhen,
        where the golden apples grow,
    Many a horseman fleet and brave, many a stainless maiden veiled in
        white, would hasten at my call;
    Would be here to wail above you,
    O Arthur O'Leary, my brave one!

XVIII.

"My heart's love, O my darling!
    Your heavy corn is garnered in;
    Your kine stand by the milking-maids;
    But my heart is full of anguish for your loss—
    Anguish that is bound within it as within a fast-locked casket,
    Whose key is lost, whose rusty hinges will not yield to pressure.
    Not all the might of Munster,
    Not all the smiths within the confines of the Fenian Isle,² can loose it
        till my Arthur comes again.

[The three foregoing verses are those recovered at Darrynane.]

XIX.

"You are my true love, you are my darling!
    Arthur, son of Connor O'Leary—Connor, who was son of Cedach,
    Who was son of Lewis O'Leary from the west, where lies the Gerah,
        and from the east where the long narrow mountain ridges rise,
    Where the wild berries grow and tawny nuts on waving boughs,
    And apples weigh the branches down in autumn days.

---

¹ She refers to the death of her father, Donal Mor (Big Daniel) O'Connell, of Darrynane; the drowning of her young brother Connell; and the long absence of her sister, the wife of Major O'Sullivan, of the Austrian Service.

² "Fenian Isle"—a poetical name for Ireland, meaning the isle of the Fenian heroes: the Fianna, or warriors of Finn-mac-Cumhal of famous memory, father of Ossian the bard.

Let them kindle fires of mourning through the country of Ive-Leary,
By the holy Gougane Barra, and the lands of Ballengeary,
For the snowy-handed rider,
For the hunter unsurpassed, who would speed from distant Grenagh,
While his fleet greyhounds lagged outstripped behind.
What befell my blue-eyed rider?
Clothed in the shirt of mail my love procured him, I thought him safe from every harm.

XX.

"O my beloved one! you counted kindred with all the great and noble in the land;
Your kinsmen were the heads of great old houses, where in old times eighteen fosterers would feast at one board.
Theirs the rich gifts, milch cows, brood mares, the sow and her litter, the mill by the ford,
Bright silver and yellow gold, silken and velvet stuffs, and rentless lands.
All these were given in guerdon for the rich milk of their bosoms—given to the offspring of fair and noble dames.

XXI.

"O my beloved, my white dove! My love for you is living in the innermost depths of my heart.
Reproach me not that three mourners are absent this day.
They lie in close and darkened chambers in a dreamless torpid sleep that wakens not.
Ah! but for the small-pox and the fever and the Black Death, they and their followers would be here, a goodly gathering.
They would be riding with slackened rein, and making the hillsides quake
As the stillness is broken by the heavy thud of trampling steeds.
Thus would they have hastened to your funeral, O my Arthur of the snowy breast.

XXII.

"O my beloved, the light of my soul, kinsman of the brave and noble company whose headlong charge at the hunt was wont to shake the valleys and the hillsides!
Many a time you led them homewards, where a hearty welcome met them.
Knives were whetted, joints dismembered, streaky flitches set before them, and sides of mutton where no bones were seen.
Full-grained oats, meet food for hunters, filled the mangers to o'erflowing.
Crested steeds and grooms to tend them might tarry 'mid plenty while their masters stayed.
These were as brothers among friends.

XXIII.

"O my loved one! O my darling! an awesome vision came to me in sleep as I slept alone in Cork, within the city's bounds.
I thought I saw the Gerah wither, as though some raging fire had swept across its trees.
The fair house where we dwelt beside it crumbled to the ground.

Your swift hound was struck dumb, the song-birds all turned voiceless,
and you lay dead on a dreary mountain-side.
I thought you lay there stiff and stark and lifeless.
There was neither priest nor cleric near you, only an aged crone who
flung her mantle's ample folds across your breast.
O Arthur O'Leary, then I saw you; there was blood in heavy clotted
masses on your garments,
And it had flowed from out your breast.

XXIV.

"My darling, my secret love, whose love is buried in the innermost
depths of my soul! well your riding garb became you;
The five ribbed stocking, the boot to the knee, the fine laced beaver
cocked in three,
Your free swinging whip, as you paced at ease on your ambling hack.
Many a modest and gentle maiden would gaze admiring as you rode by.

XXV.

"Beloved of my steadfast heart! when you entered wealthy cities,
The merchants' wives would show you great respect.
[This verse is defaced. I suppose she must have described his buying
costly goods and bringing them to her.]

XXVI.

"I swear before Christ, that if the need arise,
I will sell the coif from off my head,
The garment from my back, the shoe from my foot,
The gear within my house, ay, to the brown mare's very bridle,
And spend it all in law to seek justice for my dead.
If needs be, I will cross the seas and lay my wrongs before the king,
If he will not hearken to my tale, I will come back again to seek the
villain,
The black-blooded wretch, who tore my loved one from my side.

XXVII.

"Thanks from my heart to ye, fair women of the mill,
Who poured the tide of mournful song above my dead,
Who mourned the brown mare's rider. . . .

XXVIII.

"May pangs of anguish rend your heart, O Shawn-a-Cuniagh![1]
When 'twas for a bribe you slew him, why came you not to me?
The richer bribe would have been mine to spare his life.
A bawn of kine, or sheep and lambs, and a crested steed, who would
bear his rider scatheless through hostile ranks in days of peril.

XXIX.

"O my snowy-handed rider, whose mighty arm hangs nerveless by your
side!
Go to Baldwin,[2] harsh of feature, mean of spirit, gaunt and long and
lean of limb,

---

[1] This curse is on a peasant to whom Arthur O'Leary had been very kind, and who for a bribe betrayed him to the soldiers who shot him.

[2] It is supposed that Mr. Baldwin had the mare given up, which in the then state of the laws was the wisest thing he could have done for the widow and children. Eileen's curses are also because he refused being a party to the Corsican vendetta she set on foot.

> Make him answer for his conduct, what he did about your mare; and
> how he treated your beloved.
> May he never live to see the blooming of the six babes round his board;
> But, oh, let Mary be left scatheless!
> Not that I love her much; but that she, too,
> For thrice three months,
> Lay 'neath my mother's breast."

Note E.

Baldwin of Clohina, County Cork.

[They have for the last three hundred years, in memory of the alliance of their ancestor, quartered the Herbert arms. They bear—

Quarterly, 1st and 4th, Baldwin arg. a chevron erm. between three oak branches ppr.; 2nd and 3rd, Herbert party per pale az. and gu., three lions ra. arg., armed and langued or.]

The first of this name to come into the south of Ireland were two brothers, cadets, perhaps, of the ancient Shropshire house of Bawdewin, Baldwyn, or Baldwin, of Dodelebury, who settled in the neighbourhood of Bandon, in the reign of Elizabeth. The elder married a daughter of Herbert of Powis, by whom he had three sons, Walter (*ob. s.p.*), Herbert, and James (Colonel), who purchased, in 1678, the estate of Clohina from the celebrated Valentine Greatrakes; this he bequeathed to his nephew Herbert, second son of his brother Herbert.

Herbert Baldwin, of Clohina, married, in 1689, Mary, daughter of Colonel Hungerford, of the Island, County Cork, by his wife Mary, daughter of Sir Emanuel Moore, and was grandfather of James Baldwin, of Clohina, who in 1763 married Mary, daughter of Daniel O'Connell, of Darrynane, by whom he had three sons—Walter, Connell, and Herbert. The two elder died without issue. Herbert, who was for many years M.P. for Cork, left a son Herbert, who died *s.p.*, and a daughter Mary, wife of John O'Sullivan Beare.

The parents of James Baldwin were James Baldwin, of Clohina (married 1726, died 1776), and Elizabeth Langton, of Bary, County Limerick.—[R. O'C.]

Note F.

A Century and a Half of Dr. Leynes in Tralee.

Arms (from an ancient seal): a tree eradicated, a snake entwined descendant, supported by two lions rampant.

Crest: an arm mailed in armour, couped at the elbow, the hand grasping a dagger. Motto: "Fortitudine et prudentia."

Dr. Teigue Leyne, who may have been the Teigue O'Leyne, a cornet in Carroll's Dragoons in the army of James II., died about 1723, in which year his wife, who bore the pretty foreign name of Violetta, registered a lease to him of premises in Tralee. After him came, in 1759, Dr. Jeremy Leyne, M.A. and M.D. of the University of Avignon, who married Elizabeth, daughter of Geoffrey O'Connell,[1] of Kilkeeveragh, County Kerry, by Elizabeth, daughter of Edmond Conway, of Glanbeigh, and Joanna, daughter of John Fitzgerald, of Ballycarthy. Dr. Jeremy Leyne was succeeded by his son, Maurice Leyne, M.D., Paris, the correspondent of Captain Rickard O'Connell, to whom, on his death, succeeded his son, Dr. Jeremiah Leyne, who died in 1872.

The father of Dr. Leyne (in his diplomas *nobilis dominus Jeremias O'Leyne*) was Dermot O'Leyne, of Killarney, and his mother was Catherine, daughter of John Fitzgerald, of Adare, whose property, or a portion of it, passed into the hands of the Quinns, Lord Dunraven's ancestors.

Dr. Jeremy Leyne's wife was an aunt of Captain Rick of the Brigade, who was therefore cousin-german to Dr. Maurice Leyne. The latter was for fifty years the physician and personal friend of the principal families in Kerry.

I take from a Kerry paper the following extract respecting him:—

"Dr. Maurice Leyne, like many other sons of old Catholic families, had been educated in France before the Revolution. He was a very clever physician, and a highly educated man; a welcome guest at all the best houses in the county, but especially at Ardfert.[2] Over and above his agreeable conversational powers in French, Italian, and English, Dr. Maurice Leyne had a good voice, and a much rarer gift, almost equal to that of Theodore Hook, of improvising capital songs, into each verse of which he managed to weave a playful allusion to each member of the company he found himself in at an evening party. An old lady used to repeat a long and very clever song of this kind sung by Dr. Leyne at Lohercannon House, then the residence of Sir Edward Denny. In sparkling wit and drollery it quite equalled anything I ever read of Hook's. There was nothing ill-natured in it; for what Moore, in his

---

[1] Referred to p. 48, vol. i., where he is designated in Irish Sheara-na-mo-Mor, *Anglicè*, "Geoffrey of the Vast Herds."

[2] The Earl of Glandore's.

beautiful poem, said of Sheridan, applied equally to Dr. Leyne's improvised songs—

> ' His wit, in the contest, was gentle as bright,
> Ne'er carried a heart-stain away on its blade.' "

According to a writer in the *Kerry Evening Post*, Dr. Leyne was a descendant of Colonel Leyne, of Dingle, in 1641; and in Miss Hickson's invaluable work, "Old Kerry Records," it is stated that towards the end of the fifteenth century The MacGillicuddy of the Reeks married a daughter of one Dermot O'Leyne. Dr. Leyne married, in 1786, Agnes Ruth Herbert, daughter of Cornelius, The MacGillicuddy of the Reeks.

The Kerry O'Leynes are descended from the ancient tribe of O'Liathain, owners, before the invasion, of a large tract in the south of County Cork, which included the district called after the clan, Carrigaline, *i.e.* O'Leyne's Rock, so named from the rock at the head of the river on which still stand the ruins of De Cogan's castle, built there after he and the Barrys had expelled the O'Leynes from their territory.—[Contributed by Mr. J. Leyne, Registry of Deeds, Dublin, great-grandson of Doctor Jeremy O'Leyne above mentioned, whose Irish Christian name, Dermot (Dhiarmid), was always rendered in other languages by the name of the Hebrew prophet, Jeremias, Jeremiah, Jeremy, etc.]

BOOK IV.

COLONEL O'CONNELL.

1780-1783.

No letters from Daniel Charles O'Connell from October, 1778, to March, 1780—Captain Rickard and others fill the void—Rickard's first letter of 1780 dates from Cambray—Recruiting—Marching—Colonel O'Connell's kindness—A true friend—Flanders—Robin Conway—Eugene McCarthy—Little Maurice Geoffrey O'Connell—Sir Maurice (Charles Phillip) O'Connell and other small boys—Captain Robin Conway to Hunting Cap (Bergues, February, 1780)—A little cousin—The colonel gone to Strasbourg—Robin loses his mother-in-law—Little Robin to play the pipes for promotion—Colonel O'Connell, "my best and worthyest of friends"—Mrs. Seggerson—The Cross of St. Louis—Our hero's portraits—Paris, March, 1780: Colonel O'Connell to Hunting Cap—Thanks for money—Knowledge of the affairs of the country—Going to Strasbourg—Little Maurice to be presented to Duke de Fitz-James—Eugene McCarthy gone to Martinico as captain in his regiment—Chevalier O'Mahony—Doctor Connell—Account of Colonel Eugene McCarthy—Strasbourg, May, 1780: Dan to Hunting Cap—Old friends—Royal Swedes—Genealogy—Earl of Glandore—Counsellor Fitzgerald—Little Maurice gone to college—The O'Connells at home and abroad—Irish gossip—Knight of Kerry to Maurice O'Connell, on roads—Iveragh, the asylum of rogues and vagabonds—Maurice's reply to Knight of Kerry—On the affairs of the barony—Volunteer corps—Account of a shipwreck—Captain Rickard writes from Cambray (January, 1781)—Sentiment—An exile from Erin—Rickard's cold and cure—Colonel O'Connell, as usual, the best of friends—Poor Conway—No letters from Colonel O'Connell from May, 1780, to April, 1783—He is mentioned as with the battalion at Minorca—Quite well in Captain Rickard's letter—A letter (1782) mentions his brilliant prospects—Chevalier Bartholomew O'Mahony—Port Phillip and Gibraltar—Daniel is invited to serve in Russia—Later in Portugal—O'Callaghan on our hero—Port Mahon—The siege of Gibraltar—Allied forces of Spain and France—Drinkwater describes the times—News from Portugal—The Spanish Fleet—Fort St. Phillip besieged—Surrender of Fort St. Phillip—Lieut.-Colonel

O'Connell to Rickard O'Connell (December, 1781)—Grant's account of the landing of the Duc de Crillon—O'Connell specially and honourably noticed—Account of Minorca from the "Annual Register"—General Murray's description of the fall of Port Phillip—Captain Rickard to Hunting Cap (December, 1781)—Is in Ireland, ill—Dan with the battalion in Minorca—Dan's letter to Rickard from Gibraltar—Dan's pedigree—Captain Rickard pedigree-hunting—" Flirting the mother of mischief"—Colonel O'Connell's "College"—Chevalier O'Mahony—Captain O'Connor writes to him—Rickard speaks of Dan's brilliant success at Gibraltar—The Liberator on his uncle—Anecdotes of the Colonel—Old Kerry newspaper—Count de Vaudreuil—Fine friends—Vaudreuil on O'Connell—Our hero at Cadiz—Siege of Gibraltar, and list of officers there—Duc de Crillon-Mahon—O'Connell a member of the council of war—Names of the battering-ships—Count Fersen—"Le Beau Fersen"—Fersen's generosity—Account of the floating batteries from the "Annual Register"—Contemporary account of our hero on board the floating batteries—Prince of Nassau—"That day of wrath"—O'Connell's coolness in danger—Plot on his life—Saves his friends and others—Wounded—A shell bursts—"Annual Register" continues—Captain Curtis—Letter of a French officer—Family tradition—Mr. James Roche—Chevalier Bartholomew O'Mahony writes (Paris, October, 1782) to Hunting Cap—Congratulates him on Dan's promotion—Pedigree a necessity—Cambray, October, 1782 : Chevalier O'Mahony again—Dan wounded, but recovered—Brothers in arms—Perils at home—The penalties of smuggling—The mysterious crooked knife—Captain Whitwell Butler—The smugglers caught—Gallantry of Captain Butler—Young O'Sullivan, of Couliagh—Ow n McCrohan writes to Morgan O'Connell—Plots—Informers—Mr. Dominic Trant, M.P.—Trants of Dovea—Maurice O'Connell to Counsellor Dominic Trant—Foul plot against Hunting Cap—Honourable conduct of Judge Henn, Dominic Trant, Lord Annaly, and other Protestants—Several letters about this matter—Triumphant refutation of all calumnies, and perfect vindication of Maurice, Morgan, and Daniel O'Connell.

No letter of Daniel Charles O'Connell's can be found from October 15, 1778, to March 12, 1780. This period of a year and three months, however, is pretty fully recorded in stray sentences in other people's letters. Rickard O'Connell, of "Walsh's," gratefully and graphically describes his colonel's devoted friendship in his first letter of 1780. Rickard shall march in with the year; kind Captain Robin Conway, who is always doing good turns, and Colonel O'Connell shall then resume the pen.

Rickard O'Connell's first letter for 1780 gives a most graphic description of marching and recruiting, and such an account of my hero's unfaltering kindness as more than justifies his enthusiastic eulogies on his "almost adored patron," as he styles him.

On January 11, 1780, he writes from Cambray, from whence so many Brigade letters are dated.

At Cambray, where we are Sent for the sake of Recruiting, we shall probably stay a Long time. Our Batallion is reduced to the Company of Grenadiers, not compleat; 3 Fusileers in Health, about 20 in Different Hospittals; some Sergeants and Corporals of the lowest condition, the Ghost of our lately Compleat ... out of Brittany. You have no Idea, my Dear Maurice, of the misery of a subaltern Officer on a Long March, especially if sufficiently useful to be Much ... During the greatest part of Our last Route, I have been ... in the Morning untill midnight with the Rearguard, whose duty it is to Conduct the Sick and the Baggage. Our Pay, which we receive only at the Etappe, is, on a March, from 45 to 48 Sols, and 25 of which we are Obliged to pay for ye hire of a Horse. Ill-clad, for we always Wear our Worst cloathes on a Route; almost sleepless, Fatigued to death, Bemired from Head to Foot by the badness of the Shocking roads, Without being able to Shave or change Linen for several days, Together with an Empty Purse, and its concomitant, not Rarely,—what fine pleasure it would Afford you to see Me in this Pickle at Dreux? Besides, I had a Scheme of slipping to Paris and Surprising you, but Colonel O'Connell, to Whom I wrote to get me Leave, writes to me in his Last that he Sacrificed the pleasure of Seeing me to the Pleasure of Hearing that I was Fasting, watching, drudging, etc., etc., night and day, "pour le bien du service."

The Colonel's Unremitting Attention to my Interests is, indeed, Astonishing in these days, when Rising Men in all Professions never cast Away a thought on any Other object but their Own advancement; when it is a Maxim that to Ask favours for a Friend takes away from Your right of asking for yourself. But he Has a soul Above policy, a Soul whose passion it is to do good and to Redress the wrongs of Fortune. In his Letters he gives me distant Hints that he Has a plan.

Cambray, March 23, 1780, Rickard is coughing, choking, and shivering, unable to afford change of air.

"No, My friend; here I must Stay, at Patrolling and Dressing recruits untill His Majesty thinks proper to Order us to some other Country. Here I must Stay in this Fine Corn-field—for Flanders is Really nothing else—Consuming a

Fourth of my pay next Winter in Stinking coals to heat An infernal Stove, and strive to Exclude the Rigours of this Most disagreeable Climate."

Rickard abuses Flemish snows, regrets the fair wilds of Lower Brittany, and complains of all the reading and writing his profession entails on him.

Robin Conway's letter is a practical illustration of Rickard's assertions about our hero's kindness.

From first to last he brought out three nephews and two cousins. Eugene McCarthy, of Oughtermony, his sister Betty's son, died a lieut.-colonel in British Service. Marcus O'Sullivan, of Couliagh, his sister Honora's son, died a captain in British Service. Little Maurice, son of Geoffrey Maurice O'Connell, died a captain in British Service. Sir Maurice (Charles Phillip) O'Connell, son of Charles Phillip O'Connell, died in 1846 a British general and Governor of New South Wales. Maurice O'Connell, of Carhen, the Liberator's brother, my hero's nephew, died a lieutenant in British Service.

Captain Robin Conway writes to Maurice O'Connell, of Darrynane, what is practically a receipt in full for "Little Maurice," and the seventeen guineas he had about him.

Captain Robin Conway to Maurice O'Connell, of Darrynane.

Bergues, St. Vermoux, February 28, 1780.

Dear Cousin,—This day I rec^d your much esteem'd favour of the 19th November last, by the hands of Cousin M. O'Connell, who arrived safe at this house after 8 days' passage from Corke to Ostend. I can assure you, my dear Maurice, that your reccommendation has greater weight with me than all Ireland, but must let you know it was quite unnecessary to reccommend Maurice Connell in the strong terms you have. I hope you are fully persuaded of my desire of serving any gentleman from my Country, Especially my own flesh and Blood. Whilst he stays, we shall not make the least difference between him and my own son. He is like to remain with me a month or more. [Some references to the boy's illness are crossed out in modern ink.] I wrote to the Colonel by this post, but am afraid he parted for Strasbourg, where his regiment lays, even so we have time enough. The Child cannot well part till well cured. I have your letter before me, which draws drips of blood from my heart to hear of the situation of my poor Brother. God is Judge of my heart and way of thinking. Were it in my power, the poor dear man should not suffer one moment; but it's not. You'd oblige me if in one of your letters you asked my Brother my Situation. He is the man living who knows my circumstances best. This summer I travelled 430 Leagues, which put me to great Expence, and, to crown my fate, lost my Mother-in-law, the 1st of Ocb^{re} last, three days after I arrived to my home. The death of this good woman deranged me much, leaving a debt of £155 stg., which I was obliged to pay in the course of 21 Days. I must own, if my good Brother arrived, he could, without hurting himself, spare that poor man 7 or 8 guineas a year. I have not seen him these 3 years past, nor won't till I hear he relieves his poor brother. The Worthyest of men, your Brother, engaged me last 9bre to write to him. I did, and had no answer. My poor man expects to hear from me. Tell my poor man I shall never write to him till in my power to relieve him. I shall endeavour for next summer to send for little Robin. Wished he applyed till then, and that he made some progress in playing on the pipes, by which means Duke FitzJames will make him an officer on the spott.

My little family are composed of 2 sons and 2 daughters, the eldest now 12 years old, my eldest son 7 and the youngest child, called Daniel, 11 months. He was called Danl to compliment his Godfather, Colonel O'Connell, my best and worthyest of friends. Adieu, my dear Maurice. May the Heavens prosper you with all the sincere wishes of Your affect. Kinsman!

R. CONWAY.

The little fellow arrived here with 17 guineas in his pocket. Mrs. Segerson seems uneasy about her brother. Assure her he is well, if he had Cash enough. I mean Mr. Prendergast.

My best Compliments to Mrs. Connell and all other friends that will ask for me. I hope before now that my good Brother has wrote to Ireland, as I prayed Cousin Daniel to write him a scholding letter.

We can make out from my hero's own letters and from the contemporary account that he was chiefly engaged in pushing his fortunes through the influence of Count de Maillebois, and in severe study at Paris during the winters. He refused promotion in the East, and having been disappointed of serving in America, was then, through the influence of the Minister, sent back as lieut.-colonel to his old original regiment, the Royal Swedes, some time before May, 1778. Curiously enough, I cannot make out when he obtained the Cross of St. Louis which he wears in his miniature at Darrynane, with the uniform of the Irish Brigade.[1] The miniature represents a handsome man, with the fresh, fair complexion, blue eyes, and dark brows, seldom seen in conjunction out of Ireland. Doubtless the hair was dark too, but it is thickly powdered and tied behind in a queue. He wears a prodigious cocked hat, with silver tassels at the points, and a red coat with a blue plastron laced with silver and silver epaulettes, a black stock and white cambric frill. He wears the Cross of St. Louis on its little bit of flame-coloured ribbon—not the broad red grand cordon and star of his picture as an old general. Comparing the little miniature of the middle-aged man, and the life-sized portrait of the old one, we can get a very good idea of him. He was very tall, erect, and muscular, without a superfluous ounce of flesh. The expression is cheerful and wide awake. The eyes, larger and longer than the famous Daniel's, are the same light blue; but there all resemblance ends. The count's face is oval, with a rather aquiline nose very delicately cut about the nostrils; the mouth is small, well-formed, firmly shut, but good-humoured; the chin is full and firm, and has a strongly marked dimple. The forehead, concealed in the young man's picture, is high, very well formed, and full over the temples. The dark eyebrows are well arched and well defined, even in extreme old age, and the veteran has preserved plenty of snow-white hair. Both portraits confirm the tradition of good looks, and have that dignified old-world *bel air* for which he was distinguished through life. He makes such a point that the young nephews sent out shall be of good appearance, strength, and stature, that we can well believe he had found a handsome face, a fine person, and pleasing manners no small help in his uphill struggle with fortune.

[1] The miniature represents Daniel Charles O'Connell as Colonel of the 4th Regiment of the Irish Brigade, when King George III. had brought over the Irish-French officers, headed by the Duke of Fitz James, and formed an Irish Catholic Brigade.

Lieut.-Colonel Daniel Charles O'Connell to Maurice O'Connell, of Darrynane.

Paris, March the 12th, 1780.

I rec'd my Dr Brother's Letters of the 26th January but 2 Days Since, and return him my most warm and unfeigned thanks for the bill it contained. I had it directly presented here, and it has been accepted payable the 17th next month. This very timely succour will enable me to discharge my present *Embarras*, and to appear at my Regiment in a more easy and comfortable footing. I am perfectly sensible, my dear Brother, how necessary and incumbent on me to use the Strictest Economy, without which my appointment, tho' much beyond what I hitherto enjoyed, did not answer my Calls. Unhappily, every step we make in the career of honours in this Country brings on an Addition of Expence which is considered as an Essential part of the obligations of the Man of rank and Dignity. Nothing can repair, in the eyes of the publick, any omission or economy of this nature. However, I know from experience that with Attention and Care a small income goes far. Be assured mine shall be managed with the strictest frugality. However, there are some particular cases where it's sometimes prudent to Sow for to Reap. This consideration will induce sometimes the most prudent man to anticipate on his revenue—from an expectation of increasing it. Had I not followed this course, and had I sat down content at my Regiment, I might live and die a Captain of Infantry, whereas at present I am, Thank God, in a posture of pushing my fortune far beyond even my present Station; but no doubt that will require an Attendance on the Great, whose friendship I am beholden to, and from whom I've still more to hope; and attendance in that line of life brings on Expence. This I tell you, my Dr Brother, only to give you an idea of my position, Least you may think me inclined to spend and lavish money intemperately. Be assured I am far from it, and I venture to assure you that no character can be better established, as well in point of honour and delicacy as for prudence and economy, than mine. I wish you may be convinced that I deserve this opinion of me, and hope that experience will prove to you hereafter that the plan I've laid down to myself, and which I follow, has been conceived and is the pure result of my Observations and the Knowledge I have of the Nature of Affairs in this Country.

I rec'd your letter, which contained Mrs. Burke's receipt. But it came to hands only a few days after my letter to you was gone off. Hitherto there has been no miscarriage, so it seems quite useless to charge Mr. Hennessy to receive my letters. I should fear an omission on his part, rather than from the post. I shall be at Strasbourg towards the 15th April, therefore you'll please to direct thereafter as below.

Little Maurice is at Bergue since the latter days of February. He brought over with him a troublesome companion, of which he must be cured ere I venture to shew him. I expect him down here towards the 30th, when I shall present him to Duke FitzJames, and then send him down to College. I am of opinion Dan must send him over a supply of a dozen pounds before the end of the Summer. The first expence is heavy, but after he shall be discharged of all, or at least he shall demand only the price of a coat from time to time. Eugene is gone with part of his Reg^t to Martinico, and behaved so well on the tour he made, that on his return here I got him a Captain's Commission and a gratification. He received two wounds in a certain Engagement which made some noise in the World. I hope he is changed for the better. I have recommended him to the care of Chev. Mahony, who is with battalion of Walsh's Regiment. Our friend [name torn off][1] commands it. He promised me to take some measures, if possible, to send me something from time to time for his poor Sister Bourke. If he does, I shall be careful to remit it on the spot. It's better, I believe, not to mention it to her, lest she may conceive expectations which may prove Vain, tho' I hope they may be effected. Nothing can be done in the affair of Doctor Connell. The College is at law with his Executor. Farewell, my d^r Brother. Receive again the true acknowledgements for your extreme kindness, which I feel with the most real gratitude. My Duty and Love to my Mother. Most tender affections to my Sister. Farewell, Dr Brother once More.

D. O'C.

My address, à Monsieur O'C., Lieutenant-Colonel du regiment de Royal Suédois, à Strasbourg.

Maurice Leyne is now with us, and desires his compliments. He is a young man of great merit and parts.

I am happy to hear that my Mother is well, all to some gouty complaints which sometimes affect her. I hope my Sister is also well. How are all the others? Pray remember me to them. How is Brother Morgan and family? My compliments to Dan.

Our colonel evidently refers to Eugene McCarthy's distinguished bravery in the engagement with the British ship

---

[1] It must be Colonel FitzMaurice, as Mrs. Burke was his sister.

Serapis. The following account is quoted from a memoir of the Liberator, by his son John. The writer says Eugene escaped unhurt, but I naturally infer that his uncle, who saw him soon after, knew best.

In his memoir of the Liberator, John O'Connell tells us how a company of the Irish Brigade, under the command of Lieutenants McCarthy and Stack, volunteered as marines on Paul Jones's ship, *Le Bonhomme Richard*, and were the only officers unwounded when, in command of three French vessels of war, he engaged the British off Flamborough Head, in 1778. "He took the British frigate *Serapis*," says John O'Connell, "with the loss of his own ship, which sank as he boarded the *Serapis*. It is a singular fact that Lieutenants McCarthy and Stack, who boarded with their few surviving marines from the tops, were, although the most exposed, the only French officers unhurt in the action; and that one of them [McCarthy] died a lieutenant-colonel in the British Service, and the other [Stack] died a general in the same service."

I have received the following account of Colonel Eugene McCarthy from his niece, Miss Evelina McCarthy, grandniece to Count O'Connell, and second cousin to my dear husband. At a very advanced age she retains her faculties unimpaired, and, having spent her life abroad, knows a great deal about the Irish in France. I sent her a list of queries. Here is her reply about Eugene—

"The next person you mention is Colonel Eugene McCarthy, the youngest son of my grandmother (Betty O'Connell), Mrs. McCarthy. He was eight years older than my mother, the youngest of sixteen children. I remain alone the sole representative of that large family. Colonel Eugene went to France to his uncle [Count O'Connell] when he was about ten years old. I have heard from many who knew him that he was a splendid man, a polished gentleman and accomplished soldier, who would have risen to the highest posts of his career had not it, like that of many others, been stopped by the Revolution. He got permission from Louis XVI. to accompany La Fayette and Rochambeau to America. He sailed in the ship commanded by the celebrated Paul Jones. They put in under the Skellig Rocks, opposite Darrynane, and some of the officers, Irish and Kerry men, landed to get recruits for the cause of America. My uncle was on the point of landing also, but was kept back for the second boat. However, only one landed. Soldiers under a magistrate covered the shore, and arrested them. One of the gentlemen was able to say in Irish to my great-grandmother [Maur-ni-Dhuiv] that her grandson was safe on board. I have a rosary my uncle got conveyed to my mother that he brought from France to her. On the breaking up of the Royalist Army he was for a time *aide-de-camp* to the Duke of York. I am not quite sure, but I think he accompanied him in his inglorious campaign in the Netherlands. He died young, and left no children."

"Walsh's," in which Eugene was captain, as his uncle tells us, had gone to Tobago before the fight off Martinique between Count de Grasse and Sir Samuel Hood, in which seven hundred of "Dillon's" took part in April, 1781; however, both Irish regiments bore a part in its conquest by the Marquis de Bouillé, in June, 1781.

O'Callaghan does not give us the names of all the officers who took part in the brilliant surprise of the Isle of St. Eustache, by the Marquis de Bouillé, in the following November. He made Lieut.-Colonel Thomas FitzMaurice governor of the island. As this brave and most kind-hearted man was in "Walsh's," and was first cousin to Eugene's mother, and specially requested by Count O'Connell to look after his nephew, it is more than probable he contrived to get the young captain a place in the three hundred men from "Walsh's" who shared in the expedition where honour and profit were happily combined.

Our colonel gives the following pleasant picture of his return to the regiment in which he had first served:—

Strasbourg, May the 10th, 1780.

MY DEAR BROTHER,—On my departure from Paris I deffered writing to you until my arrival here, and since have been so occupied that I really cu'd not sooner satisfy my impatience to give you an account of the reception I met with among my old friends of Royal Sweedes. It was natural to suppose my introduction might have been disagreable to some old officers who were Captains when I enter'd the

Service, and still continue in the same rank; however, nothing can Equal the friendship and fondness I have met with from them all, and, far from discovering the least displeasure, they seem highly satisfied to serve under me. I shall leave no stone unturned to make myself agreable to a sett of brave and honest veterans with whom I hope to acquire some day honour and glory; at the same time, if fortune answers my expectations, and that of my friends, I might, before a year or two at most, quit them for a better post; but hopes are no certainty. At all events, my present rank is honourable and satisfactory, tho', I must own, I carry my views far beyond it, and flatter myself, with the assistance of the Almighty, to succeed.

There's a matter of the greatest consequence for to promote my fortune and expectations—I mean that of my Genealogy. That is a point so much looked to in this country, that without it a man, whatever his merit and capacity, will scarse ever rank amongst the great. It's indispensably necessary to be presented at Court for to roll with the Nobility, & to be admitted to that honour a genealogy must be produced, supported by authentic Deeds, records, or family acts, which prove the candidate having ranked amongst the Nobles of his Country at least since the year 1400. The genealogy you sent me cannot serve that purpose, as being divested of proofs and quoting no record, act, or deed of any kind to support any filiation sett forth therein; for which reason it may be supposed to be made up without foundation. I give you on the other side a notice of the Publick Offices where some affidavits or transactions relative to our family may be more probably met with, and where Count de Serrant [Walsh, whose brother took over Charles Edward in his merchant-ship and supplied a man-of-war] and others of our countrymen found the éclaircisments and proofs on which they built the Edifice of their Extraction in the most ample manner; but as I know how remote these ideas are from the present mode of thinking amongst you, I scarsely flatter myself that you will make the necessary searches to procure me the like. Nor does your position, so remote from the Capital, where these publick offices are, admit of it, tho' you were even disposed to go to the trouble and tiresomeness of turning over old nasty mouldering papers. The person immediately interested can alone be able to persevere in so tedious an investigation. No doubt you must put off that untill Peace shall permit me to go over myself and persue my aim; but en attendant, my Dear Brother, you can render me a most essential service by procuring a Certificate, signed and attested by several Members of both Houses of Parliament, particularly those of Munster, setting forth that Colonel Daniel O'Connell is descended of one of the most ancient and considerable of the old Milesian families of Ireland, formerly possessed of considerable properties in Ireland, particularly in the Countys of Limerick, Kerry, and Clare, and the County of Dublin, of which properties they were stripped or divested off by the Revolution of Ireland, particularly that of 1690 [torn]. Such an attestation, which I doubt not the Earl of Glandore and Counsillor FitzGerald cu'd procure you to be Signed and certified by a sufficient number of Members of both Houses, might answer my purpose and serve me in lieu of a Genealogy which cannot be obtained without considerable Expence and trouble. Pray, my dear Brother, let me know in your next whether I can expect you may be able to procure me such a Piece, and, if so, you must take care to have it Drawn out on Parchement and certified by a Notary Publick, or tabellion, who must certify the Signing and Seal of those who attest it. My receiving it before next winter, or at least for New Year, may have a most favourable influence on my fortune if it should be procur'd. It would be best to forward it to London, whence I mean to have it over. I rely on your friendship for me, my Dr Brother, and indeed you will render service therewith to more than one person of the family, as my success in life must prove favourable to all my friends and indigent relations.

Little Maurice got a severe fit of sickness, of which he had like to have died. He is gone over to join his Colledge, where he has already 3 or 4 behind him. I've not seen him, as I was forced to quit Paris ere he was in a condition to travel. Farewell, my Dear, Dr Brother. I mentioned to you in due time, and thanked you for your last remittance. May God preserve my Dr Brother and friend! How much are you not wanting to us all, and what are we not beholden to you for—surely I before any other? That all blessings may ever attend you, my Dearest Brother, is the most sanguine wish of your ever loving and most grateful brother,

D. O'C.

My most tender Duty to my Dr Mother, and most affectionate compliments to my Sister. Remember me to all friends. My address is as follows: à Monsieur, Mons. le Chev^r O'Connell, Colonel d'Infantérie, Lieutenant-Colonel du Régiment de Royal Suédois.

The publick records of Ireland are in Dublin, viz. Roll's Office, forfeiture Office, Birmingham tower, Trinity Colledge

Library, where there exist old visitations of Several Counties by Molineux King-at-Arms, with an account of the state of the Different families in his time in said Counties.

It is most probable that there exist in the records some papers relating to our family, and setting forth their ancient position and forfeitures.

How, when, or where Daniel O'Connell got made Chevalier de St. Louis we are not informed. He is "M. le Chevalier" in this letter, and to get it one had to serve in a campaign with distinguished bravery.

Count O'Connell refers precisely to the sources from which the brief account of his family prefixed to this memoir is taken. Mr. J. Leyne, Registry of Deeds Office, who has them all at command, kindly expounded them to me.

The fact of the matter was that the O'Connells, not being a large clan with a chief, had no clan-pedigree. The great clan-pedigrees were exactly like the genealogical lists of Scripture. Their object was to preserve the direct descent of the "princely" family, *i.e.* the family truly sprung from some prominent chief, who in early times had left his impress on his tribe and was the father whose name his children continued to bear. The chiefs could only be chosen from the princely stem recorded in the clan-pedigree, and the descents of certain younger branches were recorded in the margin. I saw several of these clan-pedigrees in the Royal Irish Academy, where the late eminent Irish scholar, Mr. Hennessy, explained them to me. Centuries ago, the O'Connells had been among the smaller and less powerful clans absorbed into McCarthy Mor's great following.

This the count does not seem to have known. I fancy no authentic documents earlier than the Tudors could have been found. I do not know exactly by what process that famous pedigree-monger, Chevalier O'Gorman, evolved two or three centuries of descents; but I am inclined to think he worked on some other Kerry pedigree.

Concerning the arms, several old articles of plate belonging to the count's mother bore a stag, the chief device in the arms of the family. The arms were duly registered by John of Ashtown, at the Restoration. They are, in untechnical language, a stag on a shield, white above, green below, with two green shamrocks on the white, and one white shamrock below the stag on the green. The crest is a stag's head with a shamrock on the collar.

Now, we cannot find out why Hunting Cap refused to believe a whole company of experts concerning the advantages of a pedigree. I suspect the astute elder brother knew that a really true one, going back to A.D. 1400, was an impossibility; also that he refused to believe it could get a man a rich wife. Perhaps he thought his brother's brilliant achievements, high character, and fine person would have succeeded without it.

But a time came later on when the dear old Chevalier Fagan would not have his younger friend foiled at this turning-point of his career, and the moderate fortune of the prudent veteran again came to the aid of Daniel O'Connell, but not until two years after this application to Maurice O'Connell had failed. Daniel meanwhile had pushed his fortunes to some purpose. It would seem that, in time of war, there was great difficulty about letters, and that relatives at home rather feared to receive them. This appears very clearly from a series of letters written by a Clare man, Admiral O'Houny, earlier in the century, in which that old gentleman's summaries of his adventures during each war show that all direct communication had been severed with friends at home. From persons passing through other countries tidings sometimes came. To wit, Captain Rickard O'Connell and Chevalier O'Mahony mention tidings of my hero during the Spanish War. They had reached the former through Captain Robin Conway, retired and settled at Bergues.

The great siege of Gibraltar occupied so large a space in men's memories, that the operations in Minorca, which preceded it, are difficult to trace with any clearness. The excellent old account of my hero in the *Kerry Chronicle* dismisses it in a few sentences. It mentions his appointment as lieut.-colonel in his old regiment, the Royal Swedes, where his former comrades were still simple lieutenants, but does not give the date. In a letter of May 5, 1778, Captain Rickard O'Connell writes of him as "the Colonel;" so he must have been promoted during one of the periods we were left letter-less, viz. from May, 1777, to the autumn of 1778. Doubtless, the dates of commissions are recorded somewhere, but it is not in my power to visit the archives of the French War Office for them, and O'Callaghan's "Brigade" does not enter into details of non-Irish regiments. Concerning the beginning of the Spanish War, the contemporary chronicler merely observes, "With this regiment [the Royal Swedes] he was at the taking of Minorca. Having accomplished their purpose in spite of the valiant Murray's vigorous defence, he joined the rest of the confederate army before Gibraltar."

There are at Darrynane three very interesting illustrative documents of the Irish side of life in 1780. The two letters which passed between the Knight of Kerry and Maurice O'Connell, of Darrynane, strike me as of peculiar interest. The Hill of Drung has been duly chronicled. Thirty years before the Knight's letter, Dr. Smith, in his "History of Kerry," has spoken of the public spirit of the gentlemen of the wild south-western baronies in subscribing to make roads and bridges. Hunting Cap's reply to the part of the letter concerning Catholic volunteers strikes me as full of dignity. He would have no half-loaf—nothing but the full bread of repealed penal laws. I happen to know that some Catholics were not prevented from having fowling-pieces (on licence given), but it was for wide-mouthed blunderbusses they craved. These may still be seen in many old houses.

A curious illustration of the difficulty of getting leave from the dominant caste for popish houses to set up this domestic artillery appears in letters of my husband's great-great-grandfather, Stephen Coppinger, written in 1729 to his son. He dared not live on his own land, so rented Barry's Court from the Earl of Barrymore, and there, by the kindly nobleman's connivance, his thrice outlawed and attainted father died in peace. Lord Barrymore took his tenant's son to England, and arranged his marriage with Mary, eldest daughter and co-heiress of Nicholas Blundell, of Crosby, the last male representative of that long-descended family, by his wife, Frances, daughter of the second Lord Langdale. In one of his letters to the youth, the father urges on him to get "my very good lord's written permission for heavy arms to protect the dwelling and its surrounding orchards." But what was the need of heavy arms at Barry's Court, in a thickly inhabited district, within two or three hours' drive of Cork, compared to the need at Darrynane, approached only by bridle-tracks over a mountain or by sea, and shut off by an amphitheatre of hills from help from outside ? The house might have been burned in its sheltered nook below the mountain, and people four miles off would have known nothing about it. It is odd bits of these old letters that really enable us to see what the older generations of Catholics had to endure. At the same time, the letters show the greater number of high-class Protestant gentlemen in the most honourable light.

The Knight of Kerry to Maurice O'Connell, of Darrynane.

DEAR SIR,—I am Exceedingly obliged to you for Kind Intentions and for the Pains you took for me. I have now, thank God, weathered the Storm, and, unless I Meet some Unforeseen misfortunes, I never shall Encounter such distress again.

I have no doubt You will exert yourself and Prevail on your Friends to do so for Removing the abominable Grievance of Drung Hill. I suppose Jermyn has Before now made a good Progress in tracing the proper Line. I think the Work should be Done in a style of Solidity and duration, Well guarded by Arches or stout Linterns from the Mountain Waters, and so executed as to make it an Everlasting work. For the purpose we must not Hesitate at some Extraordinary Expence, and I think we shall, by Subscription, make the Burthen up to the Barony.

I have been Thinking of a scheme for Preventing the Barony of Iveragh from being the Asylum of the Rogues and Vagabonds of the other parts of the Country. The Associations of Volunteers have done wonders all over the Kingdom, in Civilising the country and quelling Lawless proceedings. Why should not a Corps be raised in that Barony, Westward of the River Beigh ? The gentlemen of Property of your Religion, uniting with the Protestants, might soon raise a Body of men, I should Imagine, that might be Relied on for Executing the Above purpose. If a Spirit of that sort should be Raised and Carried into execution, the men Disciplined and well Officered, I will furnish them with Firelocks. In such an Undertaking care must be taken to avoid Entering into Feuds and Factions, and to have no Object in view but the Peace and Good of the Publick.

I am, Dear Sir, your most Obedient and faithful Servant,

Merrion Square, February 1st, 1780.   ROBT. FITZGERALD.

Maurice O'Connell's reply to the Knight of Kerry.

Darrinane, Feb. 10th, 1780.

DEAR SIR,—I am Extremely happy to Hear by your favour of the First that you are well. I Assure you there is not among your many Friends one who more Sincerely wishes you an Uninterrupted continuance of Happiness and prosperity. I have had Jermyn to view the Mountain of Drung, but could not at that Time attend myself, owing to a Cold which Confined me. The enclosed Billet, being a copy of One he left with me, will let you See his estimate, and also give you some idea of his Plan. His line, forming a Sweep round the mountain, must, undoubtably, not only take off the present enormous Pitch, but render the Whole a much easier and more convenient one for carriages. The Sum mentioned is heavy, but I perfectly agree that the Work should be Executed in a style of solidity and Durability, which cannot be Expected without an adequate Expence. Nothing on my part shall be wanting to promote so Useful a work; but it rests entirely with you to set out and give success to the Subscription, the aid of which will be indispensably necessary.

The observations you make with Respect to the Barony of Iveragh are very just. It is much to be wished that the land should be purged of Outlaws and Vagabonds. Not only that, but that it should possess some little Force for repelling the pillaging of scampering Privateers. You were in the country when Paul Jones was off its Coast, but had he taken it in Head to land with only 20 Men, might he not have plundered and Burned the whole Barony, naked and Defenceless as it was, without Arms for 10 men? From end to End of it the terror of the Inhabitants exceeded all Power of description. The very distinguished services of the armed Volunteer Corps are universally known and Gratefully acknowledged through the whole Kingdom, and I am Fully convinced that the Roman Catholic gentlemen of Iveragh would readily unite with their Protestant neighbours [as you mentioned] to form a Corps did they think such a Measure would meet the approbation of the Legislature. They would, in common with every Catholick of standing in Ireland, be exceedingly Happy by every means in their power to give additional Weight and strength and security to the kingdom; but what can they do while the Laws of their country forbid them the use of arms? Under such circumstances, I look upon it to be their Duty to confine Themselves to that line of conduct marked out for them by the Legislature, and with Humility and resignation wait for a further Relaxation of the laws, which a more enlightened and Liberal way of Thinking, added to a clearer and more deliberate Attention to the real interests and prosperity of the country will, I hope, soon bring about.

I have the honour to, etc., etc.,

M. O'CONNELL.

This is copied from my copy of Hunting Cap's rough draft. We notice that he now ventures to begin to use the "O'."

I shall quote another interesting letter on a different topic. It is from a shipwrecked ship's captain, who indites a formal letter of thanks.

Letter of David Murray, concerning a ship and portions of cargo entrusted to Maurice O'Connell.

August 13th, 1781.

Whereas on Sunday morning, the Twelfth of August Instant, I was chased by a privateer, and, to avoid falling into her possession, was under the severe necessity of running my ship ashore on the lands of Cummaklacane, Inside of the Skariffe Islands, as by my protest made before Whitwell Butler, Esqr., one of his Majesties Justices of the peace, may more fully appear; and whereas it is my Earnest wish and desire that such part of the cargoe of my said ship, as well as her Hull and Materialls as can be saved, be turned to the best and most advantageous account for the Owners; and whereas I have every Reason to place the utmost Confidence in Maurice O'Connell, of Darrinane, Esqr., whose distinguished Humanity to me and my people I shall ever most gratefully acknowledge;—be it known that I hereby Impower and Authorize him, the said Maurice O'Connell, to save, preserve, Collect, and Take up such part and parcels of the said Cargoe, Ship, and Materiall as can possibly be had or saved, and to Turn the same to the best accountt for the Owners, hereby investing him with every power and authority to act as he shall Judge most prudent and proper, for and on behalf of the said Owners. Witness my hand and seale this Thirteenth Day of August, 1781—eighty and one.

DAV. MURRAY.

Presentt—Andrew Connell.

I particularly desire that the two casks of Indigoe be recovered from the People that plundered it, and that they be punished as the Law shall direct.

DAV. MURRAY.

Rickard O'Connell's New Year's letter of 1781 describes my hero as in excellent health and full of kindness. I shall enrich posterity with fair Miss Rice's infallible cough syrup, as recorded by her grateful countryman. This same New Year's letter of Captain Rickard contains a few pathetic sentences.

Cambray, Jan. 22d, 1871.

I have known Afflictions, I have quitted my distressed Parents in their declining in the vale of Years, whom it was not in my Power to Assist—left them, perhaps, exposed to the Contumely of the sordid, purse-proud Wretch; and many such there are, who would delight to depress a Decayed family. I left thee, Ireland, my dear country, a voluntary Exile, to earn amongst Strangers the means of supporting the Rank to which I was born, and which Fortune denied me to maintain at Home. Yet I swear by the Honour of my Profession that Grief never sat heavier on my heart than on the day when I leaped out of your Barge on the Canal of Dunkirk.

Rickard, having caught a cold while taking some powerful expectorant medicine, was given over with a lung attack, and sent invalided from Bergues to Cambray.

Happily for me [he continues], Miss Rice,[1] sister-in-law to Countess Watters, with whom I had been a little acquainted, passed a week here. This amiable young lady gave me a Receipt to make a syrop, composed of a handful of Rue, 2 handfuls of Rosemary, a head of Garlick, boil'd in a quart of white-wine vinegar till half is consumed, strained thro' a piece of Linen, and sweetened with a pound and a half of Sugar Candy. It pleased gracious Providence to make this syrop the instrument of my recovery which, thank God, advances. . . .

Colonel O'Connell is very well, thank God. It is needless to tell you he is, as usual, the best of friends. Poor Robin Conway 'got a malignant Fever last 7ber, and still continues in a very weakly way. I much fear for him.

He requests to be addressed, "Chez M. l'Abbè Griffin, Chanoine de la Cathédrale de Cambray."

There is but one discoverable letter of Count O'Connell's between May 10, 1780, and April 16, 1783. I find mention of him as with the Battalion at Minorca, and quite well

---

[1] I think he uses "sister-in-law" for "stepsister," as Countess Watters was herself a Miss Rice, of Nantes.

in December, 1781, in a letter from Rick O'Connell, his Clare kinsman; and there is a whole letter informing his brother Maurice of his brilliant prospects in November, 1872, signed only C. B. M., which stands for Count Bartholomew O'Mahony, his devoted friend, usually mentioned as the Chevalier O'Mahony. In the letters I have seen—and I have heard of several I have not been able to get hold of—there are only four references to these sieges of Port Phillip and Gibraltar. Once he says his old comrade, the Prince of Nassau, under whom he had served in the floating batteries, wanted him to go out and serve under him in Russia. Ross O'Connell, of Lake View, found a letter there the other day about an invitation from the Portuguese Government to remodel the discipline of their army; so that, in addition to actually serving France and England, this "cavalier of fortune," as Grant very aptly calls him, had been invited to serve Holland, America, Russia, and Portugal—truly an odd agglomerate of services. His two principal chroniclers— O'Callaghan, quoting the Liberator's article in the *New Monthly*, and Grant, largely quoting the "Biographie Universelle"—make the Minorca business two years too soon. However, I quote them for want of better.

The notice of Count O'Connell in O'Callaghan states, "He distinguished himself at the siege and capture of Port Mahon, in Minorca, from the English in the year 1779, being at that time major in the Regiment of Royal Swedes. He received public thanks for his services on that occasion, and a recommendation from the commander-in-chief to the Minister of War for promotion. That promotion he immediately obtained, and served at the siege of Gibraltar in the year 1782 as lieut.-colonel of his regiment, the Royal Swedes, but attached to the corps of engineers." This is a curious mistake of dates, as Minorca surrendered in February, 1782, and he was already a lieut.-colonel. Some part of this statement is probably correct, but it is utterly inaccurate in two points: Daniel O'Connell was a lieut.-colonel before he ever saw the Island of Minorca, and he was never an engineer at all. Drinkwater gives a copy of the French Army List. Daniel O'Connell figures on the staff—"État-Major." His is the third name of the German Brigade—Daniel O'Connell, lieut.-colonel—at the siege of Gibraltar. "By confederate army" the writer means the allied forces of Spain and France. Hostilities had begun between England and France in 1777, and two years later Spain, after proffers of mediation had been refused by England, espoused the part of France, and declared war with England on June 16, 1779.

Through that year, and the winter and early spring of 1781, small ships frequently kept up a communication between Minorca and Gibraltar, though "the enemies' cruisers" kept a sharp look out, worthy Drinkwater tells us, and a privateer, which reached Gibraltar from Port Mahon, in Minorca, on February 9, "ran thro' ten cruisers, besides six gun-boats, and was chased by a xebeque, but escaped them all."

The French succours sailed in May. Drinkwater thus describes their sailing far from the Rock : "A boat arrived from Portugal on the 24th of July, with tidings that the Spanish Fleet had sailed from Cadiz on a cruise. Soon after this arrived," continues the painstaking chronicler, "a large fleet of upwards of seventy sail appeared from the west. When abreast the *Europa*, we discovered amongst them, a ship of the line, two frigates, two cutters, a bomb-ketch, and several armed vessels. They did not display any colours. This proved afterwards to be the fleet which blockaded Mahon, and conveyed the troops which besieged Fort St. Phillip, under the command of the Duc de Crillon, and captured the Island of Minorca."

The fleet was sighted off Gibraltar towards the end of July, and the landing of the troops it carried was easily effected. Occasional tidings reached the Rock.

Drinkwater tells us that, on September 5, the British prisoner exchanged for a Spaniard informed him "that the Duc de Crillon, with 10,000 men, had landed at Minorca, and that it was reported he was to be joined by a French Army from Toulon."

He also says that, on the 12th, the Spanish lines and shipping outside Gibraltar fired a *feu de joie*, commemorating some success of the Duc de Crillon at Minorca.

Fort St. Phillip did not finally surrender until February 5, 1782. Captain Rickard O'Connell, on December 29, 1781, mentions that my hero was there. He says—

"I lately had an account from Captain Conway, that the dearest and best of my Friends, your dear Brother, is with the Battalion at Minorca, ... and trust that an all-gracious Providence will restore him safe and victorious to his friends."

He most certainly was not in the artillery or engineers, whose staff lists do not contain a single Irish name, while three Irish names figure in the German Brigade—Baron Hamilton, Daniel O'Connell, and Major O'Ghier.

Mr. Leyne happily discovered and transcribed a letter from our lieut.-colonel to his cousin Rick O'Connell, written from Minorca. He only found it, and a more precious epistle describing royal and princely favour, after the type had been actually set up for this portion of the book. The sorely tried printers, worried with bad writing, Irish, French, and Latin quotations, now find fresh matter set before them. It is characteristic of my hero that, before he has done anything in particular, he wants his pedigree, so as to be qualified to ask favours when he shall have achieved distinction in arms.

Lieut.-Colonel Daniel O'Connell to his cousin Rickard O'Connell, Esq.

Minorca, the 1st December, 1781.

I received last night your most acceptable favour of the 9th October, my dear Rick, which Abbé Griffin was so Kind to forward me. I can't express my Satisfaction to hear from yourself you are on the mending hand, and likely to recover your former health and Spirits. I leave you to judge whether I shall be Zealous in promoting this happy change by exerting my powers and interest to procure the leave of Absence you want. By this very oppertunity I shall indorse your letter to our friend Chev^r de Mahony, with directions to lose not a Moment, and to inform you without delay whether or no the Certificates be required to grant y^r just demand. If so, you'll address them directly to his abode in Paris, as underneath. Sending them here would be tedious, and wou'd be losing Time. I make no doubt your request shall be Granted. Mahony will be careful to inform you on't, and how long you can stay abroad—the longer the better—until your health be solidly and firmly restored. I need not tell you, my Dr Rick, how ardently I wish for that happy event. I give the Chev^r your address. I suppose your papers have long ere now mentioned the Invasion of this island by the Spanish forces, and their being reinforced by a Corps of 4 thousand French. My Regiment is of the number, and here we are these 6 weeks. I suppose you'll not expect from me any Particulars of our operations. Your papers will put us all to death, most doubtless, and paint us as a dastardly Race, undisciplined and cruel, but the Knowing and impartial reader will, I hope, do us the honour and Justice to believe the contrary. I find myself very happy here. You know how much I love my Profession, and how much I long'd to act. Altho' I've no oppertunity of a seperate Command, by which I may expect to be distinguished, yet such an undertaking as this must Needs afford instruction. It's a Capital Point for me, and the siege of one of the strongest places in the world no bad Lesson in the art which rendered Vauban and C—— so famous. I shall endeavour to draw some Benefit from it.

I return you my hearty thanks for the Trouble you took about my family papers. It's indeed a matter of Great concern for me to have them. If I return from this Expedition they may be more than ever Wanting, and the means of making my Fortune. I already made you Sensible of their importance. The more I am Known, the more friends I make, and the more they Prove so. Therefore I Request you exert yourself to Procure them, and if you've any friends residing in Dublin, give them the charge to Search the records for some acts, titles, or transactions which make mention of this Name, and may serve to corroborate the Genealogy. I suppose you've been ere now at Darinane, where I trust you've met with a Cordial Reception. Was I Lord of the Place, it w'd be so, and I believe my Brother was not less pleased to Possess you. Farewell, Dr Rick. God grant we meet again in perfect health. I am Persuaded you wish it equally. Adieu, done, Dearest Cousin. My most affectionate wishes to all your family, and believe me,
Your steadfast friend,
D. O'C.

Address to Chev^r de Mahony, chez Mgr L'Archevêque de Cambray, en son hôtel, rue du Regard [torn]. Employ your good offices, jointly with my brother, to procure the Certificate I called for, and to have it Signed by the Nobility. It must be on Parchment, and attested by a Notary Publick, as if transacted in his presence at Dublin. Transmit Them by the first sure hand to Chev' Mahony and, if none offers, to some friend in London, who may meet frequent oppertunities of sending them to London.

Rickard O'Connell, Esq', at Fenloe, near Six Mile Bridge, County Clare, Ireland.

Par Ostende.

Grant's "Cavaliers of Fortune" gives what seems the most connected account, though with a wrong date, for the Duc de Crillon's landing: "In 1779, when France espoused the cause of America, and sought to harass the mother country in Europe, O'Connell was engaged in the expedition against Port Mahon, the principal town of Minorca, situated on a rocky promontory, difficult of access from the landward, and defended by Fort San Philipo, in which there was a resolute garrison. O'Connell, in his new regiment, served under the Duc de Crillon [who only passed Gibraltar on August 25, 1781] at the siege, and conducted himself with such honour as to be specially noticed. The operations were severe and protracted, but in three years the Spaniards and their allies captured the whole island, which, at the peace of 1763, had been formally ceded to Britain."

The mistake in the above is about the date of the Duc de Crillon's arrival, on whose staff my hero served at Gibraltar.

I shall now quote a short account from the "Annual Register," and the gallant Murray's beautiful letter about the heroism of his English veterans.

The "Annual Register" positively states that the Duc de Crillon-Mahon, by order of the Court of Spain, endeavoured to induce General Murray to give up Port Phillip for an immense bribe. "General Murray treated the insult with a mixture of that haughty disdain incident to the consciousness of an ancient line and illustrious ancestry, and with the generous indignation and stern resentment of a veteran soldier who feels himself wounded in the tenderest part by an insidious attempt upon that honour which he had set up as the great object and idol of his life."

The following is General Murray's description of the fall of Port Phillip (from the Appendix to the "Annual Register," 1782) :—

The Hon. General Murray, Governor of Minorca, to the Earl of Hillsborough, one of H.M.'s Principal Secretaries of State.

Minorca, Feb. 16, 1782.

My Lord,—I have the honour to acquaint your Lordship that Fort St. Phillip was surrendered to his Catholic Majesty the 5th instant. The Capitulation accompanies this. I flatter myself all Europe will agree the brave garrison showed uncommon heroism, and that thirst for glory which has ever distinguished the troops of my royal master. The most inveterate scurvy which I believe ever has infected mortals reduced us to this situation. The reports of the faculty fully explain the dreadful havoc it made, and that three days' further obstinacy on my part must have inevitably destroyed the brave remains of this garrison, as they declare there was no remedy for the men in the hospitals but vegetables; and that of the 660 able to do duty, 560 were actually tainted with the scurvy, and in all likelihood would be in the hospitals in five days' time. Such was the uncommon spirit of the King's soldiers, that they concealed their disorders and inability rather than go into the hospitals. Several men died on guard, after having stood sentry. Their fate was not discovered till called upon for the relief, when it came to their turn to mount again. Perhaps a more noble or a more tragical scene was never exhibited than that of the march of the garrison of St. Phillip's thro' the Spanish and French armies. It consisted of no more than 600 old decrepit soldiers; 200 Seamen, 120 of the Royal Artillery, 20 Corsicans, and 25 Greeks, Turks, Moors, Jews, etc. The two armies were drawn up in two lines, the battalions fronting each other, forming a way for us to march through. They consisted of 14,000 men, and reached from the Glacis to Georgetown, where our battalions laid down their arms, declaring they surrendered them to God alone, having the consolation to know the victors could not plume themselves on taking an hospital.

Such were the distressing figures of our men, that many of the Spanish and French troops are said to have shed tears as they passed, and the Duc de Crillon and the Baron de Falkenhayn declare it is true. I cannot aver this, but I think it is very natural; for my own part, I felt no uneasiness on this occasion, but that which proceeded from the miserable disorder which threatened us with destruction. Thanks to the Almighty, my apprehensions are now abated; the humanity of the Duc de Crillon (whose heart was most sensibly touched by the misfortunes of such brave men) has gone even beyond my wishes in providing everything which can contribute to our recovery. The Spanish as well as the French surgeons attend our hospitals. We are greatly indebted to the Baron de Falkenhayn, who commands the French troops. We feel, too, infinite obligations to the Count de Crillon; they can never be forgot by any of us. I hope this young man will never command an army against my Sovereign, for his military talents are as conspicuous as the goodness of his heart.

Lists of the killed and wounded, with the number of our guns which were destroyed by the enemy's battering artillery, which consisted of 109 pieces of cannon and 36 mortars, are enclosed. I shall wait here until I see the last man of my noble garrison safely and commodiously embarked. If my accompanying them in a transport to England could be of the smallest service to any of them, I would cheerfully go with them by sea; but as I can be of no further use to them after they are on board ship, I trust his Majesty will approve of my going to Leghorn, to bring home with me my wife and children, who fled to Italy in the evening of the day the Spanish Army landed on this island.

My Aide-de-Camp, Capt. Don, will have the honour to present this letter to your Lordship. He is well acquainted with the most minute circumstance relative to the siege, is an intelligent, distinguished officer, and is furnished with copies of all the papers I have, which he will lay before your Lordship if requisite.

The Captains Savage, Boothby, and Don, of the 51st Regiment, Lieut. Mercier of ditto, Lieut. Botticher of Goldacker's Regiment, and Lieut. Douglas the engineer, are exchanged for the officers we made prisoners at Cape Mola.

Colonel Pringle and his nephew, Lieut. Pringle, are to be left hostages until the transports return, agreeable to the capitulation.

I have the honour to be, etc.,
JAMES MURRAY.

P.S.—It would be unjust and ungrateful was I not to declare that, from the beginning to the last hour of the siege, the officers and men of the Royal Regiment of Artillery, and likewise the seamen, distinguished themselves. I believe the world cannot produce more expert gunners and bombardiers than those who served at this siege, and I am sure the sailors showed uncommon zeal. It is unnecessary, likewise, to declare that no garrison was ever nourished with better salt provisions of all kinds than we had sent to us from England; fresh vegetables we could not have, but we had plenty of pease, good bread and rice, with currants and raisins; and left in the Fort six months' full allowance of all kinds, although a magazine, containing six months' more, was burnt by the enemy's shells.

While Lieut.-Colonel Daniel O'Connell was soldiering abroad, he was busily engaged in having his pedigree looked up at home, not from any personal vanity, but as a necessary stepping-stone to fortune. His Clare kinsman writes the following graphic letter to Hunting Cap, who, however, could not be induced to take up the matter, and could not even be moved by the prospect of a brother riding in the king's coach:—

Rickard O'Connell to Maurice O'Connell, of Darrynane.

Dec. 29, 1781.

DEAR SIR,—I should have given you an account of myself, and assured you of my unalterable attatchment since I have been in Ireland, had it not been for my determined Resolution on my arrival to have waited on you at Darrinane as soon as ever I should be able. When I came to the County of Clare, I was so much reduced that I could not mount a Horse; but in some Time my native air began to have the desired effect, and last October I was so far recovered that I began to consider about the Expedition to Kerry, notwithstanding the Difficulties some of which lay in my way. About this Time I was attacked with a bilious Disorder attended with a cold, which had like to have carried me off. I got the better of it, thank God, but, tho' recovering, I am still but puny.

I lately had an account from Captain Conway, that the dearest and best of my Friends, your dear Brother, is with the Battalion at Minorca. Humiliating as it may appear, I am not ashamed to own my feelings on this occasion, But trust that an all-gracious Providence will restore him safe and victorious to his friends.

He desired I should consult with you about making out his Pedigree and getting it signed by some of the Nobility, and also that I should endeavour to procure old Deeds which might prove the Antiquity of our Family. I well know how useful such Materials as these could be, and that the Want of them has been heretofore a great Disappointment to him.

I heard since I came home that a Mr. O'Callaghan, of Shanbally, in the County of Tipperary [Lord Lismore's ancestor], a grandson of old Counsellor O'Callaghan, had my Grand Father's Papers, and when I began to mend, I went to enquire for them. If I had not been a fool, all I could do was to apply to one of the O'Callaghans of Kilgory to write to O'Callaghan of Shanbally, his intimate Acquaintance. He excused himself by telling me he would go to that County last October and do my Business, but he is not yet gone, nor in truth do I expect much from him. As it is uncertain when I may be so happy as to have the much wished for Pleasure of seeing you, I entreat you will let me know how you think these Papers may be had, and also the Proper steps to be taken to make out the Pedigree.

Permit me to wish you and Family of Darrinane many happy years. No one more ardently longs to assure you in Person how sincerely I have the Honour to be, with the greatest esteem, Dear Sir,
    Your Affectionate Kinsman,
    and most obedient Humble Servant,
          RICKD. CONNELL.

Please write me at Fenloe, near to Six Mile Bridge, County of Clare.

Rickard is at home at last. It seems strange to me to read his congratulations on Dr. Maurice Leyne's early professional successes, when I remember that my own husband was actually attended by that physician for whooping-cough when he was a small child. The letter is an old-world medical chronicle. Rickard survived a bewildering multiplicity of treatments. Dr. Spellicy went at him for bile with powders of bark, rhubarb, and some kind of salt. Old Dr. Finucane further suggested a pitch plaister in April. Then Dr. O'Loughlin and Doctor Comyn started each a perfectly opposite theory. The patient attributes his marked improvement to goat's whey. Though so reduced during his winter illness, which seems to have been pneumonia, as to "totter in his march like a man of eighty, and unable to walk half a mile or leap a potato-trench, were he to have been made a general for it," he is now getting a little flesh on his bones, and beginning to look like his former self. After sundry remarks, Rickard says (Ennis, June 2, 1782)—

"Heigh-ho! well, to be sure, flirting is the mother of mischief. I must and will leave it off, that's certain, but not this summer; for I promised to take Flavia to the salt water next week."

He expresses a great wish to visit Darrynane, but fears he may be murdered if he passes into Kerry after his old scrape there. He quotes a message from Chevalier O'Mahony, in which an expression occurs of frequent use both in English and French. Count O'Connell also speaks of his "college."[1] Was it a slang word for winter quarters? However, no man was less given to slang than Count O'Connell, and until the Emigration, when he re-learned English, he wrote it just like a foreigner. And whoever talked slang in a language in which he was not perfectly and fluently at his ease? Rickard says—

"I have *congé* until the 1st of December, and make no doubt of obtaining a prolongation of it till the 1st of May, if I think proper to ask for it; for Chevalier O'Mahony, in his last letter to me, writes, 'Vous pouvez vous donner tout le temps nécéssaire pour votre parfaite guérison. Le Comte de Serrant a trouvé le moyen à ce que vous puissez être absent du collège sans rien perdre. Ainsi restez ou vous êtes jusqu'e ce que vous reveniez bien portant;' and my worthy friend Captain O'Connor, who manages the affairs of the regiment, in his letter of the 24th of April, writes to the same effect.

"I am elated with the joy of perfect friendship at hearing that you have as much business as you can do. Indeed, it is what I always expected. Your success and prosperity, and that of your dear family, will always swell my heart with joy. . . . Yes! my Dear Maurice, I am informed of the brilliant success of the best of friends and the most amiable of men. I believe he is about this time at Gibraltar, from whence I fondly hope Providence will graciously restore him safe to the wishes of all who have the happiness of knowing him. There can be no doubt of his speedy promotion."

Now, all Count O'Connell's biographers say he signalized himself in Minorca, whence he went to Gibraltar; but I have quite failed to find any precise account of what he did. Fort Phillip seems to have been carried by a three hours' assault, in which, of course, he bore his share, but what distinguished thing he actually did seems rather hard to trace out now.

With much toil and trouble, I have picked out Count O'Connell's adventures at the famous siege of Gibraltar, and for the convenience of the reader I affix a separate heading.

[1] Littré gives as one meaning of "collége," "un corps de personnes revêtues de la même dignité." In illustration he cites "le collége des sécretaires du roi," and explains the first words as "la compagnie."

Hence the reference is to "le collége"—probably represented by "the officers' corps."—[Sigerson.]

Count O'Connell at the Siege of Gibraltar.

All my hero's biographers are agreed that he achieved special distinction on the memorable occasion of the siege of Gibraltar, served on board the floating batteries, and had the narrowest possible escape of his life, through the bursting of a shell quite near where he stood; but the real details of his adventures crop up in two letters written by his friend and old brother-in-arms, Count Bartholomew O'Mahony, and in the pages of the Duc des Cars' "Mémoires" published last year (1890). These differ in several points from the statements written long after the events in five biographical notices, viz. in "La Biographie Universelle;" in "La Biographie Générale;" in the *New Monthly Magazine* for 1833; in Grant's "Cavaliers of Fortune;" and in O'Callaghan's "Irish Brigade." Cheap editions of these two latter works are easily procurable. The account of the siege in the "Annual Register" is believed to be the work of Edmund Burke. I have condensed a considerable portion of his narrative. It tallies wonderfully with the Duc des Cars' account. I shall also make use of a contemporary Kerry newspaper, placed at my disposal by Sir Maurice O'Connell, which gives a singularly accurate account of my hero. At the siege of Gibraltar Lieut.-Colonel O'Connell made the acquaintance of a kind and valuable friend, in whose recently published letters he is most honourably mentioned. It was the Comte de Vaudreuil—"le Beau Vaudreuil" of courtly circles—a fascinating dandy, a singer, amateur actor, verse-maker, picture-collector, and fine gentleman, in the butterfly days of Versailles. He was attached to the suite of his bosom friend, the wild young Comte d'Artois, to whom he remained devotedly attached through long dark days of poverty and exile. Vaudreuil cherished a sentimental attachment to his charming cousin, the Duchesse de Polignac, Marie Antoinette's devoted friend. Even before the arrival of the famous pedigree, which enabled my hero to be presented at court and to ride in the king's coaches, he was taken up by the Polignacs, most probably through Vaudreuil. He already knew fine people at court, some of them doubtless through his friend, Chevalier O'Mahony.

Vaudreuil formed an unusually high opinion of his capacity. "O'Connell," he writes to the Comte d'Artois, in the dark days of 1790, "est encore un de ces hommes propres aux grandes enterprises." The siege of Gibraltar was the only occasion on which they served together. Vaudreuil had accompanied the Comte d'Artois, and followed him to the trenches.

As Minorca surrendered in February, and the Duc de Crillon-Mahon did not appear before Gibraltar till June, I am inclined to allocate a long sojourn my hero made in Cadiz to that period, though he was there for a while immediately after the siege. In a letter of March, 1784, defending an Irish merchant, Mr. Houlahan, from the suspicions of misapplying the funds a mutual friend had left in his hands, he mentions the opportunity he had of forming an opinion of his honourable character during his sojourn in Cadiz.

Drinkwater tells us how, on June 18, 1782, the dwellers on the beleagured Rock saw in the afternoon sixty sail, bearing the French reinforcements under the Duc de Crillon-Mahon.

"The following evening several Spanish and French general officers visited the lines, where they remained, excepting one general, who, accompanied by an artillery officer and an engineer, came forward and stood some time in the front of St. Martin's Battery. At this time, a group of those who remained in the lines were assembled on the glacis. Our artillery thought proper to give them a shot, which the general in the advanced works probably took as a hint to retire, for he immediately pulled off his hat and returned to the battery.

"On the 20th and 21st the French troops disembarked, and encamped to the east of the stone quarry, immediately under the Queen of Spain's Chair."

The following is the list of French officers given by Drinkwater from an official return (abridged from Appendix to Drinkwater's "Siege of Gibraltar"). The original is in French, and headed, "État Général de l'Armée Espagnole et Françoise employée au Siége de Gibraltar, sous les ordres de son Ex. le Duc de Crillon, État-Major de l'Armée Espagnole ; Général-en-chef, le Captaine-Général Duc de Crillon."

In modern parlance "État-Major" is rendered "staff." Count O'Connell always call it "state"-major. I find it to consist of lieut.-generals, maréchaux de camp (major-generals), and brigadiers. Save and except the illustrious Irish name of Count Lacy (spelt Lascy), "Le Comte Lascy, Commandant Général de l'Artillérie," the Spanish staff does not concern us Irish folk. They are fifty-one in all, without counting the Duc de Crillon. The "État-Major des Troupes Françoises" is much less numerous, so far as generals and colonels are concerned, but seems a real working staff. None of the Irish regiments took part in it, though three Irishmen appear.

The Duc de Crillon-Mahon is given as commander-in-chief of the whole united army.

French Staff.

Baron Falkenstein, Commander-in-Chief.
Marquis de Bouzolz, second in command.

Staff.

Marquis de Crillon, Brigadier.
de Portal, Major-General.
Baron F. le Fort, Baron C. le Fort, Adjutant-Generals.
Aides-de-Camp to Baron Falkenstein: Count de Nesle de la Fourette, Chevalier de Grave, Chevalier de Vault, Chevalier de Poncet, Count d'Argoult, Count de Périgord, Count de Lost, Marquis de Laillebit.
Marquis de Bouzolz's Aides-de-Camp: Marquis de Travance, Chevalier d'Oraison, Marquis de Montaigu.

French Brigade.

Lyons Regiment.

Vicomte de Veneur, Maître de Camp Colonel.
Marquis de Guerchy, Second Colonel.
Dubourg, Lieut.-Colonel.
de Cappy, Major.

Regiment of Brittany.

Count de Crillon, Maître de Camp Colonel.
Vidâme de Nassé, Second Colonel.
Chevalier de St. Roman, Lieut.-Colonel.
de Portal, Major.

Artillery.

Lieut.-Colonel Commandant, de Goenand.
Aide-Major (Adjutant), Captain de Barras.
Captains: d'Artan, Gromar de Quinlen.
First Lieutenants: d'Hemery, Cadman.
Second Lieutenants: Chevalier d'Alphonse, de Marten
Third Lieutenants: Fich, Fournier.
130 men.
Captain and Brevet-Colonel Marquis de Puiségur.

GERMAN BRIGADE.
Royal Swedish Regiment.
Count E. de Sparre, Maitre de Camp Colonel.
Baron d'Hamilton, Maitre de Camp, Second Colonel.
D. O'Connell, Lieut.-Colonel.
d'Osner, Major.

Bouillon Regiment.
Baron de Wimpfenn, Maitre de Camp, Colonel.
Baron de Nivenhaim, Second Colonel.
de Peyrier, Lieut.-Colonel.
O'Ghier, Major.

Engineers.
Colonel d'Arçon.
Major Doria.
Captains: de l'Hillier, de Bouleman, d'Assigny, de Sanis.
Lieutenants: Damorsean, d'Aumont.

ADMINISTRATION.
Officers in charge of French Works.
Second Captains: de Wildemonth, de Meumir.

Intendant de Boussière.
Commissaries: de Boileau, du Demaine.

Commissariat.
Inspector Mommergue.
Director Demange.

Postal Department.
Director Brochel.
Sub-Director Channel.

Hospital Department.
Thion, First Physician.
Bodner, First Surgeon.
Massol, Second Surgeon.

Regiments.	Officers.	Men.
Lyons (French Brigade)	65	1,024
Brittany, ditto...	65	1,016
Royal Swedes (German Brigade)	65	1,000
de Bouillon, ditto	52	1,025
Total French troops	247	4,055
Spanish ditto	1,667	27,067
In all	1,916	31,122
Men and officers		33,038

On August 15 the French king's brother, the Comte d'Artois, came for the great attack, and was followed next day by the Duc de Bourbon. The future godly Charles X., then an exceedingly wild, scampish, but plucky and good-natured young scrapegrace, brought on Governor Eliott's private letters (detained at Madrid), and sent them to him, with a present of game, fruit, and ice, through the Duc de Crillon-Mahon.[1] The chivalrous Englishman, though accepting the compliment, requested it would not be repeated, as he shared and wished to share every privation of his soldiery. As well as the great preparations for the sea attack, the French made great earthworks for a land attack, which were personally visited by the Comte d'Artois. On the 16th, after his inspection, they raised in the night, says Drinkwater, "a very strong and lofty epaulement, in extent about 500 yards, connecting the parallel to eastern beach, with a communication near 1300 yards long, extending from the principal barrier of the lines to east end of new epaulement." The new work of casks of sand and fascines was ten to twelve feet high, and of proportionate thickness. Ten thousand men did it in one night. On the 17th they "erected three epaulements with retiring flanks of sand-bags for mortar batteries." But the great novelty of the siege was the Chevalier d'Arçon's invention of floating batteries, of which I shall give the exceedingly graphic account furnished by the "Annual Register."

I have to pick out my hero's personal adventures among

---

[1] Louis de Berton des Balbes de Crillon, Duc de Crillon-Mahon, did not represent "an ancient noble family." The Bertons were among the forty-eight "familles illustrées par les armes ou dans les conseils du prince qui jouissent des honneurs du Louvre sans avoir fourni les preuves de 1399." This is very sufficient proof that they were not an "ancient noble family," and is an ample refutation of their claim to descend from the illustrious house of De Balbes de Chieri.

The Marquise de Crequy ("Souvenirs," vol. iii. p. 15) says apologetically, "Il est vrai que nous avons parmi nos ducs MM. de Crillon et De Coigny; mais, au moins, les auteurs de ces deux familles étaient de vaillans guerriers et d'illustres capitaines."

Louis Berton, the first traceable ancestor (a hero must be of very mysterious parentage if he cannot produce a grandfather), bought in 1456, according to Mons. Bouillet, the seigneurie of Crillon from the family of Astonaud. He is supposed to have been a shopkeeper of Charpentras. His son took the name of Crillon, and was granted lettres d'enoblissement in 1510. His son Louis de Berton des Balbes de Crillon (born 1541) annexed the name of des Balbes, was a mighty man of war, and is known to history as "le brave Crillon." To him Henri IV. wrote from the battle-field of Arques, "Pends toi brave Crillon! nous avons combattu à Arques et tu n'y étais pas." The haute noblesse might sneer at the Crillons' claim to high descent; it would have been better for France if her highest-born sons had imitated the exuberant valour of MM. de Crillon, and left pedigree to Mons. Chérin and his subordinates of the Cabinet de l'Ordre du St. Esprit.—[R. O'C.]

the mighty issues and momentous questions and brilliant deeds of the great. He was an eminently scientific soldier, who from his boyhood had studied his trade; as a lieut.-colonel he was on the état-major, or staff, and entitled to a voice in the council. His opinion had the additional weight attaching to an acknowledged student of military science. From this his biographers have set out to make him an artillery or engineer expert; but the evidence of official documents and his own letters amply shows his exact grade —an infantry lieut.-colonel. I do not deny that long and sustained study and application gave an additional weight to his opinions. This explanation was made clear to me by Daniel O'Connell, of Darrynane, who has made a most careful study of the siege, and who kindly lent me his copiously annotated Drinkwater.

Lieut.-Colonel O'Connell "served with the combined French and Spanish armament which blockaded Gibraltar during that memorable siege," says Grant, "which had commenced on January 12 the preceding year." He forgets to mention that the French only joined towards the end of June, 1782. "Having shown considerable skill as an engineer at Minorca [this error has been previously pointed out] he was one of the council of war appointed to assist the Chevalier d'Arçon in conducting the grand attempt in which France and Spain had resolved to try their full strength for the capture of that celebrated rock, the key of the Mediterranean; and for his purpose, as already stated in the 'Memoir of the Lacys,' 40,000 soldiers, with 200 pieces of cannon and 80 mortars, pressed the attack by land, while 47 sail of the line, 10 battering-ships, and a multitude of frigates mounting 1000 guns, and having 12,000 chosen soldiers added to their crews, lay before the fortress by sea; and in that fortress, to meet all this warlike preparation, were only 7000 British soldiers.

"The French Army was commanded by Louis Duc de Crillon-Mahon,[1] the representative of an ancient noble family in the Vaucluse, who had commenced his military career in the Grey Musketeers, and served under Marshal Villars in

---

[1] See note, previous page.

Italy. He had direction of the whole attack; his engineers were the most expert in Europe, and brave volunteers came from all quarters to take part in a siege which attracted the attention and roused the expectation of continental Europe.

"As a member of the council of war, O'Connell repeatedly opposed the plans of the Duc de Crillon and the Chevalier d'Arçon, and declared their system of attack 'worthless;' and in the sequel the triumph of General Eliott proved that his observations were correct."

In the next sentence Grant commits an extraordinary mistake: "In the grand attack he accepted command of one of the floating batteries."

Now, the Lieut.-Colonel of the Royal Swedes was by no means important enough for such a command, and by the enclosed official list, copied from Drinkwater, it will be seen that the Prince of Nassau was the only person not a Spaniard who commanded one of them. By my hero's letter of October, 1787, now published for the first time, it is conclusively proved that he served under the prince, consequently in the *Tailla Piedra*, the second ship on the list.

Names of the battering-ships.	Guns in use.	Guns in reserve.	Men.	Commander.
Two-deckers—				
Pastora	21	10	760	Rear-Admiral Bonaventura Moreno.
Tailla Piedra	21	10	760	Prince of Nassau-Siegen.
Paula Prima...	21	10	760	Don Gayetano Longara.
El Rosario ...	19	10	700	Don Fras. Xav. Munos.
St. Christoval	18	10	650	Don Frederico Gravino.
One-deckers—				
Principe Carlos	11	4	400	Don Antonio Basurta.
San Juan ...	9	4	340	Don José Angeler.
Paula Secunda	9	4	340	Don Pablo de Cosa.
Santa Anna ...	7	4	300	Don José Goicoechea.
Los Dolores ...	6	4	250	Don Pedro Sanchez.
	142	70	5,260 men.	

N.B.—About thirty-six men to each gun in use, besides sailors, etc., to work the ships.

Note states that Chev. d'Arçon remained on the *Tailla Piedra* until half an hour after midnight.

The Liberator makes the same mistake, and says, as quoted by O'Callaghan—

"Every one remembers the attack made by the floating

batteries on Gibraltar, and the triumphant resistance of the English garrison under General Eliott. Lieut.-Colonel O'Connell was one of the three engineers to whose judgment the plan of attack was submitted a few days before it was carried into effect. He gave it as his decided opinion that the plan would not be successful. The other two engineers were of a contrary opinion, and the event justified his judgment." Instead of "engineer" let us say "military expert," and then the story ceases to be improbable. Another mistake occurs a few lines later, in speaking of O'Connell and Count Fersen as the two Lieut.-Colonels of the Royal Swedish Regiment. Now, Drinkwater's Army List conclusively proves it had only one—agreeing with Count O'Connell's account of the officers of a French regiment in one of his letters already quoted. The Royal Swedes, however, did not lack colonels. Their colonel-proprietor was the King of Sweden; then they had Count de Sparre as colonel in command, and Colonel Hamilton as second colonel. This latter must have been transferred to make room for Count Fersen. The cheering soldiers would naturally shout for their colonel without prefix or addition, so the "Colonel en Second" might easily fancy the cheers for the lieut.-colonel were intended for himself. Let us suppose the soldiers simply shouted, "Long live our colonel!" instead of "our lieutenant-colonel!" and the whole story is quite feasible. I am sorry to say "le Beau Fersen,"[1] brave, chivalrous, and disinterested as he was, has spoken very nastily and spitefully of my hero, accusing him of getting himself promoted out of his turn, through the influence of the Polignacs, and of accepting the Revolution. In justice to Fersen, however, we must admit that Count O'Connell's serving so long in Paris was suspicious, and Fersen could not possibly know he did so by the king's express orders. He was removed from the Royal Swedes to the Salm-Salm Regiment, to make way for Count Fersen. I shall now resume the Liberator's story, correcting the grades in brackets.

"Upon a point of honour recognized in the French Army, he [Lieut.-Colonel O'Connell] claimed a right to share the perils of an attack which was resolved upon against his

[1] Vol. ii. of his "Letters and Journals."

opinion. When the attempt to storm Gibraltar was resolved on, it became necessary to procure a considerable number of marines to act on board the floating batteries. For this purpose the French infantry was drawn up, and being informed of the urgency of the occasion, a call was made for volunteers, among the rest, of course, from the Royal Swedes. Lieut.-Colonel O'Connell's regiment was paraded, and the men having been informed *he* was to be employed on the service, the whole battalion stepped forward to one man, declaring their intention to follow their lieut.-colonel. It so happened that the senior lieut.-colonel [really the Colonel en Second], the Count de Fersen, then well known as 'le Beau Fersen,' and towards whom it was more than suspected that Marie Antoinette[1] entertained feelings of peculiar preference, had

---

[1] I regret to find a person of the Liberator's intelligence deliberately repeating a monstrous calumny, for which there was no shadow of foundation.

Such stories generally owe their existence and their longevity to the type of woman so admirably described by Shelley—

> " . . . mincing women mewing
> Of their own virtue, and pursuing
> Their gentler sisters to that ruin
> Without which—what were chastity ? "

Count Fersen was a brave and true man, a devoted servant of the royal family. He risked his life for them when "glass-coachman of a thousand," he drove them the first stage of the fateful flight to Varennes; he risked it again and again when he returned to Paris in February, 1792.

Many of the queen's letters to him have been published in "Les Papiers du Grand Marechal de Suede Comte Jean Axel de Fersen."

These "wild years of the change of things," were pre-eminently a period of slander; *la sainte canaille* dragged God and the Bourbons, all things high and holy, through the mire; the mob dethroned and strove vainly to defile the Lord and the anointed of the Lord. Fersen, in this shared, and was glad to share the fate of the king and queen he served. A brief study of any authentic contemporary memoirs would have saved the Liberator from repeating a base lie. O'Connell may have derived his ideas from the "Souvenirs et Portraits" of the Duc de Levis, a work that would be reliable enough were it not for the duke's passion for sneering at anything he failed to understand. The noble devotion displayed by Fersen was entirely beyond this good gentleman's comprehension. He says, "Il était inconvenant sous plus d'un rapport que M. de Fersen occupât dans cette occasion perilleuse un poste qui devait appartenir à un Grand Seigneur Français." One is tempted to ask what that grand Seigneur Gaston de Levis-Ventadour did towards saving the life of the king who had created him Duc de Levis? He had no share in the flight. The names of Grand Seigneurs are few in the list of those impeached as accomplices to the king's flight, by M. Mugnet de Nanthon. They are MM. de Bouillé père et fils, Duc de Choiseul, Talon, De Fersen, De Maldan, Manaisen, De Raigecourt, De Mandel, and about a

arrived from Paris but a short time before to join the regiment which, since his appointment, he had scarcely seen. Attributing the enthusiasm of the men to his appearance, he rode up, and assured them he would be proud to lead them. A murmur of disappointment passed along the line, and at length some of the old soldiers ventured to declare that it was not with him they volunteered to go, but with the *other* lieut.-colonel who had always commanded and protected them. With a generosity which does him honour, Fersen immediately declared that he would not attempt to deprive Colonel O'Connell of the honour he so well deserved, but that he hoped, when the regiment knew *so* much of *him*, they would be equally ready to follow him. Colonel O'Connell was named second in command of one of the floating batteries, and this battery was one of the first to come into action."

We have his own word that he served on the prince's [1] battery. I find the following very interesting account of the floating batteries in the "Annual Register." I am sure the reader will thank my diligence for transcribing it.

The "Annual Register" states that the court of Madrid proposed the sacrifice of from ten to twenty great ships of war in the attempt to seize Gibraltar by a combined attack by land and sea. The French engineer, Chevalier d'Arçon, opposed the idea, and suggested the floating batteries, which, however excellent in theory, proved a failure in practice. This, how-

---

dozen others, most of whom were officers commanding the detachments of cavalry posted in the neighbourhood of Varennes. Many of them were utterly ignorant of the king's flight until after his arrest ("Memoires du Frère de Lait,' vol. ii. pp. 416, etc.).—[R. O'C.]

[1] Charles Henry Nicholas Otho, *soi-disant* Prince of Nassau-Siegen, was the son of Maximilian, *soi-disant* Prince of Nassau-Siegen, whose mother, Charlotte de Mailly, gave birth to him three years after she had been separated from her husband, Emmanuel Ignatius, Prince of Nassau-Siegen.

The Aulic Council of 1746 refused to entertain Maximilian's claim to the principality of Nassau-Siegen; but his title was recognized by the Parliament of Paris in 1756; his son Charles was born in 1745, and died at Paris in 1805, having served France as colonel, Spain as general, and Russia as admiral. He received from Spain three millions of francs and the grandeza as reward for his services at the siege of Gibraltar. The title of Nassau-Siegen became extinct on the death of Prince Frederick William in 1734. He left two sisters, co-heiresses, Princess Charlotte, wife of Graf Albrecht von der Lippe-Buckeburg, and Princess Elizabeth, wife of Count Frederick zu Sayn-Witgenstein.—[R. O'C.]

ever, could not be known until the experiment had been tried. "His plan," says the careful chronicler of the "Register," "was the construction of floating batteries as ships upon such a principle that they could neither be sunk nor fired. [However, they were fired.] The first of these properties was to be acquired by an extraordinary thickness of timber with which their keels and bottoms were to be fortified, and which was to render them proof to all danger in that respect, whether from external or internal violence. The second danger was to be overcome by securing the sides of the ships, wherever they were exposed to shot, with a strong wall, composed of timber and cork a long time soaked in water, and including between them a large body of wet sand; the whole being of a thickness and density that no cannon-ball could penetrate within two feet of the inner partition. A constant supply of water was to keep the parts exposed to the action of fire always wet, and the cork was to act as a sponge for retaining the moisture.

"For this purpose ten great ships from 600 to 1400 tons burthen (some of them said to be of fifty or sixty guns) were cut down to the state required by the plan, and 200,000 cubic feet of timber was with infinite labour worked into their construction. To protect them from bombs, and the men at the batteries from grape or descending shot, a hanging roof was contrived, which was to be worked up and down by springs with ease and at pleasure. The roof was composed of a strong rope-work netting, laid over with a thick covering of wet hides, while its sloping position was calculated to prevent the shells from lodging, and to throw them into the sea before they could take effect. The batteries were covered with new brass cannon of great weight, and something about half the number of spare guns of the same kind were kept ready in each ship, immediately to supply the place of those which might be overheated or otherwise disabled in action. To render the fire of these batteries the more rapid and instantaneous, and consequently the more dreadfully effective, the ingenious projector had contrived a kind of match to be placed on the lights of the guns, of such a nature as to emulate lightning in the quickness of its consumption and the rapidity of its action, and by which all the guns on the battery were to go off together, as if it had been only a single shot.

"But as the red-hot shot from the fortress was the enemy most to be dreaded, the nicest part of this plan seems to have been the contrivance for communicating water in every direction to restrain its effect. In imitation of the circulation of the blood in a living body, a great variety of pipes and canals perforated all the solid workmanship, in such a manner that a continued succession of water was conveyed to every part of the vessels, a number of pumps being adapted to the purpose of an unlimited supply. By this means it was expected that the red-hot shot would operate to the remedy of its own mischief, as the very action of cutting through these pipes would procure its immediate extinction. So that these terrible machines, teeming with every instrument of outward destruction, seemed to be themselves invulnerable and entirely secure from all danger.

"The preparation in other respects was beyond all example. It was said that no less than twelve hundred pieces of heavy ordnance of various kinds had been accumulated before the place, for the almost numberless intended purposes of the attack by sea and land. The quantity of powder only was said to exceed eighty-three thousand barrels. Forty gun-boats with heavy artillery, as many bomb-vessels with twelve-inch mortars, besides a large floating battery and five bomb-ketches on the usual construction, were all destined to second the powerful efforts of the great battering-ships. Nearly all the frigates and smaller armed vessels of the kingdom were assembled to afford such aid as they might be found capable of, and two hundred large boats were collected from every part of Spain, which, with the very great number already in the vicinity, were to minister to the fighting-vessels during the action, and to land troops in the place as soon as they had dismantled the fortress. The combined fleets of France and Spain, amounting to something about fifty ships of the line, were to cover and support the attack, and could not but greatly heighten the terrors as well as the magnificence of the scene."

Resuming the thread of Edmund Burke's narrative in the "Annual Register," we come to the following passage :—

"The preparations by land kept pace with those by sea. Twelve thousand French troops were brought to diffuse their peculiar vivacity and animation through the Spanish Army, as well as for the benefit to be derived from the example and exertion of their superior discipline and experience. The Duc de Crillon was assisted by a number of the best officers of both countries, and particularly of the best engineers and artillerists of his own."

I have peculiar pleasure in transcribing the contemporary account of my hero's adventures on board the floating battery, *Tailla Piedra*—

"Here it was [at Gibraltar] that a far wider field presented itself to Mr. O'Connell for the display of his bravery and skill; nor was the opportunity lost upon him. In every attack he bore a part either with the regiment or as a volunteer, and such respect was paid to his judgment that he was consulted by the commanders on every movement of importance. Though he disapproved of the last grand effort, notwithstanding all the tremendous preparations so happily disconcerted, yet that no occasion of acquiring glory might slip him, he volunteered with eagerness, and in opposition to the wishes of his friends, for liberty of serving in the gun-boats. No doubt there were others as gallant in the same service. The Prince of Nassau may be called Valour itself; possibly there is not existing a man who has stood the brunt of danger so often. Yet would all his courage have been of no avail *that day of wrath* were he not accompanied by Mr. O'Connell; for to his exertions he certainly owed his preservation. *Dreadful as the pelting of that pitiless storm* [allusion to red-hot shot] must have been, when the veteran, whose glorious deeds are some compensation for the many shocks the national honour has sustained during a ruinous war, was like the god of thunder hurling destruction upon his enemies, it is to Mr. O'Connell's peculiar praise that he continued as composed as if he had been only sending them hot rolls for breakfast.

"In the midst of carnage and confusion, when his companions had abandoned themselves to despair, he conducted everything with coolness, and gave his orders so deliberately that he brought sure on shore the prince's own boat on which he served. Not content with this, he gathered assistance from all quarters for the unfortunates whom he left behind, and it is acknowledged on all sides that it was by his activity that the greater part of those who escaped were saved. This generosity, however, had nearly cost him his life, for a party of Spanish sailors, averse as it might well be supposed they were to hazard themselves in such a scene, attempted to throw him overboard. Having providentially frustrated their nefarious designs, he received at last a wound on the head, which was thought for some time to have been mortal."

The Duc des Cars' "Mémoires" have just come out, and enable me to add some important details of the siege of Gibraltar. He gives one anecdote of my colonel. The Chevalier d'Arçon's great conception of the floating batteries, so graphically described by the pen of Edmund Burke, in the "Annual Register," was imperfectly carried out, owing to the carelessness of the commander-in-chief and the boyish impatience of the royal prince.

M. des Cars, then a cadet of his house, accompanied the Comte d'Artois to the siege of Gibraltar as captain of his guard. He says ("Mémoires du Duc des Cars," vol. i. p. 286)—

"We had the greatest curiosity to visit the famous floating batteries, on which the two courts had fixed their hopes for the success of the siege and the capture of the place. Messieurs de Crillon, de Nassau, and d'Arçon brought M. le Comte d'Artois to visit them in Algesiras Bay.

"We must bear in mind that everything to be used in this siege had been fixed upon, ordered, and arranged exactly a year before. But instead of finding the batteries finished, according to the engineer's plans, they were far from ready, though, the attack being fixed on for the following month, their co-operation was indispensable before the English could be able to revictual the place. Monsieur d'Arçon had the weakness to consent to do without some essential portions, for instance, some of the precautions against red-hot balls, so that, though the work proceeded with redoubled activity, the pivot on which the whole plan hinged, namely, the projected free circulation of water which he had planned, almost entirely failed, either through undue precipitation or shortness of time."

Le Chevalier des Cars, as he was then, had served in the navy, and describes with a sailor's appreciation the stately spectacle of fifty ships of the line and numerous frigates riding at anchor. These were the combined fleets of France and Spain.

In pp. 301 to 315 of his first volume he gives many interesting details of the siege. He mentions that, three months before the attack, the Chevalier d'Arçon had drawn up an exact plan of where the fire by land and sea was to open. He had marked exactly where the ten floating batteries were to be moored, so that their fire should complete the circle of fire which was to be opened from the land batteries. Will it be credited that the Duc de Crillon-Mabon lost the document; that the Chevalier d'Arçon had no copy; and that at the last moment he had to go out in a row-boat to sound for their anchorages? It was only the night before that the Duc de Crillon confessed he had mislaid the paper. The noise of M. d'Arçon's oars attracted the enemy's notice, and he had to desist.

On the morning of September 13 the ten floating batteries appeared before the eyes of Europe, propelled by a favouring breeze, but, owing to the loss of the plan, they did not get into the proper place. Instead of riding in a suitable depth of water at the precise point where land and sea fires would converge on Gibraltar, while being in partial shelter themselves all the time, they drifted in a disorderly manner to the central space between the two moles, where they were quite unprotected, and drew the whole central fire of the place.

Instead of the ten floating batteries, only three got near the beleaguered city—Moreno's, Nassau's (on which my hero was serving), and Gravino's. They were drawn up by nine o'clock in the morning. The other seven anchored outside, "Moiullèrent au large," says Des Cars, exposed in full to the English fire. He also observes that there was neither first nor second line regularly formed according to plan. No gun-boats followed or accompanied the "Empailletaos," as the Spaniards called them. "Such," he observes, " was the disorderly fashion in which the sea attack was conducted."

To revert to our colonel. The period of time during which he was thought dead must have been indeed brief, as he was the envoy sent on shore with a verbal message, and to bear back a reply on which the lives of all on board the burning ships depended. I infer that the explosion which scarred his face knocked him down and rendered him insensible, or at least partially stupefied for a few minutes, when the flow of blood from his forehead would have restored the keenness of faculties which never had greater need of coolest perception.

He himself wrote to his friend O'Mahony that he was slightly wounded by the bursting of a bomb. The Duc des Cars shall first describe, in the unconsciously graphic strain of an eye-witness, how O'Connell came to the Duc de Crillon, by whose side were the Comte d'Artois and his staff, and brought the evil tidings, and bore back the orders to evacuate the *Tailla Piedra*.

"The three floating batteries," says Des Cars (p. 306), " isolated and ill placed as they were, showed a stout front to the enemy even at three o'clock in the afternoon (having been engaged since nine), and their fire was well sustained. Crillon flattered himself he would augment it with that of the seven others, to which he was sending orders to draw near the three, when Monsieur O'Connell, slightly wounded in the forehead, arrived, sent to Monsieur de Crillon by Messieurs de Nassau and d'Arçon. They sent word to the commander-in-chief that flames had broken out on board; that they could not possibly quench them; that they were losing numbers of men; and that the best thing they could do would be to disembark the men serving the batteries, and to set fire to these, so that the English might not get the ' carcasses ' and the artillery.

" Crillon at once sent off another courier " (Des Cars has been scornfully telling of his passion for despatching too-hopeful reports to the Spanish Court)—" Crillon sent off word

'The three first batteries have suffered, but the seven others are untouched.' On receipt of their message, Monsieur de Crillon sent orders to Messieurs de Nassau and d'Arçon to come back to him, that they might concert together about taking new measures. They came back to him sure enough, but things had got far worse since O'Connell's departure."

The Duc des Cars here mentions how the Duc de Crillon's orders to the Spaniard Don Luis de Cordova, to take off the crews of the floating batteries under cover of the night, were disobeyed; how at break of day the three doomed hulks were blazing fires amid the waters; how the cries of the doomed crews reached the trenches; how two batteries blew up; and how the heroic humanity of Commodore Curtis saved the third crew just before the last one blew up.

Now, the above-mentioned anecdote of our hero seems to me of great importance. It shows the remarkable coolness of the man. A shell had burst at his feet and scarred his face, and a very short time after he is chosen to carry a message on which the lives of three crews depended. Surely no more perfect illustration of his coolness could be given. I fancy the mention of him in the Comte d'Artois's despatch must be about this message. The anecdote of his happy discovery of the designs of the Spanish sailors to throw him overboard must have occurred when he bore back the answer that the French commanders were to come on shore and confer with the commander-in-chief.

The "Annual Register" and the French "Mémoires" both say it was Captain Curtis who rescued the crews. Our colonel's boat most probably brought off the commander and some attendants, and the Prince of Nassau for his conference with the Duc de Crillon. I fancy the oft-repeated anecdote that our hero saved the life of the French prince must have arisen from his saving that of the German prince. The valiant Nassau would never have left the ship without the Duc de Crillon's orders, and these orders were given in response to O'Connell's message. Probably his knowledge of Spanish led to his selection for the task, as it certainly saved his life on his return trip.

This story is as follows, written down by Daniel O'Connell, of Darrynane:—

"After the floating batteries were set on fire at the siege of Gibraltar, Count O'Connell was endeavouring to rescue their crews with a boat manned by two Spaniards. The English were firing on the burning ships; their own guns were going off as they got heated, and, of course, there was the risk of explosion. The Spaniards, not liking the danger they must encounter by approaching the ships, agreed to throw Count O'Connell (then Colonel O'Connell) overboard and return to the shore. He understood what they said, took out his pistols, examined their priming, laid them on the seat by him, and, addressing the men in Spanish, told them he would shoot the first that attempted to stir except to row towards the floating batteries. The Spaniards submitted, and Count O'Connell saved several of his friends and others. Told me by my uncle, Morgan O'Connell."— [D. O'C.]

Count Bartholomew O'Mahony writes thus to Maurice O'Connell, of Darrynane, of his friend's escape. The letter and another are only signed "C. B. M.," but the cross of Malta, the count's coronet, and the arms conclusively prove the owner of the seal a Count O'Mahony, Knight of Malta. The admixture of snakes and lions is thus heraldically designated—

Quarterly, 1st and 4th, a lion ramp., countercharged; 2nd and 3rd, arg., a chevron gules between three snakes wavy in pale sable.

Cambray, 28th 8bre, 1782.

Your Brother, dear Sir, is in perfect health. I just now received a letter from him, date the 15th of this Month, and wrote after that business he was about was all over; so don't be in the least Uneasiness if you hear that he was wounded. He happily got but a very slight touch on the forehead, the skin of which was a little scarred by a case shot on the Bursting of a bomb. I expect that we will meet next month at Paris. Adieu, dear Sir. The departure of the Post obliges me to finish, as I would not put off to another day to quiet your anxieties, and acquaint you of a news that makes me the happiest man alive.

Thus former comrade and eye-witness exactly agree. I cannot conceive how the biographers make out that our colonel was mortally wounded, his death sympathetically mentioned in a despatch by the Comte d'Artois, and one of his ears blown right off, "une orielle d'emportée," say the French biographical dictionaries. His grand-niece, the Liberator's second daughter, who, marrying her cousin, ever remained Kate O'Connell, assured me she never saw the least thing wrong with the general's ears, and she was constantly with him all one winter. I fancy his name was mentioned in despatches in connection with the message he bore from the burning battery.[1]

I must now turn from my hero's personal adventures to the closing scenes of the great siege in which he has borne his part.

The "Annual Register" for August 8, 1782, gives a most graphic and ghastly picture of the sequel of that famous fight.

"The battering-ships were found upon trial to be an enemy scarcely less formidable than had been represented. Besides maintaining a cannonade so prodigious through the greater part of the day as scarcely admitted any appearance of superiority on the side of the fortress, their construction was so admirably calculated for the purpose of withstanding the combined powers of fire and artillery, that for several hours the incessant showers of shells and the hot shot with which they were assailed were not capable of making any visible impression upon them.

"About two o'clock, however, some smoke was seen to issue from the upper part of the admiral's ship, and soon after men were observed using fire-engines and pouring water into the shot-holes. This fire, though kept under during the continuance of daylight, could never be thoroughly subdued;

[1] In a note at the end of this chapter will be found interesting extracts from the journal of the person chiefly engaged in the destruction of the floating batteries. Alexander Ross, who commanded the English Ordnance at the siege of Gibraltar, was the great-grand-uncle of my fellow-worker, Ross O'Connell, whose other great-grand-uncle he nearly blew up on that occasion. Alexander Ross's niece, Miss Hannah Ross, married Admiral Sir Richard O'Connor, whose daughter Emily married Sir Maurice O'Connell, my hero's grand-nephew. I had first intended using the extracts as footnotes, but think they will be more interesting and more easily referred to when printed as a whole.

and in some time the ship commanded by the Prince of Nassau [on which my hero was serving], which was like in size and force to the admiral's, was perceived to be in the same condition.

"The disorder in these two commanding ships in the centre affected the whole line of attack, and by the evening the fire from the fortress had gained a decided superiority. The fire was continued from the batteries in the fortress with equal vigour through the night, and by one o'clock in the morning the two first ships were in flames and several more visibly on fire. The confusion was now great and apparent, and the number of rockets continually thrown up from each of the ships as signals to the fleets were sufficiently expressive of their extreme distress and danger.

"These signals were immediately answered, and all means used by the fleet to afford the assistance which they required; but as it seemed impossible to remove the battering-ships, their endeavours were only directed to bringing off the men. A great number of boats were accordingly employed, and great intrepidity displayed in the attempts for this purpose; the danger from the burning vessels, filled as they were with instruments of destruction, appearing no less dreadful than the fire from the garrison, terrible as that was, and that the light, thrown out on all sides by the flames, afforded the utmost precision in its direction.

"This state of things presented an opportunity for the exercise of the daring genius of Captain Curtis, in using the exertions of his gun-boats to complete the general confusion and destruction. These were twelve in number, and each carried an eighteen or twenty-four pounder; their low fire and fixed aim were not a little formidable. They were specially manned by the Marine Brigade, who were equally eager to second the designs of their adventurous commander, whether by land or by sea. He drew these up in such a manner as to flank the line of battering-ships, which were now equally overwhelmed by the incessant fire from the garrison and by that just at hand, raking the whole extent of their line from the gun-boats. The scene was wrought up by this fierce and unexpected attack to the highest point of calamity. The Spanish boats dared no longer to approach, and were compelled to the hard necessity of abandoning their ships and friends to the flames, as to the mercy and humanity of a heated and irritated enemy. Several of their boats and launches had been sunk before they submitted to this necessity; and one in particular, with four score men on board, were all drowned, excepting an officer and twelve men, who, having the fortune to float on the wreck under the walls, were taken up by the garrison.

"The daylight now appearing, two Spanish feluccas, which had not escaped with the others, attempted to get out of the danger, but a shot from a gun-boat having killed several men on board one of them, they were both glad to surrender.

"It seemed that nothing could have exceeded the horrors of the night; but the opening of daylight disclosed a spectacle still more dreadful. Numbers of men were seen in the midst of the flames, crying out for pity and help; others floating upon pieces of timber, exposed to an equal though less dreadful danger from the opposite element. Even those in the ships where the fire had yet made a less progress, expressed in their looks, gestures, and words the deepest distress and despair, and were no less urgent in imploring assistance.

"The generous humanity of the victors now, at least, equalled their extraordinary preceding exertions of valour, and was to them far more glorious. Nor were the exertions of humanity attended with less danger than those of active hostility. The honour and danger, however, all lay with the Marine Brigade and their intrepid commander.

"The firing from both the garrison and gun-boats instantly ceased upon the first appearance of the dismal spectacle presented by the morning light, and every danger was encountered to rescue the distressed enemy from surrounding destruction. In these efforts the boats were equally exposed to the peril arising from the blowing up of the ships as the fire reached their magazines, and to the continual discharge on all sides of the artillery, as the guns became to a certain degree heated. It was, indeed, a noble exertion; and a more striking instance of the ardour and boldness with which it was supported need not be given than that of an officer and twenty-nine private men, all severely and some dreadfully wounded, who were dragged out from amongst the slain in the holds of the burning ships, and most of whom recovered in the hospitals of Gibraltar."

As my hero was not among those saved by their generous enemy, I shall abridge the rest of the account of August 9. Captain Curtis was ever the first to board the burning ships, and to set the example of dragging the wounded through the flames. His pinnace was actually beside one of the largest ships when she blew up, and several of its crew were killed. General Eliott thought he had perished.

"Admiral Don Bonaventura Moreno left his flag flying," continues the "Annual Register," "when he abandoned his ship, in which state it continued until it was consumed or blown up with the vessel. Eight more of the ships blew up in the course of the day. The tenth was burned by the English when they found she could not be brought off."

The "Annual Register" calculates the Spanish and French loss at 1500. It quotes an affecting passage from the letter of a French officer, given in the foreign gazettes. It is dated the evening of August 8, 1782—

"The eye is fatigued and the heart rent with the sight and the groans of the dying and the wounded, whom the soldiers are this moment carrying away. The number makes a man shudder; and I am told that in other parts of the lines, which are not within view of my post, the numbers are still greater. Fortunately for my feelings, I have not, at this instant, leisure to reflect much on the state and condition of mankind."

Hostilities on a small scale were kept up until February 6, 1783, when the Duc de Crillon-Mahon announced to Governor Eliott that peace had been concluded among their royal masters, and that the blockade was to cease. Old Drinkwater gives a charming account of the interchange of civilities and banquets.

The generals had a solemn interview on the 12th, on the beach, where they dismounted and embraced. On the 18th the duke presented Eliott with a grey Andalusian horse, and on the 22nd personally led Generals Eliott and Greene through the Spanish works, and entertained them at dinner. On the 31st the duke and several Spanish nobles returned the visit, and were hospitably entertained. "When the duke appeared within the walls," says Drinkwater, "the soldiers saluted him with a general huzza, which, being unexpected by his grace, it is said greatly confused him. The reason, however, being explained, he seemed highly pleased with the old English custom, and, as he passed up the main street, where the ruinous and desolate appearance of the town attracted a good deal of his observation, his grace behaved with great affability."

A family tradition has always asserted that, on some occasion during the siege, my hero saved the life of the Comte d'Artois, but it is not mentioned in any of the biographical sketches I have seen. However, I came across a confirmation of it from an independent source in the "Critical Essays of an Octogenarian." The writer, Mr. James Roche, once an eminent banker, was a member of an ancient County Cork family, and a person of great erudition. I knew his daughters in after-years. He spent a great deal of time in France, and at one period collected some materials for a work on the Irish Brigade, but he never made use of them.

Mr. Roche was not in any way related to or connected with the O'Connells. At p. 40 of his Essays, which are rather a series of reminiscences interspersed with history and criticism, he says, "It is well known that a marshal's staff was destined for Count O'Connell by Charles X., whose life he had saved in 1782 at the siege of Gibraltar, and only stopped execution by that sovereign's dethronement. No one could be worthier of that or any other honour."

Mr. Roche was personally acquainted with the old gentleman and sundry other veterans of the Brigade in Paris.

[The Comte d'Artois was, one day during the siege in 1782, inspecting the lines at St. Roch. H.R.H. was accompanied by the Duc de Crillon and a numerous staff, including Count O'Connell. A bomb fell beside the brilliant party; they all threw themselves on the ground to avoid the effects of the explosion, when a Frenchwoman, who kept a canteen close by, rushed forth with two children in her arms, and, seating herself on the bombshell, extinguished the fuse, by her extraordinary courage saving many lives. H.R.H. granted the woman a pension of three francs a day, and the duc allowed her a pension of five.—R. O'C.]

There is not a discoverable scrap of my hero's writing now extant during this most momentous period of his career, but a friend takes up the tale. He signs " C. B. M." The seal is badly broken, and the armorial bearings were rubbed off in pasting it into the letter-book. Only the points of the cross of Malta appear. It was customary to put the family coat of arms in the centre, and let the cross appear outside. Now, Chevalier Fagan's name was Christopher, and it was customary to sign all formal letters with a title, so the first " C." stands for "count" or " chevalier." The writing is not Chevalier Fagan's; whose writing it is, I could not at first say, but the cross and initials all pointed conclusively to Chevalier Bartholomew O'Mahony. Since I wrote the above, Mr. Leyne, of the Registry of Deeds Office, lent me the letter quoted before, in which the perfect armorial seal proves the writer to be this gallant soldier and devoted friend. The letter, in the letter-book, corrects another mistake of all Count O'Connell's biographers. It states that he was made colonel in command of the Royal Swedes. This would also account for Count Fersen's evident jealousy. The Irish soldier of fortune was promoted by leaps and bounds, right over the head of the King of Sweden's own special friend. Later he had to make way for Fersen, by the orders of the Swedish king. O'Connell's services must have been very distinguished, when he was made full colonel, passing over the grade of second colonel and a person of such consequence as the Swedish Fersen.

Of course, there is the usual hint about the pedigree in the end of this letter. How Hunting Cap must have hated the very sound of the word " pedigree "! Yet it was a most essential and integral point. I am quite incompetent to do the court chapter single-handed, when the arrival of the pedigree finally permitted my hero to make his bow to King Louis ; but my able coadjutor, Ross O'Connell, of Lake View, will do much of it for me. I must not any longer keep the chivalrous friend waiting to describe a comrade's luck.

To Maurice O'Connell, of Darrynane, from C. B. M.

Paris, 14th 9bre, 1782.

It's, Dear Sir, with the most feeling satisfaction that I inform you of your Brother's being promoted to the place of Colonel Commandant of the Swedes Regiment. So you see him now on the high road to the most brilliant Military fortune, and Nature has bestowed upon him all the qualities that can make you expect of his following it as far as possible. This place gives him twelve thousand livres a year. I received a Letter from him dated from Cadiz, the 2nd of this month. He is in perfect health, and I hope I shall have the pleasure of embracing him very soon. It would be most useful to him to find on his Arrival here the papers he prayed you to send to him. They are absolutely necessary in the present circumstances.

I am, with sincere regards and attatchment,
Ever your most faithful and assured humble servant,
C. B. M.

All the old letters and memoirs concur in describing Cadiz as the most delightful quarters in the world. It was ruled by a valiant and distinguished, but nowise delightful person, Count O'Reilly, with whom my hero had a slight encounter, confined only to words. The Duc des Cars tells how, after the siege, he accompanied the Comte d'Artois and the Duc de Bourbon to the lovely city, which he had known well in his sailor days.

"I was enchanted to see once more, after a lapse of twelve years, a town where I had tasted of every species of pleasure. General O'Reilly was the governor, and I found the town greatly embellished by his care, also the road outside the land gate. O'Reilly held the state of a viceroy in Cadiz. He gave the princes a magnificent reception, superb cheer, and all the perfumes of Arabia breathing through the apartments."

Perhaps the veteran, who was very crusty by nature, had expended so much suavity on his illustrious guests that he had none left for humbler folk.

Says the *Kerry Chronicle*, March 9, 1785, "Governor

O'Reilly, whose rigorous treatment of prisoners during the war has been often censured, congratulated Colonel O'Connell on his good fortune, and asked to what *impegneo*, or intrigue, he owed such rapid preferment. 'To this, sir,' replied O'Connell, drawing his sword, and giving Count O'Reilly a most disdainful look. 'To this, which has procured me the favour of my sovereign.' He could not be persuaded to visit the governor again."

Any book about distinguished Irishmen will tell of the veteran's achievements, but I heard the following quaint anecdote from a reverend namesake of O'Reilly's. My informant, when a little child, had seen a very aged priest who had been bred in Spain. O'Reilly used to visit the Irish College, where the student dwelt, for he was both patriotic and devout, according to his temperament. His dream was to head a Spanish force against England, land in his native country, overturn heresy and tyranny, and the very first thing he swore to do was to burn to the ground his ancestral home, polluted by conforming kinsmen, whom he would put to the sword,[1] as he used to tell the student who related the story.

The Duc des Cars gives us a more pleasing account of another Irish veteran, Count Lacy. "Count Lacy," says the Duc des Cars (vol. i. p. 278), "was a man of most lofty stature. His appearance was most noble, his manners those of a great lord. As Spanish Minister Plenipotentiary, he had enjoyed the highest esteem of the Courts of St. Petersburg and Stockholm, and it was entirely to him that Charles III. was indebted for a superb and excellent corps of artillery. His valour, cool to a degree, was as brilliant as his appearance was imposing. Both Frenchmen and

[1] "A TRUE 'SOLDIER OF FORTUNE.'—Don Alexander O'Reilly, Count Commander of the Spanish Armies, Field-Marshal, Captain-General at the Havannah, Governor and Lieut.-General of Louisiana, which he took possession of in 1768, when surrendered by the French. Born in Ireland 1725, died in Spain 1794. There can scarcely be found anywhere a more romantic or exciting career than that of O'Reilly. He fought in Spain, Italy, Germany, France, and America. He saved the king's life, was at the head of his armies and government, was in disgrace and exile, and everywhere and always showed high spirit, the greatest bravery, and the most devoted loyalty to the king. He was a 'terror' when in command in Louisiana, and made short work of evil-doers and those who resisted the authority of 'the king, his master.'" One of the principal streets in Havana is named Calle O'Reilly after him.—[Found in a newspaper.]

Spaniards had the highest veneration for him." Surely a more noble portrait cannot be found in the long gallery of the Irish cavaliers of fortune. Such was the Spanish general-in-chief who had been pitted against the illustrious Eliott.

At the very time Count O'Connell was achieving position and distinction at the sword's point, his two surviving brothers and their cousin Daniel O'Connell, of Tarmons, had a narrow escape of their lives and liberties. Their smuggling exposed them to the machinations of an informer, and this time, but for powerful Protestant friends, things might have gone hard with them; however, they came off with flying colours, and Maurice's grim and ponderous respectability shone forth untarnished. Smuggling was not considered in eighteenth-century Kerry in the smallest degree incompatible with an "uncommon good character" and considerable "consequence," as appears from the letters of his heretical but valuable friends.

The following curious story was told me by the late Mr. Butler, of Waterville, as well as by the O'Connells and their followers. The mysterious token, "the crooked knife," was merely an old pruning-knife. Hunting Cap probably first got it for his orchard, and then used it as a token in dealing with the peasantry. Old Dan Sullivan, the Liberator's steward, told me that he had often heard a tenant would walk out and give up his holding at the bidding of the bearer of the crooked knife. It also served the purpose of the Scottish fiery cross for assembling the people. Its bearer was implicitly obeyed as Hunting Cap's mouthpiece. It was lost when the present Daniel O'Connell was a boy.

Captain Whitwell Butler, of the Revenue Force, formerly a naval officer, had become very successful in putting down petty smuggling, and now determined to try conclusions with the sage of Darrynane.

One fine September morning, the 5th of that month, 1782, while Hunting Cap, his brother, and sundry cousins and nephews, with a throng of peasants, were happily engaged in landing a valuable cargo, Captain Butler swooped down on them with the King's men, and made a seizure of all their store. Hunting Cap submitted to the inevitable, and civilly invited the officer to breakfast. Hunting Cap's wife had a French silk gown in the cargo, and expressed a wish to ransom her finery.

"You shall have it free, madam, if it costs me my commission," gallantly responded the officer, and he sent for the piece of silk for her.

Captain Butler determined to return to Waterville across country on foot, with a very small escort. Hunting Cap knew the peasants were furious at the capture, and dreaded mischief, so he besought the officer to let him send with him one of his nephews (the O'Sullivans of Couliagh), as otherwise he could not answer for the people. In Captain Butler's presence he handed the crooked knife to his nephew, bidding him escort the officer to the river-bank at Waterville.

Thus singularly guarded, the representative of law and order set out. In passing through the hamlet of Cahirdaniel they noticed lowering looks and hostile gestures, but a sight of the crooked knife caused the peasants to make way. Some distance beyond the village, Captain Butler begged young O'Sullivan to go back, and struck across the high mountain for his home. Whilst Captain Butler was crossing one shoulder of the mountain, a mob of angry peasants had skirted the other brow from Cahirdaniel. They fell on the officer, routed his men, and beat him to within an inch of his life. Old Mr. Butler told me that his grandmother saw the crowd, and ran out for help. Though expecting a baby in a few days, she crossed the river the first, leaping from stepping-stone to stone, and found her husband living, but unconscious. In a few weeks Captain Butler was well again, and the father of a fine boy—old Mr. Butler's father.

Now the papers at Darrynane take up the story. I only quote a few letters.

Mr. Owen McCrohan writes to Morgan O'Connell, on December 1, 1782, a most graphic letter, but too long to copy in full. He relates how he has been at Waterville (Currane it was called then), and had called on Mr. Butler, this interchange of civilities among opposite parties seeming the most natural thing in the world in eighteenth-century

Kerry. Mr. Butler, "in great confidence," produced a warrant from Lord Chief Justice Annaly to arrest Morgan, Maurice, and their cousin Daniel O'Connell, of Tarmons, as having instigated the late barbarous attack, and an informer also stated that Daniel had offered £100 reward for the murder of Butler. In return for this secret information, Mr. Butler requested a solemn pledge that no direct or indirect attempts should be made on his life or liberty. "A matter," observes Mr. McCrohan, "I hope you'll readily comply with, its being in ye smallest degree no reflection on either of you, in my humble opinion, particularly as I am well convinced you never had the least intention in aiding or abetting in the murder of any one; and God forbid ye should!"

The circumstances which could give colour to a charge against the kinsmen were the facts of the mob being composed of Hunting Cap's tenants. The outrage, however, was simply a piece of personal vindictiveness on the part of the peasantry, who, like their betters, found the smuggling very profitable. If the accused had to go to Dublin, however, a strange jury might very possibly hang them on the testimony of informers.

All the letters and copies are at Darrynane. I copied the next one from Hunting Cap's own rough draft. It is to a very elegant, polished, and amiable man, Counsellor Dominic Trant, M.P., an ancestor of the Dovea family.[1] The Trants were originally a Dingle family, and related to relations of the O'Connells. Dominic Trant was an ancestor of my friend Mr. Armstrong, of Mealiffe, County Tipperary, and Judge Henn, who behaved exceedingly well to the Kerry men, was the ancestor of my friend Recorder Henn, whose beautiful place, Paradise, is near my husband's Clare property.

Mr. and Mrs. Trant, of Dovea, kindly supplied me with the following information concerning Dominic Trant.

Dominic Trant, Q.C., of Dunkettle, County Cork, and Merrion Street, Dublin, was the second son of Dominic Trant the elder, of Dingle, who died in 1759, having married a Miss McCarthy, of the County Cork. Dominic Trant, the King's Counsel, married, first the widow of Judge Blennerhasset,

[1] See Note D, p. 325.

née Rice, by whom he had no issue; and, secondly, Elinor FitzGibbon, sister of the future Chancellor Lord Clare, by whom he had two sons, John and William, and one daughter, Maria, married to Lord Dunally. Mr. Trant says his ancestor was never a Member of Parliament, but the contemporary letters state that he was Member for Dingle. Mrs. Trant informs me that they possess a copy of a pamphlet in favour of the Catholic claims and a general increase of freedom, which caused such a commotion among the Protestant interest in Munster, that he had to fight a duel in consequence, in which he killed his adversary, the Sir George Colthurst of those days. Ross O'Connell has given me a good deal of information about Catholic Trants, which will be found in the note on Count Bartholomew O'Mahony,[1] whose mother was of that branch of the family. Mr. Trant, of Dovea, concludes by stating, "Dominic had an elder brother James, who for some reason was disinherited. He married, and left five or six daughters. Dominic Trant the elder had become a Protestant, and James went back again to the Roman Catholic Church with his family.

"Dominic Trant, the King's Counsel, died in 1790, and is buried at Cahir, in the County Tipperary. His portrait is at Dovea."

I give Hunting Cap's letter, with all its violent abuse of Mr. Butler, which is not to be wondered at under the circumstances. He even overlooks Mr. Butler's friendly warning in his indignation at being suspected of a share in so very silly, vulgar, and unprofitable a crime. Dominic Trant's last letter shows that Mr. Whitwell Butler had been gulled by a rural "Pigott" in the shape of one Kelly, a professional informer, and that he acted very honourably in avowing his error, and thus aiding in the triumphant display of innocence on the part of the three kinsmen.

Maurice O'Connell to Counsellor Dominic Trant, M.P.

Darrinane, 5th Dec', 1782.

DEAR SIR,—I beg leave to communicate a most Horrid and Base attack that has been made on my brother and me and Mr. Daniel Connell, by Mr. Whitwell Butler, on or about

[1] See Note B, p. 316.

the Time you were in this Country [previous October], and which we only discovered Two days since, thro' Mr. Owen McCrohan, of Portmagee, to whom he shewed Lord Annaly's warrant against us.

The warrant sets forth that we are charged on Information on Oath before his Lordship with being the persons who raised the Mob that assembled and beat Mr. Butler after making a seizure, and that Daniel Connell has att different Times offered a reward of £100 stg. to any person who would assassinate Mr. Butler, particularly on the 5th September last, being a Club Day att Nadeen, in Glanarough, where he was then; that he publickly declared he would pay the sum to any person who would perpetrate it; that Daniel Connell, my Brother, and I have repeatedly and several times uttered words to the same effect, particularly about a year and a half since at Killarney Fair, in company with a Mr. Guthrie, with several other charges which Mr. McCrohan does not recollect. At the same time that I can not express my horror at such a deep Infernal train of Iniquity, equally calculated to stabb us in the dark, and keep up his own weight and influence with the Commissioners, I shall not trespass upon your time by making any remarks on it. All I shall say is that, Conscious of our Innocence and of our just abhorence of such Barbarous, Inhuman, and Unchristian practices, We are ready to meet these abominable charges in open Day, In the fface of our Country, att the next Assizes, and to rise or fall by the Impartiall Decision of the Laws of Our Country; but as to resorting to my Lord Annaly to receive these informations and taking out his Warrant, which I apprehend is not Bailable, is a Magnificent proof of a determined Intention to add oppression and the distressing and Loathsome Confinement of Jail to accumulated Falsehoods, and we are ready and willing to enter into recognizances with sufficient Baill for our appearance at the next Assizes. I hope it will be thought equally just and reasonable to put a stop to all rigorous and severe measures, and not to distinguish our Case by a mode of procedure which, however it may be authorized by Law, is one rarely practised. It should be Considered that the most upright men and the purest and most respectable Characters have not always Escaped the Invidious and designing attacks of the Tongue of Malevolence and Slander, and I have heard it was a maxim, and indeed a very Wise and Just one, in Law that Criminality was not to be affixed till after the Tryall.

What I would take the Liberty to request from you is that you would move my Lord Annaly and prevail with him to admitt us to Baill in the County, and to grant a Copy of the Informations, etc., if it be not inconsistent with your other arrangements, and that you would be our Counsel at the next Assizes.

Mr. Frank Spotswood will waitt on you with this, and attend to any directions you shall be pleased to give him.

I give my Honour most solemnly, which I trust you'll believe, that my Brother and I have kept as clear of Mr. Butler since, either in Word or Deed, as we have of my Lord Temple, as has Daniel Connell to the best of my opinion and Belieff, and you'll see we shall baffle his plotting and poisonous Machinations.

I am, etc.,
M. O'C.

The attorney, Mr. Spotswood, retained Counsellor Trant, and they tried to get Judges Henn and Robinson, who were to go to Kerry Assizes, to take local bail, but they were unable to do anything without Lord Annaly. The Chief Justice was a great friend of Dominic Trant's brother-in-law, FitzGibbon, afterwards the notorious Lord Clare. He was down at Tenneleck, on a visit to Lord Annaly. Judge Henn, who was to join the party, conveyed the following letter from Dominic Trant to FitzGibbon, evidently intended for the Lord Chief Justice's perusal. He sends a copy to Maurice O'Connell, whose "uncommon good character" he expatiates on. The writer and recipients of this epistle evidently consider the steady and sustained pursuit of wholesale smuggling as not the least drawback to the primmest and most starched respectability. The primmest, grimmest, austerest respectability was considered evidently to be Hunting Cap's strong point.

Counsellor Dominic Trant, M.P., to Counsellor John FitzGibbon.

Stephen's Green, Dec' 31st, 1782.

DEAR FITZGIBBON,—I forgot to mention to you yesterday a circumstance relative to a particular friend of mine in Kerry, a Mr. Maurice Connell, of Darrinane. A Common man of the name of Kelly has sworn that this Mr. Connell and his brother Morgan Connell, and a cousin, Mr. Daniel Connell, threatened the life of Mr. Whitwell Butler, a commander of revenue Cruizer, and had instigated a Mob to waylay and beat him. Application was accordingly made to Lord Annaly some time last September for the purpose of apprehending these three gentlemen, who got notice of the circumstance only a few days since. I enclose you Mr. Connell's letter to me, which will give you fuller information.

I applied in vain to the Justices Robinson and Henn for an order to take Bail to any amount, and before *any Magistrate* in Kerry whom they should appoint. As this is a sort of Revenue Prosecution, and the agent Employed is the Sollicitor to the Commissioners, I proposed such Bail as to the Board thro' their Secretary and Agent.

The Justices Robinson and Henn thought they could not meddle with the Lord Chief Justice's warrant, so that unless Lord Annaly himself (who had unfortunately the day before left town) should make such an Order it must lie over until next Term, and these gentlemen must either be out on their keeping like Tories or White Boys, or, if taken, lie in the worst Jail in Europe, that of Tralee, among Felons and other Malefactors. This seems rather severe in the case of three gentlemen of reputation and Consequence in that Country (two of whom I know particularly to be men of Character and Considerable property), who are able and willing to give any Bail which may be required.

The Collector of Tralee (Mr. Blennerhassett) is a Magistrate of Kerry, and, if such order as I mention can be made, would be a proper person to take their Bail, such as might satisfie the Commissioners in the fullest manner.

If Lord Annaly should express any wish to see a Copy of the Warrant, it lies in the hands of Mr. Richard Waller, of St. Andrew's Street, the under Sollicitor to the Commissioners.

Mr. Francis Spotswood (No. 5, College Street) is the Attorney for the Mr. Connells, who would readily go down to Tencleek if you should write to him a line which might induce him to Expect success on this application to Lord Annaly.

These three Gentlemen live in different parts of the Barony of Iveragh, in Kerry, the nearest part of which is full 160 miles from Dublin—very bad roads, no Carriages to be had, and in this time of the year a Journey on Horseback seems rather dangerous to persons much beyond the middle point of Life. Two of them have very large families. If forced to come to Dublin, they must bring Bail with them at a very great expence—perhaps that Bail may be thought insufficient, or the same Bail may not be taken for the three persons accused—in either case there can be here no alteration, and the delay of sending again to Kerry for other Bail, who may be objected to, would certainly be attended with hardship and heavy expence.

On the whole, try if anything can be done in this Case before Term ; if not, you will be applied to to move the King's Bench for an Order of Bail in the Country. My apprehension is that the Warrant may be executed in the interval, and these three gentlemen thereby put to very great distress and inconvenience.

Besides that these gentlemen are my Clients, I have long known the two Brothers Maurice and Morgan [the Liberator's father], who are both esteemed men of probity and honour. Maurice is a man of singular good character. Daniel I do not know well. They are men of a very ancient Roman Catholic family, which has preserved a remnant of its former property thro' all the Revolutions of this Kingdom. Maurice is possessed of very considerable personal property. There can't be the slightest cause for supposing that such men would fly from their Country and decline a publick tryal, which the Law requires on such occasions.

Write a line to Spottswoode as soon as possible, to inform him if anything can be done by his going to Teneleek. If not, that he may be prepared for his application next Term. All here well. I am better every day.

Ever yours,
Dom. Trant.

Judge Henn, who sets out for Teneleek in the morning, will deliver this Epistle to you, will mention the point to Lord Annaly, and save you the trouble of first breaking it.

Lord Annaly granted the request, the three kinsmen appeared at their own assizes, and the grand jury threw out the bills, so that they returned without the smallest slur on their characters. Dominic Trant had evidently been away, judging from his letter.

Thurles, May 28, 1783.

My Dear Sir,—On my arrival from England, a few days since, in Dublin, I heard with great pleasure from Mr. Francis Spotswood that you had completely triumphed over the very ungenerous attempt made to distress you, your Brother, and your Kinsman, and that the gentleman who had been imposed upon by the artifices of a very paltry and contemptible and lying Informer, became in time sensible of his error, and made the proper acknowledgements of his mistake. I was much mortified that my business detained me in England when I imagined you might have had some trial on this business at the last Assizes of Tralee. Tho' I was very sensible that other Law Friends would have assisted you more ably than I could, had it been in my power to do so, yet I am well assured that none would have exerted himself with more zeal or friendship in any case in which you were concerned. That, however, is now passed, and in a manner much to your honour, in the full face of your County, and very much to my satisfaction.

It will induce gentlemen to be cautious for the future how they give credence to the lies and misrepresentations of such low fellows as that Kelly, which I believe was the name of the author of that calumny.

I formerly mentioned to you somewhat of the survey of the County of Kerry, undertaken by Mr. Henry Pelham. He has now begun this undertaking, and in his progress will call upon you for such advice and Assistance as you shall be pleased to give him. I believe I have some time since given him a Letter to introduce him to your notice. He is a very fair and well-conducted man, who will neither disgrace my recommendation nor any politeness and kindness you may be pleased to show him on my account.

My Brother-in-Law, Mr. FitzGibbon, has declared himself a Candidate for the County of Limerick at the next General Election. May I request that you will be kind enough to exert yourself for him, as I flatter myself you would for me on a similar occasion? I am anxiously solicitous for his success, not more from the bond of my connection with him, than from the incitement of a very strong personal friendship which I have had for him long before that connection subsisted.

May I request that you will be so good as to present my most sincere compliments to the good Ladies of your family, and to assure them that I do not forget their very kind attention to me during those two very agreable days I had the pleasure of spending last October at Darrinane? If I were permitted by the troublesome business of this World, I would scale Mountains much more rugged than those of Dunkerron to repeat so pleasing a visit.

The New Lord Lieutenant is expected in Dublin on Monday next, the 2nd of June. I intend to be one of his Levéers on that day, and hope to have the pleasure of a line from you with an account of the health of all the family.

Ever, my dear Sir, Most Faithfully yrs.,
DOM. TRANT.

Mr. Lecky (p. 377), in the fourth volume of his "History of England in the Eighteenth Century," mentions the curious fact of FitzGibbon's being in favour of liberal measures from

1780 to 1783, so that, in asking the support of Catholic friends, Dominic Trant was not asking anything against their principles.

After mentioning that, on the promotion of Yelverton to the Bench in 1783, FitzGibbon became attorney-general, Mr. Lecky says—

"This remarkable man, who for the last sixteen years of the century exercised a dominant influence in the Irish Government, and who, as Lord Clare, was the ablest and at the same time the most detested advocate of the Union, had in 1780 opposed the Declaration of Rights moved by Grattan in the House of Commons, and supported the policy of Grattan in 1782, and had used strong language in censuring some parts of the legislative authority which Great Britain exercised over Ireland. It is very questionable whether he ever really approved of the repeal of Poyning's Law, and his evident leaning towards authority made him distrusted by several leaders of the popular party; but Grattan does not appear to have shared the feeling, and when he was consulted on the subject by Lord Northington, he gave his full sanction to the promotion of FitzGibbon."

Mr. Lecky states there was no breach between them until 1785.

NOTES TO BOOK IV.

Note A.

A Few Brief Extracts from the Diary of Alexander Ross, who commanded the English Ordnance during the Siege of Gibraltar.

The diary begins June 21, 1779, "all communications with Spain cut off," and ends September 13, 1782. It is in the possession of Alexander Ross's grandson, the Rev. Robert Poole Hooper, of Brighton.

"*Aug.* 29, 1780.—The guard-boat with five men deserted and took the midshipman with them.

"*Sept.* 23.—The midshipman sent in that was forced off by the guard-boat's crew the 29th ult°.

"*April* 13, 1781.—The town much destroyed. The works are as yet but little injured. A wine-house set on fire in the green market, where a great quantity of spirits was. The fire-ingines were got, but the people got so drunk with the wine and spirits that they brought out the liquor in the leather buckets, and poured it into the ingine instead of water, which greatly increased the flames and burnt a house at the opposite corner of the street. The soldiers plunder the store-houses of liquor, and are in such a condition that numbers of them that are getting ready for guard can hardly stand.

"*Oct.* 6, 1781.—1343 shot and shells fired by the enemy this day.

"*Dec.* 31, 1781.—The Enemy have fired against this garrison from their batteries on the Isthmus, since the 12th of April last 141,220 shot and shells; from their gun and mortar-boats 5510.

"*April* 12, 1782.—Since this day twelve months there has not been an intermission of 24 hours in the enemy's fire.

"*June* 4, 1782.—King's Birthday. We saluted with 44 shot into the Enemy's advance works.

"*Aug.* 8, 1782.—The shot, shells, and military stores of all kinds in the Enemy's camp is inconceivable.

"*Aug.* 9.—The enemy are lining the ports of their floating batteries with tin.

"*Aug.* 15.—The Duc de Crillon with his suite in the advance works.

"*Aug.* 19.—A flag of truce from the enemy, with a present of game and fruit. By this we learnt that the Count d'Artois and the Duke de Bourbon were in the Spanish camp.

"*Sept.* 12, 1782.—This morning arrived in the bay the combined fleets of France and Spain, being 38 sail of the line, which with nine before, and a large ship of one Deck with an admiral's Flag amounts to 48 sail, among which seven ships of three decks. Besides this force there is ready for the attack of this place 10 large fortified ships as floating batteries, three bomb-ketches[1] and mortar-boats, with about 16 gun-boats, as also about 300 boats of different constructions.

"*Sept.* 13, 1782.—This morning about seven o'clock the enemy's 10 fortified ships or floating batteries began to get under way, and about ten o'clock the headmost ship or two-decker came to an anchor a little to the south of the King's Bastion, and within less than 1000 y^{ds} of our walls. The others soon came into their stations with a fine north-west breeze, the 10 between the south-west of Columbines and the Montagu Bastion, and immediately commenced an exceeding warm fire from about 144 pieces of cannon mostly 26 p^{ds}, besides a bomb-ketch, which was returned by us from all batteries that c^{ld} be brought to bear upon them with mortars, Howitzers, and guns, chiefly with red-hot shot, in all about 90 Pieces of Artillery. At the same time, the enemy kept up a heavy Enfilading fire from their Batteries on the Isthmus with 109 cannon and Howitzers, and about 80 mortars. This violent and conjunct fire of artillery was kept up without intermission from about ten in the morning until five in the aft^n, at which time the Enemy's Floating Batteries began to slacken much in their fire, and the headmost ship hoisted a signal of distress, on which a Cutter, sailing in the Bay, came near and sent her boat on board. Early in the afternoon some of them were observed to smoke in several places, and the men were observed to be pouring in water from several ingines into the holes made by the red-hot shot. From about nine at night a g^t noise was made on board their ships, which we conjectured was towing them off, but by twelve o'clock the fire was plainly to be distinguished on board the southernmost ship, and soon after on board the Admiral; great numbers of Rockets were thrown up by these two ships, as also from

---

[1] "A kind of a ship strongly built to bear the shock of a mortar" (Johnson).

several of the others, which were answered by guns and lights on board several of the ships of the combined Fleet in the Bay. Before two o'clock we c^{ld} observe two ships to flame out, soon after another; by the flames we could perceive numbers of boats passing, and between three and four in the morning our twelve gun-boats went out from the New Mole, and took two large launches full of seamen and soldiers who were leaving the vessels, some of which were now in different stages of burning, and from which Brigad. Curtis, with the greatest bravery and humanity, rescued above 350 persons from the flames, among whom were eight officers and three priests. In which humane action, by the blowing-up of two other ships, he was in the most imminent danger of perishing. . . . Nine of these batteries (*i.e.* floating batteries) were burnt by our red-hot shot and shells, and the tenth, a single-decker, was burnt by us in the afternoon of the following day, being then on shore and unable, as the navy reported, of being got off. About midday the Enemy loosened their topsails, and about three o'clock 4000 men marched into the lines fully accoutred."

Here the volume of the diary in Mr. Hooper's possession concludes. The writer, Alexander Ross, born in Holland, 1748, died at Gibraltar, 1804, was my great-granduncle (see note "O'Conor" in notes to "Descendants of Daniel O'Connell, of Darrynane," end of vol. ii.)—[R. O'C.]

Note B.

Bartholomew Count O'Mahony, sometime Knight of Malta, 1749–1819.

[Bartholomew, Knight of Malta, Count, born January 3, 1749; captain in "Berwick's," January 23, 1771; second colonel in "Walsh's," 1778; Mestre de Camp en second in "Berwick's," January 1, 1784; second colonel from October 21, 1781, to 1791; Knight of St. Louis, August 19, 1781; lieut.-general, Commander Order of St. Louis, August 23, 1814; died 1819.—From M. de la ̺ nce's manuscript relating to the Irish Brigade, R.I.A., Dublin.]

Ross O'Connell has abridged the following details from Dromore papers.

He married Marie Louise, daughter of Louis, Marquis de Goury. Only son, Marie Ives Arsein, Chevalier de Malte, died 1795.

A manuscript pedigree of Count Bartholomew is in the possession of Mr. Mahony, of Dromore. It is drawn up by Andrew Young, "Notary Publick," on a huge sheet of parchment, is exceedingly diffuse, and is thus authenticated—

"We, the several lords and gentlemen whose names are hereunto subscribed, do certify that the above pedigree is true. Dated this 25th day of August, 1763." Then follow the signatures of, on one side, thirteen "original Irish," including "O'Donnoghue of Glinn; Mcfinnin; and O'Donoghue More;" and, on the other, ten settlers, including "Saml Morris, Sheriff; Branden;[1] Maurice Fitzgerald, Kn^t. Kerry; and Ar. Denny, Provost Traly."

Bartholomew, who was born in 1749, must have taken this precious document with him when he left Kerry to seek and find a foreign fortune. It gives, with the marked absence of dates so characteristic of Irish pedigrees, a vast catalogue of great-grandmothers and great-great-great-grandmothers. If it had been necessary for Bartholomew, when he sought the honour of Maltese knighthood, to prove thirty-two instead of eight "quartiers" of gentility, he could easily have exhumed them from the now mouldering parchment that was once doubtless one of his most treasured possessions. The pedigree in the male line is, when one takes its nationality into consideration, unusually modest and unassuming, contenting itself with "Core, King of Munster in the year of our Lord 370," as starting-point.

The common ancestor of all the Kerry Mahonys was Dermod O'Mahony Mor, Lord of Kinalmeaky, *circa* 1300; his third son, Dermod, settled in Desmond in 1335, and, according to Sir William Betham, Ulster, had issue, John, who married Sheela, daughter of Aodh O'Connell, chief of his name, and was great-grandfather of Teigue O'Mahony, Seneschal of Desmond, called "Teigue the Wanton," who signed a treaty with Lord Deputy Gray in 1536, and, marrying Honora, daughter of Dermod O'Sullivan Beare, by Elinor, daughter of Gerald, Earl of Kildare, was grandfather of Finghin, *alias* Florence, Seneschal of Desmond in 1568, who married Bridget, daughter of Jeffray O'Donoghue Mor, of Ross. Their eldest son, Dermod, was High Sheriff of Kerry in 1639—Betham, with a glorious disregard for the possible, says in 1667, Dermod having died before 1652! Dermod's great-grandson, Teigue (whom Sir William erroneously calls Thady, and equally erroneously kills at Aughrim) of Kilderry, County Kerry, married Elinor, daughter of Florence Mahony, of Kilbonane, County Kerry, "by his wife, Margery, daughter of Jeffray O'Connell, heir of Ballinavlaun, in said county" (manuscript of 1763), and had an eldest son, Owen, who settled at Knockavola, in Kerry, and, marrying Elinor, daughter of Thomas FitzMaurice, of Cosfeal (erroneously called Hon. Thos. F.-M. by Betham), had two sons. The

---

[1] Crosbie, Lord Brandon or Branden, extinct 1815.

younger, Bartholomew, was in 1763 an M.D. in Paris; the elder remained in Kerry, and married Helen, daughter of Francis Holles, of Knockanagulsey, in Kerry, by his wife, Ann, daughter of Walter Fitzgerald, of Nurney, in Leinster; the said Ann, through her mother, Elizabeth, daughter of Sir John Crosbie, Bart., was great-great-granddaughter of Sir Nicholas Browne, Knight, of Rosse, and Sheela, daughter of Sir Owen O'Sullivan, fourteenth Lord of Beare. Francis Holles was the great-grandson of John Holles, who came from England in the reign of Elizabeth, and married Margaret, daughter of John and niece of Sir Edward Herbert.

Michael Mahony and Helen Holles had issue, two sons— Owen, who married a De Courcy and seems to have died *s.p.*, and Bartholomew, Count O'Mahony.—[R. O'C.]

Count O'Mahony's grandmother was of the old Catholic branch of the Trants, whose interesting pedigree I subjoin, followed by a note about the FitzMaurice family.

Count Bartholomew O'Mahony had to give up his benefice as a Knight of Malta on his marriage, but it seems to have been granted to his young son, who died in 1795. Rev. Francis Mahony[1] states that £8000 (the endowment) was lodged in London in 1795, it is presumed by Count O'Mahony, and recovered for the Order by Father F. Mahony in 1847.

FitzMaurice of Cosfeal, alias Duagh-na-Feily, now called Duagh, near Listowel, County Kerry.

Dr. Robert FitzMaurice, of Tralee, younger son of the late Maurice FitzMaurice of Duagh, lent me a somewhat fragmentary pedigree, of FitzMaurice of Duagh, or Cosfeal.

Dermod McCarthy Mor, King of Cork and Desmond, granted, in 1178, a large tract of land in North Kerry, including Cosfeal, to Raymond le Gros, as a reward for his services against the king's rebel son Cormac. These lands descended to Raymond's great-great-great-grandson John, fifth Lord Kerry, living in 1339, who gave them to his second son Garrett. They passed from father to son until forfeited by Edmund McJames FitzMaurice in the reign of Elizabeth. Duagh alone was retained; it was forfeited by James Fitz-Ulick FitzMaurice in 1688, but was restored to his grandson Garrett, a minor, called Grodemore, who died 1739; from which time it passed from father to son until the death of Oliver FitzMaurice, of Duagh, in 1859, when it became the property of his two daughters, having descended in the male line for over 680 years—a circumstance rare in any country, but almost without parallel in Ireland.

[1] Better known under his *nom de plume* of "Father Prout."

Garrett, called Grodemore, was the eldest son of Thomas FitzMaurice (eldest son of James of Cosfeal), *ob. v.p.* before 1688, and Catherine (called Anne in "Book of Claims") Trant. Their daughter Elinor married Oliver Mahony, of Knockavola, as already stated.

"Certain many-centuried oaks overhang the river Feal at Duagh; preserved by superstition, for they are the dwelling-place of countless fairies, who resent interference, and punish with festering sores or deadly disease the wretched mortal who tampers with their house beautiful."—*Tralee Chronicle*, August 9, 1861.

The descent of FitzMaurice of Duagh from Edward III. is given by Foster in "Our Noble and Gentle Families of Royal Descent," p. 647.

FitzMaurice of Duagh bears arg., saltier gu. a chief erm., never having differenced the arms of its chief, Lord Kerry, now Marquess of Lansdowne.—[R. O'C.]

Dominic Trant, of Fenitt, co. Kerry, sent to Spain, 1583, by 16th Earl of Desmond, to seek arms, etc. = Honora, daughter of James Fitzgerald, of Ballymacadam, Kerry.

Garrett = Margaret, daughter of Thomas Trant, of Fenitt. of Cahirtrant, Kerry, M.P. for Dingle, 1613.

Edmond = Barbara, daughter of Rowland Rice, of Fenitt. Ballingolin, Kerry.

Twenty-three other sons, four of whom were colonels in Spain. From one of these twenty-three descended Sir Patrick Trant, Bart., who went to France with James II., and had

Edward = Ellen, daughter of Richard of Fenitt. Trant, of Glensherune, Kerry, by his wife Catherine, daughter of Timothy O'Connor, of Tarighe (?), Kerry, who was of the O'Connor Kerrys, and his mother was daughter of Corn. O'Sullivan, 2nd son to O'Sullivan Beare.

Sir John murdered in London
? Richard.

James, killed colonel, at siege of Cork.

daughter, m. Lord Slane.

daughter, m. Prince d'Auvergne.

Catherine = Thomas FitzMaurice, (? Anne) of Cosfeal.

Elinor = Owen Mahony, Knockavola.

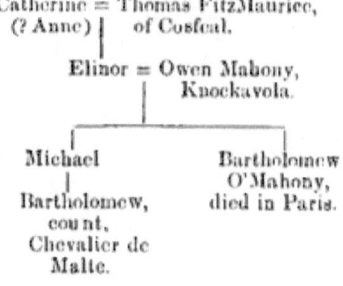

Michael
|
Bartholomew, count, Chevalier de Malte.

Bartholomew O'Mahony, died in Paris.

Another descendant of Edmond of Fenitt, David Trant, of Killeen, Kerry, was father of Garrett, Edward, and David Trant, captains in James II.'s army, of whom Garrett and Edward were killed at Aughrim, Garrett leaving an only child, Margaret, who married Richard, 4th Earl of Cavan, *ob.* 1741.

The above is taken chiefly from the manuscript pedigree of Count O'Mahony. Sir Patrick Trant must have been son or grandson of Edmund of Fenitt. Burke's "Extinct Baronetage" says he was created a baronet in 1686, and that letters patent for his elevation to the peerage as Lord Maryboro' were being made out when James II. fled. Burke ignores Sir Patrick's sons. He had at least two. A plate in Keatinge's "Ireland" (1st edit., 1723) is dedicated to Sir *Laurence* Trant, Bart. Trant bears per pale az. and gu., two swords in saltire ar., hilts and pomels or, between three (sometimes four) roses of the third.—[R. O'C.]

Note C.

"Le Brave O'Mahony:" his Descendants; their Poor Relations and Successful Kinsmen.

Daniel, "le brave O'Mahony," the preserver of Cremona, was given by Louis XIV. to his grandson Philip of Spain, in which country he distinguished himself during the War of Succession. He died a count of Spain, general, and Commander of St. Iago. He was first married to Cecilia Weld, of Lulworth, and secondly to Charlotte Bulkeley, widow of the fifth Lord Clare. His second son, Dermot, or Demetrio, was a lieut.-general, Count Commander of several Orders, and Ambassador from Spain to Austria, where he died in 1776, according to O'Callaghan, from whom I abridge the above statement (pp. 204, 205). However, from the contemporary letters I infer that O'Callaghan kills him a little too soon. At p. 602 he quotes an old London periodical ("Annual Register") of March, 1766: "On the 17th of this month, his Excellency Count Mahony, Ambassador from Spain to the Court of Vienna, gave a grand entertainment in honour of St. Patrick, to which were invited all persons of condition that were of Irish descent; being himself a descendant of an illustrious family of that kingdom. Among many others, were present Count Lacy, President of the Council of War, the Generals O'Donnel, McGuire, O'Kelly, Browne, Plunket, and McElligott, four Chiefs of the Grand Cross, two governors, several knights military, and six staff officers, four Privy Councillors, with the principal officers of State; who, to show their respect to the Irish nation, wore crosses in honour of the day, as did the entire Court." This distinguished personage undertook to find out the Irish next of kin of a relative and namesake, Lieut.-Colonel O'Mahony, of the Spanish Service, Knight Commander of a distinguished Order.

He applied to Chev. Bartholomew O'Mahony to speak to Irish friends and to Mr. French, merchant in Cork. These nephews and nieces of his kinsmen, the second or third generation since Count Daniel of Cremona had followed King James to France, had become so impoverished that it was difficult to trace them. Hunting Cap, at his brother's request, wrote to their cousin and Cork correspondent, Jerry McCrohan, who in April, 1777, replies, "According to your instructions, have sent you the above, which is a real copy taken from Mr. French for the payment he made to the above people. I asked him if he knew where they lived, which he did not know, and I believe they live in or about the parish of Killmichel."

The copy of acknowledgment runs as follows across the top of the first page:—

"We, the underwritten Cornelius O'Mahony, Kean O'Mahony, Cornelius, son of Murtough O'Mahony, Elizabeth and Mary O'Mahony, Mary and Ellinor O'Mahony, Sisters to Kean O'Mahony, Nephews and Nieces of the Late Lieut. Col. Cornelius O'Mahony, deceased in the Spanish Service, and in our quality of Heirs to the said deceased Lieut. Col. Coṁñ. O'Mahony, acknowledge to have rec^d from his Excellency Count O'Mahony, Ambassador from the Court of Spain to that of Vienna, by the hands of Martin French, Esqr., Merc^t in Cork, the sum of Ninety Pounds sterling, proceeding from the Inheritance of our said Uncle deceased Lieut.-Col. Coṁñ O'Mahony, and making with the sums heretofore transmitted to us by his said Excellency Count O'Mahony the full am^t of all the pceeds [proceeds] of said inheritance, for which we signed two rec^{ts} of the same tenor and date, the two being for one and the same payment. Cork, 19th Nov., 1776.

"Present: [Here follow signatures.]
   Revd Dominick Morrough.
   Ro^l French."

One of the signatures is affixed to a mark. There were rich and flourishing Mahonys at Dunloe, Dromore, Cullinagh, and Castle Quinn, but this especial branch had fallen into such poverty and obscurity as to be unable to educate all its children.

I was curiously brought into contact with a descendant of a brother of "le brave O'Mahony."

While Count Daniel and one of his brothers followed King James to France, and found fame and fortune abroad, a brother—probably yet a boy—was left at home. After the family sank into poverty and obscurity, his grandson married the beautiful daughter of a famous old blacksmith, and his son followed the trade. He left Kerry, and he or his son settled in Clonmel, and became a famous master farrier, where this scion of a noble race shod horses for her Majesty and for my father, Charles Bianconi, who at that time kept a great number of public cars starting from Clonmel. His son, John O'Mahony, served both potentates. He refused to follow the paternal trade, learned Latin and music, insisted on enlisting, served valiantly, came home to be a mail-coach guard, and eventually emigrated to Africa, where he died highly respected within the last seven years, having long held a responsible post in the Custom House of Durban. My father thought too much education had spoilt John O'Mahony for following the paternal trade; I think it was "le brave O'Mahony" who did the mischief, if mischief it were. I should not wonder if he left nephews and nieces who may chance to see this record of their race. Strange two sides to one shield—the ambassadorial banquet; the marks of one of the heirs of the ambassador's kinsman.

Mr. Mahony, of Dromore, was kind enough to answer some queries as well as he could from abroad. He also tells me that the present house of Dromore is the third house erected since his family settled there in 1680.

"General Count Conway," he continues, "of the Irish Brigade, was brought up at Dromore, his mother having been a Mahony. Daniel O'Mahony, in the service of France, married the widow of the Duke of Berwick.[1] I have got his pedigree. The Countess of Newburgh, who died a year or two ago, descended from him. The title became extinct with her, but I found the Mahony arms quartered on her hatchment. This Count O'Mahony is represented by Prince Giustiniani, his mother having been the last lineal descendant bearing the name of the count."

Mr. Mahony here tells the anecdote I have quoted about the Vienna banquet, but with a trifling inaccuracy. He says, "There were two other counts of the name. 'Father Prout' [Rev. Francis Mahony] gave me a letter written by one of them who lived near Lyons. Another count had a château near Bordeaux. He stayed a few days with me years ago, and was a complete Frenchman.[2] He died without

---

[1] O'Callaghan says her sister, Lord Clare's widow.

[2] John Francis, son of Darby of Dillon's Regiment, Colonel French Service, fourth son of Donell Mahony, of Dunloe, emigrated in 1792, being then Sub-Lieutenant Irish Brigade, entered English Army, served against French in Egypt; re-entered the French Service after Peace of Amiens: "commandant" third battalion Irish Regiment, 1809; served in

issue, and his nephew, a Lieut. Bourdalieue, of the French Marine, took his name and property. The Cremona champion was none of these."

All the achievements and adventures of O'Mahony are too long to tell, but I cannot resist quoting a couple of episodes from O'Connor's "Military Memoirs of the Irish Nation."

At the famous surprise of Cremona in 1703 Prince Eugene would certainly have carried the town, but for Mahony's vigilance. He was a reformed officer, *i.e.* one of those who had been retrenched from the regiments, and, in the absence of the lieut.-colonel, was in command of "Dillon's." "Mahony," says O'Connor, "was a great martinet, and had ordered his men to parade at break of day. He had thrown himself into bed, with orders to his valet and host to awake him before dawn. On hearing the trampling of horses he sprang up, began to scold those who had let him sleep, and heard they were the Imperial Cuirassiers. He ran out, watched his opportunity, reached the barracks, and had the drums beat an alarm. The Irish ran out with only their shirts and small clothes, muskets, and cartouche-boxes. In this costume they fought, fasting, for ten hours.

"During the conflict Mahony seized the bridle of Count Taaffe's lieut.-colonel, Friburg, when his Imperial Cuirassiers had broken the half-naked corps of Irish, and called out, 'Quarter for Friburg!' Friburg refused, and was shot down. When two hundred and twenty-three of his six hundred were *hors de combat*, he retreated to the battery and turned the guns on Prince Eugene's advancing column.

"No wonder Marshal Villeroy sent him to bear the despatches to King Louis. 'You have said nothing,' observed the king, 'of my brave Irish.' Mahony modestly replied, 'They fought in conjunction with the other troops of your Majesty.'"

Mathew O'Connor translates the following quaint cha-

Spain on Junot's staff: lieut.-colonel, February, 1812; Colonel "3rd Foreign Regiment," *ci-devant Irlandais*, November, 1813; Chevalier de St. Louis, August, 1814; count, March, 1815. I have been unable to trace him further, but find him mentioned as "General Count Mahony" under the citizen-king. He seems to have served with equal readiness for and against France, for and against England, and under Bourbon, Napoleon, and Orleans. He is the Colonel Mahony unfavourably mentioned in Byrne's "Memoirs," vol. ii. p. 98. He married a Miss Power, and his son Ernest, Count Mahony (*ob. s.p.*), was the "complete Frenchman" who stayed at Dromore. The foreign regiments in the service of Buonaparte were—No. 1, "of Latour-d'Auvergne;" No. 2, "of Isenberg;" No. 3, "The Irish;" No. 4, "The Prussian" (Decree of "the Emperor," February, 1812).—[R. O'C.]

racter of O'Mahony from Bellesme's "Histoire des Campagnes de Vendôme:"—"He was not only always brave, but laborious and indefatigable; his life was a continued chain of dangerous combats, desperate attacks, and honourable retreats. He might have availed himself of his descent from one of the most ancient families of Ireland, but he preferred advancement by personal merit. If he has risen to the first rank in the army he has risen gradually, and has passed through all the subordinate military stations to learn their duties. He learned to obey before he commanded, and without sudden elevation to the glorious employments which he has sustained with so much applause during this war. What did not this famous Mahony do on the day of Cremona, on which his conduct, equally bold and fortunate, procured for him the esteem of the Government and the admiration of the garrison? By his foresight, along with M. de Praslin, in cutting down the Po bridge, ten thousand Germans were prevented from joining Prince Eugene. Thus Cremona was saved by the vigilance and valour of the brave Mahony. . . . The king [of France] made him a colonel, afterwards a brigadier. He afterwards entered the service of his Catholic Majesty [of Spain], who gave him a commission to raise a regiment of dragoons. Having raised it, he, at the head of these Irish dragoons, performed astonishing feats at the battle of Almanza.

"His Catholic Majesty, convinced of his capacity, valour, experience, and devotion to his glory, sent him with his regiment to Sicily, where he served with much distinction, and by his polished and generous manners acquired the friendship of the Sicilians. The king recalled him soon after to Spain, and made him a lieut.-general, and honoured him with the title of 'Count of Castile.' He served in the campaign of Ivaris under Philip V., and made during it many successful military expeditions. He signalized himself as a captain and a soldier at the battle of Saragossa, and at the head of the Spanish cavalry charged with great vigour the Portuguese horse, whom he broke and drove into the Ebro, in which many of them were drowned. After he had performed this exploit, he got possession of the enemy's artillery, and, as he could not carry it off, he cut the sinews of four hundred artillery mules, by order of the Marquis of Rey; if the rest of the cavalry had followed the impetuous movement of the dragoons and the king's guards, we would have gained this battle, though the allies had twenty-six thousand and the Spaniards only twelve thousand men."

O'Connor also tells us that O'Mahony acquired great

glory on the day of Villa Viciosa at the head of the dragoons. The king rewarded him with a commandery of St. Iago, worth 150,000 livres a year.

It is so pleasant to find an Irishman's merits so fully acknowledged and rewarded that I have given, perhaps, a little too much space to the brave man whose son's name crops up in these pages as almoner for a kinsman to poor Irish kindred.

NOTE D.

DOMINIC TRANT AND HIS JACOBITE KINDRED.

Colonel Trant, of Dovea, kindly permitted me to rummage among the papers of his great-grandfather, Dominic Trant. He could not tell me the precise relationship between that most pleasant and cultivated gentleman and Sir Patrick, who followed King James to France. Sir Patrick's life-sized portrait, by Sir Peter Lely, in all the bravery of a long curled wig, white satin under-garb and brown and amber drapery, hangs in the dining-room at Dovea, near Dominic's own likeness. There are several papers about his descendants. I annex the will of Sir Patrick's widow, as also the letter announcing her death. Sir Lawrence Trant, their son, who announces the venerable lady's death, must have succeeded Sir John, murdered in London, who is mentioned in the papers Ross O'Connell received from Dromore. I have been unable to procure any further information about the Jacobite baronets.

Dominic Trant's picture was admirably painted in Rome. His brown hair is unpowdered, though dressed in the fashion worn with powder. He wears a light blue silk suit, and leans against a pile of books, with a drawing protruding from the heap, and a view of Italian scenery showing in the background. He is tall, stout, and florid, with large lively grey eyes and a bright genial expression. I saw several of his books, and also his pamphlet which led to the duel which ended fatally for his antagonist. It is on the tithe question, which wrought such terrible mischief in the south of Ireland. Arthur Young gives a glowing description of his beautiful home at Dunkettle, near Cork, full of treasures of literature and art within, and of the charms of landscape gardening without.

Colonel Trant showed me some very interesting letters, by which it appears that Dominic Trant did a great business as counsel for his friends, the southern smuggling gentlemen.

In a case where a ship and valuable cargo were at stake, he gets fifty guineas on his brief, and seven guineas a day from the moment of stepping into the post-chaise at the door of his town house.

I quote his graphic description of the fatigues of the managing counsel at a contested election.

Extracts from Letters of Dominic Trant, concerning the Kerry Election of 1790.

May 11, 1790.

I was obliged to come off Express to this County Election to support my friends, young J. Blennerhassett and Sir B. Denny, against the Crosbies, Herbert-Leslies, Ponsonbys, etc. This is the thirteenth day of our election, and it may continue for three, four, or five days longer, or perhaps to the next week. I am most heartily sick and tired of it, as in fact almost the whole burden of my friends' cause lies on me in various points. However, we must endeavour to get through it with honour and success at least. I have not the least doubt of J. B. Hassett's keeping far ahead of the others, and I think it also 5 to 1 that Denny must beat Herbert. My friends seem disposed to give me the whole credit of their prospects of success, which is a great satisfaction to me. I have lived here for the last fortnight in perpetual bustle and fatigue, not having had literally one half-hour to myself. And I come home from Court frequently *parfaitement rendu*. Even at this instant I have got up at six o'clock, after very little sleep, to write this scroll, with the best stump of a pen I could lay my hands on.

I lodge at my old friend's, the Collector's, where I am taken as good care of as the nature of this time of hurry will permit. In half an hour I shall have a levee of at least 50 agents, freeholders, etc., to receive directions from me; then precisely at ten we go into court, into a scene of the greatest labour and confusion imaginable till near six o'clock, and so on from day to day in the same scene of riot.

Tralee, May 14th, 1790.

Our election here will finish probably this day, or certainly to-morrow, and my two friends, Blennerhassett and Denny, will certainly be returned. All this I behold with joy, as the interest of my friends is thus fixed on a firm basis, and my labours are for the present at an end. For the two last days I was fairly wrought down, almost feverish, with a violent sore throat, loss of appetite and rest; but I kept at home those two days, issuing out my directions as occasion offered, and am at this instant much better than I have been for the last six weeks.

A strongly contested election is certainly a most severe trial to the constitution of the leading counsel, as I have felt it severely more than once, and I think it probable I shall never try the experiment again. I have had messengers to induce me to attend as council in the County of Limerick and Co. of Tipperary Elections, which my engagements here have happily enabled me to decline.

I cannot add another word, as I am just summoned into Court, where it is imagined Herbert will make a long speech and strike his colours.

JACOBITE TRANTS.

Copy of Letter from Sir Lawrence Trant to Charles Campbell, Esq., in Kapel Street, Dublin.

SIR,—I should think meself much wanting to the respect I have always had for you if I should not acquaint you with the subject of great concern to my sister and me, that my mother departed this life on Friday last, the 11th instant, in her perfect senses, after a few days' illness, in the fourscore and third year of her age. She made her will a good while ago, but, it being sealed up, will not be opened till her funeral is performed. I shall after that acquaint you with the contents of it.

I am, with my sister's well wishes and mine for your preservation and long life,

Sir,
Your most Obedient and Most humble Servant,
LAWRENCE TRANT.

London, 15th Sept., 1724.

Copy of the Will of Lady Helen Trant.

In the name of God. Amen.

I, Dame Helen Trant, of the Parish of St. Anne, Soho, in the County of Middlesex, in the Kingdom of Great Britain, widow and relict of the late Sir Patrick Trant, Bart., deceased, being of sound mind and memory, do make this my last will and testament in manner and form following (that is to say): Imprimis, I comitt my Soul into the hands of Almighty God, and my body to the earth to be decently interred. And as for my workdly Estate, I give, devize, and bequeath to the uses in that expressed hereinafter mentioned, (vizt.) I give and bequeath unto my Granddaughter, the Honbl. Mrs. Hellen Fleming, daughter of the Right Honbl. now Lord Viscount Longford, late Lord Slane, in the Kingdom of Ireland, the sum of twenty pounds, to be paid to her out of the part of the £7000 given unto me and my children by a late Act of Parliament, remaining in the hands of Charles Campbell, of the city of Dublin, in the s^d Kingdom of Ireland, Esqre, survivor of the Trustees appointed by the said Act for distributing the same. Item, I give, devize, and bequeath out of the said money remaining as aforesaid the sum of £1000 unto my dear daughter, Frances Trant, upon Trust nevertheless, and to the intent that she shall apply the same to the uses by me declared in a writing bearing the same date as this my last will and testament, and by me signed, sealed, and attested by the same subscribing witnesses to this my last will and testament. And I do likewise give and bequeath the further sum of £200 out of the said money, to be by her paid to the uses I have given her particular charge and directions for, and which I desire she shall take care to perform. And it is my will and desire that until such time as the said money so remaining in the hands of the said Charles Campbell as aforesaid can be recovered by and paid in to my Executrix, having so named my said dear daughter, Frances Trant, she shall continue to apply the yearly interest of the said two hundred pounds to the same uses for which the principal is intended. And as for concerning the overplus of the said £7000, which shall or may remain after my funeral expenses, debts, and the said several Legacies hereinafore specifyed shall be satisfyed and paid, I give, devize, and bequeath, together with all my other credits, goods, chattels, and personal estate whatsoever and wherever lying and of what nature and kindsoever, unto my dear son, Sr Lawrence Trant, Baronet, and unto my said dear daughter, Frances Trant, who most dutifully and affectionately attended me under all my circumstances and Hardships, tho' with no small inconvenience to herself, and to their assigns, to be equally divided between them, share and share alike, and to be for no other use, intent, or purpose whatsoever. And of this my last will and testament I declare, constitute, and appoint my said dear daughter, Frances Trant, sole Executrix, and the Right Honbl. Lord North and Grey Supervisor and Trustee to see the same put in execution according to the true intent and meaning thereof herein before declared. And lastly, I do hereby revoke and anull and declare void all former wills by me at any time made. In witness hereof

I have hereunto set my hand and seals the 26th day of October, in the year of our Lord God 1721.

           HELEN TRANT.
              (s.)

Signed, sealed, published, and delivered in the presence of us, who in the presence and at the request of the Testatrix have subscribed our names.
  Jo. PRENDERGAST.
  Jo. GORMAN.
  MARY DALTON.

NOTE E.

SIR NICHOLAS TRANT, K.T.S. (Major-General Portuguese Service).

It would ill become the chronicler of the last of the Irish Brigade to pass over in silence Sir Nicholas Trant's brilliant Peninsular adventures during the time he was lent by Great Britain to Portugal. Ross O'Connell and Mrs. Trant of Dovea have furnished me with memoranda concerning him, and two other friends have ransacked Napier's vast "Peninsular War" for his achievements. Owing to Dominic Trant's migrations over a century ago, his descendants at Dovea have lost touch with the tide of Kerry tradition, and cannot tell me how Sir Nicholas was connected with their line. He was also connected with the Chevalier Fagan, Count Bartholomew O'Mahony, Colonel Thomas FitzMaurice, and many more of the last generation of Irish Quentin Durwards. He was the grandson of Dominic Trant, of Erls, and one of his aunts, Helena, daughter of James Trant, of Castle Island, was married to the Chevalier Fagan's brother Stephen. Evidently the Protestant Trants, now of Dovea, and their poorer Catholic kindred who stayed on in Kerry, and the extinct Jacobite baronets, all sprang from the Trants of Fenitt. King James's Army List (D'Alton) states that Sir Nicholas was a lineal descendant of Sir Patrick, who raised a regiment for King James and followed him into exile. M. Roche, the antiquarian Cork banker,[1] talks of Sir Nicholas Trant as among the most distinguished veterans of the Irish Brigade, and he was certainly one of the Irish-French officers who followed the Duc de FitzJames into the British Service; but I fancy he must

---

[1] "Reminiscences of an Octogenarian," quoted in text.

have first served King Louis in some non-Irish regiment, as his name does not occur in M. de la Ponce's exhaustive record of the services of the officers of the Irish Brigade. We find so many Irishmen serving in the German Legion that this is quite probable.

We first find clear and certain traces of Nicholas Trant in 1794, when his commission as captain in the second regiment of the English Irish Brigade, Count Walsh de Serrant's, was signed by King George III., on October 1, 1794.

My text tells how that unfortunate corps fared.

He was one of the many British officers lent to the Portuguese Government when Marshal Beresford was sent to organize the Portuguese Army. He seems to have been made a Portuguese colonel while only a British captain. Colonel Trant, of Dovea, gave me an old newspaper with the gazette of March 9, 1816, which says, "Captain Sir N. Trant to be Major in the Army, he being appointed to serve with the Portuguese troops, *vice* Sir R. Arbuthnott, removed to the Coldstream Regiment of Foot Guards."

He seems to have been made general immediately after he took Coimbra, as the letter of thanks of his French prisoners is to "Monsieur le Général." At p. 225 of Napier's second volume we are told how, Colonel Lameth having been murdered and mutilated in the village of Arrenana, Soult had five or six villagers shot, but the principal murderers, including a Portuguese major, took refuge with Colonel Trant," who, disgusted at their conduct, sent them on to Marshal Beresford. At p. 227, vol. ii., Napier mentions that Trant was well known to the Portuguese, having commanded at Rarice and Vincera. He was at Coimbra when the news of the defeat at Braga came in. He took the command of all the armed men in the town, including a band of volunteers formed of the students of the university. "The dismay and confusion having been greatly increased by the catastrophe at Oporto, the fugitives from that town and other places, accustomed to violence, and attributing every misfortune to treachery in the generals, flocked to Trant's standard; and he, as a foreigner, was enabled to assume an authority no native of rank durst either have accepted or refused without danger." He advanced with about eight hundred men to Aviera, and joined the Portuguese generals. The people, distrusting these, continued to flock to his standard; many thousands deserted in a panic when sent to seize a bridge, which Napier considers lucky for him, as the masses of insubordinate, excited men would have ill suited his prompt and brilliant dashes.

"Trant," he says, "finally detained only about four thousand men, with whom he imposed on the French, and preserved a fruitful country from the enemy; but he was greatly distressed for money, the Bishop of Oporto having, in his flight to Lisbon, laid hands on all that was at Coimbra."

There are various short mentions of Trant and his irregulars in this chapter. The only interesting one of these says, "Trant's corps was to make its way between Paget's division and the Lake of Aviers, but late in the evening, Trant having ascertained that an impracticable ravine would prevent his obeying orders, passed the bridge of Vouga, and carried his forces beyond the defile."

Napier also mentions that he was made Governor of Oporto when the town was taken.

At pp. 319, 320 of his third volume Napier tells us how, on September 20, 1810, Trant formed the hardy project of destroying Masséna's artillery on the road about twenty miles from Viseu. "Quitting Moimento de Beira in the night, with a squadron of cavalry, two thousand militia, and five guns, on the 20th he surprised a patrol of ten men, from whom he learned that the convoy was at hand, and Montbrun's cavalry close in the rear. Nevertheless, as the defiles were narrow, he charged the head of the escort, and took a hundred prisoners and some baggage. The convoy then fell back, and Trant followed, the ways being so narrow that Montbrun could never come up to the front. At this time a resolute attack would have thrown the French into utter confusion; but the militia were unmanageable, and the enemy having at last rallied, a few men repulsed the Portuguese cavalry with a loss of twelve troopers. The whole got into disorder, whereupon Trant, seeing nothing more was to be effected, returned to Moimento de Beira." The French still fell back, and Masséna lost two days, the artillery not reaching Viseu until the 23rd.

Trant's most brilliant achievement was the capture of Coimbra, for which he was knighted. Napier, who has been telling us of Masséna's advance, says—

"Masséna followed, in one column, by the way of Rio Mayor; but, meanwhile, an exploit, as daring and hardy as any performed by a partisan officer during the war, convicted him of bad generalship, and shook his plan of invasion to its base.

"Colonel Trant reached Milheada, intending to unite with Miller and J. Wilson, the latter having made a forced march for that purpose, but they were still distant. His own arrival was unknown at Coimbra, and he resolved to attack the French in that city without waiting for assistance. Having surprised a small post at Fornos early in the morning of the 7th, he sent his cavalry at full gallop through the streets of Coimbra, with orders to pass the bridge, and cut off all communication with the French Army, of whose progress he was ignorant. Meanwhile his infantry penetrated at different points into the principal parts of the town; the enemy, astounded, made little or no resistance, and the Convent of Santa Clara surrendered at discretion. Thus on the third day after the Prince of Esling had quitted the Mondego, his depôts and hospitals and nearly five thousand prisoners, wounded and unwounded, amongst which there was a company of the marines of the Imperial Guards, fell into the hands of a small militia force! The next day, Miller and Wilson, arriving, spread their men on all the lines of communication, and picked up above three hundred more prisoners, while Trant conducted his to Oporto.

"During the first confusion, the Portuguese committed some violence on the prisoners, and the Abbé du Pradt and other French writers have not hesitated to accuse Trant of disgracing his country and his uniform by encouraging this conduct, whereas his exertions repressed it, and if the fact that not more than ten men lost their lives under such critical circumstances was not sufficient refutation, the falsehood is placed beyond dispute in a letter of thanks, written to Colonel Trant by the French officers who fell into his hands."

This letter, quoted in the appendix to vol. iii., is addressed to General Trant, Governor of the Town and Province of Oporto, by Colonel Catelot, " sous inspecteur au revue des Troupes Françaises," Staff-Surgeon Fallot, and the navy commander, H. Delahaye.

Trant's own brief and modest report of his exploit, in the form of a letter to Marshal Beresford, dated Coimbra, October 7, 1810, is given in the Duke of Wellington's despatches. He specially commends the valour of Lieutenant Dutel, and the spirited conduct of Colonel Serpa, and says nothing could exceed the state of wretchedness in which he found the city, the French having not only plundered it and set fire to some houses, but heaped up piles of clothes and furniture in the streets to be burned. He describes the fury of his troops, of whom eight hundred were natives of the town, and the difficulty he had in protecting his French prisoners from insult.

In the fourth volume Napier tells us how, in the following April, six thousand regular infantry and three hundred cavalry, under Silviera, and eight thousand five hundred of the northern militia, were called out before the allies quitted

Coru. Of these raw levies Trant led three thousand, described by Napier as "raw peasants, unskilled in the use of arms." However, by a brilliant forced march, Trant reached the bridge of Almeida, in the Cabega Negro Mountains, just in time to save it from the French, who had driven Carlos d'España before them. He arrived there, retreating with two hundred men, just as Trant got up with his division.

"Trant immediately threw some skirmishers into the vineyards to the right of the bridge; then, escorted by guides he had dressed in red uniform, galloped to the glacis of the fortress, received from the governor (Le Messurier) a troop of English cavalry, and returned at dusk. The Cabega Negro was immediately covered with bivouac fires, and Le Messurier sallied from the fortress in the evening, and drove back the enemy's light troops. Two divisions of infantry had come against Almeida, but the attempt was not made, the general commanding being startled by the sudden appearance of Trant. Trant sent back the cavalry to Le Messurier, and marched to Guarda. Here he was joined by Wilson, and should have been joined by Silviera; but that general, crossing the Douro on April 14, halted at Lamego. Thus these scarcely six thousand raw peasants were left to guard the position at Guarda, and the only squadron of dragoons in the vicinity was retained at Celorico by Bacellar. Trant and Wilson, with six thousand militia and six guns, held the post from the 9th to the 17th of April, keeping the enemy's marauders in check, and prepared to move to Abrantes in case the French should menace that fortress. Trant had formed the daring design of surprising the French marshal at Sabugal, but Bacellar's procrastination fortunately delayed the execution of this project, which would undoubtedly have failed; for on the 13th, the night on which Trant would have made the attempt, Marmont, designing to surprise Trant, led two brigades of infantry and four hundred cavalry up the mountain. He cut off the outposts, and was entering the streets with his horsemen at daybreak, when the alarm was beaten by one drummer at Trant's quarters, and the other drummers taking it up at hazard in different parts of the town, the French general fell back at the very moment when a brisk charge would have placed everything at his mercy, for there were no troops under arms, and the beating of the first drum had been accidental. The militia then took post outside Guarda; but they had only one day's provisions, and it was decided to retreat, which the regiments did in good order at first, but as the head of the troops were passing the Mondego, forty dragoons sent up by Bacellar were pressed by the French troops and galloped the rear-guard of eight hundred infantry. These, seeing the enemy dismount to fire, and finding their own powder damaged by the wet, fled also, the French following. All the officers behaved firmly, and the Mondego was passed, but in confusion, and with the loss of two hundred prisoners. Bacellar, having destroyed a quantity of powder at Celorico, retreated with Trant's people towards Lamego. Wilson remained at Celorico, and, when the enemy had driven in his outposts, ordered the magazines to be destroyed. This order was only partly executed when the French general retired, and the militia reoccupied Guarda on the 17th."

Napier mentions two other anecdotes of Trant.

Bk. XII. ch. iii. p. 465: "Wellington had ordered Bacellar to look to the security of Oporto, and directed Wilson and Trant to abandon the Mondego and the Vouga the moment the fords were passable, retiring across the Douro, breaking up the roads as they retreated, and destroying all means of transport. Trant, having destroyed an arch of the Coimbra bridge on the city side, and placed guards at the fords, resolved to oppose the enemy's passage. On the evening of March 11, 1811, the French appeared at the suburb of Santa Clara, and a party of their dragoons actually forded the Mondego at Pereiras. On the 12th the French examined the bridge of Coimbra, but one was wounded by a cannon-shot, and a skirmish took place along the banks of the river, during which a party, attempting to feel their way along the bridge, were scattered by a round of shot. The fords were practicable for cavalry, and Trant, having been obliged by Bacellar to withdraw the greater part of his force on the 10th, had only two or three hundred militia and a few guns, yet these opposed the enemy, and the French, believing that reinforcements had reached Coimbra, withdrew, and thus the same man and same militia who had captured Coimbra, saved it."

Bk. XII. ch. iv. p. 487: "Trant, crossing the Lower Coa with two thousand militia, had taken post two miles from Almeida, when the river suddenly flooded behind him. There was a brigade of the 9th corps, which had been employed to cover the march of the battery-train from Almeida to Ciudad Rodrigo, but ere they had discovered Trant's situation he had constructed a temporary bridge, and was retiring, when he received orders from British head-quarters to be vigilant in cutting off the communication with Almeida, and also notice that the next day a British force would be down to his assistance. Marching to Val de Mula, Trant interposed between the fortress and the brigade of the 9th corps. The latter were within half a mile of his position, and his destruction seemed inevitable, when cannon-shots were heard to the south; the enemy formed squares and commenced a retreat as six squadrons of British cavalry swept over the plain in their rear. The enemy only escaped over the Aqueda with the loss of three hundred killed, wounded, and prisoners."

I have far outstripped the usual limits of a note to record this valiant Kerry man's adventures. We afterwards see him in Paris, revisiting the scenes of his youth, and mixing with the little knot of veterans of the Brigade who had settled there on the Restoration. Whom he married or when, I have not been able to learn. Ross O'Connell sends me the following brief obituary notice, from which I gather a fond daughter closed the old man's eyes, and that he died in her English home.

"October the 16th, 1839, died Sir Nicholas Trant, K.T.S., formerly Major-General in the Portuguese Service, aged 70, at Great Braddon, Essex. His only daughter, Clarissa, had married, in 1832, John Branston, Vicar of Great Braddon."

END OF VOL I.